Writing
WITH THE Lights On
FROM SENTENCES
TO PARAGRAPHS

WRITING WITH THE LIGHTS ON FROM SENTENCES TO PARAGRAPHS

KRISTBJØRG EIDE

BROOKE O'HARRA

Prentice Hall, Upper Saddle River, New Jersey 07458

Library of Congress Cataloging-in-Publication Data

O'Harra, Kristbjørg Eide
    Writing with the lights on - from sentences to paragraphs /
    Kristbjørg Eide : with Brooke O'Harra.
        p.   cm.
    Includes index.
    ISBN 0-13-670100-0
    1. English language—Paragraphs—Problems, exercises, etc.
    2. English language—Sentences—Problems, exercises, etc.
    I. O'Harra, Brooke.   II. Title.
    PE1439.044   1995
    428.2—dc20

                                                95-42502
                                                CIP

Acquisitions editor: Maggie Barbieri
Project manager: Jill Schoenhaut
Buyer: Mary Ann Gloriande
Illustrations: Moore Electronic Design
Cover design: Bruce Kenselaar
Cover art: Bruce Kenselaar

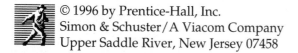 © 1996 by Prentice-Hall, Inc.
Simon & Schuster/A Viacom Company
Upper Saddle River, New Jersey 07458

Printed in the United States of America
10 9 8 7 6 5 4 3 2 1

ISBN 0-13-670100-0

PRENTICE-HALL INTERNATIONAL (UK) LIMITED, *London*
PRENTICE-HALL OF AUSTRALIA PTY. LIMITED, *Sydney*
PRENTICE-HALL CANADA INC. *Toronto*
PRENTICE-HALL HISPANOAMERICANA, S.A. *Mexico*
PRENTICE-HALL OF INDIA PRIVATE LIMITED, *New Delhi*
PRENTICE-HALL OF JAPAN, INC., *Tokyo*
SIMON & SCHUSTER ASIA PTE. LTD., *Singapore*
EDITORA PRENTICE-HALL DO BRASIL, LTDA., *Rio de Janeiro*

To
Josh, Brooke, and Sean
and, of course, Michael

$\mathcal{C}$ONTENTS

SECTION III: POINTS—PUNCTUATION: POINTS THAT MARK THE WAY FOR READERS 345

$\mathcal{P}$REFACE

This book is for anyone who wants to know more about English and writing. Its audience is all students, from those enrolled in developmental education programs to degree-carrying college graduates who are looking for answers—answers many have long been operating without.

All too often, students

- write *without* being aware that writing is a *process*, one that may take many sittings as ideas *evolve* through brainstorming on paper, organizing, revising, revising, and revising.
- are referred to an English handbook for answers to stylistic questions *without* having sufficient vocabulary to access its index or understand its explanations.
- are expected to apply punctuation rules to fix comma splices and figure out semi-colon placement *without* knowing enough about sentence structure to find these rules meaningful.
- are asked to replace sentence fragments with complete sentences, either intuitively or by looking at "good" examples, *without* really understanding why their own incomplete sentences seem so complete to them.
- are sent off to learn about grammar and usage by reading definitions and doing drills *without* experiencing any improvement in their own writing because the *explanations of how these concepts enhance writing* are missing.
- are asked to replace incorrect verb forms *without* clearly understanding why the "correct" ones actually sound incorrect in their own local dialect of English, and are asked to avoid tense shifts when the only shift they have been exposed to is a gear shift.

As we all know, this is no longer a machine age—in which the "mechanics" of writing is all students ask for. It is a computer age in which students and teachers alike will not and should not settle for less than *information.*

Writing with the Lights On offers precisely that. It is a book for writing students that sheds light on aspects of English that can help improve writing. It offers explanations in a way that students can easily understand. It is a user-friendly book that is sometimes full of passion and compassion and other times just plain playful.

But whether a section is serious or silly, *Writing with the Lights On* turns lights on for students because, though its subject is the most fundamental of writing and language concepts, its approach requires students to *think* rather than memorize. Steven Pinker writes in *The Language Instinct*, "Unlike memory, which people are bad at and computers are good at, decision-making is something that people are good at and computers are bad at." And writing involves so much decision making! But too often students are making writing decisions without adequate information. Therefore, this book is filled with information, logically sequenced so that students can acquire knowledge about English which they can then *directly apply to writing*. Its purpose is not only to en"light"en but to empower.

O THE STUDENT

Let's Talk . . .

Think back on the English classes you have taken before. Did you like English? Was it your favorite subject? Or was it your worst subject? Think back to the times you have been assigned the task of writing something. Did you welcome writing assignments? Or did you dread them? Think back on your ability to construct and punctuate sentences. Have you always felt confident that you could write correctly? Or have grammar and punctuation been something you worry about? If you answered any of these questions negatively, you have plenty of company.

In my 25 years of teaching English, not a single semester has gone by without students coming into my classes saying, "I hope we don't have to do any writing in here . . . English has always been my worst subject. . . . I never did understand when to use a semicolon . . . I couldn't tell you the difference between an adjective and an adverb to save my life. And, furthermore, what good is it going to do me to know that stuff anyway?"

And that's why I'm writing this book—for my students, and for **you**—to help you feel better about your writing; to answer your questions about punctuation; to share with you the rewards knowing the different parts of sentences that are always ready to work *for* you and *with* you to write what you want to say—exactly the way you want to say it.

In this book I don't want to prescribe unbending rules; instead, I want to describe how the English language works when you use it to write. I don't want you to memorize information; instead, I want you to understand concepts that will help you become more confident about writing. I have tried to replace my teacher voice with my own personal voice—a voice I hope you will come to trust as you try to make sense of all this "stuff" about English and writing.

I love this subject. In fact I think it was love at first sight (or first sound) with me and English. I have been infatuated with this language since I was first introduced to it as a seven-year-old child who stepped off the boat that had brought me with my immigrant family across the Atlantic Ocean from our protected, picturesque fishing village on the island of Karmøy in Norway to the scary, smog-shrouded, skyscraper-silhouetted city of New York. I couldn't speak or write a word of English then. I still remember the train ride to Oregon across the United States. I remember my mother pointing to other people's meals in the dining car to communicate what she wanted to order for her children to eat. And I remember her paying for our food by trustingly offering her cupped palm full of crumpled, strange-looking, green paper money and silver and copper coins whose value neither she nor I understood.

From there to here has been a long journey. One that, for me, has included learning to speak English, to read it, to write it, and finally to teach it to others. Your journey to mastering English and writing may be harder than mine, or easier. I am certain, at least, that it is unique. You, too, have a history with this subject. And sometimes histories are full of "ghosts."

An image of English papers returned with red marks may act as a ghost whispering to you, "You always make mistakes when you write; you don't know what you're doing." One student I know carried around a ghost of a teacher who had read his paper aloud in class and then proceeded to tear it up in front of his classmates while announcing, "This kind of writing is not acceptable." Sometimes the ghosts are visions of failing competency tests and being left behind because our English skills were not as good and everyone else's. And sometimes ghosts are just the feelings we get from knowing that we do not understand exactly what teachers are talking about when they use words like "agreement," "tense-shifts," "modifiers," and "antecedents."

If you have ghosts in your English closet, whatever they are, you can learn to leave them behind as you move forward to improve your writing skills. While you may never forget embarrassing and painful experiences, you can move beyond them. In school, as in life, the best we all can do is leave behind the pain of the past and take the *learning* with us. For whatever we have learned, even from negative experiences, we can put to positive use to create new and better experiences. Thus, we grow.

Just this morning as I was revising this message to you, my daughter, Brooke, warned me, "You'd better make this book interesting, Mom. Tell 'em all your neat stories." In response to that bit of advice, I have included for you what I call my "hooks" and "connections." Hooks to understanding and remembering are the personal stories, puns, analogies, and word histories that make learning memorable. Connections are the connections of the English language to writing, to thinking, to reading, to the world of work, and to many other aspects of your life. I hope the hooks and connections in this book will enable you to internalize and apply what you learn about English and writing.

My wish for you is that you become an owner of knowledge, rather than a temporary caretaker of information. Sharing what I know about writing is my gift to you; but, more importantly, learning about writing will be your gift to yourself. Knowledge can transform. It can transform you. I'm not offering you a "quick fix" for writing papers; I'm offering you a "fishing pole." An old Chinese proverb says, "Don't give a starving man a fish, instead give him a fishing pole." I want to give you the "pole" that will empower you so you can write with confidence.

As you work with *Writing with the Lights On*, I hope you will grow to feel good about yourself as a writer. Feeling good about yourself is the key to succeeding in whatever you set out to do whether it be to excel in sports, work, your personal life—or to excel in *writing!* I respect your limitations (we all have them), yet I also applaud your willingness to tackle the difficult and sometimes frustrating task of growing. You already know I have a passion for the English language. Coupled with that, I have a compassion for learners. I will feel honored if you let me walk with you part of the way as you travel your personal road to success as a writer.

Kristbjørg Eide

$\mathscr{A}$CKNOWLEDGMENTS

Thanks...

To the editors and reviewers: To Carol Wada, this project's first editor, for taking time to give me your personal feedback about my writing; to Maggie Barbieri, the English editor, for coming in without missing a beat and energetically following this project to the end; for Maggie Barbieri, the Mom, for understanding how important children are to working mothers; to Joan Polk, for always answering the telephone with a human voice and heart and accommodating all my deadline extensions graciously; to the reviewers, Stanley Coberly of West Virginia University at Parkersburg, Karen J. Patty-Graham of Illinois University at Edwardsville, Sharon Gavin of Salem County Community College, Wayne Rambo of Salem County Community College, and Karen Standridge of Pikes Peak Community College, for giving this book confidence; to Phil Miller, my one-time editor turned Prentice Hall College Editorial President, for continuing to believe in me for more than a decade; to Jill Schoenhaut, project manager, for tirelessly contributing your commitment to detail and excellence in publishing—thank you for the many long evenings and weekends during which we kept Oregon and New York connected via telephone—your efforts were monumental.

To my colleagues: To Jean Harmon for sharing your enthusiasm about class testing my materials and providing valuable input; to Maggie McBride for letting my book play a role in your success as a teacher; to Chrys Brown for being willing to try my approach with your students; to Jamila Barber for making your delightful contribution to Chapter 2; to John Mock for sharing your remarkable insights into the writing process and for encouraging me to explore a new path to my own writer's voice; to Bernie Knab for offering your support and your comments about the book's title; to Jerry Berger, a college president and a real human being, for supporting my professional endeavors and valuing my contributions to Chemeketa Community College; and especially to my lifetime friend and colleague, Barbara Wasson, with whom I can always share everything, thanks for giving your ear and your voice and believing so profoundly in this project.

To my students: For being dedicated, candid, and tolerant. Thank you for keeping me on track and on task during the many hours we worked together in the making of this book; thanks, too, for offering your contributions and making corrections; this truly is *your* book.

Finally, and most important, to my family: To the world's three most wonderful children: to my son R. Sean O'Harra for asking so little when I was buried deep in my writing, yet always offering so much love and good advice whenever I needed encouragement; to my son Josh O'Harra, for bringing me joy and for contributing your outstanding talent as a copy editor by devoting countless hours reading and re-reading nearly 800 pages of manuscript; to my daughter, Brooke O'Harra, my co-author, for providing enthusiasm and constant support and making your significant contributions to this work; to my mother, Alice Aksnes Eide, for understanding me; and to my father, Toralv T. Eide, the creative one, who died too soon to realize his profound influence on my life; to my Norwegian Onkel Alfred T. Eide, for forgiving me for taking time to finish my book instead of visiting my family in Norway; and most of all to Michael Bates, for providing the love and patience and kindness and enthusiasm for my work that sustained me through the longest hours of this project. Thank you all for putting your needs on hold to give me the time and strength to write this book—I love you.

THE MAIN MENU

QUESTIONS TO THINK ABOUT WHILE READING CHAPTER [1–14]

 Pre-reading questions to start you thinking about how each chapter can help your writing

DO IT YOURSELF! . . .

 Practice exercises to help you internalize new concepts.

COLLABORATE! . . .

 Activities designed to be used in group settings (but you may do them individually). *Collaborate* activities are more challenging than the *Do It Yourself* sections.

WRITE RIGHT FOR THE JOB . . .

 Ways to apply what you have learned to on-the-job writing. These sections reflect actual writing concerns expressed by employers.

JOURNAL PROMPT . . .

 Ideas for journal entries—light bulbs to start you thinking and writing.

THE READING CONNECTION . . .

 Suggestions for related reading beyond the confines of this book.

THE WRITING CONNECTION . . .

 Writing assignments that reinforce concepts presented in each chapter.

SELF TEST . . .

 Objective fill-in tests to check your understanding of the main ideas in every chapter.

FINAL JOURNAL WRITING . . .

 Invitations to reflect on your own learning.

BLOCKS
Blocks that Hinder Writers
and
Blocks that Help Writers

WRITING . . . THE HARD PART IS TO BEGIN

In creating, the only hard thing's to begin; a grassblade's no easier to make than an oak.

—JAMES RUSSELL LOWELL

QUESTIONS TO THINK ABOUT WHILE READING CHAPTER 1:

1. How can I turn my thoughts into writing?
2. How can I overcome hang-ups and negative feelings about writing?
3. How can I feel more relaxed about writing?
4. What are my writing goals?
5. How can I push through procrastination to start my writing assignments sooner?
6. How can I feel more inspired to write?
7. What resources can I draw upon when I write?
8. What are some techniques I can use to generate ideas for writing?

Ralph Waldo Emerson once said, "The ancestor of every action is a thought." This is especially true of the action of writing. Every day, important thoughts result in writing. Thoughts you explore in college classes become written papers and reports; thoughts you express on the job become memos or official documents; and thoughts you convey to people you love become cherished notes and letters. Thoughts find fulfillment in writing.

As you work through this book, I encourage you to turn your thoughts into writing. Stop reading now and write awhile. Simply write what you are thinking and feeling right now.

_____

_____

_____

_____

_____

_____

_____

_____

_____

_____

_____

HOW DO YOU FEEL: POSITIVE OR NEGATIVE?

How do you feel about writing? Do you love to write? Do you hate to write? Or do you not feel strongly about it one way or the other? What has caused those feelings?

If you love writing, have there been teachers who inspired you—teachers who valued your writing and believed in your abilities? Did your love of writing begin in a classroom?

Or did your love of writing begin with you? Have you discovered for yourself that writing can release your emotions and express your feelings? Have you learned that writing can help you through the tough times and intensify the good times? Have you learned that writing is not only communication, but discovery—a way to learn more about yourself?

Take a moment now and write any positive feelings you have about writing. Write about your *positive* writing experiences:

_____

_____

_____

_____

_____

_____

_____

_____

Maybe you hate to write. Why? Have negative experiences made you fear and hate writing? Every semester, men and women from age sixteen to sixty file into my classes. Someone always hates to write. This is what I hear:

You can ask me to do anything in this class, but please don't ask me to write. I'd rather do anything but write.

Horror stories often follow:

> *I used to like to write until I had a class where I was asked to read my writing aloud, and the teacher proceeded to point out everything that was wrong with my paper in front of my friends and classmates. I was so embarrassed I never wanted to write anything again.*
>
> *I haven't stepped foot into a writing class for ten years. My last teacher read my paper aloud to the class and then she said, 'This kind of writing is not acceptable!' After that she tore up my paper in front of everyone.*

I shudder when I hear the fear in these students' voices.

How vulnerable we all are when we share what we write! On paper for everyone to see, we lay out the ideas born in our hearts and minds—words which have sometimes painfully worked their way out from our insides. Then critics, who are often well-meaning teachers, trample on them.

At least, sometimes we feel they do; for writing, more than any other subject, is taught by criticism and correction. In writing classes, we learn ever so much more about what we have done wrong than about what we are doing right.

Write about your fears of writing. You need not share this with anyone else. But, for yourself, write your negative feelings. Sometimes writing heals.

_____

_____

_____

_____

_____

_____

_____

_____

_____

_____

_____

_____

RELAX INTO WRITING . . .

According to philosopher Bertrand Russell, "To conquer fear is the beginning of wisdom." You can make today the beginning of wisdom for you. Are you willing to meet your fears in this new class? Even if your writing *history* has been negative, your writing *future* can be positive.

First, honor your previous pain and acknowledge the tension that writing has caused you.

Then say good-bye to that pain and tension. Embrace the NOW. Welcome the new discoveries that await you, and you will begin to conquer your fear as you gain wisdom about writing.

One way to move through the tensions you (and I and most writers) feel every time you sit down to write is to start each writing session with a relaxation exercise like this one:

R-E-L-A-X-A-T-I-O-N

Crumple up a piece of writing paper into a ball and squeeze it as hard as you can in the palm of your hand—the hand you write with.

Push the tension from your body down through your arm, through your hand and fingers, and into the paper ball.

Close your eyes. Keep them closed.

Squeeze hard. Then, let go. Squeeze hard. Then, let go again. Do this several times until you feel the tension leaving your body.

Relax your shoulders; let them fall; let your arms fall to your sides. Position yourself comfortably in the chair in which you are sitting.

Let your head become heavy and let it fall to one side or let it roll around on your relaxed shoulders rather than trying to hold it up.

Breathe deeply. Take a deep breath, expand your lungs, and bring air deep into your gut. Hold it there. Then release the air gradually. Continue breathing like this.

Focus again on your hand with the crumpled paper. Gradually relax your grip on that wad of paper. Gently and s-l-o-w-l-y uncurl your fingers; release your grip a little at a time until you can barely feel the presence of the paper ball in your hand. Eventually let the paper fall out of your hand.

Relax . . . Relax . . . Then open your eyes and start writing.

Write something, anything. Write the first thing that comes to mind while remaining as relaxed as possible:

_____

_____

_____

_____

_____

_____

_____

_____

_____

_____

_____

_____

_____

_____

_____

_____

_____

_____

When first attempting this relaxation exercise, you may want to ask someone else to read the steps to you, s-l-o-w-l-y, as you follow them. Or you may want to tape yourself reading the instructions. Or you may merely read the process through several times until you can do it without being reminded of the steps. Be patient . . . it may take a while before you truly feel the freeing effects of *relaxing into writing*.

Damn braces, Bless Relaxes.

—*William Blake*

MAKE THE BEST CHOICES FOR YOURSELF

All of us are an accumulation of both positive and negative experiences; and all of us can choose what to do with those experiences.

Take *positive experiences*, for example: you can choose to

- *Treasure* them.
- *Recall* them whenever you need support.
- *Celebrate* them when you need cheers and applause.
- *Replay* them when you need courage.

Or *negative experiences*: you can choose to

- Put them into perspective.
- Not allow them to have any power over you.
- Refuse to let them hurt you any more.
- Take from them what they have taught you and leave the rest behind.

When healing from negative experiences, give yourself permission to be good to yourself. Simply say to yourself, "All your thoughts are worthwhile and worth expressing. You can say anything you want to say, any way you want to say it. Don't worry, just write."

As an adult, you no longer need to wait for approval from some other "grown up" to decide that what you do and say and write is worthwhile. You *are* the grown up. So don't wait for someone else to encourage you. Pat *yourself* of the back. **Free** *yourself* to write. Accept and honor *your own power*.

Whenever previous mistakes come back to haunt you (and they will), just remember, no one gets through life without making mistakes. As you set out to write, you can choose to lay aside negative thoughts and load up, instead, with this positive belief: you can *learn* to do anything well; you can even learn to **write well**.

Take a few minutes now to remind yourself that all can be all right in the future in spite of the past. Encourage yourself. Tell yourself all the positive things you have always wanted to hear about yourself and your abilities:

_____

_____

_____

_____

_____

_____

_____

_____

_____

_____

SET WRITING GOALS

Look forward to your writing future. Oliver Wendell Holmes once said, "The greatest thing in this world is not so much where we are but in what direction we are moving." You are already moving in a positive direction: you are taking this class, reading this book, pursuing an education. "Education" implies movement. It comes from Latin and means "to lead out of." Picture that: Being educated literally means being led out of ignorance into knowledge!

Teachers and books are only guides pointing out possible directions you may choose. Actual "learning" is a step you take on your own. The success of your writing future is up to you. *You* decide where you want to end up. No one else can do that for you. *You* plan when and how to get there. (Remember, people who don't plan often end up somewhere they don't want to be.)

Write down your *decisions* about *learning to write better*. Write down where you want to end up as a writer. Do you want to learn to write just well enough to pass your English classes? Do you want to learn to write so well that your writing ability can help qualify you for a job or a promotion? Do you want to write for your own personal satisfaction? Do you want to become a professional writer someday? Write down your goals and how and when you plan to start making them happen:

_____

_____

_____

_____

_____

_____

_____

_____

_____

_____

_____

Your written goals can help you map your writing journey. But along your writing journey, as along most journeys, you can anticipate detours and challenging barriers to cause delays. Don't let unexpected obstacles end your trip, though. Instead, resolve to face the setbacks and focus even more intently on your destination. If you make your destination a priority, even the toughest obstacles can't keep you from reaching your writing goals.

A journey of a thousand miles must begin with a single step.

—Lao-Tzu

DO IT YOURSELF!   *The First Step: A Writing Assignment*

Directions

Using all the thoughts about writing you have explored so far, create a finished piece of writing to be handed in. Include at least one paragraph devoted to each of the following:

1. Your positive and/or negative feelings about writing and your thoughts about how you acquired those feelings;

2. Your hope and vision for your writing future, including how you want it to be different from your writing past;

3. Your plan: how and when you intend to start your journey to becoming a better writer.

    To create these paragraphs, draw from the thoughts you have written so far, as you have worked through this chapter: Expand upon them. Add details. Use personal examples.

    Give this piece of writing a title; call it whatever **you** want to call it.

You may have had little difficulty completing the previous writing assignment. After all, during the first part of this chapter, you have been jotting down your thoughts about your writing experiences and goals. You may not be as well prepared to write on other subjects that teachers might ask you to write about.

How do you typically react when you are faced with a major writing assignment?

O YOU AVOID GETTING STARTED?

You have a writing assignment! What are you thinking? Are you thinking, "I'll do it later"? Many writers begin to procrastinate the minute they are assigned a writing task: "I'll start that assignment after I finish the rest of my reading . . . after I complete all my math assignments . . . after I clear my desk . . . clean my room . . . do my laundry . . . fix myself a snack . . . call my friend . . . watch my favorite TV program . . . play just one more hand of cards . . . etc., etc., etc.? William Zinsser, author of the book *On Writing Well*, says this of writers and procrastination: "A writer will do anything to avoid the act of writing. I can testify from my newspaper days that the number of trips made to the water cooler per reporter-hour far exceeds the body's known need for fluids."

I know that story all too well. Every time I write, my ritual is to wear a path to my refrigerator. How do you procrastinate? Write about what you do before you settle down to write. Write your own thoughts about getting started:

_____

_____

_____

_____

_____

_____

_____

_____

F I ONLY HAD THE TIME TO WRITE . . .

Why is getting started so difficult? Is it that you feel you need a block of uninterrupted time to write? Is it that you don't want to feel guilty about setting aside that block of time—so before you sit down to write, you feel you must complete all those chores you have been meaning to get around to for weeks?

Be realistic. Can you ever really create time when you have *nothing* else to do, when your mind can't conjure up a single activity to prevent you from sitting down to write? I never can, at least not before my deadline.

Your written goals can help you map your writing journey. But along your writing journey, as along most journeys, you can anticipate detours and challenging barriers to cause delays. Don't let unexpected obstacles end your trip, though. Instead, resolve to face the setbacks and focus even more intently on your destination. If you make your destination a priority, even the toughest obstacles can't keep you from reaching your writing goals.

A journey of a thousand miles must begin with a single step.

—Lao-Tzu

DO IT YOURSELF! *The First Step: A Writing Assignment*

Directions

Using all the thoughts about writing you have explored so far, create a finished piece of writing to be handed in. Include at least one paragraph devoted to each of the following:

1. Your positive and/or negative feelings about writing and your thoughts about how you acquired those feelings;

2. Your hope and vision for your writing future, including how you want it to be different from your writing past;

3. Your plan: how and when you intend to start your journey to becoming a better writer.

    To create these paragraphs, draw from the thoughts you have written so far, as you have worked through this chapter: Expand upon them. Add details. Use personal examples.

    Give this piece of writing a title; call it whatever **you** want to call it.

You may have had little difficulty completing the previous writing assignment. After all, during the first part of this chapter, you have been jotting down your thoughts about your writing experiences and goals. You may not be as well prepared to write on other subjects that teachers might ask you to write about.

How do you typically react when you are faced with a major writing assignment?

O YOU AVOID GETTING STARTED?

You have a writing assignment! What are you thinking? Are you thinking, "I'll do it later"? Many writers begin to procrastinate the minute they are assigned a writing task: "I'll start that assignment after I finish the rest of my reading . . . after I complete all my math assignments . . . after I clear my desk . . . clean my room . . . do my laundry . . . fix myself a snack . . . call my friend . . . watch my favorite TV program . . . play just one more hand of cards . . . etc., etc., etc.? William Zinsser, author of the book *On Writing Well*, says this of writers and procrastination: "A writer will do anything to avoid the act of writing. I can testify from my newspaper days that the number of trips made to the water cooler per reporter-hour far exceeds the body's known need for fluids."

I know that story all too well. Every time I write, my ritual is to wear a path to my refrigerator. How do you procrastinate? Write about what you do before you settle down to write. Write your own thoughts about getting started:

_____

_____

_____

_____

_____

_____

_____

_____

_____

F I ONLY HAD THE TIME TO WRITE . . .

Why is getting started so difficult? Is it that you feel you need a block of uninterrupted time to write? Is it that you don't want to feel guilty about setting aside that block of time—so before you sit down to write, you feel you must complete all those chores you have been meaning to get around to for weeks?

Be realistic. Can you ever really create time when you have *nothing* else to do, when your mind can't conjure up a single activity to prevent you from sitting down to write? I never can, at least not before my deadline.

Therefore, I often wait too long. I start writing too close to deadline time. Have you ever pulled an "all-nighter" to write the paper that was assigned a month ago and realized, too late, that you could have written it better had you started it earlier? Me, too.

Write about your experiences with missing deadlines and turning in writing assignments late:

_____

_____

_____

_____

_____

_____

_____

_____

Genius is one percent inspiration and ninety-nine percent perspiration.

—*Thomas Alva Edison*

INSPIRATION BY MEANS OF PERSPIRATION

Maybe you don't start writing because you just don't *feel* like writing. Do you believe good writers are inspired to write? Do you ever think, "Even though I have some time right now, I don't feel inspired. Whatever I would write now probably would not sound good. So I'll wait until I'm in the 'mood' "? Which do you suppose will come first, the "mood" to write or the *due date* of your paper?

When it comes to "feeling like it," I compare writing to exercising. Have you ever been on an exercise program? Have you ever walked, run, swum laps, or lifted weights regularly? I have. I was once an avid runner; every day I ventured out for five miles. Believe me, it is as easy to procrastinate about exercising as it is to procrastinate about writing. Any day, I could have thought of an excuse not to run. I could have complained that I was tired, my knees were sore, I didn't really have time, the weather was bad. . . . But to achieve my exercise goals, I pushed through my own excuses. To achieve your writing goals, you too will be pushing through your own excuses for not getting started.

As a runner, I pushed through and ran whether I felt like it or not. The first mile or two was always the hardest. I had to push through monotony, side aches, and sometimes rainy weather. Not until I was half-finished with my five-mile run, did I start to relax and feel like running. Only when I had gone half the distance, did the movement of my legs become effortless and my breathing natural. Then I no longer noticed I was performing the act of running. I was just being me, and part of me was the running.

Writing, too, is like that. The first few phrases and sentences will be the hardest and may seem forced and unnatural. It may not be until you are half finished that you will start to feel "inspired." Sometimes, if your writing task is short, you will be nearly done before you *feel* like writing; or it may be not be until you are rereading and revising your writing that the thoughts you really wanted to express in the first place finally find their way to your paper.

Unfortunately, by then you may be out of time—IF you waited too long before starting. By then it may be too late to rewrite your thoughts into the paper you are really capable of writing. If the assignment is due, you may be forced to turn in your paper when you have gone only half the distance you are capable of going, after you have written a version that is only half as good as the paper you are capable of writing.

To write, then, requires the self-discipline to **start** before you may feel like starting and the tenacity to **continue** writing no matter how much effort each phrase seems to require.

 ## TOP WORRYING AND START WRITING

You may feel nervous when you begin, and you may struggle with your first sentences and paragraphs. Even experienced writers are nervous when they start writing. Just like you, professional writers, too, worry about how their finished product will look, who will read it and find fault with it. These feelings are perfectly normal. Yet, when you devote yourself to one assignment long enough, you will eventually stop worrying about the process and be able to focus on your ideas rather than the act of writing. You may even stop noticing that you are writing at all. That is when you are just being you and part of you is the writing.

> *A professional writer is an amateur who didn't quit.*
>
> —*Richard Bach*

Write about an activity (anything at all) that was hard for you at first; but then, as you did it more and more, it became easier. Did you ever become so comfortable with this activity that you eventually reached the point where you could do it without thinking?

_____

_____

_____

_____

_____

_____

_____

_____

_____

_____

_____

_____

_____

THE WRITER AS ARCHITECT

Writing is a creative process. Whether you write a story, a poem, a business letter, or a technical report—writing is creating. Creating means you begin with something intangible, an idea or a feeling; and you eventually end up with something tangible, a real finished product you can see and touch and share with others. But how do you get from an idea, which is real only to you, to a finished piece of writing everyone can experience? How do writers create?

Building a house is another creative process that begins with just ideas. The builder first has to have a vision of the finished house. From this, he or she devises a plan, a blueprint for the house. At some point, when creating a piece of writing, you may be asked for a blueprint or outline of your paper.

But whether you are a builder or a writer, your plan is likely to change along the way as you encounter construction difficulties. You may find the materials you planned to use are not available. You may find that ideas you thought fit well together don't fit. Or you may simply change your mind about what you want your final product to be. Don't be surprised if your house—I mean your paper—ends up going beyond the boundaries you first imagined.

GATHERING RAW MATERIALS

Gathering materials is an important step in creating. To create a house, the builder gathers nails, concrete, wire, pipes, and lumber. These are raw materials for building. But what are the raw materials for writing? To make your ideas a physical reality, you need words, phrases, and sentences.

Often student writers don't think in terms of "raw" materials. Instead, they think the first sentence they write must be the first perfect introductory sentence. My students during in-class writing assignments often act like this: They think for a while, write a sentence, read it over, then crumple up their paper, and start again. Sometimes they do this several times before producing their first line of writing.

Have you ever started a piece of writing this way? Why? Do you feel you must *begin* the writing process by composing an important, memorable, and beautifully stated sentence? This is not so. Usually what ends up as the first sentence of your finished writing is one of the last sentences you actually write. After all, the first sentence introduces the rest of the paper. How could you write accurately about what is in a paper until you have *finished* the paper—including all the changes to your original outline? If you do write your introduction first, realize that you should be prepared to change it later.

If, then, the way to start writing is not necessarily by fussing over the first sentence, how do you begin? *You start by gathering the raw materials for your essay.* But where do the raw materials come from?

WHERE TO LOOK FOR RAW MATERIALS

Here are some resources you have to draw from every time you write:

1. You can usually reach back into your own memory of past experiences and knowledge and find ideas to write about.
2. You can draw from your imagination and fantasies.
3. You can observe present situations and report your immediate feelings and thoughts.
4. You could write about the knowledge of others. By reading books and magazines, watching films and television programs, you can often learn from what others know. You can use that information for raw material for your own researched papers.

You have much to draw from.

MOVING FROM IDEAS TO WRITTEN WORDS

Now, how do you transform "stuff" that is just ideas into raw materials for a piece of writing? How do you move ideas from your head onto paper? You may already have a technique that works for you. Many writers use proven techniques to start their writing. These techniques include *free writing, brainstorming, mind mapping,* and *self-interviewing*.

Technique #1: Free Writing

Free writing is one way to fill a page with many ideas in a short time. To free write, you first set aside a block of time; even fifteen minutes is enough. During this time you will concentrate exclusively on the subject of your writing.

Follow These Guidelines for Free Writing

1. Take a piece of paper; take two pieces of paper, for that matter.
2. Write your topic across the top. Think only about that topic, nothing else.
3. Write as you think, emptying every thought out of your head; YES, write *every* idea that pops into your mind.

4. Force yourself to write *nonstop.*

5. Jot down ideas in any order and any form. At this point your writing doesn't have to be good. It doesn't have to be organized; people don't think in orderly outlines. Simply write whatever comes out of your head. Ideas may emerge as just words or phrases, not always as sentences.

6. If you find that you're repeating yourself, shift gears and focus on new and different thoughts.

7. When you think of related ideas that don't quite fit your topic, note them quickly (in parentheses) without getting off track. Writing down even stray ideas in this way helps you move past a thought that may be blocking you. Once you have it on paper, you can stop thinking about it and move on to thoughts that are more related to your topic. Also, some ideas that seem unrelated at first may eventually be useful as your writing evolves.

8. When you change your mind about something, don't take time to stop and cross it out; just start your next thought on a new line.

9. Increase your tolerance for letting mistakes show; don't worry about spelling or punctuation at this point.

What can you expect to accomplish in fifteen minutes of free writing? Since you write thoughts just as they occur to you, you may fill one or two pages and yet not have a single usable paragraph. You might have several sentences next to one another that really don't belong together. Or you might have a group of sentences that do go together but one oddball idea that doesn't fit with anything else on the page. You certainly won't have anything you can hand in as a finished piece of writing. But you will have *valuable raw material* you can later expand upon, organize, revise, and eventually turn into a finished paper.
The following is a student example of free writing:

TOPIC: WHY I WANT TO BECOME A BETTER WRITER

—I want to write better because I have a ton of important thoughts and ideas . . . I don't want my thoughts and ideas to seem stupid to people who read them because my writing is bad . . . or because I made a lot of dumb mistakes in my writing

—It's important to write well because I am a student . . . I have to write term papers and essays . . . I have to take writing classes to graduate and get a degree . . .

—I am busy and I feel I spent too much time worrying about spelling and punctuation (because I'm not sure what is correct) . . . that interferes with expressing my thoughts

—If I were a better writer I would be more confident . . . stress energy wouldn't be wasted on worrying about my writing . . . instead I could spend more energy on my arguments

—I'm sure when I have a job, I'll have to write . . . then it must be perfect . . . errors in business letters could cost me my job . . . I would be embarrassed to have to ask my co-workers to correct my letters . . . I would be even more embarrassed if my boss found writing mistakes in my work . . . I am smart enough that I should be able to write letters myself without having to ask . . . at least I am smart enough to learn to write correctly. . . .

Questions and Answers about Free Writing

Q: *During free writing, what if I suddenly think of something important I need to remember that has nothing to do with my topic? How do I get it off my mind?*

A: If you think of something important (like, "I have a doctor's appointment at four today") just jot it down in parentheses so you don't have think keep thinking about it. This way it will only interfere with your free writing for an instant, and you can quickly return to focusing all your thoughts on your topic.

Q: *What if I run out of ideas to write about before my fifteen-minute free writing time is over?*

A: If you run out of ideas, go back and read the first few phrases you wrote and try to think of examples to illustrate them. Ask yourself specific questions about those ideas and write down more details pertaining to each one.

Q: *Can I free write using a computer?*

A: Of course, a computer is a wonderful tool for free writing. However, if you are tempted to correct and revise words that appear on the computer screen, you might experience fewer distractions if you turn off the screen during free writing.

DO IT YOURSELF!   *Choose a Topic and Free Write*

Directions

A. *Select from the following topics to experiment with free writing as a way to gather raw materials for a piece of writing:*

1. *My Writing History*
2. *My Neighborhood*
3. *Why Fast Food Restaurants Are So Popular*
4. *My First Day of College*
5. *My Ideal Spouse*

B. *When you have selected your topic, you are ready to start writing. These tips may help you:*

—*Sometimes free writing is easier if you do a relaxation exercise before you begin writing. Also, pleasing, relaxing music in the background helps some writers free write more easily.*

—*Remember, as you write, to give yourself permission to say whatever you want to say.*

—*When you are ready to begin free writing, check the time, and free write on one topic for at least fifteen minutes before you put your pen down. (Use your own paper for this activity.)*

COLLABORATE!   *Discussing the Value of Free Writing*

Directions

Together with a group (or on your own) read the following situation and respond.

<u>Situation</u>: One semester, in an introductory writing class, a young student complained about a required fifteen-minute free writing session. She said, "I just finished writing solid for fifteen minutes, and all I have is two pages of 'ideas.' They are not organized; I don't know if I can even use all of them. To get something I can turn in, I will have to write this all over again in a different form. Free writing is a waste of my time! If I had started the way I normally do, I would have just started writing my paper using complete sentences, organizing along the way. By the end of fifteen minutes I'd have something I could turn in instead of this stuff I have to rewrite."

Questions to Consider When Responding

1. Now that you have had some experience with free writing, discuss how you would respond to this student. Do you agree with her? Do you disagree? Why?
2. If this student had started writing the way she normally does, how would her finished product be different from the finished product she will eventually end up with as a result of beginning with a free-writing session?
3. What do you think are the pros and cons of using free writing to generate ideas for your own writing tasks?
4. When you begin the writing process by doing some free writing, do you think your finished writing will contain more interesting and varied details than if you had started writing from a prescribed outline? Why?

Technique #2: Brainstorming

Another way to begin writing is to *brainstorm* your topic with a classmate or a group of people working on the same project. In a brainstorming session, the group pools its collection of memories, observations, and research on a certain topic. Everyone contributes ideas, and the whole group keeps working to expand the pool of ideas.

Sometimes one person's idea, even if it sounds strange at first, can jar another person's mind to come up with a new approach to the topic. So don't stop the flow of ideas to criticize; keep suggesting ideas non-stop.

At the end of the brainstorming session, you can take whatever ideas seem useful and develop them into a paper of your own.

Follow These Guidelines for Brainstorming

1. State and define the subject clearly.
2. Start listing ideas on the board; list *every* suggestion—the wilder, the better.
3. Don't criticize any suggestions.
4. After all ideas have been listed:
    a. Combine similar ideas;
    b. Reject ideas, if necessary;
    c. Improve upon already suggested ideas.
5. Establish a list or outline of usable ideas. . . . then start writing!

The following is an example of students writers' brainstorming:

TOPIC: WHAT IS A GOOD STUDENT?

—hard worker

—goes to class

—does all the work

—cares about learning

—can budget time

—pays attention

—isn't disruptive in class

—flirts with the teacher

—writes all papers on the computer

—smells nice in case you have to sit next to them

—memorizes the books

—really smart and should be on Jeopardy

—is a nerd who wears glasses

—doesn't go to school just because his parents make him (or her)

—spends many hours in the library

—studies for tests

—has good study habits

—doesn't wait until the last minute to study for tests and write papers

—asks questions in class when she doesn't know the answers

—has a good attitude

—isn't just a grade grubber

TOPICS ORGANIZED

A good student has a good attitude

—pays attention

—cares about learning

—asks questions in class when she doesn't know the answers

—doesn't go to school just because his parents make him

—isn't disruptive in class

—isn't just a grade grubber

A good student has good study habits

—hard worker

—goes to class

—does all the work

—can budget his time

—spends many hours in the library

—studies for tests

—doesn't wait until the last minute to study for tests and write papers

(Subjects that were rejected: *flirts with the teacher; smells nice in case you have to sit next to them; memorizes the books; really smart and should be on Jeopardy; is a nerd who wears glasses.*)

COLLABORATE!   *Brainstorming*

Directions
Together with a group of classmates, brainstorm one of the following topics:

1. Why People Watch Soap Operas
2. The Definition of a Good Teacher
3. How Our Lives Would Be Different if We Had No Telephones
4. What Males Want from Relationships
5. What Females Want from Relationships

Technique #3: Mind-Mapping or Webbing

Mind-mapping, or webbing, is similar to free writing and brainstorming; but it is more visual and, from the start, more organized.

Start in the middle of a large sheet of paper. Write your topic and draw a circle around it. Then draw a line leading out from your topic, and write down the first thing you associate with your topic. Draw another line leading away from that idea, and write down more associations. Keep going until you run out of associations. Then go back to your subject in the center of the page and start a new set of associations.

A student mind map appears on the next page (page 20).

As you see on the mind map, the topic written in the center circle is "How to Pack for a Hiking Trip." Even though this student's ideas came out in a very random way, as he put them on the mind map, he attached related ideas to the same line. The result is a "map" that resembles a tree with branches coming out from a circular trunk. The more developed an idea becomes, the more twigs are attached to its branch.

Can you see how a mind map could easily be transformed into an outline?

COLLABORATE!   *Mind-Mapping*

Directions
Working with a group or on your own, create a mind map for one of the following topics.
Note: To make your mind map more memorable, use different colored pens to make different branches and illustrate some of your ideas with line drawings.

1. How to Find a Job

2. How to Prepare for a Natural Disaster (Hurricane, Flood, Tornado, Earthquake, Blizzard, Volcanic Eruption, etc.)

3. How to be Successful in College

4. Why American Families Have Changed Since Grandma's Day

5. My Favorite Relaxation Techniques

Example Mind Map

Technique #4: Self-Interviewing

Still another approach to gathering material for a paper is to interview yourself. Pretend you are the person who will read the paper. Make up ten questions relating to the subject of your paper. Then write out the answer to each question.

In business writing, the *self-interviewing* technique often uses the "five W's" as cues. The first W stands for *who*: write down all the *who's* you associate with your topic or any questions about your topic which begin with *who*. When you run out of *who* questions, move on to the other cues: *when? where? what?* and *why?* Of course, you can always go back and fill in more ideas about an earlier question or cue anytime they occur to you.

The following is a sample set of self-interviewing questions:

TOPIC: THE IDEAL DIET TO LOSE WEIGHT

1. Who should diet?

2. What kind of diet is best for losing weight? Why?

3. What kinds of diets do not work? Why? Which diets do work? Why?

4. How many calories should I consume each day?

5. How much fat can I eat?

6. Which foods should I eliminate from my diet?

7. Which food should I include in my diet?

8. How much water should I drink?

9. How often should I eat and when?

10. What about eating out? Where should I go (or not go)?

DO IT YOURSELF!   *Try Self-Interviewing*

Directions

A. *Write a brief memo about a meeting to be held by a club or organization to which you belong. Use the five W's as a guide.*

B. *Create self-interviewing questions and answers pertaining to one of these topics:*

1. A Description of My Favorite Place

2. When Divorce **Is** the Answer

3. When Divorce **Is Not** the Answer

4. The Role Music Plays in My Life

5. My Favorite Movie Character

WRITE RIGHT FOR THE JOB

Creating a piece of writing on the job involves all the same processes that we have discussed so far in this chapter. In addition, however, the workplace can present extra challenges. For example, finding a place and time to write may not always be as easy at work as it may be at home or at school. At work you may be stationed at a desk in a busy office with many distractions including interrupting phone calls that require your attention. In order to find even fifteen minutes to free write ideas for your next report, you may need to have your calls forwarded or find a quiet conference room where you can shut the door for a short time. If you have no such haven to retreat to, you might consider investing in some earphones. Your co-workers might assume you are listening to dictation when in reality you are piping in soothing music that helps to free you up to write.

Often, on-the-job writing is done by committee. Proposals and policy statements are drafted by groups of people. Techniques such as brainstorming and mind-mapping are excellent approaches to writing as a group.

COLLABORATE! *Deciding and Drafting by Committee*

Directions

Working with a group (or on your own) develop raw materials and then recommendations in preparation for drafting a proposal to address one of the issues that faces your school. The following are some suggested topics:

1. A Plan for Making the Campus Environment Free from Physical Obstacles

2. A Plan for Eliminating Cheating

3. A Plan for Streamlining the School's Registration Process

4. A Plan for Making the Campus a Safer and More Secure Environment

5. A Plan for Better Assimilating Foreign Students into Classes and the Learning Community

Step 1: Gather the raw materials for your proposal by brainstorming or mind-mapping or both. Decide which ideas you want to keep, reject, combine, and expand upon.

Step 2: After you have done this, create a list or outline of your ideas—an organizational plan for a finished paper. This plan may even be in the form of a mind map. Jot down not only the order of your ideas but the specific details, explanations, and supporting examples that will accompany each idea.

Step 3: After this, prepare for the first draft of your proposal by writing a list of recommendations.

MAKING THE READING CONNECTION

Writers not only spend much time creating, many of them spend time trying to learn more about the creative process. The following is a partial list of books that have been written about the writing process. Obtain a copy of one of these from your library, school resources center, or local bookstore. Skim the book, stopping occasionally to read carefully sections that particularly interest you. Share with your classmates what you learn about creating and writing.

1. *Walking on Alligators: A Book of Meditations for Writers*, by Susan Shaughnessy, uses quotations from other writers to explore aspects of writing from the pitfalls of perfectionism to the trials of distractions to the pain of the loneliness that accompanies the art of writing. This book helps inspire writers to say, "I can."

2. *One Writer's Beginnings*, by Eudora Welty, provides insights into the creative process, glimpses into different writers' development, and tips for becoming inspired to write.

3. *On Writer's Block: A New Approach to Creativity*, by Victoria Nelson, teaches would-be writers to adjust the way they approach their work. It offers solutions for "writer's block."

4. *Writing Down the Bones: Freeing the Writer Within*, by Natalie Goldberg, offers practical exercises to bring out creativity.

5. *Drawing on the Right Side of the Brain: A Course in Enhancing Creativity and Artistic Confidence*, by Betty Edwards, is a guide to intuitive thinking.

6. *Writers Dreaming*, by Naomi Epel, is full of insights to understanding how dreams often intermingle with the work of writers and their creative process.

7. *Creating Poetry*, by John Drury, for those who are interested in writing poetry, offers thoughtful and motivating instruction to make poetry writing more rewarding.

MAKING THE WRITING CONNECTION

In upcoming chapters of this book you will often see the heading "Journal Prompt." These "prompts" are *invitations* for you to write freely in a journal on a suggested topic.

A journal can be just a notebook full of writing paper that you reserve for jotting down ideas whenever you feel like it. Some people prefer to buy a special book or a diary just for this purpose. In fact, you may already have a personal journal or a writing journal from a previous class. Regardless of what your journal looks like, journals:

- are a wonderful way to practice putting thoughts into writing;
- provide a storehouse for ideas for topics you may want to develop into papers at a later date;
- are good places to jot down questions that come to mind as you work through your classes.

For your first Writing Connection, begin a journal. In your journal, write your responses to *one or several* of the following quotations:

1. *I will not reason and compare. My business is to create.*—William Blake

2. *Art [including writing] is not a handicraft, it is the transmission of feeling the artist has experienced.*—Leo Tolstoy

3. *A man may write at any time, if he will set himself doggedly to it.*—Samuel Johnson

4. *If there's a book you really want to read but it hasn't been written yet, then you must write it.*—Toni Morrison

5. *There's nothing to writing. All you do is sit down at a typewriter and open a vein.*—Walter "Red" Smith

6. *Writing, like life itself, is a voyage of discovery.*—Henry Miller

7. *I write to discover what I think.*—Daniel J. Boorstin

8. *To me, the greatest pleasure of writing is not what it's about, but the inner music that words make.*—Truman Capote

9. *I never travel without my diary. One should always have something sensational to read on the train.*—Oscar Wilde

10. *Writing is the hardest work in the world not involving heavy lifting.*—Pete Hamill

SELF TEST FOR CHAPTER 1

1. _____ exercises can help release the tension you experience when getting started on a piece of writing.

2. You can learn and grow not only from positive experiences but even from _____ experiences.

3. Getting started writing—especially when you don't feel like it—requires self–_____.

4. By setting _____ for yourself, you can begin your journey to becoming a better writer.

5. If you subscribe to James Russell Lowell's philosophy, in creating a piece of writing, the hardest thing is to _____.

6. Writing is a creative process because it begins as an _____ and ends up as a tangible product.

7. When using the "getting started" technique called _____, you write non-stop without worrying about spelling, punctuation, or complete sentences.

8. _____ is an effective way for a *group* to generate ideas.

9. _____, or webbing, is a more visual way of generating and organizing ideas for writing.

10. _____, or asking questions, is another way to generate raw materials for writing.

FINAL JOURNAL WRITING

In your journal, write about what you have learned by working through this chapter. Which one of the "getting started" techniques did you prefer? Were there any techniques you weren't comfortable using? After reading this chapter, how do you plan to approach your next writing assignment differently? Which sections of this chapter related most directly to your own experiences with writing? Which ideas about writing were new to you? Which suggestions were the most useful? What kinds of frustrations did you encounter as you worked through this chapter?

$\mathcal{P}$ARAGRAPHS . . . $\mathcal{U}$SEFUL $\mathcal{W}$RITING $\mathcal{B}$LOCKS

$\mathcal{I}$f you have built castles in the air, your work need not be lost; that is where they should be. Now put foundations under them.

—HENRY DAVID THOREAU

QUESTIONS TO ASK YOURSELF WHILE READING CHAPTER 2:

1. How do I decide where to break my writing into paragraphs?
2. What are some ways to come up with interesting topic sentences for my paragraphs?
3. What kind of techniques can I use to come up with effective supporting details in the paragraphs I write?
4. How can I spot a sentence that does not belong in a paragraph I have written?
5. What are some different ways to organize paragraphs for the different kinds of writing I do?
6. How can I write an introductory paragraph that will make my reader want to read what I have to say?

$\mathcal{I}$N THE BEGINNING, THERE WERE NO PARAGRAPHS

What is a paragraph, and where does it come from? Manuscripts written and hand-copied hundreds of years ago were not divided into paragraphs. Nothing was *indented* on a page; all the margins were even. Therefore, readers had difficulty separating out the different ideas in written texts. To solve this problem, a plan was devised to break up the text by inserting a ¶ at the beginning of every new idea in a manuscript. This symbol was called a *paragraphus* (Latin for *para* meaning "part of" and *graphus* meaning "writing"). The paragraphus was the beginning of dividing writing into meaningful parts called *paragraphs*.

Nowadays, teachers and editors use the paragraphus only as a proofreading mark to point out when a writer should have started a new paragraph, but didn't. New paragraphs are signaled by indenting a line of writing five spaces. Another way to indicate paragraphs, especially in business correspondence, is merely by making two hard returns on a word processor or typewriter. This skipping of a line creates a noticeable space which divides one block of text from another.

HOW CONSCIOUS ARE YOU OF PARAGRAPHS?

When you are in the middle of reading a book or long report and want to stop because you are tired or have something else to do, do you ever stop reading in the middle of a paragraph? Or do you not stop until you have completed the paragraph you are reading? I always read until the end of a paragraph. I know that, by reading to the end of a paragraph, I have come to the end of something, even if it is just the end of one complete, developed idea.

That is, after all, what a paragraph is: one developed idea in a piece of writing.

DO IT YOURSELF!   *Proofread a Modern Manuscript*

Directions

How much do you already know about paragraphs? The selection below is laid out like an ancient manuscript with no indentation to mark where one developed idea ends and the next one begins. Using your present sense of what you think makes up a paragraph, decide where you think each new paragraph should begin. Mark the spot by inserting a paragraphus (¶).

Today visual arts can encompass much more than just sculpting, drawing, or painting realistic scenes. Modern artists vary dramatically in their approaches to art. Therefore, today's college art departments employ a variety of art instructors. This ensures students of opportunities to train in any style of art they desire to pursue. The art of sculpting itself is incredibly diverse and ingenious. Today, there are sculptors who create art works out of rusted garbage. One artist in the South makes human-looking sculptures out of garbage in his backyard. Many of these "masterpieces" now decorate the mantels of some of the most prestigious penthouses in New York City. There are also sculptors who make asymmetrical sculptures that balance on tightropes. One of these two-thousand-pound sculptures rides, perfectly balanced, across a tightrope above a large open area of a major shopping mall. Today visual art is also created on computers. One computer artist makes art from photos of butterfly wings. He scans the photos onto the computer screen and then zooms in on different patterns until a picture of something specific manifests itself in the wing. His designs appear on posters and calendars. His pictures often look like pictures of babies, trees, owls, and other natural objects; but, in reality, they are just photos of butterfly wings! Other modern artists, called abstract expressionists, make art that doesn't look like any specific object. Their pictures and sculptures are meant to be expressions of the painters' feelings or views. Many of these artists create abstract paintings that are simply black or white or blue canvasses. Other abstract expressionists splatter paint on a surface and then paint crooked lines across the splatters. One such artist calls this an expression of "pulsating energy."

- What difficulties did you encounter as you tried to divide the above selection into paragraphs?
- What understanding of paragraphs did you use as you worked with this selection?

JOURNAL PROMPT

Write about any experiences you have had with modern art. Discuss any part of your education that touched upon art. Do you ever create your own art? Do you enjoy viewing art? Or do you not believe that art is important or worth the high prices and praises it sometimes receives? Have you ever considered art as a career? Explain.

TOPIC SENTENCES TAKE CONTROL

If a paragraph is typically a group of sentences that develops <u>one idea</u>, then it must be possible to simply state that idea in a single sentence. Look back at the paragraphs you marked in the previous "Do It Yourself." Can you locate a single sentence that states the main idea developed in each paragraph? Do you agree with my choices below?

Paragraph 1: *Today visual arts can encompass much more than just sculpting, drawing, or painting realistic scenes.*
Paragraph 2: *The art of sculpting itself is incredibly diverse and ingenious.*
Paragraph 3: *Today visual art is also created on computers.*
Paragraph 4: *Other modern artists called abstract expressionists make art that doesn't look like any specific object.*

A sentence expressing the main idea of a paragraph is called the TOPIC SENTENCE or the CONTROLLING IDEA. *In the topic sentence, you, the writer, state your position on the topic of the paragraph.* You may already be familiar with topic sentences and controlling ideas. Even if you were not conscious of them, the topic sentences in the previous "Do It Yourself" activity may actually have been what enabled you to separate that unmarked "manuscript" into paragraphs.

TOPIC SENTENCES HAVE THEIR LIMITS

While being able to spot topic sentences is a useful skill for readers, the challenge at hand for you is *creating* your own topic sentences as a writer. To begin with, an effective topic sentence should be both specific and thorough. Often writers end up not controlling their ideas sufficiently because they have made their topic sentences too broad or too vague. An out-of-control topic sentence can throw the entire paragraph out of control; and the reader will be unable to identify the point the writer is trying to make. For example, a topic sentence which states, "Reading books is boring," is too broad. A more specific and thorough topic sentence might instead read like this: "Reading technical textbooks for my homework assignment is boring."

COLLABORATE!   *Choosing Controlling Topic Sentences*

Directions

Working as a group or on your own, choose the sentence in each set which would make the best topic sentence—the sentence that would help you, as a writer, maintain the most control over a paragraph. Underline your choice.

1. a. Cats are very interesting animals.
    b. Cats are easy pets to care for.
2. a. On Sunday I go to church.
    b. Sunday is the day I celebrate my religion by attending church.
3. a. Hobbies can be fun and exciting and even thrilling.
    b. My hobby, rock climbing, adds excitement to my life.
4. a. Many Japanese car models sell well in America because they are small and get good gas mileage.
    b. Japanese cars are small and get good gas mileage.
5. a. Riding a bicycle in heavy traffic areas can be dangerous.
    b. Sometimes bicycle riding is dangerous.
6. a. Foreign languages often frustrate people.
    b. Foreign language students are often frustrated by the difficulty of learning so many new words.
7. a. Many jobs require concentration and commitment.
    b. To maintain a good job, the worker must concentrate and be committed to the work.
8. a. A stamp collector does more than gather bits of paper.
    b. Stamp-collecting is a good hobby.
9. a. I have many friends.
    b. Making friends is easy for me because I am an active person.
10. a. Last Saturday Ralph and Tom fished all day.
    b. Last Saturday Ralph and Tom had great luck fishing for trout on the Santiam River.

JOURNAL PROMPT

In your journal, write about one or several of the above ideas.

WRITING YOUR OWN TOPIC SENTENCES

You can learn to write your own effective topic sentences by practicing with broad subject areas from which you create your own controlling ideas.

- Begin by choosing a broad subject area. For example, your subject might be "My Family."
- Next, take a stand on that subject. You must take a *specific* stand in order to create a controlling topic sentence. Perhaps your stand would be one of the following:

Topic sentence possibility #1:

<u>My family</u> *enjoys spending time together during the holidays.*

Topic sentence possibility #2:

<u>My family</u> *appreciates good food.*

Topic sentence possibility #3:

<u>My family</u> *is more important to me than my friends.*

What are some other topic sentences you could write to express a position you may have on the subject of "My Family"? Write three of your own topic sentences:

1. _____

   _____

   _____

2. _____

   _____

   _____

   _____

3. _____

   _____

   _____

DO IT YOURSELF! *Write Your Own Controlling Topic Sentences*

Directions

For each general subject area listed below, write three different topic sentences with controlling ideas that would work well for developing a paragraph.

1.   SUBJECT: Watching TV

    Topic sentence with controlling idea #1:

    _____

    _____

    _____

    Topic sentence with controlling idea #2:

    _____

    _____

    _____

    Topic sentence with controlling idea #3:

    _____

    _____

    _____

2.   SUBJECT: Owning Pets

    Topic sentence with controlling idea #1:

    _____

    _____

    _____

    Topic sentence with controlling idea #2:

    _____

    _____

    _____

    Topic sentence with controlling idea #3:

    _____

_____

_____

3.   SUBJECT: The President of the United States
     Topic sentence with controlling idea #1:

_____

_____

_____

     Topic sentence with controlling idea #2:

_____

_____

_____

     Topic sentence with controlling idea #3:

_____

_____

_____

4.   SUBJECT: Exercising
     Topic sentence with controlling idea #1:

_____

_____

     Topic sentence with controlling idea #2:

_____

_____

     Topic sentence with controlling idea #3:

_____

_____

_____

5. SUBJECT: When I Think . . .

Topic sentence with controlling idea #1:

_____

_____

_____

Topic sentence with controlling idea #2:

_____

_____

_____

Topic sentence with controlling idea #3:

_____

_____

_____

JOURNAL PROMPT

Write in your journal using one or several of your own controlling ideas from this activity as your starting point.

STARTING FROM OTHER DIRECTIONS

Did you have difficulty coming up with three workable topic sentences for each of the above subject areas? If you did, you may want to try some other approaches to creating topic sentences.

Remember the techniques you learned in Chapter 1, the techniques that helped you move ideas from your head to the written page. *Brainstorming* and *free writing* (sometimes used together with relaxation exercises) were two of those approaches. If you can't easily think of topic sentences just by looking at a broad subject heading, begin instead by using the subject heading as a stimulus for brainstorming or free writing. For example, you might free write for ten minutes on "My Family." Then read through all your ideas and pick out ones you can use as topic sentences for paragraphs.

DO IT YOURSELF!   *Free Write Your Way to Topic Sentences*

Directions

A. *Listed below are three different subject headings. On your own paper, free write for ten minutes on EACH of these. Follow the guidelines for free writing described on pages 14–15 in Chapter 1.*

SUBJECT AREA #1: Earning Money (Write for ten minutes.)
SUBJECT AREA #2: Learning about Computers (Write for ten minutes)
SUBJECT AREA #3: Listening to Music (Write for ten minutes.)
Attach your pages of free writing to this assignment.
B. *After you have finished your free writing for each subject, carefully read over what you have written. From each free writing, formulate three usable topic sentences that express controlling ideas. Write your sentences in the spaces provided:*

1.   SUBJECT: Earning Money
     Topic sentence with controlling idea #1:

     _____

     _____

     _____

     Topic sentence with controlling idea #2:

     _____

     _____

     _____

     Topic sentence with controlling idea #3:

     _____

     _____

     _____

2.   SUBJECT: Learning about Computers
     Topic sentence with controlling idea #1:

     _____

     _____

     _____

     Topic sentence with controlling idea #2:

     _____

     _____

     _____

     Topic sentence with controlling idea #3:

     _____

_____

_____

3.   SUBJECT: Listening to Music

Topic sentence with controlling idea #1:

_____

_____

_____

Topic sentence with controlling idea #2:

_____

_____

_____

Topic sentence with controlling idea #3:

_____

_____

_____

What were the advantages and/or disadvantages of using free writing to come up with topic sentences that contain controlling ideas for paragraphs?

_____

_____

APPING YOUR WAY TO TOPIC SENTENCES

Still another way to come up with topic sentences for paragraphs is to generate a mind map for a broad subject area. To review the technique of mind-mapping, turn to pages 19–20 in Chapter 1. If you pay close attention to the main branches on a mind map (those lines coming directly from the center), you will find they often suggest excellent topic sentences for paragraphs.

DO IT YOURSELF!   _Map Your Way to Topic Sentences_

Directions
A. Below are two broad subject areas. On your own paper, mind-map each of these following the guidelines for mind-mapping on pages 19–20 of Chapter 1.

SUBJECT AREA #1: Going to School
SUBJECT AREA #2: Building a Successful Marriage
B. *When you have finished your mind maps, study them carefully and formulate three or more usable topic sentences that express controlling ideas for each subject area. Write your sentences in the space provided:*

1.   SUBJECT: Going to School

Topic sentence with controlling idea #1:

_____

_____

_____

Topic sentence with controlling idea #2:

_____

_____

_____

Topic sentence with controlling idea #3:

_____

_____

_____

If you came up with more usable topic sentences, write them here:

_____

_____

_____

_____

_____

2.   SUBJECT: Building a Successful Marriage

Topic sentence with controlling idea #1:

_____

_____

Topic sentence with controlling idea #2:

_____

_____

_____

Topic sentence with controlling idea #3:

_____

_____

_____

If you came up with more usable topic sentences, write them here:

_____

_____

_____

_____

Of all the techniques for creating topic sentences that contain controlling ideas for paragraphs, which technique do you prefer? Why?

_____

_____

_____

_____

HEY, I NEED A LITTLE SUPPORT HERE!

When you wrote the topic sentences for the subjects suggested in this chapter so far, did specific incidents, situations, or examples come to mind that made you arrive at those topic sentences? Can you now think of some reasons the controlling ideas expressed in your sentences are true or arguable? If you were asked to explain why you took the position you did, could you support your idea?

Examples and reasons are called SUPPORTING DETAILS. Writers use supporting details to back up the controlling ideas expressed in the topic sentences of their paragraphs. For instance, from the subject of "My Family," I came up with a topic sentence that read like this:

My family enjoys spending time together during the holidays.

That sentence expresses a controlling idea I can write about because I see my entire family only during the holidays; and when we do see each other, we enjoy the time we spend together. I can support my topic sentence by writing down examples of what my family does during the holidays to have fun together.

COLLABORATE!   *Uncover My Supports*

Directions

Work with a group or on your own. In the following paragraph about "My Family," I have underlined my topic sentence.

A. *Read the following paragraph carefully, looking for supporting details.*

B. *In your own words, list at least FIVE different details used in the paragraph to support the controlling idea expressed in the underlined topic sentence.*

<u>My family enjoys spending time together during the holidays</u>. Since the holiday season is the only time all of us can come together each year, we make the most of this special time. My children each come home from their respective colleges and jobs to see me and one another. When we first gather, we talk for hours, excitedly sharing our new experiences and ideas. Since my children like to spend time in the kitchen, they sometimes make gourmet meals. Other times they make not-so-good meals. But then we all have a good laugh and usually end up going out for pizza. My favorite part is sharing our creative efforts. My daughter usually brings home some of her artwork. I share books I have written; sometimes we have a good laugh about that too. In the evening we usually stay up late playing board games or asking one another trivia questions. My youngest son always wins at trivia, but no one seems to mind. At least once every holiday season, we rent one of our favorite old movies and watch it together and reminisce. Our family seems to enjoy holidays even more now that everyone has grown up and moved away.

JOURNAL PROMPT

Write about what it is like when you see family members you haven't seen for a long time. Do some of your closest relatives live far away? Are there certain times you can always plan on seeing those people? Do you have some family members you want to see but are not sure when that will happen? What do you share with someone you haven't seen for a long time?

*M*ORE THAN ONE WAY TO SUPPORT AN IDEA

Depending on what you are writing, you may need to use different types of supporting details. Some of the most common supports writers use to develop paragraphs are *specific examples* (such as in the paragraph you just read about "My Family"); *sensory images; comparison and contrast; and reasons that demonstrate cause and effect. Specific examples* include information, illustrations, specific incidents and circumstances which prove your controlling idea. The following paragraph uses specific examples for supporting details:

> *Before I sign up for a course, I always make an effort to learn about the teacher because I know the quality and style of my instructor will have a significant effect on how well I learn. I learn best from a teacher who is confident in his or her subject area. When I feel a teacher knows the subject well, I am more comfortable asking questions. I also appreciate a teacher who values my comments and treats my input as significant during class discussion. But, since school can be frustrating and tiring, the quality I look for most in a teacher is an enthusiastic personality that includes a good sense of humor. A teacher that brings enthusiasm and humor into the classroom can make even the dullest subject exciting.*

Sensory images are descriptive details that appeal to the five senses: sight, sound, smell, touch, and taste. The following paragraph uses sensory images for supporting details:

> *Usually, I'm too broke to go out to eat, but whenever I splurge on going out to a fancy restaurant, I savor the experience. Restaurants that set the tables with candles seem dreamlike to me as I look across the table at my dinner partner whose face is illuminated by flickering shadows. Being served by waiters with a crisp manner and an erect posture makes me feel as if I am royalty. The food, however, brings me the most joy. The gourmet chefs at fancy restaurants always seem to create meals with just the right balance of seasonings to stimulate my taste buds. And the food doesn't just taste good, it looks good too. It is usually artfully placed on the plate in a visually stimulating pattern that juxtaposes soft, smooth foods to coarsely textured foods and emphasizes the contrast between dark foods and light-colored foods. As I admire the picturesque design of the fresh, hot food being placed before me, the tantalizing scents of the food provide an aromatic preview of the taste experience that awaits me. All this makes me enjoy my meal before I even eat it.*

Comparison and contrast refers to using examples of familiar objects or situations to show how your topic is the same or different. The following paragraph uses comparisons and contrasts for supporting details:

> *My freshman year of college was hard enough to adjust to without having my school place me with a roommate that was completely different from me. There I was, a black, six-foot-tall, city girl from the east coast; and I was stuck with a white, five-foot-two-inch, suburbanite from Oregon. Immediately, I knew it was going to be a miserable year because we could not possibly have anything in common. But this wasn't the case. It turned out that we both liked to listen to the same background music when we studied in our room. Of course, I thought we would never hang out with the same friends. But that was not true either. While my roommate and I did not have all the same friends, we had many friends in common. We both seemed to get along with the same kind of people. In addition to that, we both loved to go to plays, liked the same movies, and watched the*

same television shows. We had differences, of course, but that gave us something interesting to talk about because we were both "talkers." After the shock of my first impression had worn off, I decided that spending a year living with my "opposite" was not so bad. In fact, we remained roommates until we graduated.

Cause and effect emphasizes reasons that contribute to your controlling idea and/or results that occur as an outcome of your controlling idea. The following paragraph uses supporting details that emphasize cause and effect:

> *Even though most of us are aware that good health can best be maintained by exercising regularly, many of us slip into unhealthy lifestyles because we lack self discipline. Instead of getting up early and exercising before school or work, we stay up late and watch TV because we don't have the self discipline to turn off the late night talk show. Therefore, we are too tired to jump out of bed in the morning when the alarm first rings. Instead we push the snooze button and sleep an extra half hour. That, of course, gives us a late start. As a result, we end up rushing all day long. Because we are "stressed out" by the time we arrive home from work or school, we "unwind" by watching television or taking a nap. Exercise is usually not an option because it takes too much effort to change clothes and put on a pair of athletic shoes.*

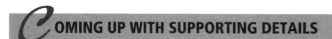 COMING UP WITH SUPPORTING DETAILS

At this point, you may be thinking that coming up with supporting details is a big order. But you already know how to use supports for your ideas. You use them every day in conversation. When you voice an unusual opinion or tell an interesting story, whomever you're talking to might not agree with you or believe your story. Sometimes you have to back up what you say—with supporting details. For example, you might *list reasons* for forming your unusual opinion. You might *describe incidents* in graphic detail to make your story believable. In other words, you use supporting details to develop and back up your ideas.

Often the person you're talking to draws supporting details out of you by asking questions like

When?

Where?

How?

Why?

What do you mean by that?

What is it like?

If you ask yourself these same questions, coming up with supporting details for your paragraphs can be quite easy. Other questions that are especially useful for generating supports for controlling ideas expressed in topic sentences include the following:

How do I know?

What example or illustration would make my point clear?

How can I appeal to my reader?

One of the easiest ways to generate supporting details for paragraphs is to ask yourself specific questions—and then **answer them**!!

DO IT YOURSELF!   *Interview Yourself*

Directions

Choose three of the controlling ideas you wrote in any of the previous exercises in this chapter. Ask any of the following questions that could apply to each idea:

When?

Where?

How?

Why?

What do you mean by that?

What is it like?

How do I know?

What example or illustration would make my point clear?

How can I appeal to my reader?

Since different topic sentences will naturally require different types of supporting details, not all the above questions will apply to every topic sentence, or controlling idea, you write. Answer as many as you can, however. In addition, you may make up your own questions that apply more directly to the controlling idea.

1.   Controlling Idea:

_____

_____

_____

Question: _____

Answer: _____

_____

_____

Question: _____

Answer: _____

_____

_____

Question: _____

Answer: _____

_____

_____

Question: _____

Answer:_____

_____

_____

Question: _____

Answer: _____

_____

_____

2.   Controlling Idea:

_____

_____

_____

Question: _____

Answer: _____

_____

_____

Question: _____

Answer: _____

_____

_____

Question: _____

Answer: _____

_____

_____

Question: _____

Answer: _____

_____

_____

Question: _____

Answer: _____

_____

_____

3.   Controlling Idea:

_____

_____

_____

Question: _____

Answer: _____

_____

_____

Question: _____

Answer: _____

_____

_____

Question: _____

Answer: _____

_____

_____

Question: _____

Answer: _____

_____

_____

Question: _____

Answer: _____

_____

_____

WHICH SUPPORTS REALLY SUPPORT?

When writing supporting ideas, you need to be thoughtful and careful to use only specific details that support your topic sentence. Readers read your writing to learn something new or to understand your perspective, which may differ from theirs. They will become skeptical if they perceive your statements are untrue or vague. They will become bored if you only give them generalizations. They will become disillusioned if you merely restate your topic sentence over and over in different words rather than provide reasons and examples to support your ideas. They will lose interest if you wander from the subject and head off on an unrelated tangent. "Supports" that don't relate directly to the topic sentence and supports that lack detail only weaken your paragraph. Remember, the purpose of providing supporting details is to strengthen your paragraph—to strengthen the position you have taken and stated in the topic sentence.

Be sure that all the sentences in your finished paragraph clearly relate to the topic sentence. This will give your writing "unity." After you have finished writing a paragraph, ask yourself, "Do all the sentences fit within the parameters of the controlling idea I expressed in my topic sentence?" If the answer is NO, rid your writing of any sentence that disrupts your paragraph's unity.

COLLABORATE!   *Throwing Out Weak Supports*

Directions

The following paragraphs contain some sentences that are either vague or don't support the topic sentence. Working with a group or on your own:

A. Find the vague and unrelated sentences and circle them.

B. Decide whether to cross out these sentences OR revise them to fit within the parameters of the controlling idea of the paragraph.

C. In the space provided, write the kind of supporting detail that predominates in each paragraph: example, sensory images, comparison-contrast or cause-effect.

D. The topic sentence in each paragraph has been underlined for you.

Paragraph #1:

I enjoy going to toy stores because the atmosphere is stimulating. When I first enter a toy store, I am immediately struck by the brilliant colors of the toys. The "Nerf" toy section attracts me with its neon, multi-colored sports equipment. I can't help but reach out to touch the "Nerf" toys because they are soft and bouncy and fun to play with. "Nerf" is an awesome brand if you ask me. Toy stores are often filled with upbeat sounds. I have a friend who is deaf; of course, the sounds don't bother her. In the background, there are squeals of excited children. The crisp tones of musical toys, the rhythmic choo-choo of toy trains, and the distorted speech of talking computers create a symphony one hears only in toy stores. Some toy companies make talking computers; other companies just make ones with screens that display printing.

Predominant kind of supporting details used: _____

Paragraph #2:

Shopping for kids' toys can be frustrating for adults. Typically, toy stores are large and packed with aisles and aisles of toys. In our town there are three toy stores; they are Olson's, Toys-Я-Us, and Toy Time. Because the stores are so large and full, a busy adult has difficulty deciding what to buy. Video games are sold at toy stores, and you can buy books there too. If the adult shopper doesn't have any idea of what to buy in the first place, the overwhelming selection only makes the job more difficult. Often the lights and colors in big stores are so bright and stimulating they distract and wear down the shopper. Toy stores are just bad news as far as I'm concerned. Also, toys nowadays are so different from the toys that were popular when adult shoppers were younger; this makes choosing the right toy an even tougher problem.

Predominant kind of supporting details used: _____

Paragraph #3:

There are three main reasons I love going to toy stores. First, I enjoy watching the children as they look at the toys. Some children do not mind their parents very well. Seeing youngsters become excited about toy dinosaurs, fire engines, and life-like dolls makes me feel like a child myself. I also love to walk through toy stores just to see the new toys that toymakers have invented. Every year the shelves display creative new playthings for children, playthings that are the products of the creative minds of adults who have not forgotten what it is like to be a child. Some toys are not suitable for young children under three years of age. I have a grandson who is two. Finally, I love toy stores most of all because they provide an escape from the reality of daily life. In a toy store I can become caught up in the fantasy world of children. Toys surround me instead of concrete buildings, and traffic, and parking lots. The cheerful sounds and lively colors make my spirits soar; and, for a few moments, I forget my worries and stresses. Toys are a multi-million dollar business.

Predominant kind of supporting details used: _____

Paragraph #4:

Modern toys do not allow children to be as creative as did the toys I bought for my children when they were toddlers. Today toys are complex and intricate, so children don't need to "pretend" they have interesting characteristics. When my children were toddlers, there was only one "Barbie." My daughter would pretend that Barbie was a movie star or a pet trainer or whatever my little girl's imagination inspired her to invent. She really has a great imagination. But today there are dozens of different kinds of Barbies. There are Barbie doctors, Barbie rock n' roll stars, Barbie horse trainers, and more. Barbies also cost much more than they did fifteen years ago. Children who play with those specialized Barbies don't have to <u>pretend</u> that their dolls have different occupations or lead different lives. After all, life choices often begin forming in childhood. Legos have changed too. Today Legos come in kits that are already designed to be made into specific buildings or ships or towns. Years ago, when I bought Legos for my children, I bought snap-together colored blocks that came in simple boxes or buckets; and the children were expected to build whatever their imaginations inspired them to create.

Predominant kind of supporting details used: _____

JOURNAL PROMPT

Write about experiences you have had with toys or toy shopping. Consider how you felt about your toys as a child. Do you have many opportunities today to play with children's toys? How do today's toys differ from the toys you played with as a child? How do you feel when you go into a toy store? Why?

PUTTING PARAGRAPHS IN ORDER

So far, we have discussed topic sentences and supporting details. What else do you need to know to write a good paragraph? It might be helpful to know how to decide which sentences to put where in your paragraph. After all, readers place much greater trust in writers who appear to be organized. I'm sure you've heard writing teachers tell you to "organize your thoughts." But how do you do that?

To organize sentences in a paragraph, you first consider the possibilities: What options are available to you as a writer? Four common ways to organize sentences in a paragraph are:

1. Spatial (space) Order
2. Chronological (time) Order
3. Order of Importance
4. Cause and Effect Order

Spatial Order

When writers use spatial, or space order, they present information about people, places, or things in terms of spatial relationships—how they are arranged. Space order is most often used when writing *descriptive paragraphs*. For example, if you were describing a room using spatial order, you could start from the door where you enter the room and describe each object as you move your gaze around the room beginning with the wall on one side of the door and moving clear around the room until you end up describing the wall on the other side of the door. Or you could choose, instead, to describe the room from the ceiling down to the floor, or the center to the outside, or using any logical spatial sequence.

Chronological Order

Chronological order means that details in paragraphs are arranged in a *time* sequence. Writers use chronological order to tell stories and describe events (*narrative writing*); they also use this order when writing instructions or explaining processes (*process writing*). If you were to write a paragraph arranged in chronological order, you would begin by telling about what happened first, then next, and finally what happened last or most recently.

Order of Importance

While order of importance can be used for many different types of writing, it is especially useful in *expository writing* which "exposes" information to readers. Paragraphs using order of importance to present supporting ideas can be organized in several ways. The supporting details can be arranged in an order from least important to most important or from most important to least important. Some writers prefer to begin with the second most important idea; then put the least important idea in the middle of paragraph where it is more likely to be skimmed over by the reader; and finally, place the most important idea at the end where it makes a lasting impression. Which arrangement you choose depends on your subject, the reader, and the purpose of your writing.

Comparison and contrast paragraphs often use order of importance to arrange details; the similarities or differences compared and contrasted become more severe or less severe as the paragraph develops.

Cause and Effect Order

Still another way to organize supporting details in paragraphs is to use cause and effect order. Cause and effect order is used for cause and effect paragraphs. In this kind of paragraph, a cause may be followed by its effect; or an effect may be followed by its cause. Sometimes the topic sentence is the effect and all the supports are the causes. For example, the following topic sentence expresses an *effect*:

> *Smoking is hazardous to your health.*

The supporting details that may lead the reader to accept this as a credible effect may include the following causes:

> *Smoking increases your risk of getting lung cancer.*
> *Smoking increases your risk of having a heart attack.*
> *Smoking increases your risk of becoming a stroke victim.*
> *Smoking increases your risk of contracting upper respiratory diseases.*

DO IT YOURSELF!   *Get Organized*

Directions

Carefully read the following lists of supporting details that support each topic sentence. In the space provided, write the type of order that has been used to organize the sentences: space order, chronological order, order of importance, and cause and effect order.

1. Order type: _____

    Topic sentence: **Every weekday morning my routine is the same.**

    Supports:

    1. My first physical task each day is shutting off my alarm clock.

    2. After I do that, I lie in bed, staring at the ceiling while I remind myself what day it is and what I have to do.

    3. Next I get up and head directly for the shower.

    4. Once the shower water warms up, I jump in and clean up for the new day.

2. Order type: _____

    Topic sentence: **I still remembered when I first stepped foot into the castle.**

    1. The door was old and creaked when I opened it.

    2. As I stepped into the room, I was startled by the cold hard floor.

    3. But the center of the floor was covered by a brilliant, expensive looking, oriental rug.

    4. Illuminating the rug were filtered rays of sunlight which entered from the window cut in the wall opposite the door.

3. Order type: _____

    Topic sentence: **I know of at least three reasons people go to school.**

    1. Some people go to school because they believe it provides them with an opportunity to obtain higher paying jobs.

    2. Other people are students because they love to learn.

    3. There are also people who don't have anything better to do than to go to school.

4. Order type: _____

    Topic sentence: **When I go shopping for a new car, there are certain factors I consider.**

    1. To me, the most important consideration when buying a car is whether or not I can afford it.

    2. Once I find cars that are within my price range, I make sure that the models are safe and sturdy.

    3. Then I look to see if the cars get good gas mileage.

    4. The least of my worries is whether or not the color is attractive.

COLLABORATE!   *Write Your Own Orders*

Directions

A. *Working with a group or on your own, write four supporting details for each topic sentence listed below. Each set requires a different kind of order; the order is specified for you.*

B. *After you have written the sentences containing the supporting details, identify the* <u>*type*</u> *of paragraph you have developed. Is it descriptive, narrative, expository, comparison and contrast, or cause and effect?*

C. *When you are finished, trade your work with another group and check for any vague sentences or sentences that don't support the controlling idea.*

Note: ALL your supporting details must be written in COMPLETE SENTENCES!!

1. Spatial order (space)

    Topic Sentence: **Our classroom is/isn't a typical classroom. (pick one viewpoint)**

    Supporting detail 1:

    Supporting detail 2:

    Supporting detail 3:

    Supporting detail 4:

    Type of paragraph: _____

2. Chronological order (time)

    Topic sentence: **I have a foolproof system for preparing for tests.**

    Supporting detail 1:

    Supporting detail 2:

    Supporting detail 3:

    Supporting detail 4:

    Type of paragraph: _____

3. Order of importance

    Topic sentence: **There are many factors to consider when choosing a class.**

    Supporting detail 1:

    Supporting detail 2:

    Supporting detail 3:

    Supporting detail 4:

    Type of paragraph: _____

4. Cause and effect

    Topic sentence: **There are numerous ways I can improve my writing.**

    Supporting detail 1:

Supporting detail 2:

Supporting detail 3:

Supporting detail 4:

Type of paragraph: _____

DO IT YOURSELF!   *Make Sentences into Organized Paragraphs*

Directions

Select ONE of the above topics you developed in the previous collaborate activity. <u>On your own paper</u>, write a paragraph that uses all those sentences. Pay attention to the wording of your sentences to ensure that one sentence leads smoothly into the next.

*L*ET'S SHAPE UP!

Now that you have learned some approaches for organizing the supporting details in your paragraphs, you might be thinking about *where to place the topic sentence* that expresses the controlling idea of your paragraph. Or did you just naturally assume it would be the first sentence of every paragraph? That is not necessarily the case. While topic sentences are most often located at the beginning of a paragraph, they are not always. Sometimes writers don't state the controlling idea of the paragraph until the very last sentence! Just where writers choose to place the topic sentence depends on the kind of logic they are using to process the information in their paragraphs.

Writing and reading teachers often use the term "paragraph shapes" to talk about the placement of the topic sentence in relation to the supporting sentences. The three most common paragraph shapes are depicted this way:

Paragraph Shape #1:

This is the paragraph that begins with the topic sentence—the controlling idea. The supporting details follow. Writers arranging information this way are using *deductive reasoning* because they first state the main idea and then from that they come up with examples that bear out the truth of their statement.

Paragraph Shape #2:

This kind of paragraph ends with the topic sentence. This shape is most often used for persuasive paragraphs. Writers first present a series of supporting details which can only leave the reader to agree with whatever the topic sentence concludes. The logic used is *inductive reasoning*. Because the individual details, when added together, create a powerful argument for the concluding idea, which is the topic sentence, the reader is cleverly led to believe something he or she may not have accepted unless the proof had been presented first.

Paragraph Shape #3:

Can you guess where the topic sentence goes in this paragraph? It is located both at the beginning and the end. That is, it is stated at the beginning; but, then, it is restated in different words at the end. This is a particularly strong paragraph shape. When writers want to emphasize the idea in a certain paragraph and ensure that the readers have understood the point, square paragraphs are the best choice.

There may be times when experienced writers write paragraphs with no stated topic sentence. Instead the topic sentence is *implied* by the writers' choice of supporting detail. For now, however, we will focus on mastering the traditional three paragraph shapes just described.

DO IT YOURSELF! *Draw the Paragraph Shapes*

Directions
Read the three paragraphs below. Underline the topic sentence (or sentences) in each. Then indicate the paragraph's shape by drawing it superimposed on top of the paragraph.

1.   Stereotypes are most often not true and can cause a person who believes in them to make foolish decisions. The Hickydoodumb Company had a manager, Mr. Droll, who believed in stereotypes. When Mr. Droll needed to hire a computer engineer, he hired a Japanese man named Sazo. Even though Sazo had come into the office seeking a job in the shipping department, Mr. Droll hired Sazo as the computer engineer because he had heard that all Japanese people were computer geniuses. But Sazo didn't know anything about computer engineering; he was a weightlifter who had recently won the U.S. weightlifting championship. The Hickeydoodum Company's shipping department also had an opening for a dock loader, so Mr. Droll hired Jack, an African American, to fill the dock loader position. Droll believed all African Americans were strong and could work hard. But Jack had just received his degree in computer engineering and knew much more about programming computers than he did about loading docks. Thus Mr. Droll's two new employees were not effective in their new positions, and the Hickeydoodum Company's efficiency suffered. Since stereotypes are most often not true, believing in them is foolish.

2.   For me, buying my books each semester is a skill. My first plan of attack when buying books is to obtain my schedule as early as I possibly can. If I'm one of the first students to obtain my course schedule, then I can be one of the first students to go to the bookstore. And that's exactly what I do after I find out my schedule; I go directly to the bookstore. Arriving early at the bookstore allows me the opportunity to buy used books which are considerably cheaper than new ones. Once I have picked up all the used texts for my classes, I check to see if I have to buy any books that aren't textbooks (like novels or poetry books). I write down the names of those books and head for the used paperback store near my home. There I can sometimes find a $10 book for $1! Every semester that I use my book buying technique, I manage to save between $100 and $200.

3.   Until this year I've always lived in dormitories at college. Now I live in a

house with two roommates. Because there is more space, there is more dust. So every week my roommates and I take turns dusting the furniture. In my dormitory I didn't have a kitchen; but in the house there is one. It doesn't take long for the three of us to accumulate a sink full of dirty dishes. To avoid attracting insects and other critters, one of us has to wash the dishes every day. Of course, we also have a bathroom in our house. In the dormitory the bathroom was cleaned by the cleaning staff every day. In our house we are the cleaning staff, so we have made it a rule to clean up after ourselves every time we use the bathroom. Living in a house requires much more responsibility than living in a dormitory.

JOURNAL PROMPT

Write about stereotypes. Do you think others stereotype you? Why? Do you stereotype others? Give specific examples. How do you feel about stereotyping? What are some of the stereotypes you know of? Are they accurate? Give reasons for your answer.

JOURNAL PROMPT

Write about any unique ways you save money on books. What do you do with your books after a class is over? Why? Do you write in your textbooks? Why or why not? What has been your favorite textbook since you began taking classes? Why?

JOURNAL PROMPT

Have you ever lived in a dormitory? Do you know anyone who has? Do you prefer living in a dormitory to living off campus? Why? Have you ever lived with a difficult roommate? What made the person so difficult to live with? Do you think others would consider you a difficult roommate to live with? Why?

*N*OW THE ESSAY COMES MORE EASILY

Usually when we write, we are asked to write more than just a paragraph. We may be asked to write proposals, letters, or essays. In my case, I was asked to write this book. I planned this book just as I would plan a paragraph. I have a controlling idea (knowing more about English can help students become better writers), and my supports for this idea are the different chapters I chose to include in the book. In a way, that is just like organizing a paragraph, except paragraph supports are sentences rather than chapters.

In essays, which consist of many paragraphs, the controlling idea is stated in a sentence called a *thesis statement*. A thesis statement is like a topic sentence for an entire essay. All the paragraphs in the body of an essay support the thesis statement in the same way the sentences in a paragraph support the topic sentence.

The thesis statement typically appears in the first paragraph of the essay which is called the *introductory paragraph*.

Another purpose of the introductory paragraph is to make the reader want to read the essay. In other words, the introductory paragraph tries to attract the reader's attention. Therefore, introductory paragraphs require some thought: "What will attract the reader's attention to the subject of my writing?"

Some beginnings that **will not** attract the reader's attention in a positive way include the following:

In this paper I will explain. . . . This is too obvious and does not need to be stated. I don't know very much about this, but. . . ." Apologizing for what you are about to say will not give your reader cause to read further.

Instead, beginnings that **will** attract the readers' attention in a positive way include:

- *Beginning with an interesting quotation*:
  You can find thought-provoking and fitting quotations on almost any subject in a book of quotations. Your library or local bookstore probably stocks a selection of such books. The most well-known is *Bartlett's Familiar Quotations*. The daily newspaper is also a handy source of quotations.

- *Beginning with a thought-provoking question*:
  The best kind of question to introduce a piece of writing is a *rhetorical question*. A rhetorical question is one you ask not because you expect a direct answer, but in order to plant the question or idea in the reader's mind. Whether you begin with a rhetorical question or a direct one the reader can answer, the question should be challenging enough to make the reader think about the answer. A well-chosen question will start your reader thinking about the topic you are about to present.

- *Beginning with an interesting personal story*:
  Everyone is curious about the personal lives of others. Perhaps that comes from the fact that we can all relate more directly to personal aspects of peoples lives than to impersonal information. Therefore, one way to attract your readers' interest to a subject is to tell a personal story that somehow relates to that subject. For example, if you were writing about alcoholism, you might begin with a personal story about how your own life has been touched by alcoholism.

- *Beginning with a startling statistic*:
  As long as they are not offensive, startling statistics or statements will attract your readers' attention. You can wake up readers if you shock them a little.

- *Beginning with a background of the subject*:
  Begin with historical background, explanations as to why the topic is interesting to you, or arguments often made on the topic.

THE CHALLENGE OF THE INTRODUCTORY PARAGRAPH

The hardest part of writing an introductory paragraph is to move *naturally* from your attention-getter to the thesis statement of your paper. For example, suppose you begin with the question, "Do you like water sports?" From this, it would be too abrupt to jump directly to the thesis statement, "There are three skills you must master in order to become an expert water skier." Somewhere in between your attention-getter and your topic sentence you need transitional or background information that smoothly moves your reader from your attention-getting question to the thesis statement of your essay:

> *Do you like water sports?* Many people do. My favorite water sport is skiing. It is a sport that requires both instruction and practice. *There are three skills you must master in order to become an expert water skier.*

COLLABORATE! *Focusing on Introductory Paragraphs*

Directions

Working with a group or on your own, read the following paragraphs carefully.

A. *Underline the part of the paragraph you believe is the attention-getter. In the space provided, write which kind of attention-getter the paragraph uses: quotation, question, personal story, statistic, or background.*

B. *Circle the sentence you believe to be the thesis sentence of the essay being introduced.*

C. *Discuss your thoughts about how the writer of each paragraph makes the transition from the attention-getter to the thesis statement.*

Paragraph #1:

Type of attention-getter:_____

How often do you let the people you love know how much you love them? Every one of us has responsibilities and personal issues to deal with on a daily basis. And sometimes we become so busy we don't take time to say "I love you." Yet it is healthy for us and our loved ones to remind each other of our love. In fact, the presence or lack of love in a person's life can mold self-concept, predict future success, and affect longevity.

Paragraph #2:

Type of attention-getter:_____

The most common killer of young adults ages 25 to 40 is now AIDS. Just a few years ago, the leading cause of death for this same age group was accidental death. Since the AIDS virus has been discovered, the epidemic has grown more severe and more threatening. Still, many people ignore or avoid the crisis. They think if it doesn't interfere in their personal lives, then they shouldn't make it their problem. But AIDS <u>does</u> affect everyone's life. People in every community, in every walk of life, with every sexual orientation are dying slow, painful, and undeserving deaths. As living, breathing human beings, we are all part of humanity; and we are all affected by this horrendous disease. Therefore, we should all be taking positive steps to fight against the AIDS virus.

Paragraph #3:

Type of attention-getter:_____

"There is room for everybody in America, has he any particular talent, or industry," wrote St. Jean de Crevecoeur in his *Letters from an American Farmer*. Crevecoeur believed that all people could live and prosper in America as long as they worked and had survival skills. He was right. There is room for everybody in America; but, unfortunately, not everybody makes room for one another. Talent and industry are not the only features that identify Americans. Every American also possesses a culture, a heredity, and a religious belief that is not necessarily the same as his or her fellow American's. Although, ideally, all one should have to possess to be a member of a community is talent or industry, many Americans do not make room for other Americans because of differences in ethnic background, race, and religion.

Paragraph #4:

Type of attention-getter:_____

I never thought I could live without meat! I was a carnivore in every sense of the word. Each meal that entered my digestive system contained either juicy red meat or deep-fried chicken or tender pork. This was until I read a book about maintaining a healthy heart. The book made me incredibly aware of my body. It made me realize that, by eating meat, I was harming my body—the body that constantly worked to keep me alive and healthy. For the first time, I became acutely aware of the fact that my body and I had a relationship. In my case, the relationship was one in which I was doing all the taking and my body was doing all the giving. So I took some steps to become a vegetarian, some steps to create a healthy relationship with my body.

Paragraph #5:

Type of attention-getter:_____

For centuries, society has placed great importance on ability—the ability to succeed in certain areas. People with extraordinary abilities have traditionally been referred to as "gifted." A boy in my high school was an all-state basketball player. A girl I grew up with now has a lead in a Broadway musical in New York City because she is a gifted singer. Unfortunately, people who are recognized most for their abilities are often people like athletes and performers who have rare or peculiar abilities. Society has too long overlooked that each one of us is "gifted." Perhaps your gift is being a good listener or my gift is being a good parent or someone else's gift is being a good friend. The society we live in would be stronger if we celebrated certain gifts that are more universal and more important than the peculiar gifts of athletes and performers.

THE CONCLUSION, AT LAST

Another type of paragraph you will need when writing an essay is the concluding paragraph. The concluding paragraph is the last paragraph of an essay. An effective concluding paragraph usually begins with a summary of the thesis and the supports that were presented in the body of the essay. A strong concluding paragraph ends with some final remarks that reinforce the significance of the material to the reader.

An example of a concluding paragraph for this chapter might read like this:

> *In this chapter you have been introduced to paragraphs. First you learned to write topic sentences with controlling ideas and to support them with details such as examples, sensory images, comparison-contrast, and reasons. Next came paragraph organization. In this section you learned different ways to organize paragraphs according to space, time, order of importance, and cause and effect. Finally, you learned about introductory and concluding paragraphs. Clearly there is much more to paragraphs than simply indenting five spaces. Paragraphs help writers organize their thoughts and present them to readers in an orderly fashion. Now that you have learned the intricacies of paragraph writing, you can apply your new knowledge every time you create a piece of writing.*

THE READING CONNECTION

1. Look carefully at the paragraphs in an essay. In the library you will find books of essays; your teacher might have a collection of essays you may look at; or you may simply go back over essays that you or your classmates have previously written.
2. Another source of paragraphs is magazine articles that interest you.
3. Or you may simply look through a textbook and study the paragraphs in a chapter you have recently read.

Bring examples of any of the above kinds of writing to class and be prepared to discuss different writers' use of paragraphs. The following is a list of suggestions and questions to help you prepare for your discussion:

- Look for *controlling ideas* in the paragraphs you read. Can you find some clearly expressed topic sentences? Do some paragraphs seem to lack topic sentences? Why do you think that may be?

- Look for *different kinds of details.* Can you find *examples, sensory images,* and *reasons* in the paragraphs you are looking at? Do any of the paragraphs use *comparison-contrast* for support? Why do you think the writer chose the kinds of supports he or she chose?

- Look for *different kinds of organization.* Can you find examples of spatial organization, or chronological organization? Can you find ideas organized by order of importance or cause and effect? Why do you think the author chose a particular kind of organization? Would you have made the same decision? Explain.

- Pay careful attention to *introductory and concluding paragraphs.* Has the writer taken care to write an interesting introduction that attracts your attention? If so, what kind of attention-getter does the writer use? How effectively does the writer move from the attention-getter to his or her statement of what the piece of writing is about? Give examples.

THE WRITING CONNECTION

1.   Using "My Favorite Store" as your broad subject, write a carefully thought out paragraph that emphasizes sensory details as supports. Be sure to include a clear topic sentence in which you take a position that suggests why this store is your favorite. To develop supports for your topic, pay special attention to smells, sounds, visual stimuli (such as colors, arrangement of displays, etc.). What are some ways in which your sense of feel is affected (by surfaces of counters, textures of goods being sold, etc.)?

2.   Write a paragraph that tells a story; in other words, write a narrative, about either "The Worst Party I Ever Attended" or "The Best Party I Ever Attended." State your controlling idea clearly in a complete sentence, the topic sentence. Use *chronological order* to arrange your supports: When did the party take place? How did the party begin? What were some specific occurrences or actions of people that made the party "the worst" or the "best"? When did you leave the party . . . ?

3.   Write a paragraph about "Why I Like Traveling" or "Why I Dislike Traveling." State your topic sentence clearly. Arrange your paragraph using cause and effect order. You may want to use examples and reasons for supporting details: Are your feelings about traveling caused by a particular positive or negative experience? Does money affect your attitude towards travel? Does your fear of flying or driving long distances affect whether you like to travel? Or do you love to fly . . . ?

4.   Using one of the following quotations as an attention-getter, write an introductory paragraph. Decide *what* the paragraph will be introducing. In other words, formulate a thesis statement for the bigger piece of writing your paragraph is designed to introduce. Be sure the quotation you choose is suitable for the thesis statement you formulate. Work thoughtfully to move your reader naturally from the attention-getting quotation to your thesis statement.

It is never too late to be what you might have been.—George Eliot

A good reputation is more valuable than money.—Publius

Govern a family as you would fry small fish—gently.—Chinese proverb

The only way to have a friend is to be one.—Ralph Waldo Emerson

Don't be afraid your life will end; be afraid that it will never begin.—Grace Hansen

No one can make you feel inferior without your consent.—Eleanor Roosevelt

To me, old age is always fifteen years older than I am.—Bernard Baruch

Marriage is our last, best chance to grow up.—Joseph Barth

A divorce is like an amputation; you survive, but there's less of you.—Margaret Atwood

5. Write a paragraph of your choice. Pay careful attention to creating a workable topic sentence and strong supports. Choose the kind of organization that best fits the paragraph you are writing.

SELF TEST FOR CHAPTER 2

1. The word *paragraphus* means _____.

2. The controlling idea in a paragraph is also called the _____ sentence.

3. Four types of supporting details discussed in this chapter include

    _____, _____, _____, and _____.

4. When all the sentences that make up a paragraph relate to the topic sentence, we say that paragraph has _____.

5. Sentences that are _____ or _____ should be eliminated from paragraphs.

6. _____ order means time order.

7. When writers describe the locations of things in a paragraph, that paragraph is said to have a _____ order.

8. The order _____ is most often used in expository writing.

9. Cause and _____ order is used for cause and _____ paragraphs.

10. The "shape" of a paragraph is determined by the placement of the

    _____.

FINAL JOURNAL WRITING

In your journal write what you learned about paragraphs in this chapter. What was the most useful part of the chapter? How can you apply what you have learned in this chapter to your own writing and reading? Do you have any questions about paragraphs that were not answered by this chapter? If so, what are they?

$\mathcal{R}$EVISING . . . $\mathcal{B}$ARRIERS TO $\mathcal{R}$EWRITING

$\mathcal{J}$t is the best of all trades, to make songs, and the second best to sing them.

—HILAIRE BELLOC

QUESTIONS TO THINK ABOUT WHILE READING CHAPTER 3:

1. How well does my writing communicate my ideas?
2. Do I ever avoid using words I can't spell?
3. Do I avoid "fancy" punctuation, like semicolons?
4. Do I ever hope my grade depends more on content than mechanics?
5. Do I feel bad about myself when I get a paper back full of red marks?
6. Do I feel embarrassed about asking questions in my writing class?
7. When my sentences don't sound right, can I figure out how to improve them?
8. Could I spot a "fragment" in my own writing?
9. Do I understand the *reasons* behind any of the "rules" I've learned in English classes?
10. How much do I really know about English?

Creating is the first important part of the writing process. Without the creating step, there would be nothing for readers to read. But what if you write something and no one reads it? Nearly two thousand years ago, the philosopher Martial wrote, "He writes nothing whose writings are not read." Having your writing read—communicating what you have written—is, in some cases, as important as writing it.

$\mathcal{N}$OW IT'S TIME TO TAKE RESPONSIBILITY

Does your writing communicate to your reader? This is a thought you put aside when you were creating—when you were concentrating on relaxing and permitting thoughts and emotions to flow freely—when you were brainstorming and free writing words and phrases and sentences with no logical arrangement. In the creating step, you could bask in permissiveness and allow yourself to run free. The focus was on you, the writer.

In the communicating step, however, the focus moves to the reader. In this step, your role as a writer is to prepare your writing for the outside world—the world where teachers grade papers and bosses write evaluations and readers refuse to read anything that isn't interesting as well as clear. To prepare your writing for these audiences, you move from being permissive to disciplining; you move from creating to revising.

When you revise, you take on the responsibilities of a disciplining parent. You prepare the writer to whom you gave so much permission during the creative step to face the demands of the real world. This is the time to gently, but firmly, remind that part of you who was free to create that, with freedom, often comes responsibility.

You see, writing is first generating ideas, then organizing them; and finally it is revising those ideas so they communicate to an audience or reader. As your writing evolves, your role as a writer changes from creator to communicator.

I see but one rule: to be clear. If I am not clear, all my world crumbles to nothing.

—*Marie Henri Beyle Stendhal*

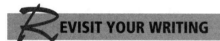

REVISIT YOUR WRITING

Which one is you?

Is This You?

- You carefully proofread and edit before handing in your writing.
- You meticulously check and re-check your paper for correct spelling and punctuation.
- You make sure you have written only complete sentences and avoided fragments and run-ons.
- You painstakingly revise your first draft to make your writing clear, accurate, and readable—as perfect as you can make it.

OR

Is This You?

- Once you have written the assigned number of words, you hand in your paper "as is."
- Knowing your paper will be returned with red marks anyway, you leave it up to the teacher to find spelling errors, insert commas, point out fragments and run-on sentences.
- You do not seriously proofread for mistakes until after the teacher has graded your paper and given you a second chance to re-write.

- By not taking responsibility for your own revisions, you ensure your teacher actually gets much more practice inserting punctuation and repairing misspelled words than you do.

Careful editing and proofreading for mistakes become your responsibility as you prepare your writing to be read. A simple *misspelled word* can be distracting and may cause your reader to question your credibility and competence. *Punctuation*, incorrectly placed, can actually make your message say something entirely different from what you intended. Careless *word choices* can create a tone that communicates an attitude you had not meant to convey. *Incomplete sentences* can confuse your reader and cause your writing to make no sense at all. Yet, your finished writing may contain all these errors if you do not surmount the barriers posed by revising.

REVISING BARRIER #1: PRACTICING "SAFE WRITING"

I suspect student writers sometimes skip the revising step. I believe this happens because, in the writing process, as there are *blocks* to creating, there are also *barriers to revising*.

Have you ever avoided having to revise and rewrite by choosing what I call "safe writing"? Safe writing is what happens when you want to use a word you can't spell, but you choose another, less appropriate, word instead just because it is easier to spell. You make the "safe" choice, not the "best" choice, because you don't want to be marked down for spelling. Safe writing means you might choose to avoid semicolons because you are worried about putting them in the wrong place. Instead, you "safely" use commas or stick to writing short sentences.

True, safe writing may help you avoid mistakes. Yet, too much safe writing may also stifle your style. Safe writing may actually keep you from developing as a writer. Growing as a writer involves taking risks—risks such as:

- exploring new word choices;
- experimenting with words you have only read or heard but have never used yourself;
- pushing every punctuation mark to its limit—discovering all the applications of different marks including semicolons and colons;
- playing with word order—attempting new ways of arranging your ideas.

By taking chances, you will learn new ways to communicate through writing. Free writing is not the only step in the writing process where you can be creative. You can be creative and innovative in the revising step as well.

Don't allow safe writing to become a barrier. Don't be afraid to take risks even though that may mean making some new mistakes. Ultimately, the lessons you learn from your mistakes can improve your writing skills. We often learn best from our mistakes.

Experience is the name everyone gives to their mistakes.

—*Oscar Wilde*

DO IT YOURSELF!   *Write About "Safe Writing"*

Directions

Write about mistakes you have made in writing and how you have learned from them or how they have caused you to avoid trying new ways of communicating. Have you ever practiced any type of "safe writing"? Explain in detail.

_____

_____

_____

_____

_____

_____

_____

_____

_____

_____

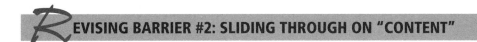

REVISING BARRIER #2: SLIDING THROUGH ON "CONTENT"

Have you ever been in a writing class where your assignments received two grades, one for "mechanics" (spelling, punctuation, sentence structure) and the other for "content" (your ideas)? I sometimes grade papers that way. But for some students, this grading approach justifies putting less effort into revising and rewriting. Have you ever thought like this student:

> *I don't need to revise my paper before I turn it in. After all, I feel I have good ideas and can receive an 'A' for my content. Then even if I get an 'F' on mechanics, I could still average a 'C' for the paper. A 'C' in English is good enough for me.*

Have you ever been careless about proofreading and revising your writing because you planned to pass on the merits of your content?

In life, teachers who give out two grades will not always be your reading audience. And then what? Most readers will evaluate your writing holistically. That is, they will not separate content and mechanics. They will not separate *what* you say from *how* you say it. In fact, your powerful content may be overlooked if readers are distracted by misspelled words, confusing punctuation, and incomplete sentences that make your writing difficult to read. In the final reading, content and mechanics blend together for an overall effect—the finished product.

Consider the world of work. How many employers will praise you for your content if you produce documents with incomplete sentences and misspelled words? The professional world expects finished pieces of writing to be clean and polished—mechanically perfect. The major concern is that written documents *communicate*. A negative impression created by a letter full of errors may become a negative impression that a reader—a customer—will associate with the company whose name appears on that letter. Employers know this and, therefore, view mechanics sometimes as *more important* than content!

COLLABORATE! *Talking about Revising*

Directions

Working with a group of students, discuss the role revising plays in your own writing process. (You may answer some of these questions in writing if you do not have access to a group setting.)

A. Ask one another how you proofread and edit your writing before turning it in.

B. Consider issues such as outside help:

1. Do you use a spell-check, or consult a thesaurus, a dictionary, or other references before turning in a piece of writing?

2. Do you consult a tutor for assistance with punctuation and spelling?

3. Do you ask a parent or spouse to help you do your final revision?

C. Discuss the value of being able to be your own editor.

 EVISING BARRIER #3: FEELING "PUT DOWN" BY RED MARKS

- Do you ever feel you need help proofreading your writing because you feel unsure of yourself as a "writer" and even more shaky about being a "proofreader and editor"?

- Have you ever felt bad about your writing abilities simply because your papers were returned full of corrections? "Look at all these red marks! I must really be a lousy writer."

- Have you ever, out of frustration, tossed a corrected paper in the garbage (without trying to understand the errors you made) because you didn't want to deal with your mistakes and fix them?

- Has seeing what you considered a "stupid" mistake on a paper ever made you feel as if *you* were stupid?

Writing is usually a private act; you write alone. Therefore, when someone points out your writing errors, you may react by feeling personally attacked. That is a perfectly normal reaction. But be careful not to let writing criticism affect *who* you think you are. Why should writing errors alter your self-concept? After all, if a teacher gives you an "A," are you a smarter person on that day than you were the day you received a "C"? Do you give corrections on papers the power to influence how you see yourself—the more red marks you receive, the lower your perception of your own intelligence?

It is illogical to think that your intelligence goes up and down from day to day just because your grades go up and down. Who you are remains constant, no matter how other people's opinions of your work may vary from day to day. Of course, you are capable of growing and learning, of becoming more intelligent. Corrections on your papers can inform you and make you wiser. But no red mark can ever make you more ignorant.

COLLABORATE!   *Putting Corrections in Perspective*

Directions
Discuss these questions in a group setting or answer them on your own in writing:

1.   Does what others think of you affect your self-concept?

2.   Do grades or other accomplishments or failures affect who you think you are?

3.   Has acquiring a valued position (a job or a group membership) or a possession (a house or a car) ever made you feel like a more worthwhile individual?

4.   What are the dangers of letting such external influences determine who you are?

*I*F YOU DON'T KNOW, ASK!

Maybe you feel that you don't know enough about writing to clean up and polish your own work. When a teacher or tutor points out your mistakes, are you sometimes still baffled? Even when you see detailed corrections on your graded papers, do you still wonder *why* your original writing was corrected?

For example:

• Do you ever write "fragments," and not realize you are writing them? Even when someone points them out to you, do you still sometimes not recognize why they are not complete sentences?

• Do you shift tenses, even though you may not know a tense shift from a gear shift?

• Do you change from the first person point of view to the second person point of view without realizing you ever had a point of view to start with?

• Do you put apostrophes in the wrong place because you somehow haven't figured out the right place?

The solution may simply be that you need some explanations. Don't be afraid to ask for them!

One way to move beyond revising barriers and grow as a writer is to ask questions. Ask questions for clarification when a piece of writing is assigned. Ask questions about the corrections when your graded paper is returned. Why not **ask**?

- *Do you worry that you'll have so many questions you'll take up too much class time?* Then start by asking just one or two questions each session.

- *Do you worry that teachers don't want you to ask questions?* I certainly want students to ask questions. I believe most teachers do. Questions give me feedback about what my students understand and don't understand. Spontaneously answering *relevant* questions during my instruction makes teaching more interesting for me, especially on a day when I am presenting the same lesson hour after hour. After all, I sometimes tire of being in class just like you do. Provocative questions make classes more stimulating for everyone.

- *Do you worry that your questions will make your classmates think you're not very bright?* If you have a question, I guarantee other students are sitting in the same class thinking exactly the same question. They are just afraid to ask. By speaking up, you will do others a favor.

If you're shy about speaking up in class, write down your questions and ask the teacher after class. This way, you will become more comfortable with the process and more sure of how your teacher will respond. Eventually you may decide it is okay to ask your questions in class.

JOURNAL PROMPT

Write any questions you can think of now. Continue to write down questions as you are taking this class. When you are doing your homework and think of questions, write them down so you can remember to ask them in class.

WHY CAN'T I GET A STRAIGHT ANSWER?

Have you ever avoided asking a question because you feel you will get a response that will not really answer your question or a response that you will not fully understand? One student told me, "I never ask questions about spelling, punctuation, and grammar because I don't get an answer. I only get, 'That's the rule!' " She was right. "That's the rule" or "that's the exception to the rule" is often an automatic response to questions about mechanics, but it certainly isn't a *real answer*.

RULES EVERYWHERE

That doesn't mean that English should have no rules: All disciplines have rules. Science, for example, has lots of them. "Water boils at 212 degrees Fahrenheit" is a rule. But when science students ask *why* water boils at 212 degrees, they usually don't get "That's the rule" as an *answer*. A science teacher would be laughed out of a classroom were he or she to offer this response: "Water boils at 212 degrees Fahrenheit because *that's the rule.*"

So the science teacher *explains* instead, "Given a certain altitude and pressure, water boils at 212 degrees because it is made up of molecules that are always moving. The more the water is heated, the faster its molecules move. By 212 degrees the molecules are moving so fast they bump and push one another far enough apart to change water from a liquid state to the gaseous state we call steam. When we see the steam bubbles form, we say the water is boiling." That's the *reason behind* the rule!

Scientists can conduct experiments to observe the rules in science because science is empirical. Language isn't empirical. That means we can't conduct observable experiments to demonstrate the reasons things are the way they are in our language and our writing system. But that doesn't mean reasons don't exist. It just means that reasons in language are different from reasons in science.

OUR LOGICAL LANGUAGE

Language is a logic system rather than a physical science—a logic system dramatically influenced by culture and history. Therefore, the "rules" of English can often be explained by applying critical thinking to the logic of the English language and by looking at past peoples and events.

Memorizing grammar "rules" won't make you a better writer, but understanding the logic of English will. English is based on a consistent system that can be explained, understood, and, therefore, remembered. This logical, orderly system is the basis for how words work together in sentences to communicate your ideas. Every time you write a sentence you create a recognizable pattern.

"Rules" that apply to sentences are *consistent.* Impossible, you say? "I've read in books where English is reputed to be an arbitrary, unpredictable mess." But no language is arbitrary or unpredictable. Consistency is exactly what makes languages work. I'm prepared to back up my statement. Just read on . . .

YOU, THE COMPUTER

If you are a native English speaker, regardless of your educational background, you already know much more about English sentences than you may realize. After all, you didn't start learning about sentences in your first English class. You started long before that. You started speaking by the time you were two years old; and even before that you were hearing and understanding English words and sentences.

The way you acquired your native language is much the same as the way computers acquire information. Think of yourself as a computer possessing a certain amount of memory. Early on, you are loaded with a program called "English"—in other words, "English" is your *software.* That means, if I enter a sentence into your computer-like system, you will use your "English" software to try to make sense of that sentence.

If, on your keyboard, I type, "The dog bit Charles," these four bits of information, entered in precisely that **order,** will create a picture on your mind's screen. You and all the other human computers using "English" will come up with the same picture: a four-legged canine embedding its teeth into a male person.

But if, instead, I type the same four words in a different order: "Charles bit the dog," then what happens? Even though all the words are the same, the picture is different: this time, it is a male person embedding his teeth into a four-legged canine—a slightly more unusual picture.

When a dog bites a man, that is not news . . . but when a man bites a dog, that is news.

—*John B. Bogart*

You and all English speakers will see the same unusual picture when you read, "Charles bit the dog." But why? You are seeing the picture that you see because you all know something about how English word order creates meaning in sentences. You know, for example, if "dog" comes *before* "bit," the sentence says the dog did the biting. Using the same word-order logic, you also know if "Charles" comes *before* "bit," Charles did the biting. You also know that the word that comes *after* "bit" is the thing or person being bitten.

What if, instead, I wrote these same four *understandable* English words but experimented with other *word orders:* "Dog Charles the bit" or "Charles dog bit the"? You, relying on the way you've been programmed, would then decide these word arrangements make no sense because they do not compute in "English." Even though the words are familiar, the utterances make no sense because the order of the words is not recognized by your language.

PECIAL ARRANGEMENTS FOR SENTENCES

What makes some word orders result in meaningful sentences while other word orders do not? The answer is *syntax.* Syntax comes from the Latin roots *syn,* meaning "together," as in *syn*thesis (if you play music, you know what a synthesizer is), and *tax,* meaning "arrangement," as in a *tax*onomy table (if you've ever studied biology, you've seen one of these). So syntax means "together arrangement." Syntax is how words are arranged together in sentences; and certain arrangements create certain meanings.

You have been using syntax to make sentences mean what you want them to mean every day of your English-speaking life. Therefore, a good place to begin learning about writing effective sentences is with your present knowledge of syntax. Even though you may think you know nothing about syntax, you actually do.

COLLABORATE!   *Out-of-Order Sentences*

Directions

English is what linguists call a "word-order" language. This means writers of English create meaningful sentences by consistently placing words in a certain order. The particular meaning readers derive from a sentence depends on that order, or the arrangement of the words in a sentence.

A. Working with the following sets of words, write at least three different sentences for each set using __all__ the words in each sentence. Retain the shapes and underlining that go with each word you write. The first sentence is done for you as an example.

1. kissed (little)(purple)(silly)(the) [Susan] [frog] (cute) .

Sentence 1: (Cute)(silly) [Susan] kissed (the) (little)(purple) [frog.]

Sentence 2: _____

Sentence 3: _____

2. followed (greasy)(crazy)(new)(weird) (the) [secretary] [manager]

Sentence 1: _____

Sentence 2: _____

Sentence 3: _____

3. whacked (happy)(speedy)(strong)(dirty)(the) [Mike] [baseball]

Sentence 1: _____

Sentence 2: _____

Sentence 3: _____

B. *Together with a group (or on your own in writing), discuss the following questions about word order:*

1. What kinds of words did you place at the beginnings of your sentences? (circle words, square words, or wiggly words)

2. What kinds of words did you put at the ends of sentences?

3. Where did you place round words in relation to square words?

4. Where did you place the one wiggly word in relation to the two square words?

5. What happens to the meaning of your sentence when the square words trade places?

6. What happens to the meaning of your sentence when you position a round word next to the other square word?

7. Do you still have a complete sentence if you remove some of the round words? Why or why not?

8. Do you still have a complete sentence if you remove the single wiggly word? Why or why not?

9. Do you know the grammatical names of the circle words? the square words? the wiggly words? If so, what are they?

10. What have you learned about your own knowledge of syntax by looking at the relationships of the word arrangements in the sentences you just created?

As you learn more about sentence writing, you will increase your understanding of these different kinds of words and how they interact to create the communication you intend.

AVOID ACCIDENTS BY BEING ALERT . . . TO SYNTAX

Bringing your knowledge of syntax from your unconscious to your conscious thoughts can help you gain more control of your writing. This is especially useful at that point in your writing when you are revising to communicate. Too often I watch students revise by "accident." That is, they have written something that doesn't "sound right," so they try to fix it like this:

> Well, let me move these words around . . . Hmmm . . . no that doesn't make it sound better. *(Pause.)*
>
> Well, let me try taking this part out . . . No that doesn't help either. (*Pause and scratch head*.)
>
> I'll add a few words here . . . still no good. (*Pause and scratch head and nibble on a fingernail*.)
>
> Maybe I can take this word here and move it to the front . . . that's it. . . . Finally, that's the way I wanted it to sound. (*Breathe a deep sigh and move on to the next sentence.*)

A person who approaches writing and revising this way is much like someone who punches keys on a computer keyboard without understanding the program. Eventually even a cat scampering across a keyboard can produce something meaningful on a computer screen, but can he do so on pu-r-r-pose? (I couldn't resist the pun.)

If the above student scenario resembles the way you revise, you too may be revising "by accident" rather than on purpose. Instead of rewriting a sentence five times before you end up with an acceptable product, wouldn't you like to know enough about arranging sentences—enough about syntax—to write the sentence you meant to write on the first or second try?

The more conscious you are of syntax, the more confident you will become about revising sentences. Rather than being a victim of unmanageable sentences that never seem to communicate what you really mean, you can make your sentences say exactly what you want them to say if you master the syntax of English.

> *He who is not a master of his language becomes its slave.*
>
> —*Unknown*

DO IT YOURSELF!   *Reflect on Revising*

Directions

In the space provided write your own thoughts about revising.

How do you revise sentences that don't "sound right" to you? What would you like to know more about when it comes to revising?

_____

_____

_____

_____
_____
_____
_____
_____

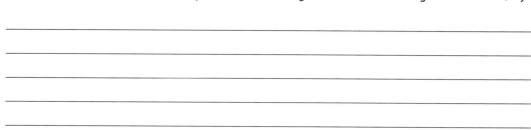

ENTENCES: BIG WRITING BLOCKS OR LITTLE BUILDING BLOCKS?

Sentences are often referred to as the building blocks of writing. Yet, for some students, playing with these blocks is not so easy. Just deciding where to begin and end a sentence can present a real challenge. As thoughts come spilling out of your brain, they may *all* seem to belong together. They may appear to be one long "stream of consciousness"—ideas that flow one into the other with no clear endings or beginnings. Brainstorming and free-writing can produce writing like this, making revising a nightmarish chore.

Very young beginning writers wrestle with the same dilemma: where does one sentence end and the next one begin? My best friend's 8-year-old son came home from school one day with a insightful answer to that puzzle. He proudly proclaimed, "I finally figured out where to put the period, Mom! You put it after you write eight words!" Evidently all the model sentences he had seen in his workbook that day had contained exactly eight words, so he deduced a sentence was a series of eight words. Of course, *you* know the formula is not that simple.

But what is the formula? Exactly *where* should you insert that periodic dot? Most students insert end marks such as periods after they have written a "complete idea." But even then, they sometimes make mistakes.

DO IT YOURSELF!   *Write About Sentences*

Directions
In the space provided, write about what you already know about sentences.

How do *you* decide when to end a sentence? What definitions have you learned for sentences in the past? How would you tell an eight-year-old where to place a period?

_____
_____
_____
_____
_____
_____
_____
_____

THE RULE ANSWER TO THE SENTENCE QUESTION

Have you ever received the mark "FRAG" somewhere on a paper? *Frag,* of course, is an abbreviation for *fragment.* Fragments are incomplete sentences. When I was a freshman taking my first college writing class, my professor announced that one sentence fragment in an essay would result in an automatic "F" for the entire essay. That's when I became serious about proofreading carefully for sentence fragments.

Now, after teaching English for many years and reading thousands of sentence fragments, it occurs to me that most students write fragments without realizing they have written them. They simply place periods where they truly believe they have finished a complete idea. Some incomplete sentences actually appear complete to the untrained eye and ear. So when students see "FRAG" scribbled like graffiti on their "masterpieces," they are often puzzled.

When you don't know why a sequence of words you've written is a fragment, **ask** *why.* Practice with a partner by reading this scene:

STUDENT: What is this FRAG marked on my paper?

TEACHER: That stands for "fragment"; it means you have written a sentence fragment.

STUDENT: What exactly is a sentence fragment?

TEACHER: A fragment is a piece or a part of something; so a sentence fragment is a part of a sentence, rather than a complete sentence.

STUDENT: What makes *this* a fragment? The statement sounds complete to me.

TEACHER: For one thing, it doesn't contain both a subject and a verb.

STUDENT: (*Thinking:* the teacher here has started using jargon—grammar terminology. This makes me feel even more bewildered and confused. . . . What if I can't remember what subjects and verbs are exactly? Do I ask? Or do I just act as if I understand and go sit down? After all, I have heard these terms before; and I should remember all about subjects and verbs; but I don't. [*Sensation of guilt and discomfort*])

STUDENT: (*Aloud, now*) I think I need to be reminded of what a subject and a verb are.

TEACHER: I can't believe you don't know that! You should have learned subjects and verbs in 5th grade!

STUDENT: (*Thinking:* Should I ask Mr. Smith if he remembers everything <u>he</u> learned in 5th grade? . . . no, not a good idea) Well, I don't remember . . .

TEACHER: Well then, let me explain. The *verb* is usually an action word; it shows the action in the sentence. The *subject* is a word that names the person or thing doing the action. A doer and an action . . . that is a subject and verb.

STUDENT: Thank you. (*Then turns to leave, but after a few steps realizes:* I have only learned definitions for subjects and verbs. I still don't understand *why* they are necessary for complete ideas or sentences.)

STUDENT: (*Returning*) But *why* do I have to have subjects and verbs in order to have complete sentences? *Who says* statements with subject and verbs are more complete than statements without them? Why do I *really* need a subject and verb to make a complete thought?

TEACHER: . . because that's the rule (*a non-answer rather than an answer*). Subjects and verbs create the complete ideas that make up sentences; and sentences are made up of subjects, verbs, and complete ideas (*a circular definition*).

STUDENT: (*Thinking:* Are there any real answers in English?)

If you really want to know what makes a fragment, read on . . .

THE REAL ANSWER TO THE SENTENCE QUESTION

Yes, Virginia, there *are* real answers to questions you ask in English classes, answers that go beyond "that's the rule." English *can* be explained.

Why do we really need subjects and verbs to create complete English sentences? What is it about the presence of a "doer" and an "action" that makes us feel a statement is suddenly complete? The answer is related to how we think. We think using logic, and our language reflects that logic. English uses the same logic as most Western civilization languages. If you have ever taken a class in logic, you probably began by studying the ancient Greek and Roman philosophers, the founders of Western thought. These ancient people taught future generations like us how to think. More specifically, they taught us that thinking in complete thoughts requires—you guessed it—*subjects and verbs*!

The notion of subjects and verbs came from the fact that the ancient Greeks, who were great scientists as well as philosophers, believed in a fundamental premise of *cause and effect*. In other words, they believed if something happened (an effect—or action), something must be making that effect or action happen (a cause—or doer of the action).

Among other things, the ancient thinkers' unwavering commitment to cause and effect enabled them to discover *gravity*. When they experimented with dropping objects from the top of a building, they observed that every object hit the ground. No matter how heavy or light, no object stopped in mid-air or sailed off into outer space; even a feather fell to the ground—eventually. The observable *effect* was that everything landed on the ground.

But what was the *cause?* There had to be one. Logic demanded that every effect must have a cause; every action must have something making it happen. "Gravity" became the name—the name for what caused the effect—which was that dropped objects consistently hit the ground. Even though they could not see gravity or measure it with their simple scientific instruments, ancient scholars knew it existed because, logically, it had to.

Today, you and I still think and reason like our Western civilization ancestors. Every time we read about an effect or an *action,* we wonder *who or what* is causing the action to happen. That logic is reflected in the way we form sentences: if the verb is an action, then there has to be something making it happen—the subject. Actions (verbs) are not completely explained until we know who or what causes them (subjects). The *reasons* we need subjects and verbs to make complete English sentences stem from our culture's history—our unwavering commitment to cause and effect.

JOURNAL PROMPT

Have you ever thought about how language affects the way you think? Do you always think in words? Do you think in pictures or images? How do you make sense out of the words and pictures in your thoughts? Has learning new words ever affected the level of your thinking? What kind of logic do you use to do critical thinking? For example, when you decide which answer to mark on a true or false test, do word arrangements affect your choice? What has learned math concepts taught you about logic and thinking? Does the logic of math have any connection to the logic of English? What do you think?

*I*F IT'S LOGICAL IN <u>ONE</u> LANGUAGE, IS IT LOGICAL IN <u>EVERY</u> LANGUAGE?

If subjects and verbs are sentence requirements that come from Western civilization, does that mean sentences in other cultures may *not* necessarily need subjects and verbs?

Yes, Native American Navajos had language long before they knew Western civilization even existed. And in their language, *pure action* can be a *complete idea* all by itself.

That means, if you speak Navajo, you don't need both subjects and verbs to make complete sentences. A Navajo speaker standing in a canyon, suddenly drenched by a rain shower, can merely respond with a one-word sentence, "Raining." (Of course, he would use the Navajo word for "raining.") The point is, this sentence contains only an *action* (a verb) and needs *no cause* (no subject). The verb alone, pure action, is the complete idea.

This, as you are reminded every time you see "FRAG" on your papers, is not the case in English. If you and a friend were standing on a street corner waiting for a bus and a rain shower drenched you, could you merely exclaim, "Raining!"? Saying this as if it were a complete sentence, you would probably produce a puzzled look on your English-speaking companion's face. Your friend might think she had not heard everything you said. For what she expects you to say, and what you, in fact, would likely say is, "<u>It</u>'s raining," not just, "Raining." Think of how many times in your lifetime you have said "It's raining." (If you live in Oregon, where I live, the opportunities will have been countless.)

Don't you ever worry when you say and write statements like "It's raining"? Don't you worry that your listener or reader will make you accountable and ask *what* is raining? "What's the *it*—the *it* that rains?" I'll wager you never stopped to worry about the "it." In fact, I'll even make a bet that no one has ever insisted you explain the "it" in, "It's raining." Why? My theory is, your friends are so delighted to hear you speak in *complete* sentences, they don't think to question the *meaning* of your sentences.

You've probably never thought about what kind of "it" rains. And that doesn't much matter because no one who will read your writing will ever expect an explanation. What readers of English do expect is complete, logical sentences containing both subjects and verbs. And "It's raining" fulfills that expectation. In other words, the fact that a sentence has both a subject and a verb is sometimes more important than what the subject and verb actually mean!

JOURNAL PROMPT

Do you know another language in which syntax is different? What about street talk or American slang? Do you ever express what you think is a complete idea without using both subjects and verbs? Can you think of some examples? Do you think that your examples may <u>imply</u> subjects or verbs even though you don't actually state them? Does it seem logical to you that actions are always caused by something or someone? Or do you believe that actions just occur without anything or anyone causing them? Explain.

*B*REAKING THROUGH THE BARRIERS TO REVISION

As you work through the remaining chapters in this book, the sentence parts that make up syntax will be presented a little at a time with *explanations*, not rules. Each explanation will be accompanied by practical writing, revising, and reading applications. You will be challenged to *understand* how to use arrangements of words in sentences to communicate the meanings you intend.

Rules you may have learned before are just shortcuts to recalling explainable concepts. If you want rules to help you remember, you will be able to write your own rules as your understanding of English grows.

Writing is a unique gift. Humans are the only species on earth who have the ability to use language *symbols* to share experiences, express feelings, and pass on information. The more you understand your language and how it works, the more confidence you will have as a writer as you create and revise. As I write this book, my wish for you is that you grow—not only as a writer, but as a thinker, and a communicator—and that you become increasingly aware and appreciative of the precious gift your culture has given you—your language.

THE READING CONNECTION

Reading is to the mind what exercise is to the body.

—*Richard Steele*

Reading can help you get your writing in shape. There are many books you can use as references when you set out to revise and edit your creations. The following is only a partial list of such books. At your library, resource center, or bookstore, obtain one or several of these books and look through them carefully. Decide how they could be useful to you as a writer. Share your impressions with your classmates.

1. An English handbook; most major publishers publish one. You may already possess an English handbook. If not, your teacher will be able to recommend one. English handbooks are handy references for looking up answers to questions you may have about usage, punctuation, spelling, and writing formats.

2. *The Writer's Art,* by James J. Kilpatrick, is a well-written book that contains valuable information about writing and revising.

3. *On Writing Well,* by William Zinsser, is one to which I refer often. Zinsser is a professional writer who gives practical advice about creating and revising. It is a good reference that is enjoyable to read.

4. Any up-to-date secretarial handbook may serve you well if you write primarily on the job.

5. *The Elements of Style,* by William Strunk with E. B. White, can be a versatile resource for student writers as well as working writers.

6. *Plain English for Lawyers,* by Richard Wydick, is designed for anyone who does legal writing; and it is filled with enlightening suggestions for anyone who writes on the job. The book is easy to read, contains clear explanations, and even includes practice exercises with answer keys.

7. *The Writing of Economics,* by Donald N. McCloskey, is a compact book packed with useful tips for writing and revising in any professional field, not only economics.

8. Finally, *A Dictionary of Modern English Usage,* by H. W. Fowler, is a classic work that is well worth exploring. Its most recent edition, the second edition, revised by Sir Ernest Gowers, is packed with information. It may be a little difficult to read: but by the time you have finished with *Writing with the Lights On,* you should be able to make good sense of it.

THE WRITING CONNECTION

Reading can sometimes be used as a "springboard" from which you can jump into writing about a certain subject. Just reading this chapter may have given you some ideas to write about. Develop a piece of writing using one of the following quotations as a springboard:

1. *True ease in writing comes from art, not chance.*—Alexander Pope
2. *Proper words in proper places make the true definition of style.*—Jonathan Swift
3. *Good style must, first of all, be clear.*—Aristotle
4. *Often you must turn your stylus to erase, if you hope to write anything worth a second reading.*—Horace
5. *I have made this letter longer than usual because I lack the time to make it short.*—Pascal
6. *Of every four words I write, I strike out three.*—Nicolas Boileau
7. *Not that a story need be long, but it will take a long while to make it short.*—Henry David Thoreau
8. *Language is the archives of history.*—Ralph Waldo Emerson
9. *An idea does not pass from one language to another without change.*—Miguel de Unamuno
10. *No tears in the writer, no tears in the reader.*—Robert Frost

SELF TEST FOR CHAPTER 3

1. You can _____ from mistakes you make when you write.
2. Some employers emphasize _____ more than content in writing.
3. Corrections on your paper can make you _____.
4. Most teachers welcome relevant _____.
5. Rules have _____ behind them.
6. Language is a _____ system.
7. The arrangement of words together to create meaning is called _____.
8. English is classified as a _____ order language.
9. The building blocks of finished pieces of writing are _____.
10. Because our culture believes in cause and effect, our language requires _____ and _____ for complete sentences.

FINAL JOURNAL WRITING

In your journal, write your thoughts about revising to communicate. Consider any barriers that may be keeping you from revising and editing the papers you turn in. Write about the areas of revising that are most difficult for you. What would you like to learn about usage, punctuation, word choices, spelling, etc.? Has this chapter affected your attitude towards revision? Explain.

PARTS
How Every Part of a Sentence Writes

VERBS BRINGING SENTENCES TO LIFE

W*ords are also actions, and actions are a kind of words.*

—RALPH WALDO EMERSON

QUESTIONS TO ASK YOURSELF WHILE READING CHAPTER 4:

1. What is the most important word in a sentence?
2. What kind of words attract readers' attention?
3. How can action verbs make my writing more lively and more interesting to read?
4. How do the kinds of verbs I choose determine what my sentences can or can't communicate?
5. Why do we use terms like noun, verb, adjective, and adverb to talk about writing sentences?

POWER AND LANGUAGE

Power and language go hand in hand. Just look at today's world in which America is powerful. Our English language is everywhere. Many American words are international; *jet, camping*, and *weekend* are only a few examples. Certain professionals, such as air traffic controllers, use English no matter where in the world they work, just because America has power.

Long ago, the Latin-speaking Romans had more power than anyone else in the Western world. Even the English-speaking Britons recognized that. Therefore, they incorporated Latin into many important aspects of British life. In England, Latin became the language of the church, the language of law, and the language of grammar (or "glamour," as envious uneducated people called it).

Therefore, English scholars, studying their own language, used Latin language terms to label counterpart structures in English. They analyzed sentences by categorizing individual words into word classes (the parts of speech) which were given Latin names such as verbs, nouns, adjectives, and adverbs. Each of these word classes represented different jobs English words performed in sentences. Modern English handbooks still use these labels. So even today, when you study English, you will learn a few Latin words.

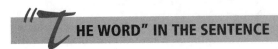

"THE WORD" IN THE SENTENCE

What should you know about the sentences you write—the sentences that make up all your paragraphs? What is the most important word in a sentence? What is the most important word class in English? And why do sentence parts matter to you as a writer?

The most important word class in English is a group of words called verbs. *Verb* is Latin for *the word*. "The word" is a fitting label because the verb is the most powerful word in a sentence. Romans and Englishmen alike were quick to recognize the verb's power.

Without a verb, you cannot write a complete sentence. The verb is a sentence's most vital organ; it provides the heartbeat that brings a sentence to life. Or, as one student put it, "The verb is the motor of the car."

Once you have learned about verbs in this chapter, you will understand more about how your sentences communicate. You will be able to begin writing—writing "with the lights on" rather than in the dark—sentences that really say what you want them to say. Once you befriend verbs, you will discover for yourself how you can energize your writing by letting verbs write.

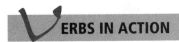

VERBS IN ACTION

Just how do verbs energize writing and bring sentences to life? What jobs do verbs do in sentences? Since you have probably studied verbs before, you may already think of them as *action words*. Writers usually write about actions. When you write letters, for example, don't you normally write about what you *do* every day, what *happens* in your life, what *goes* on around you, what you *think,* and what you *feel?* These are all action verbs. If you need to re-acquaint yourself with action verbs, work through the following:

DO IT YOURSELF!   *Look for Action*

Directions

Circle the word you think is the action verb in each of the following lists. The first one is done for you as an example.

1. kitten   it   lamp   (played)
2. with   ran   they   towel
3. tulip   sit   the   however

4.	read	now	newspaper	later
5.	bedspread	happily	laugh	eyelid
6.	clever	bright	eat	tortilla
7.	under	him	watched	three
8.	purple	wiggle	in	joyful
9.	gangster	for	gently	jumped
10.	pineapple	never	squeezes	giant

All the action verbs you found in the above lists express *physical actions*. But action isn't always physical. Action may be *mental* and *emotional* as well. A mental action might be "think" or "understand." An emotional action might be "love" or "worry." Like physical actions, mental and emotional actions consume energy. Doesn't it sometimes take as much energy to "think" as it does to just "sit"? Isn't "worrying" every bit as exhausting as "walking"?

DO IT YOURSELF!   *Look for All Kinds of Action*

Directions

Read the following paragraphs. Circle the physical, mental, or emotional action in each sentence. To find the action verb, ask yourself, "What does someone or something <u>do</u> in this sentence?" or "What is happening in this sentence?" In this selection, each sentence contains only <u>one</u> action verb.

On sunny Sunday afternoons my family and I often drive through Central Oregon. Juniper trees grow in this part of the state. Defiant red rim rock surrounds the high plateau.

Ranch hands in old jalopies move slowly ahead of us on the narrow highway. The sun reflects off their metal bumpers. Ranchers inhabit this area. One rancher, alone, owns ten thousand acres of land. Cattle graze on the open range and along the river bank. They roam freely twenty-four hours a day.

We always enjoy the trip through central Oregon. Cool mountain air passes through the open car window. The fresh breeze touches our faces. We relax in this setting. We love the scenery. Everyone in the family has a good time on sunny Sunday afternoons in central Oregon.

Did you find a verb in each sentence?

JOURNAL PROMPT

Take a few minutes to write about something you and your family enjoy doing when you have time off. After you have written about your activities, go back and see if you can spot any action verbs in what you have written.

BEING VERBS WITHOUT ACTION

After reading about action verbs, you might be asking yourself, does every sentence I ever write really show action? Do I always write about something that's happening or about something someone is doing either physically, mentally, or emotionally? The answer is **no.**

When you wrote in your journal, you may not have written an action verb in every sentence. Yet, just a few paragraphs ago, in the exercise about driving through central Oregon, every sentence did contain an action verb. While verbs are usually actions, they are not always actions.

At times you will write sentences that contain no action verbs. For example, you could write a sentence merely to *identify* something or someone:

Melinda is president.

Here *Melinda* names a person, and *president* identifies or re-names the same person. Where is the action? There is none.

You could also write a sentence to *describe* something or someone:

Melinda is smart.

Here *Melinda* still names a person, and the word *smart* tells something about her. *Smart* describes Melinda; being smart is one of Melinda's qualities. Again the sentence contains no action verb.

Yet these sentences still express complete ideas:

Melinda is president.
Melinda is smart.

Which word in these sentences is "the word"—the necessary word that makes the sentences complete? *IS* is "the word"; in other words, *IS* is the *verb.* Without *IS,* we would have

Melinda president
Melinda smart

These are not sentences. The addition of *IS,* however, turns these expressions into sentences with complete ideas. But, *IS* is not an action, not even an emotional or mental action. *IS* is, therefore, called a BEING VERB.

BEING VERBS include the following:

am	is	are	was	were
seem	seemed	become	became	

These words look familiar, don't they? That's because being verbs are the most common verbs in the language.

DO IT YOURSELF!   *Find Verbs that Are Just Being*

Directions

In the following sentences, circle the being verbs.

1. The sun was bright.
2. The mountains are a majestic sight.
3. The drive is enjoyable.
4. The cattle were on the road.
5. Mary and Anna became ranch hands.
6. Tony is on his horse.
7. My son seemed happy yesterday.
8. Normally he never becomes upset.
9. I am an enthusiastic sightseer.
10. The cowboy seems confident.

DO IT YOURSELF!   *Distinguish Action from Being*

Directions

In the following paragraphs, the verbs have already been underlined for you.

1. Decide whether each underlined verb is an action verb or a being verb. Write the word "action" or "being" in the numbered space under each verb.

2. Some sentences will contain several verbs. When more than one verb appears in the same sentence, writers often use commas or a connecting word like "and" between the verbs. Anytime the word "and" appears in a sentence, it will connect equal or identical sentence parts. Circle any comma or "and" that signals the presence of more than one verb in a sentence.

A.   Harvest mice are midget acrobats. They stretch and twist and

1._____   2._____ 3._____

swing from one blade of grass to another. They flick their long

4._____   5._____

tails from side to side. They are hilarious. Suddenly one mouse

6._____

dashes down a stalk of grass and scurries up another. His companion

7._____   8._____

follows. Up and down they go. Then they screech to a halt. Each one

9._____   10._____   11._____

perches at the tip of its own stalk. The wind blows. It seems dangerous

12._____   13._____ 14._____

for the mice. But it is not so. These mice are experts. They wrap their

15._____   16._____   17._____

tails around the grass, grab the stems with their hind feet, and hold on

18._____   19._____

tightly. Back and forth they swing with the wind.

20._____

Did you find 5 being verbs and 15 action verbs? If so, your answers were probably correct. If not, ask your teacher for help.

B.   Tears rolled down our unshaven faces, and we sang "Silent

1._____   2._____

Night." Somehow we forgot our wounds and our hunger. We raised

3._____   4._____

prayers of thanks for our homes and our fatherland. There was a

5._____

new feeling in our hearts. For this brief time, our burdens were gone. We

6._____

clung to one another. We even exchanged crude gifts.

7._____   8._____

Some men exchanged dog tags. Some gave I. O. U.'s as imaginary

9._____   10._____

presents. The gifts were only fantasies. But the spirit of giving

11._____

was genuine. We cried tears of thanks and shared hugs of

12._____   13._____   14._____

gratitude. On December 25 even the guards left us alone.

15._____

Did you find 4 being verbs and 11 action verbs? If so, your answers were probably correct. If not, ask your teacher for help.

JOURNAL PROMPT

Write about the behaviors of animals you have enjoyed watching either in the wild or in a zoo; or, if you have a pet, write about its antics. If you are a people-watcher instead, write about activities or behaviors of people you have observed.

JOURNAL PROMPT

Write about a special family holiday (like Thanksgiving or Christmas) that was particularly emotional for you. What made it so emotional? Was it the presence or absence of certain people? Was it the place where you celebrated the holiday? What do you think is the value of family holidays? Why?

THE DIFFERENCE BETWEEN ACTION AND BEING

Why is the *difference* between action and being verbs so important? Why don't we just lump these two categories of verbs together and make all verbs one big happy family?

The answer has to do with *logic.* The language you use to write is the same language you use to think. Since logic is an important part of thinking, it is also an important part of writing. The logic of a sentence is determined by the verb: A *being verb* sets up one kind of logic in a sentence, allowing you to express certain kinds of thoughts. An *action verb* sets up another kind of logic, allowing you to express other kinds of thoughts. By choosing to use a being verb instead of an action verb, you create different relationships between the words in a sentence. Relationships of words, or syntax, is what makes a sentence say what it says.

For example, let's presume you write

> *Joe <u>is</u> the manager.*

This sentence contains the being verb *IS.* Look at the words that come before and after the verb: *Joe* and *the manager.* What is their *relationship?* Who are Joe and the manager to each other? They are the same person!!!

The sentence has reversible logic. That means "Joe is the manager" would have the same meaning if you reversed it and wrote, "The manager is Joe." If the sentence were a math problem, you could write it two ways:

> *Joe = the manager*
> OR
> *the manager = Joe*

In other words, a being verb can act as an equal sign when placed between two of the same kinds of words (for example, between two *people* like Joe and the manager). That's one kind of logic!

What happens to the logic of this sentence, however, if you change the *being* verb to an *action* verb? Let's say you write

> *Joe <u>hit</u> the manager.*

When the verb changes to action (hit), the *relationship* of the words in the sentence also changes; that means the logic changes. When an action verb enters the sentence, *Joe* and *the manager* are no longer the same person. In fact, Joe is a person who *does* an action; and the manager is a different person who *receives* the action. Joe hits, and the manager gets hit. Action verbs do not act as equal signs. Action verb sentences are not reversible. That's another kind of logic!

Therefore, as a writer, when you want to introduce someone or something and provide identifying information or descriptive details, you will be wise to use *being* verbs. But when you write about events that have occurred or interactions between people, you will find *action* verbs work better.

COLLABORATE!   *Thinking Through the Action . . . Or the Being*

Directions

Working with a group of classmates or on your own, read the following sentences carefully.

1. Circle the verb in each sentence.

2. In the space provided, write whether the verb is action or being.

3. If the sentence is reversible, write out the sentence in reverse. If the sentence is not reversible, simply write "not reversible."

The first two are done for you as examples.

ACTION OR BEING?

_____*being*_____ 1.   Croup (is) a viral infection.

Reversible? A viral infection is croup.

_____*action*_____ 2.   Small children sometimes (have) croup.

Reversible? not reversible

_____ 3.   They usually survive the illness.

Reversible?_____

_____ 4.   One croup symptom is a cough.

Reversible?_____

_____ 5.   A treatment for croup is humidity.

Reversible?_____

_____ 6.   Humidity clears the airway.

Reversible?_____

_____ 7.   Steam from a hot shower was a comfort.

Reversible?_____

_____ 8.   A humidifier is also a good solution.

Reversible?_____

_____ 9.   Sick children drink warm liquids.

Reversible?_____

_____10.   Cold liquids trigger more coughing spells.

Reversible?_____

Check yourself: Did you decide the sentence was *reversible* every time you spotted a *being verb*? Did you decide the sentence was *not reversible* every time you spotted an *action verb*? If you did, your logic is correct.

JOURNAL PROMPT

Write about an illness you or someone close to you has had. Include some of its symptoms. Write about its treatment. Was the illness difficult to diagnose? What kinds of tests did doctors administer to discover the cause and extent of the ailment? Do you ever diagnose your own illnesses and decide how to treat them? Explain.

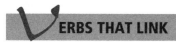
VERBS THAT LINK

Sometimes being verbs are followed by words that *describe* instead of words that *identify* or *rename*.

> *Joe is the <u>manager</u>.* ("manager" identifies or renames Joe)
> *Joe is <u>handsome</u>.* ("handsome" describes Joe)

Sentences in which being verbs are followed by descriptive words do not easily reverse because a descriptive word is not equal to a naming word. (It is not in the same word class.) Therefore, *handsome* and *Joe* cannot easily trade places.

> *Joe is the <u>manager</u>.*

may be reversed:

> *The <u>manager</u> is Joe.*

However,

> *Joe is <u>handsome</u>.*

does not read well when reversed:

> *<u>Handsome</u> is Joe.*

In any case, however, the verb *IS* links information in the back of the sentence to information in the front. Since being verbs have this ability to link different sentence parts, BEING VERBS are also known as LINKING VERBS.

DO IT YOURSELF!   *Link Sentence Parts Together*

Directions

Draw circles to show how being verbs link information in the front of each sentence to information in the back of each sentence. The first one is done for you as an example. A helpful hint: Your task will be easier if you circle the verbs first.

1. (Jeanne)(is)(a Canadian citizen.)
2. Newfoundland is a Canadian province.
3. This province is new.
4. The English settlement was old.
5. Its weather is harsh.
6. The people are tough.
7. Most Newfoundland towns are seaports.
8. Fish were plentiful.
9. The most important fish was the cod.
10. The sea is the provider.

JOURNAL PROMPT

Write about the sea as an influence in your life. What has the sea provided for you? Have you ever lived near water? Have you worked on the sea? Do you vacation near water? Do you like food that comes from the sea? Do you enjoy activities such as water sports? Explain your responses.

THE AMBIDEXTROUS TWO-WAY VERBS

Now that you better understand the difference between action and being verbs, I'd like to introduce you to a small group of versatile verbs: the "two-way verbs." Two-way verbs can act either as action verbs or as being verbs, depending on the sentence in which you use them.

Most of these verbs involve your senses. *Look, smell, taste, feel, and sound* head the list of two-way verbs. Occasionally *appear, grow, and remain* can also be two-way verbs, even though we usually think of these verbs as action verbs.

Carefully study two-way verbs at work in the following pairs of sentences. Ask yourself, in which sentence is an action really occurring?

Samantha *smells* the flower.	(Action—Is Samantha *doing* something?)
The flower *smells* sweet.	(Being—Is the flower smelling anything? Or is sweet just a descriptive word being linked to "flower"?)
The referee *sounds* the buzzer.	(Action—Who is doing what?)

The buzzer *sounds* loud.	(Being—Could you replace "sounds" with "is" and still retain the same relationship between "buzzer" and "loud"? Yes, the verb is simply linking the buzzer to the descriptive word "loud.")
Juan *looks* at the pictures.	(Action—Is Juan "looking" at something? Yes.)
The pictures *look* old.	(Being—Are the pictures looking at anything? No!)
The surfer *feels* the sand.	(Action—Why?)
The sand *feels* hot.	(Being—Why?)
The chef *tastes* the soup.	(Is the verb action or being?—Why?)
The soup *tastes* salty.	(Is the verb action or being?—Why?)

Can you explain why the following verbs, too, sometimes qualify as two-way verbs?

Jamie <u>appeared</u> in my dream. (Action—why?)
Jamie <u>appeared</u> happy. (Being—why?)

Ray <u>grew</u> beefsteak tomatoes. (Action—why?)
Ray <u>grew</u> tired. (Being—why?)

Fred <u>remained</u> in the house. (Action—why?)
Fred <u>remained</u> friendly. (Being—why?)

Did you notice that when two-way verbs act as being verbs they always link *descriptive* information rather than re-naming information?

Did you also notice that two-way verbs working as being verbs can be replaced with verbs such as "is" or "was" without changing the logic of the sentence: "The flower *smells* fragrant" becomes "The flower *is* fragrant." Both sentences have the same kind of logic. Since both are being verb sentences, the relationship between "flower" and "fragrant" remains the same.

But if you try substituting "was" or "is" for an *action* verb, the logic changes: "Samantha *smells* the flower" becomes "Samantha *is* the flower"?? The action verb sentence clearly has a different logic! The relationship between "Samantha" and the "flower" becomes quite different when the verb changes from action to being.

DO IT YOURSELF!   *Decide Action or Being*

Directions

A. *Decide for yourself whether the underlined two-way verb is an action verb or a being verb in the following sentences. Write <u>action</u> or <u>being</u> in the space provided. If you are unsure of an answer, review the above examples.*

1. Sean <u>feels</u> the warm sun on his back. (_____)

2. Brooke <u>looks</u> at the lovely view. (_____)

3. The chocolate <u>tasted</u> delicious. (_____)

4. The kitten tasted the milk. (_____)

5. The policeman sounded the siren. (_____)

6. The campground appeared empty. (_____)

7. The wind felt cold. (_____)

8. George felt Santa's beard. (_____)

9. The hunter suddenly appeared. (_____)

10. The car looked new. (_____)

B. *The following paragraph contains many two-way verbs. Determine whether the underlined verbs are working as action or being verbs.*

The night felt bitter cold. The ground looked frozen. To the small child, the

1._____   2._____

wind sounded eerie and frightening. He looked around the corner cautiously. Then

3._____   4._____

he felt the path with his foot and ventured carefully toward the lighted entrance.

5._____

As he approached, he smelled the hickory aroma of the wood burner. It smelled

6._____   7._____

inviting and cozy. He sounded the doorbell to announce his arrival. The door flew

8._____

open, and a warm embrace greeted him. The hug felt comforting. As if from

9._____

nowhere, a little girl appeared offering him a bowl of freshly-popped popcorn.

10._____

He tasted it. It tasted heavenly to the cold, hungry boy. He appeared reassured

11._____ 12._____   13._____

about his homecoming.

COLLABORATE!   *Going on a Verb Hunt*

Directions

Together with your classmates or on your own, read the following passages and circle the verbs. Then decide which verbs are action and which are being. Each passage contains a total of 20 verbs.

A.   The wind was sharp and cold. The gray sky threatened snow. Last year's hard, granular snow still lay in the depressions at the base of the trees and around the rocks. Joey pulled his hood over his head. He protected himself against the wind. It was terribly cold.

   The sky became dark. Joey lost all track of time. Finally he found a protected place and sat down in a thicket of junipers. His face ached from the cold. Pain shot up the back of his weary legs. He pulled his hood more tightly around his ears, and sat, and shivered. He kept his knees tight against his chest. He was a frozen little bundle. The area was snow covered. There were no tracks left. Was he lost forever?

(The last sentence in the above paragraph may cause some debate. It is a *question.* This means the word order has been turned around. Move the words around to make it a *statement,* then decide which word is the verb: "He was lost forever.")

B.   Some people actually like housework. I am one of them. I enjoy my daily chores. I make my bed every morning. Briskly, I pull the bottom linen taut. The top sheet floats lightly over it. Then a warm thermal blanket covers them both. I gently tuck in the corners. And the bed looks like a picture out of a magazine.

   I think best when I iron. My mind skims over the wrinkly surfaces. And my problems find smooth solutions. I work my way through a mountain of laundry and solve my dilemmas.

   Food preparation, however, is more complex. Even simple meals require full attention. But it is worth it. The rewards are the greatest with this household task. After all, a succulent filet mignon tastes better than a tidy sheet or a wrinkle-free shirt collar.

JOURNAL PROMPT

Write about an experience in the outdoors that was suspenseful for you. Have you ever been lost? Have you ever <u>thought</u> you were lost? Have you experienced staying outdoors in adverse weather conditions? What did you do to withstand the conditions? What kind of planning do you do before outings to prepare yourself for the unexpected?

JOURNAL PROMPT

Write about daily chores. What are some tasks you do every day? How do you feel about responsibilities such as housework, laundry, cooking, and home maintenance? Have you developed ways to motivate yourself to tackle jobs you don't enjoy? Explain.

WHEN VERBS WRITE . . .

You may already have noticed that the list of being verbs is short, so short you could probably write them all on a half sheet of notebook paper and memorize them in less than five minutes. Action verbs, on the other hand, are so numerous you could fill several notebooks just trying to list them. The list would include thousands (perhaps hundreds of thousands) of words. Yet, for writers, the two different categories of verbs may be equal in importance.

BEING VERBS are absolutely necessary for writing sentences that *identify* or state the existence of people, places and things: "Charles Dickens *was* an English author." "Albany *is* the capital city of New York state." "Personal computers *are* a part of student life." Being verbs are also necessary for sentences that *describe* people, places, or things: "My friend *is* considerate." "The city *was* dirty." "The weather *was* humid."

When you write such sentences, you will find yourself using the same verbs over and over again because you have so few being verbs from which to pick. But you're not the only one who repeats being verbs. Skim through any book or magazine article. How often do words like "is" and "are" appear in sentences? **V-e-r-y often!** Yet frequent use of these verbs doesn't make writing sound repetitious. Have you ever said, "Boy, that writer sure uses *is* a lot!"? The word *is* will rarely distract a reader. Being verbs are so quiet they slip by readers almost unnoticed. What readers do notice, instead, are the sentence parts that precede and follow these inconspicuous verbs. Which words do you notice most in the following sentences?

> *The cow is purple.*
> *The story was silly.*
> *Amanda and Gertrude were my pet rocks.*

Probably you are most struck by the descriptive words, "purple" and "silly"; or the names, "Amanda" and "Gertrude"; or the things, "cow," "story," or "pet rocks." The powerful elements in being-verb sentences, then, become the descriptive and naming elements. This means that when you, as a writer, want your readers to focus on names and descriptions in your sentences, *being verbs* can help you create that focus—since the being verbs themselves are not particularly noticeable.

But even though readers overlook being verbs, these subtle verbs are still the most important element in making their sentences complete. For without the "is" and the "was" and the "are," your reader would only read snatches of images and incomplete ideas. And I would be compelled to take my red pen out and write FRAG (for "Fragment") next to each of these word groups:

> *The cow purple*
> *The story silly*
> *Amanda and Gertrude pet rocks*

So while your reader might not notice the presence of being verbs, he or she would notice their absence.

(Note: When we speak rather than write, we usually contract these verbs and make them almost disappear. For example, we say: "The cow's purple." "The story's silly." The apostrophe and the letter "s" take the place of IS.)

ACTION VERBS, however, play an entirely different role. Just read the following sentences and circle the most noticeable word in each sentence:

> *The bacon sizzles in the pan.*
> *Her heart aches for him.*
> *She burst into the room*
> *The fans screamed with joy.*
> *Joe hated the darkness.*

Did you circle the action verbs—*sizzles, aches, burst, screamed,* and *hated*?

HERE YOU GO AGAIN—ACTING LIKE AN ANIMAL

You are naturally drawn to strong action verbs. Do you know why? It's because you're an animal. That's right. All living things respond to stimuli. Animals, in particular, respond to light, sound, and movement. Look at the first sentence in the above list. Doesn't the word "sizzles" suggest both sound and movement? That's why you circled it. You're reacting with your animal instincts. In fact, action verbs are sometimes so strong they make the entire sentence move. Compare the following sentences:

> *The bacon sizzles in the pan.*
> *The bacon is in the pan.*

In the first sentence, the action verb energizes the entire sentence. "Sizzles" causes the bacon to move and make noise while the pan smokes and emits heat and greasy spatters. But in the second sentence the verb "IS" has a calming effect on the entire sentence. The bacon becomes limp and cold while the pan is lifeless.

If you respond to strong action verbs because you're an animal, that means your readers will respond to action verbs too. After all, your readers are also animals!

Carefully chosen action verbs jump out and grab readers, for everyone can participate in the actions these verbs denote. When you write sentences filled with action verbs, you bring energizing sensations, emotions, and life to the written page. Action verbs move your sentences *and* your readers. These words really are the heartbeats that throb in every sentence. They dance; they sing; they leap and cry; they love; they worry; and they even *sizzle.* They express every physical and mental and emotional action our language acknowledges. Thousands—possibly hundreds of thousands—of action verbs are at your disposal, offering more word choices than you will ever have the opportunity to write or see or hear in a lifetime. Is this exciting, or what?

Remember, both being verbs and action verbs help us communicate to readers about the world around us and within us. As writers, we can use being verbs to create still-life portraits and action verbs to create moving pictures.

WRITE RIGHT FOR THE JOB: Scary Verbs

One of the most challenging and rewarding opportunities I have had during my career as an English teacher is the opportunity to train workers on the job. Since I live in Salem, Oregon's state capital, many government workers are employed in my neighborhood. I am often invited to work sites to teach seminars that focus on writing in the work place.

For people who write on the job, verbs are especially important. Energetic verbs can make documents more powerful. Most employers encourage their workers to replace submissive being verbs with power-packed action verbs.

But some verbs can have the wrong kind of power. Verbs with negative overtones can have scary consequences in the business world. A careless word choice that offends a customer can be very costly to a company.

Therefore, I have created the following list of verbs to avoid in business documents. If you read them carefully and react to them personally, I believe you, too, will feel their negative tone:

claim	misrepresented
complain	mistrust
failed	misunderstood
misinformed	must
misled	neglected

- The word "claim," for instance, can make readers feel as if they're being accused of lying.
- "Complain" conjures up an image of "whining."
- "Failed" is a very scary word for many people; it can be a reminder of every failure in their past from an "F" in math to a "failed" marriage that ended in divorce.
- "Misinformed" implies, "You don't know what you're talking about."
- "Misled," "misrepresented," and "mistrust" suggest dishonesty.
- "Misunderstood" may imply the reader was wrong because he or she was not bright enough to be right.
- "Must" is a really scary, policing kind of word that forces readers into submission and will make some readers want to rebel.
- "Neglected," of course, conjures up images of sloppiness bordering on abuse.

What a nasty list of verbs!

COLLABORATE!   *"Re-Verbing" a Document*

Directions

The following document, a business letter, contains many action verbs, some of which convey powerfully negative overtones. Working with a group of classmates or on your own, read the document aloud; circle the "nasty" verbs, and then REWRITE the letter, making it more positive. Be sure your resulting letter conveys all necessary information—but has a positive tone.

Dear Miss Ledd:

It has come to my attention that you complained about our company's services. As manager of this office, I would like to respond to your statements. First you claimed you called our office on May 15 and spoke with Mrs. Kerring about the injuries for which you are seeking compensation. You reported that she told you our company would not pay for any medical expenses you incurred as a result of your on-the-job injury. I believe you misrepresented that conversation, as Mrs. Kerring said we would not pay 100 percent but we would pay 80 percent of the expenses. In other words, you misunderstood her.

Furthermore, to collect your benefits, you must fill out the enclosed form and mail it to us as soon as possible. If you fail to do this, we cannot even pay you the 80 percent figure. If you mistrust the postal system, you may bring in the completed form in person to our office on Main Street. It is important that we have this information in our files, so please do not neglect to return the form.

As always, we look forward to serving your health care needs.

Sincerely,

I. B. Scarry

Check yourself: How positive is your tone?

- In revising the letter, did you acknowledge Miss Ledd's hurt feelings and concerns and take responsibility for correcting the misunderstanding?
- Did you notice that overusing the word "you" seems to place blame on the customer? How could you reduce the number of times "you" appears in this letter?
- Does your revised letter include an apology of some sort? Explain why or why not.
- Did you avoid repeating the complaints in too much detail and concentrate instead on solutions?

WRITE RIGHT FOR THE JOB: Getting the Job Done without the "Get"

Another concern that often comes up when I work with companies is the desire to sound "professional." That, too, is often a word choice issue. One group of verbs I suggest writers watch out for is "get," "got," and "gotten." Many people, including student writers, habitually overuse "get," "got," and "gotten." In fact, they seem to insert one of these verbs just about any time they can't come up with the precise word choice to fit a certain situation. To see what I mean, look at the following examples.

1. Please stop by and *get* your papers.
    Please stop by and <u>pick up</u> your papers.

2. When you *get* here, report to my office immediately.
    When you <u>arrive</u>, report to my office immediately.

3. Did you *get* my message yesterday?
    Did you <u>receive</u> my message yesterday?

4. You can *get* the information you need by making a few phone calls.
    You can <u>obtain</u> the information you need by making a few phone calls

5. When you go to the store, would you *get* me a newspaper?
    When you go to the store, would you <u>buy</u> me a newspaper?

In these examples "get" means "pick up," "arrive," "receive," "obtain," and "buy." Clearly none of these words are even remotely related to one another in meaning. In other words, the message you give readers every time you use the word "get" is this: I'm too lazy to think of the word I mean, so you figure it out. . . .

COLLABORATE! *Getting Rid of Get, Got, and Gotten*

Directions

Working with a group or on your own, read the following sentences and replace the vague expressions that include <u>get, got, and gotten</u> with more precise, professional-sounding word choices:

1. The weather got too hot on Monday.

2. If you work for 30 years, you will get retirement benefits.

3. I got the intruder to leave the room.

4. You can always get me by telephone.

5. When I work long hours, I get exhausted.

6. I didn't get your last name.

7. I got a lesson from the mistake I made.

8. Try to get a hold of him before 5 PM.

9. Try to get to her before she turns in the final report.

10. He got 20 years in jail.

11. I will get him to turn in the report early.

12. He will get the facts together for us.

13. I will get there late because I have to get dinner ready for my family.

14. Have you got a cold?

15. Her silly remarks really get me.

16. His tears got to me.

17. The bullet got him in the leg.

18. This report may be clear to an engineer, but I don't get it.

19. If you get to the office late, the door may be locked.

20. You will get to leave early, if you have gotten your work done.

21. I got promoted to manager yesterday.

22. I don't get into town very often.

23. Do you think the company can get through another recession?

24. I got $50 when I typed the manual.

25. He told us to get going. (Can you change this <u>two</u> different ways?)

26. The fire chief really got across to the children the fact that pulling a fire alarm was a serious offense.

27. If I work hard, I will get ahead in this company.

28. He refused to let anyone get ahead of him in sales.

29. If I could only get around the inspection, the house could get done on time.

30. I no longer have to get out on the road to conduct business.

31. In order to get at the top shelf, you may need to use a step ladder.

32. The purpose of this committee is to get at the source of the problem.

33. He tried to get away, but the police were closing in.

34. What are you getting at?

35. I didn't get away from the office until 6:30.

36. When will you get back?

37. Let's get down to the matter at hand.

38. Nothing gets me down as much as a common cold.

39. The pill was so large I couldn't get it down.

40. They wanted to get going on the construction yesterday.

41. They both got in on the same flight.

42. He forgot his key and couldn't get the door open.

43. He got in with some unscrupulous business partners.

44. We are all getting older.

45. Please get your work done by tomorrow.

46. You'll never get there, if you don't try.

47. Joe got over his illness and is healthy again.

48. I can't believe he got through college.

49. I simply cannot seem to get through to her.

50. He said he would get together a portfolio of stocks.

51. The board members get together once a month.

52. They can't seem to get together on policy issues.

53. Have you got the tickets?

LITTLE BIT OF KNOWLEDGE CAN BE A "GOOD" THING

By now you may be thinking in terms of applying what you have learned about verbs and appreciating the fact that one bit of knowledge can have many different applications.

I would like to share with you still another application for your newly acquired knowledge about verbs—an application I have never seen in a textbook before but one I find useful to share with students.

Do you ever have trouble using the words "good" and "well" correctly in your writing? In spoken English those words are so often confused that I have given up correcting my students—and my children. But in writing, I am always watchful to ensure that students use the appropriate word. Explaining the use of "good" and "well" can be confusing, however.

Even in English handbooks, explanations for the use of "good" and "well" are often confusing. For example, they usually begin with some mention of the fact that "well" sometimes means "good" and other times means "healthy." This is hardly a point anyone should spend time worrying about. After all, do you *ever* mistakenly use "good" instead of "well" when you mean "healthy"? When was the last time you told someone you were released from the hospital because you "got *good*"? Furthermore, have you ever gone to a stationery store and asked for a "Get *Good* Card" to send to your sick friend? I think not.

Another situation in which I suspect you always use "good" and "well" correctly is when you place these words in front of something they describe. You certainly know the difference between a *"good* baby" and a *"well* baby," and you would not confuse the two.

The only confusion about "good" and "well," then, comes at or near the end of a sentence. Do you say, "My car runs *good*"? Or do you say, "My car runs *well*"? Don't answer that. I don't really want to know what you SAY. I want to know what you think you should **write**!

How can you know when to use "good" or "well" correctly? Rather than telling you the answer to this dilemma, I know you can figure it out by yourself. The following exercise will help you. The only clue I will give you for now is: The *secret* lies in the VERB!

DO IT YOURSELF! *Using <u>Verbs</u> for the "Good" of Your Sentences*

Directions

A. *The following sentences all contain the word "good." In some cases, however, "good" should be changed to "well." To correct the sentences <u>you believe</u> need to be changed, cross out the word "good" and write the word "well" in its place. If <u>you think</u> a sentence is requires no change, make no mark.*

1. My car runs good.
2. The movie was good.
3. The rock group sang so good.

4. The pizza tastes good.

5. The golfer hit the ball really good.

6. It works good now.

7. The lecture was very good.

8. You did good, Honey.

9. I played good today.

10. The coffee smells good.

Did you change sentences 1, 3, 5, 6, 8, and 9 to "well"? If so, you did very WELL!

If not, correct your answers now.

B. *The big question, however, is how can you always know when to use "good" and when to use "well" correctly? After all, nowadays these words are so often confused that it has become difficult to "hear" when the wrong form is being used.*

Here is a clue: Circle all the VERBS in the above sentences. Write the letter "B" above all the <u>being verbs</u>, and write the letter "A" above all the <u>action verbs</u>. (Remember, any two-way verbs will be acting either as <u>being</u> or as <u>action</u>. Therefore, ask yourself, is the verb "taste" in sentence 4 used as an action or a being verb? How about "smells" in sentence 10? Remember, if the coffee is not doing the smelling, "smells" is acting as a being verb.)

Now, answer these questions:

1. After which kind of verb do you always use "good"?_____

2. After which kind of verb do you always use "well"?_____

3. Write a "good" rule of your own to help you remember which verb takes "good" and which verb takes "well":

_____

_____

_____

_____

If you can't remember rules (even your own), just remember this bit of advice: **always be good**! This will remind you of the correct answer to the "good" and "well" dilemma:

BEING VERBS ARE FOLLOWED BY "GOOD." ACTION VERBS ARE FOLLOWED BY "WELL."

(But don't forget, this has nothing to do with your health!)

You have just witnessed an important concept: Words in sentences work together and affect one another. While the verb is an important part of speech, it is only "part" of the sentence picture. There is more to learn about how words work together in sentences.

THE READING CONNECTION

1. Look through magazines, newspapers, or books. Find articles or paragraphs that contain interesting verbs. Circle action verbs that appeal to you. Bring these readings to class and share the verbs you found.

2. If you find interesting readings that you cannot make copies of or mark on, make a list of the interesting verbs they contain and bring the list to class.

3. Compile all the verbs you and your classmates have collected. Either as a group or as individuals, write a paragraph that uses some of these verbs.

THE WRITING CONNECTION

Now that we have explored what verbs are and how they affect writing, apply what you have learned to your own writing. As you work with one of the following assignments, don't be satisfied with your first draft. Revise your first version, paying close attention to your use of verbs. Replace any boring verbs with more unusual and interesting ones (a thesaurus may help you). Experiment with action verbs that are snappy and energetic. As you write and revise, remember, too, that being verbs can help you create descriptive sentences by linking words in the front of the sentence to other words that describe them from the back of the sentence.

Suggested topics for making the writing connection with verbs:

1. Write instructions. Write explicit, step-by-step instructions your reader can follow. Consider such topics as How to: Diaper a Baby, Mow a Lawn, Put on Make-up, Register for Classes, or anything else you have done or watched someone else do. Break the process into manageable steps, and sequence the steps carefully. Choose precise verbs that vividly communicate the actions your readers should perform to duplicate the process you are explaining.

2. Option A: Interview several people about their jobs or hobbies or favorite forms of entertainment. Compare one person's responses to another's. Ask each individual what he or she likes best and least about his or her job (or hobby or favorite entertainment).

   Option B: Interview yourself about all the different jobs you have had. Compare and contrast your jobs. You may want to discuss what you liked best and least about each one. Use energetic action verbs to make your finished piece of writing interesting and lively.

3. Write about your hobbies and your favorite pastimes. Give reasons as to why you have chosen particular hobbies and pastimes. What are some of the benefits? When do you do these activities? What do you have to show for the time you have spent with your hobbies or favorite pastimes? Be alert to the verbs you use throughout your writing.

4. Write from observation. Find a busy place to sit: the lunch area at school, a street corner where people congregate, a popular study area on your campus, a park where people go for outings, or any other busy place. Jot down your observations. From these observations write a description of what you saw. In particular, note actions you observed.

5. Write a chronological narrative. Describe something that occurs in a specific time period. What happens at your home from the time your alarm goes off until the time you leave for school or work? What happens from the time you enter a doctor's or dentist's office until the time you leave; from the time you enter a restaurant where you eat lunch or dinner until the time you leave? Write about one of these or any other event that happens in a given time period. Use energetic verbs to hold your reader's interest.

6. Develop one of your journal entries into a finished piece of writing. Pay careful attention to your use of verbs.

Share your writing with other students in the class either by making copies for everyone, reading yours aloud to others, or trading papers and reading one another's work. You may want to select one paper to revise and rewrite as a group. Pay special attention to effective and creative use of verbs, both action and being.

SELF TEST FOR CHAPTER 4

1. The word *verb* comes from the Latin word meaning _____.

2. The two major categories of verbs are _____ and _____.

3. In addition to *physical* actions, verbs express _____ actions and _____ actions.

4. _____ verbs can act as equal signs in sentences.

5. Two-way verbs can express either _____ or _____.

6. Some examples of two-way verbs are: _____, _____, _____, _____, _____.

7. Being verbs are also called _____ verbs.

8. Words linked by being verbs may either _____ or _____ the subject in the front of the sentence.

9. Readers are drawn to strong _____ verbs in sentences.

10. Readers hardly notice _____ verbs in sentences.

FINAL JOURNAL WRITING

Write in your journal about what you have learned about verbs in this chapter. What did you already know about verbs before you read the chapter? Which concepts were new to you? How do you plan to use verbs in your writing differently from the way you have used them before? How can you use your knowledge of verbs to revise sentences you have written? Which verb concepts still seem vague or confusing to you? How can you clear up this confusion?

CHAPTER 5

Verb Tenses ... The Writer's Timekeepers

*Time present and time past
Are both perhaps present in time future,
And time future contained in time past.*

—T. S. Eliot

QUESTIONS TO ASK YOURSELF WHILE READING CHAPTER 5:

1. How can learning about verb tenses improve my writing?
2. How do verbs tell time in every sentence I write?
3. How can my misuse of verbs label me as having "bad grammar"?
4. How can knowing more about verb tenses actually make me more employable?
5. How can I shift tenses in my writing without confusing my reader?

THE TIME OF OUR LIVES

As English speakers, we live in a time-obsessed culture. When we turn on a television program, we expect it will start exactly on time—not five minutes late or even five seconds late. In fact, television programs are broadcast so predictably "on time" that people often set their watches by them. Many other aspects of our lives, such as school, work, and even leisure activities like going out to dinner or attending plays, demand careful attention to time. So serious an offense is tardiness at school that an excessive number of "tardies" could cause a student to be expelled; such an act of irresponsibility is tardiness in the work place that not reporting on time could cause a worker to be fired; so grave an insult is arriving late for a social event that an unexplained delay may seriously threaten a friendship.

Since language reflects culture, no wonder the English language, like its speakers, is obsessed with time. Even this book reflects that obsession; it devotes an entire chapter just to the treatment of time. (That reminds me, I have a deadline to meet; this chapter has to be in on time!)

COLLABORATE! *Comparing Stories*

Directions

A. *With a group of classmates or on your own, read paragraphs 1 and 2 aloud and compare them.*

1.   Henry secretly smiled at his reflection in the mirror. He observes his masterful disguise. Then quietly he will open the door and looks down the hall. The moonlight was shining faintly through the skylight. He steps back again quickly. His heart will beat rapidly. Nervously Henry waited to make his surprise appearance at the Halloween party.

2.   Henry secretly smiles at his reflection in the mirror. He observes his masterful disguise. Then quietly he opens the door and looks down the hall. The moonlight is shining faintly through the skylight. He steps back again quickly. His heart beats rapidly. Nervously Henry waits to make his surprise appearance at the Halloween party.

Questions to discuss or think about:

1.   Which paragraph do you like best? Why?
2.   Which paragraph sounds better to you? What makes it sound better?

B. *Now read paragraphs 2 and 3 and 4 aloud and compare them:*

2.   Henry secretly smiles at his reflection in the mirror. He observes his masterful disguise. Then quietly he opens the door and looks down the hall. The moonlight is shining faintly through the skylight. He steps back again quickly. His heart beats rapidly. Nervously Henry waits to make his surprise appearance at the Halloween party.

3.   Henry secretly smiled at his reflection in the mirror. He observed his masterful disguise. Then quietly he opened the door and looked down the hall. The moonlight was shining faintly through the skylight. He stepped back again quickly. His heart beat rapidly. Nervously Henry waited to make his surprise appearance at the Halloween party.

4.   Henry will secretly smile at his reflection in the mirror. He will observe his masterful disguise. Then quietly he will open the door and look down the hall. The moonlight will be shining faintly through the skylight. He will step back again quickly. His heart will beat rapidly. Nervously Henry will wait to make his surprise appearance at the Halloween party.

Questions to discuss or think about:

a.   How do paragraphs 2, 3, and 4 differ?

b.   As a writer, when would you use paragraph 3 instead of paragraph 2?

c.   When would you use paragraph 4?

d.   How is the first paragraph you read (paragraph 1) different from 2, 3, and 4?

e.   What may have influenced your initial reaction to paragraph 1?

JOURNAL PROMPT

Write about a Halloween when you dressed up in a certain costume or when something scary happened to you or someone you know. Write about taking your children trick-or-treating or planning a Halloween party for them. How important is Halloween compared to other "holidays"? Explain. Is Halloween different today than it was when you were growing up? Elaborate.

ONE, TWO, THREE TIMES

Do you realize it is impossible to write an English sentence without indicating time? What is the time in each of these sentences?

Sentence A: *Olga spills the coffee today.*
Sentence B: *Olga spilled the coffee yesterday.*
Sentence C: *Olga will spill the coffee tomorrow.*

In the first sentence, the action takes place in the present (today); in the second sentence, the past (yesterday); and in the third sentence, the future (tomorrow). But what happens when we remove the last word of each sentence?

Sentence A: *Olga spills the coffee.*
Sentence B: *Olga spilled the coffee.*
Sentence C: *Olga will spill the coffee.*

Without the words "today," "yesterday," and "tomorrow," can you still tell *when* each sentence takes place? Of course you can. But *how* can you tell?

HOW TIMES ARE CHANGING

Even without the words "today," "yesterday," and "tomorrow," you still know that sentence A is present, sentence B is past, and sentence C is future. But *how* do you know?

Since "Olga" and "coffee" are the *same* in all three sentences, the clues you use to determine when the time *changes* lie in the VERB—the only word that *changes.*

Look closely at the three verbs:

Sentence A: *spills*

Sentence B: *spilled*

Sentence C: *will spill* (this verb is called a *verb phrase* because it is expressed by more than one word)

How do these verbs tell time?

By adding ENDINGS and by adding the HELPING VERB "will."

Even though you can easily spot different time signals when you *read,* can you confidently *write* in a specified time frame if a writing assignment requires you to do so? For example, if your teacher says, "Write your entire paper in the *present tense,"* do you know exactly what to do? Or does the mention of "present tense" make you *feel* tense?

ENSE TIMES

You may have heard the terms *present tense, past tense, and future tense.* Since the Latin word *tense* means "time," these terms simply mean "present time," "past time," and "future time." We English speakers divide time into three distinctly separate categories. In some, less time-obsessed cultures, time is not so neatly compartmentalized.

Looking at the verb "spill" has already taught you something about how English makes time distinctions, that is, how verbs change tenses:

- An "-s" ending can create the PRESENT TENSE.
- An "-ed" ending can create the PAST TENSE.
- The helping verb "will" can create the FUTURE TENSE.

But what if, instead of *spill,* the verb were *drink?*

Sentence A: *Olga <u>drinks</u> the coffee.*

Sentence B: *Olga <u>drank</u> the coffee.*

Sentence C: *Olga <u>will drink</u> the coffee.*

What is different about how the verb *drink* changes to past? Instead of adding an "-ed" ending, *drinks* changes to *drank.* In other words, it **changes spelling** rather than adds an ending.

Three Ways Writers Can Change Verb Tenses

1. Adding endings to verbs (spill*ed*)
2. Adding helping verbs (*will* spill; *will* drink)
3. Changing spellings (*drink* becomes *drank*)

COLLABORATE! *Reading for Tense Times*

Directions

Do this activity together with a group of other students or work on your own.

A. The verbs are underlined for you in the following paragraphs. Pay close attention to the verbs as you read each paragraph aloud.

B. Decide whether each paragraph is in the present tense, past tense, or future tense. Write the <u>tense</u> here:

> Paragraph 1_____
>
> Paragraph 2_____

C. *Change each paragraph to a different tense; you decide which tense. (For example, if a paragraph is originally written in the present, you may want to change it to past or future.) To change the tense, cross out the verbs and replace them with verbs in the new tense you have chosen.*

Before you begin, here are SOME HINTS FOR CHANGING TENSES:

- When rewriting to create the PAST tense, you will sometimes add endings <u>or</u> sometimes change the spelling of the verb. A trick that will make converting to past tense easier is to say the word "yesterday" aloud before revising each sentence.
- When rewriting into the FUTURE, you will use the helping verb "will" repeatedly. A trick to make changing to future tense easier is to say the word "tomorrow" before each sentence.
- When rewriting sentences into the PRESENT, you will sometimes use the ending "s" or "es"; *or* sometimes you will use no ending at all. Converting a sentence into the present tense becomes easier if you say the words "right now" in front of each sentence you are about to change.

Paragraph #1
Decide the tense; then change it.

Harvest mice are midget acrobats. They <u>stretch</u> and <u>twist</u> and <u>swing</u> from one blade of grass to another. They <u>flick</u> their long, skinny tails from side to side. They <u>look</u> hilarious. All of a sudden, one mouse <u>dashes</u> down a stalk of grass and <u>scurries</u> up another. His companion <u>follows</u>. Up and down they <u>go</u>. Suddenly they <u>screech</u> to a halt. Each one <u>perches</u> at the tip of its own stalk. The wind <u>blows</u>. It <u>seems</u> dangerous for the mice. But it <u>is</u> not so. These mice <u>are</u> experts. They <u>wrap</u> their tails around the grass, <u>grab</u> the stems with their hind feet, and <u>hold</u> on tightly. Back and forth they <u>swing</u> with the wind.

A **question** to discuss or think about: How did you change the verbs <u>are</u> and <u>is</u> into other tenses?

Paragraph #2
Decide the tense; then change it.

Tears rolled down our unshaven faces, and we sang "Silent Night." Suddenly we forgot our wounds and our hunger. We raised prayers of thanks for our homes and our fatherland. There was a new feeling in our hearts. For this brief time, our burdens were gone. We clung to one another. We even exchanged crude gifts. Some men exchanged dog tags. Some gave I. O. U.'s as imaginary presents. The gifts were only fantasies. But the spirit of giving was genuine. We cried tears of thanks and shared hugs of gratitude. On December 25 even the guards left us alone.

ERB PRINCIPAL PARTS (NOT A SCHOOL ADMINISTRATOR SAYING GOOD-BYE)

When you look at *spills, spilled, spill* and *drinks, drank, drink,* how many different verbs do you see? Would you say there are *six* different verbs, or would you say there are *two* different verbs? If you answered "two," you are thinking like a linguist. Even though there are six different *words,* there are only two different *verbs.* Each verb simply has three forms. If you look up *drink* in an English handbook, you will discover it has even more forms: *drunk* and *drinking.*

The different forms of verbs are called their *principal parts.* English handbooks often list verbs and their principal parts to help writers, like you, recall how verbs change from one tense to another. Here is how the verbs *spill* and *drink* would be listed in a typical handbook:

Verb Principal Parts

Present	Past	Present Participle	Past Participle
spill/spills	spilled	spilling	spilled
drink/drinks	drank	drinking	drunk

As you look at the principal parts of the above verbs, you may notice two forms for the present. You may have already realized that you add an "s" when *one* person is doing the action, for example, "The *girl spillS* the water." But you do *not* add an "s" if *two or more* people are doing the action: "The *girls spill* the water."

HAT ARE *PARTICIPLES* A PART OF?

Two of the principal verb parts are the *present participle* and the *past participle.* Participle means "part" in Latin. These two forms are called that because they always occur as *parts of a verb* rather than alone as verbs. Would you ever say, "I *drinking* water. It *spilling* onto my chin." Of course not! To use "drinking" as a verb, you would add a helper like "am" or "is": "I *am drinking* water. It *is spilling* onto my chin." **Present participles, which always end in -ING, never occur as verbs unless they have helpers.**

Past participles, like "drunk," also occur with helpers. You would not say, "I *drunk* a whole glass of water in five seconds." Instead the correct form would be, "I *drank* a whole glass of water in five seconds." (No wonder you made a mess on your chin!) In what setting, then, do you use the past participle "drunk"? **The past participle functions as a verb when you, the writer, provide a helper such as "have," "has," or "had"; "I had drunk the whole glass of water in five seconds."**

If you look back at the chart entitled Verb Principal Parts, you will notice that the verb "spill" is much less confusing than "drink". Its past participle ("spilled") looks just like its past tense (also "spilled"). Many English verbs use *the same spelling* for both the past tense and the past participle. Therefore writers don't worry much about the fact that most verbs even have past participles. But a verb whose past participle is *different* from its past tense, like "drunk," which is different from "drank," can confuse writers. For example, some writers might mistakenly write "I drunk the water" instead of "I drank the water." Or they might make the opposite mistake and incorrectly use a helper with the wrong form and say, "I have drank the water" instead of correctly saying "I have drunk the water." Mixing up past tenses and past participles is a common problem that can cause some English speakers to be accused of having "bad grammar." Could this be happening to you?

The following is a list of commonly misused verbs that cause problems mainly because their past tense forms are *different* from their past participles:

Principal Parts of Problem Verbs

Present	Past (need no helpers)	Past Participle (always need helpers: have, has, or had)
become(s)	became	become
begin(s)	began	begun
blow(s)	blew	blown
break(s)	broke	broken
bring(s)	brought	brought
build(s)	built	built
burst(s)	burst	burst
come(s)	came	come
cost(s)	cost	cost
do/does	did	done
drink(s)	drank	drunk
drive(s)	drove	driven
eat(s)	ate	eaten
fall(s)	fell	fallen
fly/flies	flew	flown
get(s)	got	gotten
give(s)	gave	given
go/goes	went	gone
have/has	had	had
hide(s)	hid	hidden
is/am/are	was/were	been
know(s)	knew	known
ride(s)	rode	ridden
ring(s)	rang	rung
rise(s)	rose	risen
run(s)	ran	run
see(s)	saw	seen

shake(s)	shook	shaken
shrink(s)	shrank	shrunk
sing(s)	sang	sung
sink(s)	sank	sunk
sit(s)	sat	sat
steal(s)	stole	stolen
swim(s)	swam	swum
take(s)	took	taken
tear(s)	tore	torn
throw(s)	threw	thrown
wake(s)	woke/waked	woken/waked
wear(s)	wore	worn
write(s)	wrote	written

COLLABORATE! *Convert "Bad Grammar" to "Good Grammar"*

Directions

In the following paragraphs circle the correct verb form. In each pair of verbs the <u>past tense is listed FIRST</u> and the <u>past participle is listed SECOND</u>. Before you begin, answer the following questions:

1. Of the past tense and the past participle, which verb form <u>never</u> needs a helper?

    _____

2. Which verb form <u>always</u> needs either "have" or "has" or "had" as a helper?

    _____

Looking for "have" or "has" or "had" in each sentence will help you arrive at the right answer. But remember, expressions such as <u>I've</u> stands for <u>I have</u>; <u>he's</u> stands for <u>he is</u>; and <u>you'd</u> can stand for <u>you had</u>. So be on the watch for those "flying commas" (also known as apostrophes)!!

Over the years, Joe and I have <u>became/become</u> good friends. Yesterday he <u>come/came</u> to me with an interesting question. He asked if I'd ever <u>stole/stolen</u> anything before. Since I <u>saw/seen</u> he was serious, I answered him seriously. I told him about the time I'd <u>went/gone</u> to a restaurant with my wife, Louise.

We <u>went/gone</u> to a fancy restaurant. I had never <u>took/taken</u> her there before. But that day was her birthday, so I wanted to do something extra special for her. We <u>did/done</u> the evening up in style. We <u>drank/drunk</u> champagne with our dinner. (I had never <u>drank/drunk</u> champagne before.) The waiters <u>sang/sung</u> "Happy Birthday" to Louise as she <u>sank/sunk</u> down in her chair from embarrassment. She'd <u>wore/worn</u> a red dress that night; and after being serenaded, she had a complexion to match her dress.

The dinner was great! After we had <u>ate/eaten</u>, the waiter brought our bill. I made out a check including a twenty percent tip, and then I escorted my wife to the "powder room" before we left. It wasn't until we arrived home that I realized I had stole/stolen something at the restaurant: our meal!! When I emptied my pockets before bedtime, I looked at my check book. I had wrote/written the check, but had not tore/torn it out of the checkbook and left it with the bill.

I panicked. Nothing has shook/shaken me up quite like that for some time. Of course, I called the restaurant right away and they graciously took my credit card number over the phone.

Joe laughed at my story. But he never did/done tell me why he asked me if I had ever stole/stolen anything? I wonder if he's keeping something from me . . .

JOURNAL PROMPT

Write about an embarrassing experience you have had. Where did it occur? What happened? What did you learn from the experience? Or write about embarrassing experiences of others that you have observed? Tell about an embarrassing experience in the form of a story or narrative.

WRITE RIGHT FOR THE JOB: How the Right Participle Can Keep Food on Your Table

"So what?" you may be asking by now, "Are participles really worth all this discussion? It's not as if my life depends on knowing the difference between past tenses and past participles." Or does it?

Let me ask you this: Does your life depend on getting a good job? Getting a job can affect your life, can't it?

Often I train workers on the job in addition to teaching classes in a college setting. Recently a personnel director of a major insurance company approached me with a concern about employees. He complained that many "front-line" employees (receptionists, secretaries, and service people who deal with the public representing the company) use what he called "bad grammar." He had overheard them using expressions such as

> I *seen* it.
> He *has sang* that tune once too often.
> I *done* it just the way you said.
> I've *went* ahead and filed those papers.

These were just a few examples. To me, all these examples demonstrated that the workers did not know how to use some of the most common verbs in their own language. Specifically, they couldn't differentiate a *past tense* from a *past participle*.

After a lengthy discussion, the personnel manager and I came to the discouraging conclusion that this kind of usage problem was too big to fix in the type of short-term training employers typically offer their staff on the job. Consequently, the manager decided he had no choice: The only certain way to eliminate "bad grammar" from the company's workforce would be to screen all the new applicants. In other words, he decided to design specific interview questions to which the applicants would naturally respond with certain verbs. Thus, early in the interview, he could eliminate any candidates with "bad grammar."

Why would a receptionist's grammar be important to a major corporation? It has to do with corporate image. If a receptionist sounds uneducated, then customers might also think he or she is incompetent. The customers might assume that a company employing "incompetent" workers is an incompetent company. And this assumption could cause valuable customers to take their business elsewhere.

The dilemma faced by the insurance company is not an isolated example. Since that discussion, I have been approached by several other businesses. One was a retirement housing facility. The director worried that the maids, maintenance crew, and kitchen workers who came in contact with some of the dignified, well-educated, elderly residents would create a negative image for the facility. After all, these workers, many of whom didn't use commonplace verbs correctly, were responsible for the welfare of other human beings. Residents might infer that if workers are careless with their language, they might also be careless about other important aspects of their jobs. Therefore, the manager was concerned about whom she hired. In such contexts, knowing the difference between certain past tense verb forms and their past participles suddenly takes on a new importance.

Making a seemingly insignificant ungrammatical remark in the wrong place at the wrong time could have significant implications in your life. Even if incorrect use of verbs does not cost you a job, your language skills will influence how certain people treat you and to what extent they have confidence in your abilities.

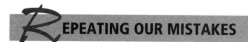

REPEATING OUR MISTAKES

If you confuse verb forms, chances are *you* only confuse a couple of the common problem verbs listed on pages 108–109 . But the problem is magnified by *repetition.* For example, if you are used to saying "I is" instead of "I am" or "you is" instead of "you are," think how many times you repeat those expressions during the course of just one conversation. Even though that may be only two different mistakes, their negative effect on your language image is multiplied every time you open your mouth. Even if your verb confusion is limited to saying "I seen" instead of "I saw," think how often you repeat that phrase during a single day. In other words, confusing just a couple of verbs can dramatically affect how people perceive you.

DO IT YOURSELF! *Pick the Right Verbs for the Job*

Directions

The following letter is full of verb forms misused by many English speakers. This is an exaggeration; few English speakers make as many errors as this writer does. But remember, just <u>one</u> verb error in a letter of application may keep you from getting the job you desire. That means you should be satisfied only if you find 100% of the errors in this letter.

A. *Read the letter carefully.*

B. *Circle any verb forms you believe are incorrect.*

C. *Change your circled verb forms to correct forms by writing the correction above each verb. If you cannot think of the correct forms of the underlined verbs, refer to the list of problem verbs on pages 108–109.*

Dear Mr. Jenkins:

     I is applying for a job with your company. I seen your ad in the paper yesterday just as I come out of the hardware store. I had went to the hardware store in the first place because I had broke the handle off my bathroom door. I had took the ruined knob with me. That way I be sure I gots the right kind of knob to replace it. I still does not have a clue what I done to make it fall apart. I just begun to turn it in a normal way, and it bursted into about five pieces, just like that. I have came to the conclusion that my whole house just weren't built right to start with. I knowed it the minute I moved in. I ain't had anything but trouble, and it has costed me a pile of money since I done moved in.

     Anyway, the reason I have set down today and have wrote this letter is that I seen you has a job for a carpenter. As you already have saw from my letter, I has got lots of experience fixing things. Besides that I have took some classes where I builded things. In those classes, I have gave speeches; and I have wrote reports about my work. So as you can see, I be not only experienced, I be educated as well. Do you think you has a job for me in your company?

Sincerely,

Shirley Qualified

Compare your answers to those of other students. Which verbs caused you problems? Why?

    Based on how well you did with this letter, do you think you should work harder on learning different verb forms and how to use them? One way to begin is by paying close attention to the verb errors your teachers mark on your papers. Also, go back over this chapter more than once.

SECOND-LANGUAGE AND DIALECT SPEAKERS—COULD THIS BE YOU?

Some people will naturally have more problems with verb forms than others. I grew up in an American home speaking Norwegian as my first language. I had to work especially hard to learn to speak and write correctly. My mother, who has never attended an English-speaking school, still uses incorrect endings on her verbs. If English is your second language (for example, if your first language is Spanish, Russian, German,

Japanese or Vietnamese), verb forms will be more difficult for you than for native speakers of English. You may, in fact, want to go to your school library or bookstore to obtain some additional aids to help you with verbs. There are many books available designed just for second language students.

Even if English is your first language, you may have severe problems with verb forms—especially if you were raised in certain parts of the United States. In some areas, dialects of English are common. For example, in some parts of the United States people use expressions such as "I is" and "you is." Some speakers also leave "s" endings off verbs when they should be there and put them on when they shouldn't, or they overlook the use of "ed" to communicate past tense.

American Black English (ABE) is a dialect of its own that uses verb forms differently.

One ABE speaker who attended a writing seminar I conducted for a local business was very discouraged because her employer kept telling her that her writing didn't "sound right." She was near tears as she shared her response with me: "It sounds right to me." And it did because she had grown up speaking a special dialect of English. Her family and all her childhood friends spoke the same way. Unfortunately, the fact that her dialect used forms that were not the same as standard written English put her at a disadvantage on the job even though she had lived in the United States and spoken English all her life—English that was perfectly acceptable where she came from.

What this means is that "bad grammar" may not be "bad" at all. Instead it is often an acceptable form of English in a certain setting. Unfortunately, that does not mean it is a dialect that is acceptable in all settings. In business and academic settings, "standard" written English is required for documents and papers.

The dialect issue is one I understand all too painfully myself. I came from a small fishing village in Norway where I learned to speak the local dialect of Norwegian. But when I now use that language in conversation with professional people who have studied at universities in Norway, they look at me like I'm a "hick" from the Norwegian "sticks." The fact that people use language as a tool for discrimination may not be fair, but it is universal.

THE WELL-WORN IRREGULARS

The list of problem verbs whose participles we have been working with are called *irregular verbs*. They are known as "irregular" because they are nonconformists that refuse to add *-ed* endings like the majority of verbs do. The majority of verbs, which do use *-ed* endings, are called *regular verbs*. The English language has thousands of regular verbs while it has only a hundred or so irregular verbs. Instead of using *-ed* endings, irregular verbs change their forms unpredictably. For example, "sing" changes to "sung" instead of "sing*ed*." But that does not mean "bring" will change to "brung." Instead "bring" changes to "brought." In fact, there is no such word as "brung."

Irregular verbs are important in English because they are verbs we use all the time. Irregularity is a characteristic of things frequently used. Have you ever walked up very old stairs in a very old building? Did you notice the steps had become irregular and dipped in the center where they had been subjected to the most traffic over the years? Rarely used steps, on the other hand, remain new-looking and straight, conforming to their original shape. Just like frequently used steps are irregularly shaped, frequently used verbs are also irregular.

And the most frequently used forms are the most irregular. Look at the *being* verb, the most common verb in our language. See how irregular it is:

The Verb of Being

Verb	Present	Past	Present Participle	Past Participle
be	am/is/are	was/were	being	been

How many different forms of the verb of being do you count?_____

If you feel you need to review the verb of being, here are some examples of how its different forms are used:

The Verb of Being at Work

Present Tense
AM—   I am
IS—   he is/she is/it is/the child is
ARE—   you are/we are/the children are (plural present tense)

Past Tense
WAS—   I was/he was/she was/it was/ the child was
WERE—   you were/we were/ the children were

Future Tense
BE—   with the helping verb "will": I will be, he will be, everybody will be

Participles Used in Verb Phrases
BEING—   this present participle is used with helping verbs: am being, is being, are being, was being, were being
BEEN—   this past participle is used with helping verbs: has been, have been, had been, will have been.

DO IT YOURSELF!   *Practice Using the Highly Irregular Being Verbs*

Directions

In the following paragraphs, fill in the appropriate form of the being verb. The first one is done for you as an example:

Today <u>is</u> the day I *am* taking my first mid-semester exam. I _____ scared about how difficult the test will _____. My friend, Wendy, _____ worried, too. She has never _____ in a college class before.

Last night, she and I _____ up until three o'clock studying together. She wanted to stay up all night, but I _____ too tired. At the time, I felt I was _____ a bit of a baby about needing my sleep. But today, Wendy and I _____ both glad that this afternoon we _____ taking the test after having five hours of sleep instead of no hours of sleep.

JOURNAL PROMPT

Write about how you deal with test taking. Do you suffer from test anxiety? Which kinds of tests are most difficult for you? Which kinds of tests are the easiest? How do you prepare for a test? Have you ever stayed up all night to study for a test? What was the outcome? What role does having plenty of rest play in your performance on a test? What can you do to improve your test scores?

HERE'S MORE TO TENSES THAN MEETS THE "I"

Since verbs are valuable tools for writers, the more you understand about them, the more confident you will become as a writer. By now you have probably noticed that some verbs in sentences are single words and other verbs are phrases comprised of two or more words (like "have broken" or "will be writing"). Each of these different ways of expressing verbs is actually a different tense; and English has many different tenses with different names.

For, you see, the English language is so time-obsessed it is not satisfied with just one present tense, and one past tense, and one future tense. It needs several ways to express each one of these times because time is a "big deal" in English-speaking cultures.

In fact, *time* is about as important to a speaker of English as *snow* is to an Eskimo. Snow is such a big deal in the Eskimo culture that the Eskimo language has at least ten different words for *snow*. Eskimos need to differentiate between wet snow and powdery snow and light snow and dense snow and . . . I don't know what other kind of snow because I'm not an Eskimo. (I'm an American who doesn't even ski.) All I need to know about snow is that it makes roads difficult to drive on and may cause schools to close so I won't have to go to work. One word for snow is all I need!

There may be languages in the world that are satisfied with one set of verb tenses, too. But English is not one of them. In English just having one way to express present tense is not enough:

> I *eat*, is not enough to express the present tense of the verb *eat*.

There is also

> I *am eating* . . . a special present tense that emphasizes the action of eating is presently in progress. Therefore, we call this the present *progressive* tense.

But that's not all; there is also

> I *do eat* . . . a third kind of present tense, which creates emphasis. It's called the present *emphatic* tense.

English speakers use different *tenses* to communicate more precisely about *time* conditions—just like Eskimos use different words for *snow* to communicate more precisely about *snow conditions.* Languages really do tell us much about the culture of their speakers.

Summary of Three Different Verb Tenses

Tenses	Regular Verb (Example)	Irregular Verbs (Example)

<u>Simple Tenses</u>: The simplest way to express a verb—sometimes requires only *one* word.

simple present	play or plays	sing or sings
simple past	play*ed*	*sang*
simple future	*will* play	*will* sing

<u>Progressive Tenses</u>: Verb in progress—uses being verb as a helper together with present participle (ending in -ING)

present progressive	*am* play*ing*	*am* sing*ing*
	is play*ing*	*is* sing*ing*
	are play*ing*	*are* sing*ing*
past progressive	*was* play*ing*	*was* sing*ing*
	were play*ing*	*were* sing*ing*
future progressive	*will be* play*ing*	*will be* sing*ing*

<u>Emphatic Tenses</u>: Emphasizes verb—uses form of "do" as a helper with no ending on main verb

present emphatic	*do* play	*do* sing
	does play	*does* sing
past emphatic	*did* play	*did* sing

(There is no future emphatic.)

THE SIMPLE TENSES: SAY IT IN A WORD . . . OR TWO

The simplest forms for expressing past, present, and future are called the *simple tenses.* Here again is what the simple tenses of the regular verb "play" and the irregular verb "sing" look like:

Simple Present	Simple Past	Simple Future
play or plays	played	will play
sing or sings	sang	will sing

Notice, it takes only one word to express the simple past or the simple present; and it takes only two words to express the future ("will" plus the verb).

Since "play" is a regular verb, its simple past tense is formed by adding an "ed." The past tense of all regular verbs will do the same. But since "sing" is irregular, its way of forming the past is different (changes spelling to "sang"). Other irregular verbs will have their own unique ways of forming the simple past. So, when you use irregular verbs in your writing, you may sometimes want to refer to the list of problem verbs on pages 108–109 to ensure you are writing the simple past tense correctly.

DO IT YOURSELF!   *Make It "Simple"*

Directions

A. *Fill in <u>simple present tense</u> verb forms to complete this paragraph. Remember, sometimes you will add "s" endings, and sometimes you will not. The first one is done for you as an example.*

Fred *plays* (play) with his son. Fred _____ (wear) blue jeans. His son _____ (being verb) in rompers. The music _____ (blare) from the stereo. "I _____ (love) dancing," _____ (squeal) little Adam. His father _____ (pick) him up and Adam _____ (wrap) his legs around his father's waist. The two _____ (glide) across the room to the rhythm of the latest hit song. The volume _____ (being verb) up, so they _____(feel) every beat of the music. "This _____ (being verb) one of the joys of being a parent," _____ (think) Fred to himself, "This _____ (being verb) a moment to treasure."

B: *Fill in the <u>simple past tense</u> verb forms to complete this paragraph. Remember, some verbs add "ed" endings, some change their forms entirely, and some verbs do not change at all. Refer to the verb charts on pages 108–109 whenever you are unsure of an answer.*

In the old days, baseball _____ (being verb) a family affair. The whole country _____(come) together during the week of the World Series. At the end of every game, kids _____ (re-create) every play on their own neighborhood street corners. At some high schools, students _____ (sit) in school parking lots and _____ (listen) to the series on the radio. At other schools, principals _____ (announce) scores over the loudspeakers at the end of each inning. Everyone _____ (stay) up to listen to the night games, even business men who _____ (have) early morning appointments at the office. In the old days, all Americans _____ (feel) the vibration of the World Series at home, school, and work.

C. *Fill in the <u>simple future tense</u> verb forms to complete this paragraph. Remember, in the simple future tense, "will" always precedes the verb.*

The Los Chiles Mexican Restaurant _____ (celebrate) Cinco de Mayo on the fifth day of May. The featured menu _____ (include) chimichangas, chile rellenos, taquitos, and, of course, nachos. On this day children _____ (eat) free. Pinatas _____ (hang) over every table. The management _____ (play) Mexican and Spanish favorites, and loudspeakers all over the restaurant _____ (vibrate) with Latin rhythms. Even if you are not Mexican, you _____ (enjoy) this celebration of Mexico's independence.

JOURNAL PROMPT

If you are a parent or aunt or uncle, write about an activity you enjoy with your child or niece or nephew. Or, write about a time you recall from your own childhood when an adult spent special time with you. If you have ever participated in a big brother program or worked with young people as a coach or troop leader, write about your experiences. What do you hope young people will remember from the time you spent with them? Do you feel you can teach youngsters anything of value by sharing your time with them? If so, what have you learned from adults with whom you spent time when you were younger?

JOURNAL PROMPT

Write about a sport you enjoy watching. Do you have traditions associated with championship games like the Super Bowl, basketball playoffs, World Series or any other major sports championship? Do you have a team you particularly favor? Why? How avid are you as a fan? When your team plays, what do you do to demonstrate your support? Why do you think you enjoy watching one particular sport more than others?

JOURNAL PROMPT

Write about a special holiday that is a part of a culture you are familiar with (that includes the American culture, as well). Describe, in detail, how the holiday is celebrated. Are there certain activities associated with the holiday—certain music, certain food? Do people wear special clothing for this celebration? Is much preparation done ahead of time? Write about the last time you celebrated this holiday. Write about the <u>most memorable</u> time.

THE PROGRESSIVE TENSES: ACTIONS IN PROGRESS

Progressive tenses are always expressed by verb phrases instead of single-word verbs. The additional words in the phrase suggest specific conditions that go beyond the time categories. Let's look at what I mean.

The verb phrase "is walking," is an example, of the progressive tense (also called the "continuous" tense). In addition to communicating time, this tense communicates that the action of the verb is *in progress* or *continuous*. Compare the progressive tenses to the simple tenses you have just learned:

	Simple Tense	**Progressive Tense**
PRESENT	I *play*	I *am playing*
	you *play*	you *are playing*
	he *plays*	he *is playing*

PAST	I or he *played*	I or he *was playing*
	you *played*	you *were playing*
FUTURE	I, he, or you *will play*	I, you, or he *will be playing*

Analyze the differences between the SIMPLE and PROGRESSIVE tense lists:

1. What do you think is the difference *in meaning* between the simple tenses and progressive tenses?

    _____

    _____

    _____

2. Why do you think the progressive tenses are called progressive or continuous and the simple tenses are called simple?

    _____

    _____

    _____

    _____

3. Which ending do all the progressive tense verbs have in common?

    _____

4. What do we call a verb form with this ending?

    _____

5. Which verb is used as a helper in the progressive tense?

    _____

    Did your answers to the above questions reveal

    - progressive tense verbs communicate continuous action or action in progress and?
    - they always use the -ING form of the verb (the present participle)?
    - they always use being verbs as helpers?

    Here is a formula for how progressive tenses are formed:

PROGRESSIVE TENSE = HELPERS (verbs of being) + -ING form of verb (present participle)

DO IT YOURSELF!   *Pick the Progressives*

Directions

A. *In the following paragraph, <u>underline</u> only the progressive tense verb phrases.*

B. *Above each, write <u>present</u> progressive, or <u>past</u> progressive, or <u>future</u> progressive.*

Hint: First look for present participles ending in <u>-ing</u>. Then look to the being verb HELPERS to help you decide the time.

This afternoon, I will be buying a new car. I will be going on a shopping spree for my dream vehicle. Last night, when I was reading the paper, I noticed all the dealers in town are having sales now. It is the end of the year. This year's cars are selling at big discounts because next year's cars will be coming out soon. This seems like the right time to invest my savings and finally realize my dream. I am picturing a bright red four-wheel drive pick-up with a black interior. I am thinking it should be a mini model rather than a full-sized truck. That way I will be spending less on gas, and I will have more money left to spend on extras like a CD player with high-quality speakers. I also am considering an air conditioner for the truck since I will be venturing out into the desert to try out my four-wheel drive. Right now I am feeling so excited. My heart is beating faster than normal as I think about what lies ahead for me today. Just imagine, a few hours from now I will be sitting in my new truck!

JOURNAL PROMPT

In your journal, write advice you would give someone who is about to make a big purchase, such a car, motorcycle, house, etc. Share your own experiences that have taught you something about making big purchases. Discuss what should and should not influence someone's decision.

WRITE RIGHT FOR THE JOB: When Progressive Tenses Are not so Progressive

The progressive tenses are used frequently in business and professional writing. In fact, they are overused. Often writers of business letters choose two- or three-word progressive expressions when a single simple verb would do just as well.

Most employers want to eliminate any kind of "excess verbiage," or extra words. They typically do not want their employees using more words than necessary to say what needs to be said. Yet workers, who may think longer sentences sound more important than shorter ones, often end up producing bulky documents containing many unnecessary words. This makes their writing both time-consuming and confusing to read.

One way to reduce bulk in business writing is to look for sentences that contain progressive tense verbs and, whenever possible, reduce those verbs to simpler forms. Where writers have used *progressive* forms out of habit, without thinking, in situations where continuous action does not really need to be communicated, the sentence loses nothing when the verb is changed to a simpler form. In fact, the simply stated message actually sounds more energetic and more compelling because it is shorter and more to the point.

COLLABORATE!   *Doing Business without Progressive Tenses*

Directions

Below is a paragraph from a business document. It contains numerous unnecessary progressive tense verb phrases; they have been underlined for you. Working together with a group or on your own, RE-WRITE the paragraph changing these progressive forms to simple forms.

Dear Mr Wang:

As I <u>am looking</u> through my stack of applications, I see you have applied for a job with our company. Your resume demonstrates you meet all the qualifications and have the experience we <u>are desiring</u>. Therefore, I <u>will be recommending</u> that our screening committee consider your application.

Presently I <u>am serving</u> on that committee as its chairperson. We <u>will be meeting</u> next Monday, November 6; and, at that time, I <u>will be presenting</u> a list of qualified candidates to be interviewed for the computer technician position.

As usual, we <u>are interviewing</u> on Wednesdays. We <u>will be scheduling</u> an interview time for you within the month. I, personally, <u>will be notifying</u> you about the specific date and time.

Thank you for your interest; I <u>am looking</u> forward to meeting with you.

Sincerely,

Maria Lopez

Personnel Director

- How does changing the tenses change the document?
- How is the length affected?
- How is the tone of the communication affected?

This exercise carries a message:
When writing on the job:

DO use the progressive tenses deliberately and conscientiously **only** when simple tenses cannot accurately express the situation about which you are writing.

DON'T use the progressive tenses in place of simple tenses just because you think they make your writing sound more "professional" and just because they make your business documents longer. Most employers want to avoid unnecessary words.

JOURNAL PROMPT

In your journal, draft a letter in which you apply for a job. Either make up a job or use a job you have seen advertised in the newspaper or on a placement office bulletin board. Write about your qualifications for the job. Mention how you heard about the opening. Tell the perspective employer when you will be available to begin work. Politely request an interview. Include anything else you think is important.

THE EMPHATIC TENSES: WHEN YOU REALLY MEAN IT

A third category of tenses is called the *emphatic tenses*. These tenses, as their name implies, allow you to create *emphasis* in the sentences you write.
Emphatic verbs look like this:

> PRESENT EMPHATIC TENSE: I *do play*, he *does play*
> PAST EMPHATIC TENSE: I *did play*, he *did play*

(The emphatic has no future tense.)

Look carefully at the emphatic verb forms and answer these questions:

What are the helpers?

_____

Are there any endings?

_____

Did your answers to the above questions suggest the following formula for the emphatic tenses?

EMPHATIC TENSE=HELPERS (do, does, or did) + THE VERB STEM WITH NO ENDING

Compare the following expressions:

A.   I *understand* the lesson. (simple present)
B.   I *do understand* the lesson. (present emphatic)

A.   Don *likes* your dress. (simple present)
B.   Don *does like* your dress. (present emphatic)

A.   She *looked* tired. (simple past)
B.   She *did look* tired. (past emphatic)

How does using the emphatic tense change the meaning of your sentence?

_____

_____

_____

Does the emphatic tense help create more emphasis? How?

_____

_____

_____

Even though the emphatic form can be quite useful in just the right situation, you may not use it very often in *statements*. But if you take a closer look at everything you say and write, you will find the emphatic tense frequently hiding out in *questions*. This is the most common place English speakers use the emphatic tenses:

<u>Do</u> you <u>drink</u> coffee?
<u>Did</u> Mary <u>dance</u> with Fred?
<u>Does</u> Alexander <u>speak</u> English?
<u>Do</u> you <u>have</u> the time?

The emphatic tense is a little harder to recognize in these expressions because in questions the word order is not the same as the order we are used to seeing in statements. In questions, the verb and its helpers become separated:

You <u>do drink</u> coffee," becomes "<u>Do</u> you <u>drink</u> coffee?

Nevertheless, the verb in the both of these sentences is *do drink.*

DO IT YOURSELF!   *Ask the Emphatic Question*

Directions
A. *Using the emphatic tense, write questions that will produce the answers provided. Remember to use <u>present</u> emphatic to elicit present tense answers and <u>past</u> emphatic to elicit past tense answers.*

1.   Question:_____

     Answer: Yes, I like milk.

2.   Question:_____

     Answer: No, I don't play the piano.

3.   Question:_____

     Answer: Oh, yes. I ordered the onion soup.

4.   Question:_____

Answer: That's right: John ate all the french fries.

5.   Question:_____

Answer: Obviously, Mary does not speak Spanish.

6.   Question:_____

Answer: Of course, I love you.

7.   Question:_____

Answer: Yes, she took the keys.

B. *Make up five questions of your own using the emphatic tense.*

1.   _____

2.   _____

3.   _____

4.   _____

5.   _____

COLLABORATE!   *Reviewing the Different Tenses*

Directions

Working with a group or on your own, read the following selection aloud. Underline all the verbs and verb phrases. Label each as simple (S), progressive (P), or emphatic (E) by writing the appropriate letter above the verb. For a comparison of these tenses, refer back to the SUMMARY OF THREE DIFFERENT VERB TENSES on page 116.

Too much cholesterol in the bloodstream will endanger a healthy heart. Therefore, many Americans are monitoring their cholesterol levels carefully. Consequently, today thousands of Americans jog or walk daily. They also eat healthful foods.

Just how many Americans really do have a cholesterol problem? In the U.S., 52 million adults have high cholesterol. That is 29 percent of our entire adult population.

Three-quarters of the people with high cholesterol do not need medication. Their cholesterol level will drop as a result of exercise, weight loss, and a low-fat diet. Others do need medication. Cholesterol levels over 220 suggest a possible need for medication. Many different factors do play a role, however. Your doctor will understand these factors.

Today researchers are working on treatments for this life-threatening condition. They are making many advances. Effective cholesterol-lowering medication is presently on the market. Doctors are prescribing these medications for patients with severe cholesterol problems. Nowadays these patients have a chance for a long life.

Do you have high cholesterol?

JOURNAL PROMPT

Have you ever had your cholesterol measured? What were the results? Are there factors other than cholesterol that present health risks for you? Do you exercise to maintain good health? How do you think your diet might be affecting your health? What could you do to lower your health risks? What are you presently doing? What do you plan to do? When?

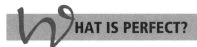

THE PERFECT TENSES: A FINISHED LOOK TO YOUR WRITING

Another important group of tenses is the perfect tenses. These tenses are usually the most difficult tenses to readily understand. Therefore, if you do not grasp the concepts immediately, you may want to read this section more than once.

The perfect tenses are important because they are used so frequently by speakers and writers of English. In fact, the present perfect tense is the most frequently used verb tense in our language; it is even used more often than any simple tense.

WHAT IS PERFECT?

To begin to understand the perfect tenses, first focus on the word "perfect." What does "perfect" suggest to you? Does it suggest flawless? If you came up with a similar answer, you are on the right track.

Now apply that definition to a verb. That is, apply it to an action set in a certain time frame. What does flawless or perfect mean when applied to actions?

Before you commit yourself to an answer, read this story:

The Perfect Cake

Let's pretend I am a superb baker. (I really need to use my imagination for this one.) I am especially good at making cakes. One day I come to class with a treat for my students. It is a *perfect* chocolate cake. Absolutely perfect! Everyone enjoys it and tells me how *perfect* it is.

A week later, a student comes up to me and whispers that his classmate, Jenny Eide, has an upcoming birthday. He implores me to bake the *perfect* chocolate cake once more and bring it to class for Jenny's birthday. I agree to do so. And I think to myself, "The last time I made that cake, I used two eggs. This time I think I will use three eggs instead."

Is that a good idea? What do you think will happen to my *perfect* chocolate cake if I add another egg? Will it still be perfect?

The answer, of course, is NO. If the first cake were truly perfect, adding more to it would only make it imperfect. In other words, perfect means finished, or "perfected." If you continue to do more to something perfect, you will ruin it. What if you had a perfect machine and you added a part to it? What if you had a perfect painting and you added a few more strokes? (Imagine painting a moustache on the *Mona Lisa*.) What if you had a perfect action and you added a little more energy? It would not be perfect any more. In other words, if your action is perfect, it is a finished action. In your writing, then, all perfect verbs communicate *finished* actions (or finished states of being).

> *Nothing quite new is perfect.*
>
> —*Cicero*

WHEN DO FINISHED ACTIONS ACTUALLY OCCUR?

The next question is, "If an action is finished, *when* did the action occur?" You are correct if you answered, "Finished actions must have occurred in the past." For this reason, all perfect tenses include the *past participle*. Remember, the past participle of regular verbs ends in *-ed* and looks just like the simple past tense. But the past participle of irregular verbs usually changes spelling and often looks different from the past tense. To refresh your memory of irregular past participles, refer to the list of Principal Parts of Problem Verbs on pages 108–109.

For now, let's look at how one regular verb (*play*) and one irregular verb (*sing*) form the perfect tenses:

The Perfect Tenses

Present Perfect	Past Perfect	Future Perfect
(I) have played OR (he) has played	had played	will have played
(I) have sung OR (he) he has sung	had sung	will have sung

The formula for the perfect tenses may be written like this:

PERFECT TENSES = HELPERS (have, has, had, or will have) + PAST PARTICIPLE

As you can see the past participles (*played* and *sung*) lend a feeling of *past* to all the perfect verb phrases. This is helpful since all perfect verb tenses communicate finished or completed actions. When you change a *perfect* verb from one time frame to another (from present perfect to past perfect to future perfect), you merely change *the time at which the action was finished* rather than the time it actually occurred.

For example, if you and I are having a conversation at noon and you say, "I have played handball this morning," I know you are *presently finished* with the activity. I would not necessarily know exactly what time of the morning the playing had actually occurred. But I would know that it is finished now in the present. *Have played* expresses *the present perfect tense which communicates action that has been finished by the present time.*

But if instead you say, "By nine o'clock this morning I *had played* handball for an hour." I would know that you finished the action by a specific time in the past. You were finished by 9 A.M., and I am talking to you at twelve o'clock noon. I would still not necessarily know the exact time the playing actually occurred, but I would know that at least an hour's worth of play had been finished by 9 A.M. *Had played* expresses *the past perfect tense which tells me the action was finished by a specific time in the past.* Notice that the past perfect is like a double past: both the helper "had" and the participle "played" communicate past—and something finished in the past actually occurred in the past of a past time!

If "perfect" means "finished," how can there possibly be a *future perfect*? That seems like a contradiction: a *future* action that is *finished.* But, again, imagine you and I are talking at noontime. I suggest we meet for coffee later at 1 P.M. But you respond, "I will meet you at 3 P.M. instead because right now I am heading to the handball court. But by three o'clock I *will have played* as much handball as I can play in one day. So, at three, I will be ready for a break." *Will have played* expresses *the future perfect tense which communicates a specific time in the future when you anticipate being finished* with the action of playing. You still haven't explained the exact time you will actually do the playing, although I can figure out it is somewhere between noon and three o'clock. Yet the point of your communication is not to tell me when you will be doing the playing, but rather when in the future you will be finished with the playing.

To summarize the perfect tenses:

Present Perfect = presently *finished*

Past Perfect = *finished* at a designated time in the past

Future Perfect = anticipates being *finished* at a designated time in the future

A Perfect Timeline

"I had played"	"I have played"	"I will have played"
(I *was* finished by 9:00 A.M.)	(I *am* finished now at 12:00 noon.)	(I *will be* finished by 3:00 P.M.)
Past Perfect	**Present Perfect**	**Future Perfect**

HAT??? RUN THAT BY ME ONE MORE TIME

If you study the perfect verb tenses very carefully, one difficulty is that the *present* perfect tense seems like a type of *past* tense. And, in fact, it is. Yes, that is correct! The *present perfect tense is really PAST*: "I have played" suggests the action was done in the past.

Why, then, is it called *present* perfect?

Take a close look at the helpers in the present perfect tense: "have" or "has." Those helpers are in the present tense. "Have" or "has" used alone as simple verbs in sentences such as, "I have a car" or "Larry has a car," clearly communicate present. That is one reason the tense is called present perfect. The *helper* in a verb phrase is always the word that determines its time category.

DO IT YOURSELF!   *Play with "Perfect"ion*

Directions

In the sentences below, circle the perfect tense which best suits the situation. Remember "had" should be the helping verb when the sentence designates a <u>time in the past</u> when an action was finished. "Will have" should be the helpers when the sentence designates <u>time in the future</u> when an action will be finished.

1. This year <u>has been/had been/will have been</u> an unusual weather year.

2. Last November, by Thanksgiving, the nearby mountains already <u>have received/ had received/will have received</u> so much snow that the ski areas were open for business.

3. But by last Christmas, the weather <u>have changed/had changed/will have changed</u>.

4. It is now January; and this month, so far, we <u>have experienced/had experienced/will have experienced</u> five inches of rain and mild temperatures.

5. The rain <u>has made/had made/will have made</u> the snow melt.

6. The weatherman predicts that by next week so much snow <u>has melted/had melted/will have melted</u> that we may experience some flooding in the valley.

7. By last week, however, the rains <u>have stopped/had stopped/will have stopped</u> and the sun began to shine.

8. Just now I <u>have been/had been/will have been</u> at the garden center shopping for primroses and pansies.

9. I plan to work in the yard this weekend; and by next Monday I <u>have planted/had planted/will have planted</u> my window boxes with colorful flowers.

10. But I just heard the weather report; an arctic storm front <u>has come/had come/will have come</u> into the weather picture and my colorful flowers may soon be covered with a cold, white blanket.

TIME FOR ALL THE TENSES

Let's look more closely at the time communicated by the different tenses you use in your writing:

Verb Tense Chart

PRESENT TIME—

SIMPLE present:	I play/she plays I sing
Present PROGRESSIVE:	I am playing/she is playing/they are playing I am singing/she is singing/they are singing
Present EMPHATIC:	I do play/she does play I do sing/she does sing

PAST TIME—

SIMPLE past:	I played I sang
Past PROGRESSIVE:	I was playing/they were playing I was singing/they were singing
Past EMPHATIC:	I did play I did sing
Present PERFECT:	I have played/she has played I have sung/she has sung

BEFORE PAST TIME—

Past PERFECT:	I had played I had sung

FUTURE TIME—

SIMPLE Future:	I will play I will sing
Future PROGRESSIVE:	I will be playing I will be singing
Future PERFECT:	I will have played I will have sung

COLLABORATE! *Naming the Tenses*

Directions

A. *Together with a group or on your own read the following excerpts aloud. Underline all the verbs.*

B. *Decide which verb tense is being used in each excerpt. Your choices are: simple present, simple past, simple future, present progressive, past progressive, future progressive, present emphatic, past emphatic, present perfect, past perfect, or future perfect. Write the tense in the space provided. Refer to the VERB TENSE CHART on page 129 to recall what each tense looks like. (The first one is done for you as an example)*

_____*simple past*_____ 1. I <u>drove</u> my daughter to Los Angeles for transfusions daily. After a few months, the ride <u>became</u> routine. She <u>had</u> company there. Twenty other children <u>received</u> transfusions regularly for the same illness.

_____ 2. Here is a fresh idea from Quasicook. Our microwave makes meals in seconds. You just push the buttons. We do the rest.

_____ 3. The tiny country had refused aid before. The government had hoped for other solutions. But the solutions had not presented themselves.

_____ 4. Soon computers will forecast the weather. They will calculate day-to-day weather statistics. They will be more accurate than our present weatherman.

_____ 5. The businesses have changed the land. They have destroyed the wilderness. They have left nothing for our children.

_____ 6. I did walk up the stairs to my apartment, and I did put the ashtrays away. But my desire for a cigarette did not diminish.

_____ 7. Americans had helped the drought victims. They had distributed food and water to all regions. Experts had trained the Ethiopians in agricultural skills.

_____ 8. The first wind of autumn is blowing through the trees. John is digging out his woolens. He is preparing for winter weather.

_____ 9. I do attend classes regularly. I do study hard. But I do not always get good grades.

_____10. By next year, I will have been a student here for four years. I will have played tennis for three of those years.

_____11. Too much stress will affect you in many ways. Tension will disturb your stomach. Sometimes anxiety will cause severe headaches.

_____12. A leopard had killed a springbok. The jackals had eaten the remains. We had seen it all through our telescopic lens.

_____13. I lived in Washington, but I made the trip to New York weekly. I visited Andre there. We kept in touch during all those years.

DO IT YOURSELF!   *Find the Time*

Directions

In the following paragraph, verbs are underlined for you. Identify the specific verb tense of each. Your choices are: simple present, simple past, simple future, present progressive, past progressive, future progressive, present emphatic, past emphatic, present perfect, past perfect, or future perfect.

Write the tense above each underlined verb and verb phrase. Refer to the VERB TENSE CHART on page 129 to recall what each tense looks like.

Dear Diane,

This <u>is</u> my senior year. I <u>am graduating</u> on June 16. I <u>am</u> sad. I <u>have attended</u> the same school my entire life. Some of my classmates <u>have been</u> my friends for twelve years. That <u>is</u> a long time.

The teachers here <u>were</u> the best. I <u>learned</u> so much from them. They <u>prepared</u> me for my next big step: college. I <u>have</u> not <u>decided</u> on a major yet. But I <u>do know</u> the general area of study. I <u>have</u> always <u>enjoyed</u> science. Perhaps I <u>will become</u> a medical technician. <u>Do</u> you <u>think</u> the medical field is a good choice?

What <u>is</u> new with you? <u>Are</u> you still <u>studying</u> Accounting? I <u>admire</u> your ability in math. I <u>will</u> never <u>be</u> a mathematician myself. That <u>is</u> certain! <u>Do</u> you <u>have</u> as many classes this term as last term? <u>Don</u>'t <u>work</u> too hard!

Well, I <u>will finish</u> this letter now. My friends <u>are waiting</u> for me. We <u>will be practicing</u> our graduation walk this evening. Afterwards, we <u>will celebrate</u> with a party at my house. Maybe graduation <u>is</u> not so bad after all.

Love,

Frank

- Did you notice that some of the verb phrases are split up because the writer has inserted the word "NOT" or a descriptive word like "ALWAYS"?
- Did you notice that in questions the verb is also split up, making the different parts of the verb harder to find?

JOURNAL PROMPT

Write about the last school you attended before this one? How did you feel about leaving? Do you feel that particular school prepared you well for what you are doing now? Explain. What do you miss about that school and the people who were there? What kinds of feelings do you think you will have when you leave the school you are attending right now?

WHEN TENSES SHIFT . . .

A common concern of writing teachers is something called *tense shift*. Have you ever had a teacher mark "tense shift" on one of your papers? What exactly does that mean? Tense shift means you have shifted from one tense to another in your writing for no apparent reason. Most teachers will tell you to be consistent in your use of tenses. That is, if you start telling a story in the past tense, you should stick to the past tense throughout the story; if you set the story in the present, you should stick to the present throughout.

But tenses often *do* shift, even in a well-written piece of writing. After all, as human beings, we have the ability to mentally move our thoughts from one time frame to another. That is one characteristic that distinguishes us from other animals that have language.

Yes, some animals, like dolphins, have language; so do chimpanzees. Dolphins and chimps both use verbs; that is, they both make specific sounds that represent specific actions. But neither of these brilliant mammals is able to comprehend or communicate different *tenses*. If animals communicate an action, that action is always immediately obvious. If they utter "eat" or "jump," they mean an action occurring immediately, rather than an action that happened three days ago or one that might take place a week from now. But we human beings are much more sophisticated and intelligent animals. Any one of us is capable of discussing actions that occurred years ago, and we can also imagine future events that have not occurred yet.

If we are so bright, then why do shifts in tenses sometimes confuse us?

LEADING YOUR READER

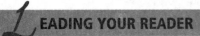

Think of it this way. When you write something, you are essentially leading a reader across a page with your words. Writing is designed like a one-way street in that readers read one direction, from left to right. When they finish one line, they move down to the next line, beginning at the left again and working their way to the right-hand side of the page. All the while, you, the writer, are leading them on their one-way journey because you have written what they read.

But when you consider tenses in your writing, it is as if your one-way street has three lanes: the present tense lane, the past tense lane, and the future tense lane. As you, the writer, enter into a piece of writing, you immediately decide which lane you want to be in. If you decide on the present tense lane, for example, your reader will follow, understanding that all events in the writing will be in the present tense.

But what if, suddenly, you decide you want to move into another lane? Let's say you remembered a past incident that somehow relates to the events happening now in your story, so you want to share that earlier, but related, incident with your reader. Can you just arbitrarily begin using the past tense? If you are driving down a three-lane highway, can you just suddenly move from one lane to another? The answer is *you can*; but if someone is following you, you must first *signal*. Your readers deserve the same courtesy as motorists who follow your lead. In a piece of writing, if you signal your intent, you can smoothly change tenses; and you can do so without upsetting or confusing your reader. Signaling is important, however.

How do you signal in a piece of writing? You signal with words, of course. Words that suggest time, such as *yesterday, today, earlier, later, now,* and *then,* are a few of the words you can use to signal tense shifts in your writing.

COLLABORATE! *Shifting Tenses Smoothly*

Directions

Compare the two following selections:

A. *The first one shifts tenses frequently. The changes in the verbs are not signaled ahead of time, so the tense shifts detract from the smoothness of the paragraph. The verbs are underlined for you.*

1. *Read this paragraph aloud in a group.*
2. *Above each verb, write the tense.*
3. *Discuss the effect of the different verb tenses on you as a reader.*

I <u>have</u> a childhood friend. Her name <u>was</u> Katie. I <u>meet</u> her in sixth grade. There <u>have been</u> thirty students in that sixth grade class, but Katie <u>is</u> special. She <u>was</u> so much like me. We both <u>share</u> the same interests. For example, we <u>liked</u> the same music and <u>are watching</u> the same television programs. Besides that, we both <u>play</u> video games and <u>enjoyed</u> the same kinds of books. Katie and I <u>will be telling</u> each other all our secrets. We <u>had known</u> not to tell anyone else. Katie <u>makes</u> my sixth grade year special because she <u>was</u> my best friend.

B. *The second selection also shifts tenses frequently. Here, however, the writer signals frequently so the reader can anticipate that the tense of the verb will change. The different tenses, therefore, seem logical and the paragraph makes sense even though the reader is frequently moved from one time frame to another. The verbs have been underlined for you.*

1. *Read the passage aloud.*
2. *Above each verb, write the verb tense.*
3. *Then circle words you believe help signal the reader that the tense is about to shift.*
4. *Discuss the effect signals have on you as a reader.*

I <u>bought</u> a camera yesterday. Now, when we <u>take</u> our vacation next summer, I <u>will be taking</u> pictures of everything. On our last vacation, which <u>was</u> to Glacier National Park, I <u>took</u> no camera. I <u>was</u> so sorry. The first sight we <u>saw</u> as we <u>entered</u> the park <u>was</u> a giant grizzly standing just ten feet from the road. And there I <u>was</u> with no camera. I <u>have learned</u> my lesson: next time I <u>will take</u> a camera with me.

My best friend Rick always <u>takes</u> one along. He <u>has</u> more time off than I do. So he <u>goes</u> on hunting and fishing trips several times a year. Wherever he <u>is</u>, he <u>is snapping</u> pictures left and right. In fact last summer, Rick <u>invested</u> in a video camera. So now he <u>films</u> his adventures. When he <u>returns</u> from a trip we all gather at his house and <u>watch</u> his vacation on video. Someday, maybe I <u>will buy</u> a video camera, too. But for now I <u>am</u> happy with my 35 millimeter Kodak.

C. *Now that you have observed how writers signal tense shifts, rewrite the paragraph about Katie (Paragraph A) into one consistent tense; if you need to shift tenses, however, insert appropriate signals to make the tense shifts easier for your reader to follow.*

THE READING CONNECTION

Use your awareness of verb tenses to explore the tenses used in what you read every day. For example, look through the newspaper and read various NEWS ARTICLES. What tenses are used most often? Do the journalists shift tenses? If so, do they *signal* sufficiently?

Does your newspaper have a section with RECIPES, or do you have any magazines or books at home that contain recipes? Which tense is used most often in recipes?

How about ADVERTISEMENTS—are there any in your newspaper or magazines? Or has the mailman delivered an advertisement to your address recently in the form of "junk mail"? Can you spot any verbs in these ads? If so, in what tenses are they written?

From your reading, bring some examples of various tenses to class. Newspaper or magazine articles, recipes, and advertisements are a good place to start. You may also bring in books you may be reading, including textbooks. Discuss the use of different tenses and why you think the authors chose to use the tenses they did.

THE WRITING CONNECTION

The following are suggestions for writing topics. As you work with one or several of these topics to produce a finished piece of writing, pay special attention to your own use of tenses. Be especially careful about shifting tenses; remember to signal. After you have completed your writing, read what you have written aloud to yourself or a friend or a classmate. Listen for your use of verb tenses.

1.   Compared with the present, project in what ways your life will be different five years from now. Describe your lifestyle in detail. Pay careful attention to your use of present and future tenses.

2.   Narrate an incident that happened to you during a special time in your past. It may have occurred when you had a certain job (or when you were in the military) or when you were involved in a certain relationship. Or it may have occurred at any specific time in your development from childhood to adulthood. Pay careful attention to your use of past tenses.

3.   Think back on how your life was different before you decided to go to college. Describe your lifestyle then: how you spent your time, what you used to do,

how you felt about your future, and more. Think about your life now and describe your lifestyle, including how you spend your time and how you now feel about your future. As you write, pay special attention to your use of all tenses and be careful to signal.

4. Write a persuasive piece to convince your reader to give up a "bad" habit, such as smoking, overeating, frequent dieting, excessive drinking, etc. Project what the benefits will be if the reader takes your advice. Pay special attention to your use of present and future tenses.

5. Develop any one of your journal entries into a finished piece of writing.

SELF TEST FOR CHAPTER 5

1. The word "tense" means _____.

2. Three ways in which verbs change tenses are:

    (1) _____

    (2) _____

    (3) _____

3. The _____ tenses are the simplest way to express time in your writing.

4. Present participles *always* end in _____.

5. *Regular* past participles end in _____ and look just like the _____ tense forms.

6. *Irregular* past participles may vary in appearance and often do not look like the _____ tense forms.

7. The most common verb, _____, is also the most irregular verb in English.

8. What some people call "bad grammar" is often caused by confusing the _____ participles with the _____ tense forms of a few common irregular verbs like "see" and "go."

9. The formula for creating _____ tenses looks like this:
    being verb helper + verb + ING _____

10. The formula for creating _____ tenses looks like this:
    a form of "do" + verb with no ending _____

11. The formula for creating _____ tenses looks like this:
    a form of "have" + past participle _____

12. Writers can shift tenses smoothly in writing, if they first _____ using words like "yesterday" or "tomorrow."

FINAL JOURNAL WRITING

Write in your journal about what you have learned in this chapter that will help you in your writing. Comment on which concepts were difficult for you and about which ones you still have unanswered questions. Decide how to find the answers to your questions. Which part of this unit was the most helpful? Why? Which part was the least helpful? Why? Now that you know more about verb tenses, is there anything you will do differently the next time you write and revise?

CHAPTER 6

Nouns . . . The Pattern Makers of Sentence Design

. . the close affection which grows from common names . . . These are the ties which, though light as air, are as strong as links of iron.

—EDMUND BURKE

QUESTIONS TO ASK YOURSELF WHILE READING CHAPTER 6:

1. What roles do nouns play in the sentences I write?
2. Why should I pay attention to whether I am using singular or plural nouns?
3. How can my use of nouns make my sentences more interesting to read?
4. How can nouns help me create variety in the sentences I write?
5. What kind of nouns should I avoid using when I write on the job?

What is a noun? Write your answer below before reading anything else on this page.

_____

_____

Did you write, "A noun is a person, place, or thing"? Congratulations, you have remembered the most frequently recited definition of a word class. In Latin, *noun* means "name"; and that makes sense: for persons, places, and things have names.

PERSONS, PLACES, AND THINGS EXPLAINED

A *person* is easy enough to explain. "Boy," "girl," "Tom," "Nancy," "children" are all persons. List ten more noun persons:

1. _____

2. _____

3. _____

4. _____

5. _____

6. _____

7. _____

8. _____

9. _____

10. _____

A *place,* too, is easily explained. "Chicago," "city," "country," "Japan" are all places. List five more noun places:

1. _____

2. _____

3. _____

4. _____

5. _____

But what is a *thing*? Is it a "rock," "table," "chair," "pen"? Yes, these are things. You could easily name hundreds of noun things: just look around you and start naming every*thing* you see!

But does "thing" refer only to objects?

What about the feelings we give names to—feelings like "love," "joy," "frustration," and "anger"? Are feelings "things," too? What about ideas like "democracy," "freedom," and "values"? Are ideas "things"? They ARE things, but they are not *concrete.* Instead, ideas and feelings are *abstract.* Therefore, another way to look at nouns is to divide them into these two categories:

Concrete nouns: people, places, and things you can see or touch or experience with your senses.

Abstract nouns: ideas and feelings you can name.

DO IT YOURSELF!   *Decide Abstract or Concrete*

Directions
Read the following list of nouns (people, places, and things) and write "concrete" or "abstract" next to each word.

1. _____ pizza

2. _____ mountains

3. _____ virtue

4. _____ teacher

5. _____ president

6. _____ anxiety

7. _____ Harry Truman

8. _____ committee

9. _____ freedom

10. _____ flag

11. _____ house

12. _____ computer

13. _____ shyness

14. _____ love

15. _____ pumpkin

16. _____ excitement

17. _____ boredom

18. _____ tree

19. _____ singer

20. _____ peaches

Wait a minute. Wasn't *love* on that list of nouns? And isn't *love* a verb? In Chapter 4 *love* was defined as "a verb expressing emotional action." So how can *love* be a noun?

OW WORDS CHANGE CLASSES

If a word is in one word class (verb), it cannot also be in another word class (noun)—can it? Yes, it can. In fact, words change classes all the time. They change from one word class—or *part of speech*—to another depending on *where* you, the writer, choose to place them in sentences.

Remember "syntax"—the arrangement of words in sentences? *Where* you place words in relationship to one another is the key to what your sentences mean.

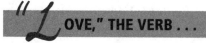 OVE," THE VERB . . .

See how *love* changes from one word class to another as its sentence position changes:

> I <u>love</u> you. (Love is in the *second* position.)
> I experience <u>love.</u> (Love is in the *third* position.)

1. In the first sentence, which word is the verb? _____

2. In the second sentence, which word is the verb? _____

3. Which position in a statement is associated with the verb? _____

In the first sentence, did you identify *love* as the action verb? But in the second sentence, did you identify *experience* (not *love*) as the action verb?

To test your answers, change both sentences into the past tense:

I lov<u>ed</u> you.
I experien<u>ced</u> love.

Which words change tense? Again the answers are first *love* and then *experience*. That settles it. Those words must be the verbs because only verbs can change tense.

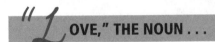"L**OVE," THE NOUN . . .**

Again look closely at *love* in the sentence, "I experience *love*." Here *love* is an abstract noun. To test this out, just place the word *THE* in front of *love*.

THE can be placed in front of nouns but not in front of verbs. Try it. Could you say "*the* boy" and "*the* girl"? Yes! Even "*the* Harry" makes sense in a sentence like, "*The* Harry in my math class is not the same person as *the* Harry in my English class." Try putting *the* in front of all the nouns you have listed so far. Does *THE* work in front of abstract nouns as well: the love, the joy, the hate, the anger? It does!

Apply the "THE test" to the two sentences we have been working with:

I <u>the</u> love you. (Oops!)
I experience <u>the</u> love. (Bingo, it works!)

THE fits only into the second sentence because, in that sentence, *love* is a noun, not a verb. Nouns can easily be preceded by *THE*.

<u>THE</u> Noun Marker, <u>A</u> Noun Marker, <u>AN</u> Other Noun Marker

In English, *THE* marks nouns, so do the words *A* and *AN*. For that reason, *THE, A,* and *AN* are called *noun markers* (some sources also call them *articles*). These three words mark nouns in sentences. For example, you can write "the love" or "a love"; you can write "the apple" or "an apple." (Notice, *A* is always used in front of words that begin with *consonant sounds*, while *AN* is used in front of words that begin with *vowel sounds*.)

COLLABORATE!   *Marking the Markers and the Nouns*

Directions
Work with a group or on your own.
A. *Circle all the noun markers (a, an, the).*

B. *Then draw an arrow from each marker to the noun it marks.*

C. *Finally, draw a rectangle around the noun. The first one is done for you as an example. Notice that sometimes the noun immediately follows its marker; but other times the noun is separated from its marker by one or more descriptive words.*

1.   Have you decided to buy ⓐ new mattress 〔set〕? You should invest in the very best. The materials, the quality, and the size of the set determine the price. A good mattress is an important investment. A sound night's sleep can have a dramatic effect on your performance during the daytime hours.

2.   Hank Aaron is an American baseball player born in the South. The Braves first signed him to a major league career. At that time, Aaron, a right-fielder, became the highest paid player in the history of the game. He signed a three-year contract for a reported total of $600,000. He retired after the 1976 season with a record of 755 home runs.

JOURNAL PROMPT

In your journal, write about your sleep habits. Reflect on your reaction to getting too little sleep, too much sleep, or just enough sleep. Do you use sleep as an escape? Are you a night person who is more awake and active at night? Or are you a morning person who has more energy in the morning? Write about the role of sleep in your life.

JOURNAL PROMPT

In your journal write about a sports hero, past or present, who has inspired you. The person may be a local sports star whom you know personally, or he or she may be someone famous whom you only know from television and the newspapers. Why does this particular athlete inspire you? How do you personally relate to this individual? Even though you may not be an athlete yourself, what can you learn from your hero that you can apply to your own life?

COLLABORATE!   *Differentiating Nouns from Verbs*

Directions

A. *In the following selection, the underlined words sometimes act as nouns and sometimes as verbs. Working in a group, or on your own, using what you have learned about word classes so far, decide when the words are acting as <u>nouns</u> and when they are acting as <u>verbs</u>. Discuss the reasons for your answers.*

I <u>dream</u> (_____) about having my own apartment. I know the <u>dream</u> (_____) of having my own place will come true someday. At least, I <u>hope</u> (_____) so. To me, an apartment <u>means</u> (_____) independence. I would no longer need <u>support</u> (_____) from my parents. However, while I <u>work</u> (_____) for minimum wage, I cannot afford to move out. <u>Work</u> (_____) at that low pay will not <u>support</u> (_____)

both an apartment and me. Someday, though, I will have the <u>means</u> (_____) to become independent. I will not give up <u>hope</u> (_____) of eventually being on my own.

B. *Together with a group of students (or on your own), write a paragraph using the following words as NOUNS.*

the attack

     the rain

     the ride

     the sweat

     the fight

     the struggle

Discuss with your classmates how the words *attack, rain, ride, sweat, fight,* and *struggle* could also be action verbs.

JOURNAL PROMPT

In your journal, write your thoughts about being on your own and living alone. Explore what it would be like not to be living in the environment in which you are presently living. If you are already living on your own, explore the challenges created by your independent lifestyle.

NOUNS WITH MANY HATS

Nouns do much more than just name persons, places, and things. Nouns work hard in sentences. In fact, they are workaholics! A noun never enters a sentence to just idly "hang out"; you'll never come across a noun that is just "nouning around." The instant you place a noun into any part of a sentence, your noun becomes a highly specialized worker. The extremely versatile noun is capable of performing at least six different jobs or functions in sentences.

How can one noun play so many different roles? The best way to understand this is to look at yourself. After all, you are a noun. You, too, are capable of performing many different functions. I'll illustrate what I mean by using myself as an example (since I'm a noun, too).

My day begins at school where I stand before groups of students and share what I know about writing. In this setting, I function as a *teacher*.

As soon as I arrive home in the afternoon, I am greeted by my son with "What's for dinner, Mom?" My function has changed to *mother* (i.e., cook and feeder of children). I still look the same as I did in the classroom earlier, yet my function has changed.

After dinner (i.e., hot dogs or macaroni and cheese), I drive to my mother's house. When I arrive there, I immediately transform again, this time into a *daughter*—another different function for the same me.

On my return trip home, I stop at my favorite department store which is having its semi-annual storewide clearance sale. My function changes again, and I become a frenzied *crazywoman* waving a plastic card at every salesperson who makes eye contact with me.

In one day, I have functioned as a teacher, mother, daughter, and crazywoman. The key to my different functions is my setting—my location and my relationship to the other nouns near me. And so it is with all nouns in sentences: as their settings change, their functions change. With nouns (as with real estate), **location** is everything!

JOURNAL PROMPT

As you read about my different functions, perhaps you thought about all the different functions you yourself perform. Before you continue reading about noun functions, write about your own functions. What different jobs do you perform during the course of one day? How does your location determine your function? How does your relationship to others in the setting determine your function? Do you always perform some function that you can label, even when you are alone? Do other people you know perform the same functions you do when they are in analogous, or similar, settings?

JOB SHADOWING WITH THE NOUN

Now, let's follow a noun around and see how its different functions are associated with its different locations in a sentence.

Function #1—The Noun Subject

The first and most common function of a noun is the job of *subject*. Just what does a subject do in a sentence? Typically, the subject is the "doer" of the verb. The following sentence contains two nouns:

> <u>Martha</u> *throws the* <u>ball</u>.

Of *Martha* and the *ball*, which one is the subject? Ask yourself, which one is doing the verb? Which one does the throwing? Martha, of course, is the subject because she is the noun who throws the ball. Martha is the doer of the verb; in this sentence, she does the action.

You may have learned before to think of subjects as *what the sentence is about*. But it seems to me that this sentence, like most sentences, is about several things. It is about *Martha*; it is about *throws*; and it is about the *ball*. Not all of those are subjects. Only the noun in front of the verb is the subject here.

DO IT YOURSELF!   *Search for Subjects*

Directions

A. *The following paragraph contains many nouns. Circle only those nouns that are <u>subjects</u>. Remember, in statements, subjects typically occur BEFORE verbs.*

Cats are cautious creatures. Our cat certainly is. Felix always runs and hides when we have company. The laundry basket is her usual hideout. Strangers will never look for her there. Dogs scare her, too. Sparky, from next door, always manages to drive Felix under the house. Neighboring cats, however, are not quite as threatening. Felix stands her ground with most of them. Felix has lived to be an old cat. My children believe that is because of her cautious personality. (Yes, Felix is a strange name for a female cat. That story will appear in a later chapter.)

B. *Write your own sentences using the following nouns as subjects. Remember, the subject is the doer of the action and generally comes before the verb. The first one is done for you as an example.*

1. soup *The soup was cold.* _____

2. Lois _____

3. veterinarian _____

4. illness _____

5. county _____

JOURNAL PROMPT

In your journal, write about a pet you have or once had. Pick one of its personality traits and discuss it in detail. Has the pet's personality changed as it has grown older? How is its behavior affected by different surroundings and the presence of different people? In what way does the animal act differently toward you than toward others? If you do not have a pet, write about a pet of someone you know. Or, write about a pet you would like to have and why.

THE NUMBERS GAME: SUBJECT-VERB AGREEMENT

Another characteristic of nouns is that they have *number*. What does that mean? Do nouns walk around wearing little uniforms with numbers on their backs? Perhaps they would if words wore clothes, had feet, and could walk around. *Number* simply means something can be counted. Can you count nouns? Can you throw *two* rocks instead of just *one* rock? Can you kill *three* flies that way instead of *one* fly? Can you follow that act up by drinking *four* glasses of water instead of *one* glass before you set *five* traps instead of *one* trap to catch *five* mice instead of *one* mouse? Whether or not you can do all that successfully, you can do one thing: **you can count nouns**. You can even count abstract nouns, if you insist: *six* loves, *seven* freedoms, or *eight* joys . . . what is your pleasure or what are your pleasures?

What happens to nouns when their number changes from one (*singular*) to more than one (*plural*)?

Singular	Plural
rock	rocks
fly	flies
glass	glasses
trap	traps
mouse	mice
love	loves
freedom	freedoms
joy	joys
pleasure	pleasures

As you can see, most nouns add "s" to create plurals. Yet, some nouns, like *glass* which already ends in "s", add "es" instead. Nouns ending in "y," like *fly*, create plurals by replacing the "y" with an "i" before adding "es." Still others are even more irregular. They don't add "s" or "es." Instead they change their spelling. *Mouse*, for example, changes to *mice*. Can you think of other words in English with irregular plurals?

Number can be more than just a spelling problem, however. It can be an **agreement** problem. Nouns functioning as subjects have to agree with their verbs in number. For example, if the subject of a sentence is singular, the verb that follows it has to be in a singular form also. This means if the noun subject changes to plural, its verb may change, too, to agree in number.

DO IT YOURSELF!   *Make Subjects and Verbs Agree*

Can you find the agreement problems in the following sentences?

Directions

Rewrite each sentence in the space provided. Change <u>verb</u> forms to agree with subjects. Reading aloud may help you detect the errors.

1. The dancers moves across the stage. _____
2. The dancer move across the stage. _____
3. The lady play the piano beautifully. _____
4. The ladies plays the piano beautifully. _____
5. The boys has talent. _____
6. The boy have talent. _____
7. The young woman are the director. _____
8. The young women is the directors. _____

- What kinds of changes occurred in the verbs when the subjects were singular?
  _____

- What kinds of changes occurred when the subjects were plural?
  _____

B. *Here's a quick quiz on agreement: answer TRUE OR FALSE:*

_____ 1. Plural forms of regular <u>verbs</u> in the present tense drop the "s."

_____ 2. Plural forms of regular <u>nouns</u> add an "s."

_____ 3. Singular forms of present tense regular <u>verbs</u> add an "s."

_____ 4. Singular <u>nouns</u> do not use the "s" endings.

_____ 5. Some of the most common irregular verbs such as <u>be</u> and <u>have</u> change from singular to plural in irregular ways.

Did you mark "TRUE" in front of all the above statements? Congratulations, your answers are correct.

DO IT YOURSELF!   *Put Only "Agree"able Verbs in the Paragraph*

Directions

Fill in the blanks in the following paragraph by picking the correct form of each verb provided. Be sure the verb agrees in number (SINGULAR or PLURAL) with the noun subject of the sentence in which you place it.

1.	attend or attends	**10.**	follow or follows
2.	involve or involves	**11.**	have or has
3.	are or is	**12.**	are or is
4.	run or runs	**13.**	wear or wears
5.	are or is	**14.**	enable or enables
6.	fill or fills	**15.**	are or is
7.	build or builds	**16.**	are or is
8.	comprise or comprises	**17.**	determine or determines
9.	are or is	**18.**	contribute or contributes

Many people _____1_____ plays. But I once saw a play in its production. Production _____2_____ much teamwork. The director _____3_____ the one in charge. This person _____4_____ all the rehearsals. An assistant director _____5_____ also a part of the team. The assistant director _____6_____ in for the director whenever necessary. Other people _____7_____ the set and make scene changes. These people _____8_____ the stage crew. Their "boss" _____9_____ the stage manager. Members of the stage crew always _____10_____ the stage manager's orders. The stage manager _____11_____ many responsibilities. One responsibility _____12_____ attending every practice and every performance of the play. Crew members and the stage manager _____13_____ headphones. Head-phones and microphones _____14_____ them to communicate with one another during performances. This _____15_____ necessary. After all, timing _____16_____ extremely important for a smooth performance. Good actors only partly _____17_____ a play's success. The production crew _____18_____ greatly to every performance.

JOURNAL PROMPT

In your journal, write about a play you have attended. Or, write about a play in which you have participated in some way; explain your role. If you are not a play-goer, write about a movie you have seen. Consider what might be going on behind the scenes to create some of the movie's special effects.

Function #2—The Noun Direct Object

Instead of writing "Martha throws the ball," what happens when the noun *Martha* moves to a different location in a sentence? Just as you and I assume new tasks when we change location, so does the noun *Martha*.

Let's move Martha to the back of a sentence and see how her function changes.

Fred greets Martha.

In this sentence, Fred is the subject because he does the greeting. What is Martha's function? She gets greeted; the greeting is done *to* her. In other words, she receives the action of the verb. Her new job is called *direct object*; in a sentence, the direct object is a noun that *receives the action* rather than *does* the action.

DO IT YOURSELF!   *Follow the Action to the Direct Object*

Directions

A. *In the following paragraph, the underlined nouns are either subjects or direct objects. Above each underlined word, write either S (for subject) or DO (for direct object). Remember, the subject does the action and normally occurs <u>before</u> the verb in the sentence; the direct object receives the action of the verb and is located <u>behind</u> the verb.*

Computers have changed the world. Today people use computers at school, on the job, and even at home. Some homemakers now keep their recipes in files in their personal computers. Families maintain records of their monthly bills on home computers. Children's medical records take up space on many households' hard disks. My brother's computer answers the telephone and takes messages. Soon no American home will be able to function smoothly without the help of the electronic servant.

- Did you discover that some noun subjects and direct objects are preceded by one or several descriptive words?
- Did you discover that some sentences containing the word "and" can have more than one noun subject or more than one noun direct object?

B. *All sentences with direct objects contain action verbs, NOT being verbs. The direct object, by definition, must "receive action"; therefore, a direct object must be in a sentence with an action verb. That means you will <u>never</u> find direct objects after being verbs.*

Write five of your own sentences with both subjects and direct objects. Use the action verb suggested for each sentence. To come up with direct objects, ask yourself <u>what</u> or <u>whom:</u> Jack throws <u>what</u>? Jack throws the <u>ball</u>. (direct object)

1. (throws) _____

2. (watched) _____

3. (followed) _____

4. (reads) _____

5. (likes) _____

JOURNAL PROMPT

In your journal write about how computers affect your life. Thanks to computers, how different is your life now compared with five years ago? What do you feel you have lost as computers have made inroads into your life? What do you feel you have gained? How do you imagine computers will affect your future life?

Function # 3—The Noun Indirect Object

In order to accommodate an indirect object, a sentence must have <u>three</u> nouns instead of two:

<u>Clancy</u> throws <u>Martha</u> the <u>ball</u>.

In the above sentence, how many nouns come before the verb? How many come after the verb? *Clancy*, the noun before the verb, is clearly the subject; he is the noun doing the action. Which of the nouns behind the verb is the direct object—*Martha* or *ball*? The answer is *ball* because the ball is receiving the action and getting thrown. Clancy is not throwing Martha, is he??

But what is Martha if she is not a subject and not a direct object? Notice, she has a slightly different position in this sentence than she has had in previous sentences. She is wedged between the action verb *(throws)* and the direct object *(ball)*. In this new setting, Martha assumes a new role. She's not doing the passing; that is *Clancy's* job. She's not receiving the action; that is the *ball's* job. What does *Martha* do in her new location? Read the sentence again:

Clancy throws <u>Martha</u> the ball.

What Martha does is receive the ball! In other words, Martha receives the direct object. Martha's new job is called the *indirect object;* the indirect object's function is to *receive direct objects.* Indirect objects are always located **between** the action verb and the direct object.

Notice, just like direct objects, indirect objects, too, can only occur in sentences with action verbs, not being verbs. Here's the logic:

If action verbs are needed for direct objects
AND direct objects are needed for indirect objects,
THEN action verbs must be needed for indirect objects.

In other words, it takes an ACTION VERB to create a sentence that contains both a direct object and an indirect object.

COLLABORATE!   *Writing Sentences with Subjects and Objects*

Directions

Work with a group or on your own.

A. The word order of sentences with indirect objects looks like this:

subject + action verb + indirect object + direct object

Study the arrows carefully. They show the relationships of the nouns and the verb in the sentence.

- *Following this sentence "pattern," use each set of suggested words to write a sentence with an indirect object.*
- *After writing each sentence, label the action verb (AV) and all the different nouns and their functions: subject (S), direct object (DO), indirect object (IO).*
- *Draw arrows to show the relationships of words to each other.*
- *Study the following example before you begin:*

Example: paintings/artist/students/showed
Your answer could be:

      S   AV   IO   DO
The artist showed the students the paintings.

Or you could have written:

      S   AV   IO   DO
The students showed the artist the paintings.

Note: To find the indirect object, ask *to whom?* The artist showed *what* (direct object) *to whom?* (indirect object).

1. package/sent/Mrs. Jones/store

_____

2.   sold/dealer/car/man

_____

3.   Jan/Sara/present/gave

_____

4.   read/class/story/teacher

_____

5.   gave/kiss/mother/baby

_____

B. *In the following paragraphs*
- *Identify the action verbs (write "AV" above them);*
- *Above each underlined noun, write subject (S), or direct object (DO), or indirect object (IO).*

Do you want a <u>mate</u>? <u>Scientists</u> have studied human mating <u>behaviors</u> for many years. Some <u>behaviors</u> are predictable. <u>People</u> choose <u>mates</u> who resemble themselves. <u>Intellectuals</u> choose other <u>intellectuals.</u> Athletic <u>women</u> like athletic <u>men</u>.

In general, <u>men</u> value physical <u>attractiveness</u> and <u>youth</u>. A pretty <u>woman</u> gives a <u>man</u> romantic <u>ideas</u>. To an older man, a younger <u>woman</u> creates an exciting <u>challenge</u>.

<u>Women</u>, on the other hand, value <u>ambition</u>, <u>status</u>, and <u>wealth</u>. They pursue rich <u>males</u>. A <u>woman</u> may earn a good <u>income</u>, herself. She still wants a good <u>provider</u>.

Both <u>males</u> and <u>females</u> desire <u>companionship</u>, however. Sometimes they will compromise other <u>requirements</u> in return for a loyal companion. Sooner or later, most <u>males</u> and <u>females</u> give <u>marriage</u> a <u>try</u>.

JOURNAL PROMPT

Write about your ideal mate. Do you fit into the male and female categories described in the above paragraph? Or are you looking for something entirely different in a partner? How high is "the ability to communicate" on your list of a mate's desirable qualities? What physical requirements do you have in mind? Is a person's family background or religious affiliation important to you? How important is educational level? How closely do your ideals match the person to whom you are presently married or the person to whom you might end up being married some day? How will you feel if you don't end up with your ideal?

Function #4—The Noun Subject Complement

Action verbs precede direct objects and indirect objects in sentences, but what happens when *being verbs* precede nouns?

The catcher <u>is</u> Martha.

This simple sentence contains a being verb, <u>IS</u>. What is its subject? <u>Catcher</u> is the subject; it comes *before* the verb.

What is *Martha* in this sentence? Be careful not to call her a direct object. Remember, direct objects receive action; and this sentence has no action; so this sentence cannot contain a direct object.

What, then, is Martha doing in this sentence? *Martha* is telling *who* the *catcher* is. In other words, Martha provides a more complete picture of the subject. Martha is therefore called a *subject complement:* subject complements complete the subject—that is, they give more information about the subject. Subject complements occur only in sentences with BEING verbs.

Sentences with noun subject complements are reversible. "The catcher is Martha" and "Martha is the catcher" both say the same thing. The only difference is that, in the first version, Martha is the subject complement and in the second version, Martha is the subject. In English sentences, **location is everything.**

DO IT YOURSELF!   *Use Nouns to Complement Subjects*

Directions

A. *Using any combination of nouns and verbs from the following lists, write five sentences containing subject complement nouns. You will need two nouns and one verb for each sentence.*

B. *Label each subject (S), being verb (BV), and subject complement (SC).*

C. *An example is done for you.*

Nouns	Verbs
meal	is
lunch	was
sweater	will be
cardigan	has been
scene	were
beach	
place	
city	
driver	
James	
citizens	
Americans	

　　　　　　　　　S　　BV　SC
Example: *The meal will be lunch.*

1. _____

2. _____

3. _____

4. _____

5. _____

COLLABORATE! *Figuring Out Four Noun Functions*

Directions

In the following sentences, the VERBS are underlined and labeled for you. The NOUNS are underlined, but NOT labeled. Your job is to label each noun as a subject (S), direct object (DO), indirect object (IO), or subject complement (SC).

Remember, while all sentences contain subjects, direct objects and indirect objects occur only in sentences with ACTION verbs; and subject complements occur only in sentences with BEING verbs.

The first one is done for you as an example.

1. The <u>students</u> *S* <u>will attend</u> (ACTION) the <u>program</u> *DO* .

2. The <u>boys</u> _____ <u>have done</u> (ACTION) good <u>work</u> _____.

3. The <u>presentation</u> _____ <u>contained</u> (ACTION) very few <u>errors</u> _____.

4. <u>Fred</u> _____ <u>was showing</u> (ACTION) the <u>participants</u> _____ their <u>seats</u> _____.

5. <u>Fred</u> _____ <u>is</u> (BEING) a <u>senior</u> _____.

6. <u>Seniors</u> _____ always <u>run</u> (ACTION) this <u>show</u> _____.

7. <u>Are</u> the <u>juniors</u> _____ <u>doing</u> (ACTION) an important <u>job</u> _____?

8. The <u>juniors</u> _____ <u>are</u> (BEING).

9. Their <u>class</u> _____ <u>is selling</u> (ACTION) <u>tickets</u> _____.

10. The class <u>treasurer</u> _____ <u>sold</u> (ACTION) his <u>family</u> _____ five <u>tickets</u> _____.

11. <u>Mary</u> _____ <u>is</u> (BEING) his <u>girlfriend</u> _____.

12. <u>Mary</u> _____ <u>gave</u> (ACTION) her <u>mother</u> _____ a <u>ticket</u> _____.

13. The <u>performance</u> _____ <u>was</u> (BEING) a <u>success</u> _____.

14. Every <u>night</u> _____ <u>was</u> (BEING) a <u>sellout</u> _____.

15. The <u>seniors</u> _____ <u>gave</u> (ACTION) the <u>juniors</u> _____ the <u>credit</u> _____.

Function #5—The Noun Object Complement

The fifth function of a noun in a sentence is to be an *object complement*. Object complements are located after direct objects. That brings us back to sentences with action verbs again. Remember, ACTION verbs are needed to create a setting for direct objects. The following sentence contains three nouns: a subject, a direct object, and an object complement:

The <u>umpire</u> called the <u>catcher</u> <u>Martha</u>.

The action verb is *called*. You have probably already identified the subject as the *umpire*. The direct object is *catcher* because the catcher is getting called (receiving the action of the verb). But what is *Martha* in this sentence?

Even though this sentence has two nouns following the action verb, this is not a sentence with a direct object and an indirect object; after all, the catcher does not receive Martha. Instead the catcher and Martha are the same person. Martha completes the picture of who the catcher is. Martha is the *object complement:* object complements provide a more complete picture of the direct object.

The difference between an object complement and an indirect object:

A noun *object complement* and the direct object are the same person:

The umpire called the catcher <u>Martha</u>.

(object complement "Martha" = the direct object "catcher")

An *indirect object* and the direct object are NOT the same person. Instead, the indirect object RECEIVES the direct object:

The umpire handed <u>Martha</u> the ball.

(the indirect object "Martha" receives the direct object "ball")

The difference between an object complement and a subject complement:

A noun *object complement* completes or renames the DIRECT OBJECT.

The umpire called the catcher <u>Martha</u>.

(the object complement "Martha" = the direct object "catcher"; the sentence contains an ACTION verb)

A *subject complement* completes or renames the SUBJECT.

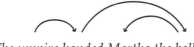

The catcher is <u>Martha</u>.

(the subject complement "Martha" = the subject "catcher"; the sentence contains a BEING verb.)

In both sentences with complements, *catcher* and *Martha* refer to the same person: catcher = Martha.

COLLABORATE! *Differentiating between Complements and Indirect Objects*

Directions

Read the following sentences.

A. Label the underlined nouns as indirect objects (IO), object complements (OC), or subject complements (SC).

B. Draw arrows and equal signs to show relationships of words.

C. Discuss your decisions.

If you need to review indirect objects, subject complements, and object complements, go back and review the marked sentences in the section you just finished reading.

1.   Jason loaned <u>Jennifer</u> his car.

2.   Jason considered Jennifer a <u>friend</u>.

3.   Jennifer is a <u>friend</u>.

4.   Jennifer baked <u>Jason</u> a cake.

5.   Jason is a <u>charmer</u>.

6.   Jason gave <u>Jennifer</u> a kiss.

7.   The cake made Jason and Jennifer even better <u>friends</u>.

Function #6—The Noun Object of a Preposition

The sixth and final function of a noun is to be the *object of a preposition*. Martha is the object of a preposition in the following sentence:

> *Clancy passes the ball <u>to Martha</u>.*

In this sentence *Martha* seems to be doing much the same job as an indirect object because she receives the direct object, *ball*. But since Martha follows the word "to," she becomes the object of a preposition rather than a direct object. This noun function is explained in more detail in a later chapter on prepositions. I mention it now just so you know that nouns can perform six different functions rather than just the five functions this chapter discusses in detail.

O WHAT?!

So what is the value of learning about subjects and objects and complements? Isn't this just more "stuff" to clutter your brain? How can knowing functions of nouns help you write better?

Compare the following two selections:

1. Susan loves John. Susan kisses John. John says some words. John says, "Sweetheart." John loves Susan, too.

2. Susan loves John. Susan gives John a kiss. John responds. John calls Susan "Sweetheart." John and Susan are a happy couple.

I realize neither selection will receive the Pulitzer Prize for great literature. But if you had to choose between these two sorry examples, which one would you send in to the judges?

Did you select the second one? I did. Re-read the sentences in both selections. This time label all the nouns and their functions.

How do the sentences in the second selection differ from the sentences in the first selection?

_____

_____

Do you see that the second selection contains a *variety* of different sentence arrangements or patterns? In the first selection, however, the pattern of every sentence is the *same:* **subject** + **action verb** + **direct object**.

 ## "SHAPES" IN WRITING

The point is that sentences have **shape**. *Sentence patterns* literally create shapes on a written page. Writers create designs on a piece of paper just as artists create designs on canvas. However, using the same shape over and over is as limiting for a writer as it is for an artist.

In the same way that art enthusiasts respond with certain feelings to shapes in drawings and paintings, readers also respond with certain feelings to shapes in writing: shapes of words and shapes of sentence patterns.

If, as a writer, you constantly repeat one shape, that recurring shape may distract your reader and keep him or her from appreciating that your ideas have variety.

If your sentence shapes are always predictable, your writing will seem uninteresting and lifeless. But if, instead, you use a variety of sentence shapes, your writing will stimulate your reader and arouse interest. As your writing becomes less predictable, your reader will begin to anticipate and delight in the sentence surprises that lie ahead.

> *Variety's the very spice of life,*
> *That gives it all its flavor.*
>
> —*William Cowper*

Sentence variety can spice up your writing and profoundly affect how a reader reacts to your content.

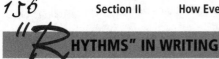

"RHYTHMS" IN WRITING

Shape in writing is not only visual, it is auditory as well. Readers not only see the shapes of your written sentences, they hear them. If you don't think readers hear your written words, consider this: when was the last time you looked at a sentence you had written and said, "That doesn't sound right"? Much in the same way that musicians "hear" sounds and feel rhythms just by looking at a series of black and white notes on a sheet of music, readers hear sounds and feel rhythms just by seeing a series of black and white letters on a page of writing.

So how can you, as a writer, create different sounds and rhythms that will captivate and dazzle your readers? You can do so partly by choosing your words carefully and partly by varying the shapes of your sentence patterns when you write.

THE PATTERNS IN SIMPLE SENTENCES

Achieving variety in your writing begins with mastering sentence shapes. And mastering sentence shapes begins with mastering simple sentence *patterns*. Simple sentences in English come in only *five* distinct patterns. These different sentence patterns are determined by different arrangements of *verbs* (action or being) and *nouns* (subjects, objects, and complements).

The Five Simple Sentence Patterns

Pattern #1:

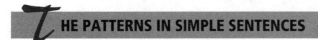

subject + verb (either action or being verb)

Example: John jogs.
Write two sentences of your own that follow this pattern:

1._____

2._____

Pattern #2:

subject + action verb + direct object

Example: John jogs a mile.
Using the verbs provided, write two sentences that follow this pattern.

1. (watches) _____

2. (understands) _____

Pattern #3:

subject + action verb + indirect object + direct object

Example: John gives Fred the baton.
Using the verbs provided, write two sentences that follow this pattern.

    1. (told) _____

    2. (sold) _____

Pattern #4:

subject + being verb + subject complement

Example: John is a runner.
Write two sentences that follow this pattern. Remember to use a noun on each side of the being verb.

    1. (was) _____

    2. (is) _____

Pattern #5:

subject + action verb + direct object + object complement

Example: The judges named John the winner.
Write two sentences that follow this pattern.

    1. (called) _____

    2. (elected) _____

Read the examples of the above patterns aloud and feel the rhythm each creates in your body and mind. To feel the rhythms more distinctly, clap your hands as you read each word. NOUNS clearly are the words that decide the shapes of sentences.

USING DIFFERENT PATTERNS IN THE SAME BLOCK

I always marvel when I think that every sentence I write can be reduced to one of only five sentence patterns. That is hard to imagine when, outwardly, all my sentences look so different.

    But sentence patterns are like house plans. Have you ever looked at houses in a brand new housing development? In the area where I live, developers sometimes build entire communities with streets full of new houses. Visiting these communities always makes me think of sentence patterns. (Remember, I teach English.) When I walk along one block in a housing development, I am impressed with the *variety* of different houses. Each house seems unique. The first house I see has brick on the front; the next one has wooden siding; the next is a two-story house; after that comes a one-story house; then there's one with a tile roof, and another one with wooden shakes—so much variety!!

But when I go inside the houses and walk from room to room, I soon realize that the first house on the block is made from the same floor plan as the third house on the block. The second house is built from the same blueprint as the house across the street. In fact, the builder clearly has used only five different floor plans in the entire development! He has just trimmed each house uniquely. The effect, however, is stimulating and interesting. A community built using only five floor plans can be an interesting place to visit—if it is well planned.

Your paragraphs, too, can become interesting blocks for readers to visit even though you only have five different sentence patterns to write with. After all, you, as a writer, can dress up each sentence with different details and descriptive words, making even the sentences that are the same pattern seem different. But just as a builder does not put too many houses with the same floor plan on the same block, you, too, will want to use a variety of patterns in each paragraph block you create.

COLLABORATE! *Creating a Variety of Sentences*

Directions

The following selection is somewhat awkward to read. Part of its problem is that each sentence is the same pattern: subject + action verb + direct object.

A. *Working with a group (or on your own), read the selection carefully.*

B. *Rewrite the selection using a greater variety of words and more interesting rhythms. The meaning of your new paragraph may end up being different from the original. Be as creative as you like.*

Chester has a low-paying job. He spends much time alone. At work, Chester sees Margaret daily. Margaret has a high-paying job. Other men in the office invite Margaret to parties. But Margaret never accepts their invitations.

Margaret adores Chester secretly. Chester loves Margaret. But Chester hides his feelings, too. Both people fear rejection.

Ernest employs Chester and Margaret. Ernest wears glasses. Chester and Margaret also wear glasses. One day after lunch, Ernest accidentally picked up Chester's glasses. Chester unknowingly grabbed Margaret's glasses. And Margaret took Ernest's glasses. The mixed-up glasses severely impaired their vision that afternoon. Chester entered the "Ladies" restroom by accident, shortly after Margaret. He addressed the mirror (thinking he was alone). "Margaret will never notice your homely face." Margaret touched his shoulder saying, "Not with these glasses on." Margaret kissed Chester. Chester kissed Margaret.

Meanwhile, blind Ernest accidentally added an extra zero to their pay checks that month. Chester married Margaret. He also received a promotion. Now both Chester and Margaret have high-paying jobs.

WRITE RIGHT FOR THE JOB: Beware of Nominalizations

Understanding the difference between nouns and verbs can help you when writing on the job. In a previous chapter, I mentioned that most employers discourage excess *verbiage* (using more words than necessary).

However, many workers, thinking excess words make documents more official and important sounding, deliberately write long sentences and intentionally select big words. Thus, business documents become swollen with unnecessary <u>verbiage</u> (could this word be a blend of "verbs" and "garbage"?). Wordy documents end up being skimmed over rather than read thoroughly. If you want someone to read every word you write, the trick is to eliminate unnecessary words.

In his book *The Elements of Style*, William Strunk writes, "Vigorous writing is concise." Anthony Robbins, author of *Unlimited Power*, expands on this idea:

> *Vigorous writing is concise. A sentence should contain no unnecessary words, a paragraph no unnecessary sentences, for the same reason that a drawing should have no unnecessary lines and a machine no unnecessary parts. This requires not that the writer make all his sentences short, or that he avoid all detail and treat his subjects only in outline, but that every word tell.*

One cause of bulky writing is a group of nouns called *nominalizations*. Nominalizations come from verbs. They are created by adding any of the following endings to verbs:

-al	-ment	-ant
-ence	-ion	-ent
-ancy	-ance	-ity

When writers use nominalizations.

> *Please consider my proposal.*

becomes

> *Please take my proposal into consideration.*

Other typical business phrases containing nominalizations include:

Nominalization	Verb
take into consideration	*instead of* consider
make a recommendation	*instead of* recommend

put on a demonstration	*instead of* demonstrate
come to a conclusion	*instead of* conclude
make a reference	*instead of* refer
effect an agreement	*instead of* agree
make a proposal	*instead of* propose
make a decision	*instead of* decide
make a contribution	*instead of* contribute
give a referral	*instead of* refer

As you can see, the bulk created by nominalizations is not just a matter of word endings. In order to fit nominalizations into sentences, the writer needs to add several extra words including a verb to replace the one that was made into a noun nominalization. The new verb usually has nothing to do with the meaning of the original one. For example,

- What does the verb *make* really mean in "make a decision" and "make a contribution" and "make a recommendation." Isn't the meaning of those phrases really just "decide," "contribute," and "recommend"?
- What does *come* have to do with concluding something?
- What does *put* have to do with demonstrating something?

The point is that nominalizations and the extra baggage that goes with them rob strong, capable action verbs of their identity. The real verb becomes lost in meaningless, excess verbiage.

COLLABORATE!   *Taking Out the Garbage (I Mean Verbiage)*

Directions

A. *Underline all the NOMINALIZATIONS in this business document excerpt. Refer back to the list of nominalization endings to help you.*

Section One has pertinence to any law that makes provision for legal fees. Although we are in agreement with you, if your intention is to avoid the charges, we will stand in opposition to you. If there is a continuation of this practice, our office will effect an immediate termination of services. Since cooperation with you is our desire, we hope you are willing to undertake serious reconsideration of this matter. Your refusal to do so, and your failure to take into consideration our warnings, will cause us to ask the court to commence the impoundment of your funds.

B. *In the space provided on the following page, re-write the above paragraph by changing the nominalizations to their original verb forms. For example, in the first sentence, change "has pertinence" to "pertains."*

_____

_____

_____

_____

_____

_____

_____

_____

_____

_____

_____

- Does this kind of revision make the message more direct and easier to understand?
- What is the difference between "give" and "take" in the expressions "give consideration to" and "take into consideration"? If these opposite words do not create opposite meanings in these phrases, does that suggest the verbs "give" and "take" are meaningless in this document?

MORE NOUNS THAT LOOK LIKE VERBS

Another especially energetic group of nouns are verb look-alikes that end in "ing." Words like *fishing*, *driving*, and *exercising* certainly look like verbs; they communicate actions. But as verbs these "ing" words always occur in phrases together with being-verb helpers (*is* fishing, *was* driving, *are* exercising). In a piece of writing, these verbs look like this:

At home tonight, Marcie <u>is hunting</u> for her old tennis shoes. She <u>is fishing</u> them out of the laundry basket. She has worn high heels all day at work. Her feet <u>are killing</u> her.

However, when "ing" words are used in sentences without helping verbs, they can act as NOUNS. They name activities which are a part of the broad noun category of "things":

The <u>fishing</u> was good this weekend.
<u>Driving</u> was difficult on the icy roads.
Juan enjoys <u>exercising</u>.

When these verb forms act as nouns, they have a special name: they are called *gerunds*. In Chapter 11, you will learn more about using gerunds in phrases. For now, just be aware that gerunds are nouns with a little extra verb-like energy. Here's an example of gerunds at work in a paragraph:

> *My favorite sport is <u>hunting</u>. However, <u>hunting</u> is not for everyone. My wife prefers <u>fishing</u>. She will not give <u>hunting</u> a try. She considers <u>hunting killing</u>. I believe controlled hunts actually help improve the quality of life for herds of game animals.*

Did you notice the functions or jobs these gerunds are doing in each sentence?

My favorite sport is *hunting.*—subject complement
However, *hunting* is not for everyone.—subject
My wife prefers *fishing.*—direct object
She will not give *hunting* a try.—indirect object
She considers *hunting killing.*—direct object (hunting); and object complement (killing)

Anything a noun can do, a GERUND can do!

THE READING CONNECTION

The following excerpt is from Stephen Vincent Benet's *American Names*:

> *I have fallen in love with American names,*
> *The sharp names that never get fat,*
> *The snakeskin-titles of mining-claims,*
> *The plumed war-bonnet of Medicine Hat,*
> *Tucson and Deadwood and Lost Mule Flat.*

Have you ever traveled somewhere and been intrigued by unusual place names? Names are a special group of nouns that begin with capital letters. These capitalized nouns are called *proper nouns*, while nouns that are not capitalized are called *common nouns*.

1. Find your own intriguing place names and product names.

    a. Read a detailed map of your local area. List any names that you find interesting, such as street names or names of rivers and lakes, etc.

    b. Read a larger map of an area in the United States and list thought-provoking names of cities or mountain ranges or deserts, etc.

    c. If you know another language and have access to a foreign map, translate some of the interesting names you find on your map.

    ALSO

    d. Explore names of local businesses. Skim through the yellow pages of your telephone book or the advertisement pages of your local newspaper. Look for names of businesses such as hair salons, exterminator services, car washes, and others whose names you find particularly clever.

e. Walk through your favorite supermarket and read product names on labels. Write down the ones you find especially memorable.

f. Choose a particular section of the store, such as the cat food section, the laundry detergent section, or the cereal section. Write a list of the different brand names given to similar products.

2. Bring to class a list of at least ten of the most intriguing names you have discovered on maps or products. Use your contribution and other students' collections as a basis for a discussion about proper nouns:

a. Which names appeal to you? Why or why not?

b. What do names tell you about the history of places?

c. What do names tell you about the physical appearance of places and products?

d. Do any of the business names have double meanings that suggest more than just the service the business provides?

e. Do certain brand names of products make some products more appealing than their competitors? Why?

e. Compare the different brand names given to similar products in the same section of a supermarket (different names for soaps, for example). What images do the names suggest that would make you choose one product over another?

f. Discuss the power of names that make certain places seem more desirable to visit; certain businesses more desirable to patronize; and certain products more desirable to purchase.

You may not have realized how often you read NOUNS: taking trips, going shopping, and making telephone calls involve reading, particularly reading proper nouns. Raising your awareness of proper nouns may keep you from being persuaded to travel places, employ services, or buy products just because their names appeal to you. *Caveat emptor*; raise your noun awareness!

THE WRITING CONNECTION

Develop a finished piece of writing on one of the following topics. As you revise and edit your writing, pay special attention to the sentence variety you create by using different arrangements of nouns and verbs. Remember to capitalize all proper nouns.

1. Describe a person you admire. Tell what it is about him or her that fills you with admiration. Use sensory details to create your predominant impression of this individual.

2. Write in detail about a relationship. Identify whether you are writing about a relationship you perceive to be short term or long term. Include examples that reveal the nature and quality of the relationship. Include examples that demonstrate how the relationship has grown or changed. Project how you think the relationship might change in the future.

3. Write about the names given to a group of similar products or businesses. Discuss what you like or dislike about specific names in the group. Explore how the words sound, the images they conjure up in your mind, any previous associations you have with those place names or brand names that might affect your likes and dislikes.

4. Write about your own parents, or ideal parents, or yourself as a parent. Explore the characteristics you feel make a parent effective in today's world. If you like, you may write a set of instructions for how to be a good parent.

5. Develop one of your journal entries into a finished piece of writing, paying special attention to your use of nouns and sentence variety.

SELF TEST FOR CHAPTER 6

1. A noun is a _____, _____, or _____.
2. In Latin, the word *noun* means _____.
3. Nouns that you can see and touch are called _____ nouns; nouns that name ideas and feelings are called _____ nouns.
4. The words _____, _____, and _____ are used in front of nouns as markers.
5. Another name for a noun marker is _____.
6. "Number" refers to the fact that nouns have _____ and _____ forms.
7. In sentences, _____ and _____ must agree in number.
8. The noun that is "doing" the verb in a sentence is called the _____.
9. In statements, subjects are usually *located* _____ verbs.
10. The direct object in a sentence receives _____.
11. Sentences with direct objects always contain _____ verbs.
12. The noun that receives the direct object is called the _____.
13. The _____ is located *between* the action verb and the direct object.

14. The _____ completes the idea of the subject while the _____ completes the idea of the direct object.

15. _____ complements only occur in sentences with being verbs.

16. _____ complements occur after direct objects in action-verb sentences.

17. A _____ is a verb-based noun ending in *ING*.

18. The endings *ion, ment, al,* and *ity* are added to verbs to create nouns called _____.

19. In English, you can use _____ (how many?) different simple sentence patterns to create variety in your writing.

20. According to William Strunk, "Vigorous writing is _____."

FINAL JOURNAL WRITING

Write in your journal what you have learned about writing in this chapter on nouns. Which sections were most useful? Which material was new to you? How can your new knowledge of nouns enable you to do a better job of revising and editing your writing? What are some aspects of nouns and their use in writing you still feel you need to understand better?

CHAPTER 7

ADJECTIVES ADDING DETAILS TO DESCRIPTION

S he was a powerful old lady, six feet tall, with the big bones of a man, and a heavy full-jawed face, sensuous and complacent, and excellently equipped with a champing mill of strong yellow horse-teeth. It was cake and pudding to see her work on the corn on the cob.

—THOMAS WOLFE

QUESTIONS TO ASK YOURSELF WHILE READING CHAPTER 7:

1. How can knowing about adjectives help me write better descriptions?
2. How can adjectives help me write longer, more detailed papers?
3. How can I know which adjectives to eliminate from my writing?
4. How can adjectives make my writing more persuasive?
5. Which details should I include when I describe something or someone? Which details should I leave out?
6. Which adjectives will make my writing more energetic and lively?
7. How can adjectives actually help me eliminate excess words from the writing I do on the job?

The strangest sounding label for a word class is "adjective." I can't seem to find any English word that resembles it or even rhymes with it. I experimented with "gladjective," "badjective," "madjective," and "radjective" before I made the "sadjective" decision that "adjective" was not a suitable word for poetry. Only by looking at its Latin roots did I make any sense of it at all. The "ad" in "adjective" means "next to" or "added to"; and the "jective" part merely refers to a "ject." Aha! *Added to a ject!* There you have it: the adjective explained.

But what's a "ject"? You know what a "ject" is. Don't let the old brain turn to jello now that you're just starting to think like a linguist. If you read the last chapter, you know the "jects." Remember the subJECT, the direct obJECT, the indirect obJECT, the subJECT complement, and the obJECT complement. "Jects" are nouns at work in your sentences. *Adjectives are words that ADD to those nouns.*

COLLABORATE! *Adding to Nouns*

Directions

A. *Together with a group of students (or on your own), read this paragraph ALOUD exactly as it is written. (Nouns are underlined.)*

> Francesca looked out the window. The mansion on the cliff overlooked the river. On the side of this river was a resort. It was located in a cove and was made up of a cluster of bungalows and a hotel. The town of Waldport was a village.

1. Invite each group member to **think** about the paragraph. In your mind, picture *Francesca, the mansion, the river,* and *the hotel.* Once you have a clear picture of each noun, share your ideas with one another.
2. Did you all come up with the same images after reading the same paragraph?
3. Has the writer created a vivid picture for you? Can you see Francesca (is she smiling or frowning?); the mansion (is it made of brick or wood?); the river (is the water moving slowly or is it rushing?); the hotel (is it modern or old?)?

B. *Read the following paragraph ALOUD (adjectives have been added):*

> Sleepy Francesca looked out the open window. The impressive greystone mansion on the nearby cliff overlooked the winding river. On the other side of this river was a lively summer resort. It was located in a sandy cove and was made up of a cluster of colorful bungalows and a historic coastal hotel. The town of Waldport was a straggling picturesque fishing village.

1. Compare the two paragraphs you just read. The actions (verbs) are the same in each. The people and places (nouns) are the same, too.
2. But what is different about *Francesca, the mansion, the river,* and *the hotel* in the second paragraph?
3. What has the addition of adjectives done for this paragraph?

In the second paragraph about the fishing village, *adjectives describe the nouns.* Described nouns communicate more vividly. Francesca is "sleepy"; you can imagine her with a drowsy expression, a yawn, stretching gestures, a soft and husky voice. The mansion is "impressive" and "greystone"; gone is any notion of a crumbling brick facade or a haunted wooden edifice. The river is "winding," which means it is neither roaring nor rushing; strong rushing waters usually follow a straight path, not a winding one. The bungalows are "colorful," and the hotel is "historic"; this eliminates a modern skyscraper. By the end of the paragraph, your own picture of Waldport, the "straggling picturesque fishing village," may even include fishing vessels, some nets, and a few "old salts" sitting on a boat dock. Do you see how adjectives make writing more vivid for readers?

Adjectives also make writing more precise. If Francesca is described as "sleepy," all readers will share the same image of her, the image the writer wants them to have.

Without detailed descriptions, readers must fill in their own details and often end up picturing scenes that are altogether different from what the writer intended.

JOURNAL PROMPT

Write about a resort or a place you have visited during a vacation. Try to paint a verbal picture of the spot. Use adjectives to help you be specific.

SO WHAT'S A MODIFIER?

That's what I wanted to know when I was in fourth grade and my teacher introduced adjectives as "modifiers." No one else seemed confused when she announced, "Adjectives are modifiers"; so I figured I was the only one who didn't understand her definition. Coming from a bilingual home, I often felt left out when teachers used unfamiliar words. So instead of embarrassing myself by asking questions about something everyone else already seemed to know, I just memorized exactly what the teacher said. On "adjective" day I rode home on the school bus repeating the teacher's words in my little fourth grade head: " *'Adjectives are modifiers. Adjectives are modifiers . . .' Modifiers, modifiers, what does that mean adjectives are?"*

I survived fourth grade without understanding modification. Not until six years later was the mystery solved.

One day, my high school pal, Diane, ran up to me in the hall and excitedly blurted out, *"Krisby, you won't believe this."* (Everyone called me Krisby because no one could pronounce Kristbjørg.) Diane continued breathlessly, *"The PE teacher brought her <u>modified</u> car to school today!"*

"Can you imagine that," I thought, *"a car covered with adjectives! Could it really be?"*

Of course, it *wasn't*—covered with adjectives, that is. But it was *modified*. When I looked at the old '56 Chevy owned by Miss Pitts (my PE teacher was Miss Pitts), I saw a vehicle with bondoed back fins that looked more like a fish than a car, an automobile with a grill resembling an open-mouthed shark. I saw a modified car—a '56 chevy that had been *changed*. Why hadn't it hit me before? **Modify meant to change!**

Immediately, I understood adjectives differently. Adjectives not only describe nouns, but they can actually modify or change them. To discover for yourself what this can mean for your writing, try an experiment with me:

WOMAN

Focus on that word. Close your eyes and picture "woman" in your mind. Have you got it?

Now, I'll give you an adjective to add to the noun "woman." Add "giant": **giant woman**. Does my adjective modify your original woman?

If it doesn't, I must have caught you fantasizing about a giant woman. Try another adjective. This time add "green": **giant green woman**. Do you see how modifiers can change nouns?

Adjectives, then, add description to nouns. This description sometimes changes nouns into something very different from what your reader might otherwise have envisioned. When you let adjectives write, your nouns become more vivid, precise, and even surprising!

DO IT YOURSELF!   *Use Adjectives to Change Your Story*

One way to alter a story is by changing the adjectives. Have you ever walked away from a scene viewed by several people only to hear another witness later describe that scene entirely differently from the way you saw it? You may both agree upon the actors and their actions, yet you may perceive the descriptive details *very* differently.

Directions

Rewrite the following paragraph, replacing the underlined words with different adjectives. I mean DIFFERENT! Change the story as drastically as you can by changing ONLY the modifying adjectives. The first sentence is done for you as a suggestion only; you may replace the word underlined *repulsive, if you like, with an adjective of your own.*

The <u>enchanting</u> woman was Audrey. She wore an <u>expensive</u> necklace of <u>valuable</u> pearls that her <u>wealthy</u> husband had once given her. Audrey was a <u>tall</u>, <u>slender</u> woman. Today she wore a <u>light summer</u> coat which accented the <u>soft</u>, <u>curly</u> locks that framed her <u>pale</u> face. Her smile was <u>genuine</u> and <u>warm</u>. She seemed <u>friendly</u>. This <u>lovely</u> vision walked toward me across the room.

The revised version:

The <u>repulsive</u> woman was Audrey. _____

_____

_____

_____

_____

_____

_____

_____

JOURNAL PROMPT

Write in your journal about a woman. She may be someone you know well and admire. She may even be you. Or, describe a woman whom you have only seen from a distance. Perhaps the woman is a television or movie personality. Describe her physical appearance and describe actions that may be clues to her personality. Experiment with writing both positive and negative descriptions of the same woman.

HELP ME, I HAVE TO WRITE A 500-WORD ESSAY

How can your knowledge of adjectives help you write a 500-word essay? I sometimes jokingly suggest to students that one way to expand an essay is to start with whatever you have written so far and locate all the nouns. Then put one or two adjectives in front of each one. Or, if you're too busy to locate all the nouns, just find the first one and put 200 adjectives in front of it. Of course my prescription isn't entirely serious, but it's not entirely ridiculous either. One way to expand a piece of writing is to add detail in the form of adjectives.

You use nouns in virtually all your sentences. But do you take time to describe those nouns? For example, instead of writing that you are sitting in a chair, would you write "comfortable" chair (or "uncomfortable," as the case may be)? Would you say you are looking at your book or at your "favorite" book? Do you prefer to write with a pen or a "ballpoint" pen (or any other kind of pen, for that matter)? Is your latest idea a "creative" idea (or an "innovative" or "refreshing" or "unusual" or even a "weird" idea)?

But how far can you or should you carry your adjective frenzy? How far is too far? Many writers and language experts caution aspiring writers about the *overuse* of adjectives. William Zinsser, a 20th century authority on writing, puts it this way:

> *Most adjectives are . . . unnecessary . . . they are sprinkled into sentences by writers who don't stop to think that the concept is already in the noun. This kind of prose is littered with . . . lacy spiderwebs . . . and friendly smiles.*

After all, your average spiderweb is always *lacy*. And smiles are normally *friendly*. The only smiles worth describing are the ones that aren't: the *wicked* smile, the *sarcastic* smile, the *insincere* smile.

Many years before Zinsser's time, H. W. Fowler, an expert on English usage, expressed the same notion:

> *Adjectives . . . ought to be good friends of the noun. In fact, as has been well said, they have become its enemies. They are often used . . . as if their users thought that the noun by itself was either not impressive enough or too stark, or perhaps even that it was a pity to be content with one word where they might have two. The habit of propping up all nouns with adjectives is seen at its worst in those pairs in which the adjective is . . . adding nothing to the meaning of the noun; such are* grateful thanks, true facts, usual habits, consequent results, definite decision, unexpected surprise *and scores of others . . .*

Fowler is right. It's obvious that surprises are *unexpected* and that facts, unless *true*, are not facts at all. On the other hand, *unusual* habits rather than *usual* ones and *tentative* decisions rather than *definite* ones may well be worth writing about.

Yet amateur writers continually "litter" their writing with adjectives that describe what is already obvious. Do you need to say *green* grass and *brownish* dirt? If the grass is *brown*, it is worth describing; and if the dirt is *red*, it merits a comment. Otherwise you should heed Mark Twain's no-nonsense advice on the subject: "As to the adjective: when in doubt, strike it out."

COLLABORATE!   *Redundant Adjectives*

Directions

A. *With a group (or on your own), read the following adjective-noun pairs and decide which adjectives you would strike out because the concept is already expressed in the noun.*

1. inexperienced writer
2. blue water
3. cold snow
4. funny situation
5. scheduled appointment
6. loyal husband
7. glass window
8. scary story
9. round ball
10. dirty windows
11. puzzling mystery
12. bright lights
13. hard rock
14. pink Cadillac
15. hot fire
16. young child
17. green grass
18. smoldering fire
19. naughty child
20. older child
21. sweet sugar
22. interesting class
23. suspenseful book
24. previous history
25. fascinating history

B. *Working as a group, in pairs, or on your own, select at least ten of the above nouns to use in a creative paragraph. Change some of the adjectives, however, to ensure that the nouns you select are not being described with redundant adjectives.*

_____

_____

_____

_____

_____

_____

_____

_____

_____

_____

_____

JOURNAL PROMPT

Use any one of the 25 adjective-noun pairs (above) as a stimulus to begin a journal entry. For example, write about an interesting class, a suspenseful book, a funny situation, or a scary story.

WRITE RIGHT FOR THE JOB: Eliminate Redundant Clichés

On the job, redundant writing is viewed as wasteful. Yet repetitious statements are common in professional writing, especially in the legal field. Business writing has its own collection of *clichés*. Clichés are trite and predictable expressions that writers write and readers read without paying much attention. Many clichés are adjective-noun combinations.

COLLABORATE!   *Removing Unnecessary Adjectives from Clichés*

Directions

A. *Read the following business letter and cross out the adjectives that are redundant and may be eliminated.*

Dear Mr. Jawb Hunter,

I have read your application and have given much thoughtful consideration to your qualifications. The written document you submitted candidly expresses the honest truth about your previous experience. (4 redundancies in this paragraph)

The enlightening information you shared in your written essay included valuable factual data that will be useful in our decision-making process. I appreciated the fact that you didn't limit your comments to broad generalities but included many specific details. So far, I have been impressed with your personal attitude. (6 redundancies in this paragraph)

I have arranged a scheduled appointment for you to participate in an employment interview on Friday, December 29. However, our committee will not convene to make their definite decision about the qualified finalists for the job until January 20. Because the unfilled opening is an important position, my personal preference would have been to complete the entire process much earlier. (How many examples did you find in this paragraph?)

In the meantime, if I can provide you with any helpful assistance, please write to me at my mailing address which is 1700 Sam Houston Boulevard, Billings, Texas. (How many examples in this paragraph?)

Sincerely,

Jeffrey Peat

JOURNAL PROMPT

In your journal, draft a thank-you letter you might write to someone who has interviewed you for a job. Make up the job or write the letter about a job you have actually applied for. Remember to thank the interviewer for his or her time; comment on what you feel you gained or learned just by participating in the application and interview process; end the letter by restating your appreciation. Avoid asking whether or not you got the job.

HE ANSWER IS THE ADJECTIVE, BUT WHAT IS THE QUESTION?

You have already had some practice finding adjectives in sentences. Would you like to learn a way to make your adjective search easier? *Asking questions* is one way to locate adjectives. This does not mean, however, that "Adjective, adjective where are you?" will make them instantly come out at you.

What kinds of questions, then, will adjectives answer? Remember, adjectives add to nouns—people and places and things. If you read about a noun like "cars," for example, what more would you want to know? How about *"What kind of cars?"* To this question, the answer might be adjectives like *foreign* cars, *blue* cars, *old* cars, *antique* cars, *model* cars. You could find thousands of adjectives just by asking *"What kind?"*

Another question that will bring adjectives out of the woodwork is simply, *"Which?"* The writer may have written about *his* cars, or *her* cars, *these* cars or *those* cars, the *first* cars or the *latest* cars, *Japan's* cars or *Detroit's* cars. You, too, can easily come up with adjectives if you ask, *"Which* cars?"

"His cars" and *"her* cars" are two possible answers to the question, *"Which cars?"* These two adjectives are examples of **possessive adjectives** that show ownership. Other possessive adjectives are based on nouns. In *"Japan's* cars" and *"Detroit's* cars," place names become adjectives describing which cars the writer is talking about. You, too, can create possessive adjectives simply by placing a possessive word in front of a noun it possesses, and "BINGO" you have written an adjective that answers the question *"Which?"*

By now, you have probably asked another adjective question: *"How many?"* How many cars is the writer talking about? The answer is more adjectives: *two* cars, *five* cars, or a *hundred* cars; *few* cars or *many* cars. The third question adjectives answer is *"How many"*?

DO IT YOURSELF!   *Question the Adjective*

Directions

A. *Practice using the three questions, "What kind?" "Which?" or "How many?" to expose adjectives:*

If the ANSWER is—	Then the QUESTION is—
(the underlined adjective)	*(circle one)*
1. Minerva is a toy poodle.	What kind? / Which? / How many?
2. She has black hair.	What kind? / Which? / How many?
3. Minnie is her nickname.	What kind? / Which? / How many?
4. She is my pal.	What kind? / Which? / How many?
5. I enjoy Minnie's company.	What kind? / Which? / How many?
6. She has many charms.	What kind? / Which? / How many?
7. She is an affectionate pup.	What kind? / Which? / How many?
8. She even sleeps on my bed.	What kind? / Which? / How many?
9. Minnie has three brothers.	What kind? / Which? / How many?
10. But she only has one master: ME.	What kind? / Which? / How many?

B. *Read the following paragraphs. The adjective-noun combinations have been marked. In parentheses, next to each set of words, write the question the adjective(s) answers: What kind? Which? or How many?*

1. "This is an emergency!" In a *neat, white* house (_____) next to the lake, the *elderly* woman (_____) was reading in *her* den (_____). She remembers hearing *no* sounds (_____), but something suddenly made her put *her* book (_____) down, go to the *nearest* window (_____), and look out. She spotted *some* movements (_____) on the *frozen* lake (_____). Then she saw *flailing* arms (_____) and heard *frantic* cries (_____) for help. "My God," she thought, "what can I do?"

2. *Many* women (_____) go to work today simply because they need the money. Indeed, *working* homemakers (_____) today really hold *two* jobs (_____); they put in a *double* day (_____). After being secretaries, *lab* technicians (_____), *factory* workers (_____), janitors, teachers, nurses, or physicians for *eight* hours (_____) or more, they race home and become cooks and *bottle* washers (_____) for another *five* hours (_____), leaving *their* cleaning (_____) and marketing for their days off.

JOURNAL PROMPT

Write about an emergency situation in which you participated or were a witness. Did you or someone call 911? What actions were taken? What was the outcome of the emergency? Describe the events as they happened. Describe your feelings during this experience.

JOURNAL PROMPT

If you are a student or a worker in addition to being a homemaker, describe your responsibilities. If you are a male in this situation, how are your responsibilities the same or different from females in the same situation? If you are a female in this situation, how are your responsibilities the same or different from males in the same kind of situation? Describe your feelings about the roles you play.

PLACE FOR LOST ARTICLES

Do you remember the noun markers, or articles, *A, AN,* and *THE?* These are actually adjectives. After all, *A, AN,* and *THE* clearly tell about nouns. *A* and *AN* tell how many. "*A* popsicle" and "*an* anteater" can mean "*one* popsicle" and "*one* anteater." They could also mean "*any* popsicle" and "*any* anteater." For this reason, *A* and *AN* are often called the *indefinite articles*; instead of pointing out a definite noun they can be referring to any noun. That makes them different from *THE*; *THE* is the *definite article*. "The popsicle" and *"the* anteater," suggest a specific or definite popsicle and anteater. Just any old popsicle or anteater won't fill the bill when someone is using THE as an article.

DO IT YOURSELF!   *Read for Definite and Indefinite Articles*

Directions

A. *Select a page of something to read—anything will do. You can use a page from a textbook, or a novel; you can pick a newspaper article or a page from a magazine.*

B. *On your own paper, make a list of all the definite and indefinite articles you find, including the nouns that go with them (for example, "the frog" or "a turtle"). If you discover other descriptive words between the article and its noun, write the whole phrase on your list (for example, "the jumpy frog" or "a speedy turtle").*

C. *Bring your list to class. If possible also bring a copy of the page you read. Share your examples with your classmates.*

LOCATING ADJECTIVES

> *Where have all the adjectives gone?*
> *Long time passing . . .*
> *Gone to <u>nouns</u>, everyone.*
> *When will they ever learn . . .*

(Or was it . . . ?)

> *O give me a home where the adjectives roam . . .*
> *Home, home on the <u>noun</u> . . .*
> *Where the deer and the antelope play . . . ?*

(No, that's not it either . . .)

I have the toughest time remembering the lyrics of old songs. How about you? Maybe there isn't a song about where adjectives are located, but who needs one anyway? When you're looking for adjectives in writing, you don't have to look far. They stay close to home. And "home is where the noun is." You won't find maverick adjectives straying far from their nouns.

Look back over all the paragraphs that contain adjective examples you've worked with so far. Where were the adjectives always located? Did I say *always*? Did you answer, *"Right in front of their nouns"*? From "sleepy Francesca" to "the elderly woman" (remember them from your exercises?), adjectives predictably plant themselves *in front of nouns.*

Can they function anywhere else? It is possible, but unusual. You can sometimes place adjectives *right behind the noun.* Remember the description about the "powerful old lady" at the start of this chapter. Author Thomas Wolfe describes her *". . . full-jawed <u>face</u>, sensuous and complacent . . .".* Instead of putting all the adjectives in front of the noun (*full-jawed, sensuous, and complacent <u>face</u>*), Wolfe creates a more interesting effect by placing two of the adjectives in a position where the reader doesn't expect to find them—**behind** the noun. This placement is usually reserved for two or more adjectives describing the same noun. And only certain adjective combinations, those with parallel meanings, lend themselves to this unusual word order.

DO IT YOURSELF!   *Relocate the Adjectives*

Directions

Experiment with the following sentences to discover what kind of adjective combinations, when rearranged, produce desirable results in writing.

A. Rewrite the following sentences by repositioning the underlined adjectives behind the noun they describe. You will need to add the word "and."

B. If the word order works, write **"Sounds great!!!"** *after the sentence you have created. If the word order does not work, write* **"Absolutely not!!"** *after the sentence you have created.*

The first two are done for you as examples.

1. The <u>blooming healthy</u> plant extended its leaves in all directions.

    The plant, blooming and healthy, extended its leaves in all directions. *Sounds great!!*

2. This <u>first</u> semester Sean struggled with Accounting.

    Semester, this and first, Sean struggled with Accounting. *Absolutely not!!!*

3. The <u>new</u> driver's license displayed Josh's most recent picture.

    _____

4. The <u>cracked dirty</u> windows obscured the pastoral landscape.

    _____

5. The <u>young second</u> mate took command of the ship.

    _____

6. The <u>hot delicious</u> stew tempted the hungry campers.

    _____

7. The <u>weary starving</u> campers ate heartily.

    _____

8. The <u>wooden nail</u> kegs were stacked in the deserted warehouse.

    _____

9. The <u>bright lively</u> fish was a challenge for the fisherman.

    _____

10. Brooke studied for <u>four long</u> hours.

    _____

TRINGING UP ADJECTIVES

You will often place more than one adjective in front of a single noun. This is especially true if one of the adjectives is just an article *(a, an, the)*. Images like "a towering barn," "an unusual event," "the energetic people," each contain two adjectives if you're counting articles. You could add still more: "a towering, weathered hay barn"; "an unusual main event"; "the energetic, joyful, bubbly young people." This is called *stringing adjectives.*

As a writer, you decide how far you dare to string your reader along. My advice is:

Two, three, four, five adjectives placed in front of every singular or plural, proper or improper noun will quickly result in a cumbersome, unwieldy, awkward, unmanageable writing style that the average, common, general, ordinary, typical reader will avoid!!

The final decision about stringing adjectives is up to you, however.

WRITE RIGHT FOR THE JOB: Adjectives in Advertising

Sales is one profession that turns strings of adjectives into profits. Leaf through some magazines and look at the advertisements, read descriptions of entrees on a restaurant menu, or inspect your most recent junk mail to discover how adjectives lure you into spending money.

COLLABORATE!   *Write an Ad with Adjectives*

Directions

A. *Together with a group (or on your own), read the following first draft of an advertisement. So far, it lacks enticing adjectives that might inspire the reader, the consumer, to make a purchase.*

B. *Locate all the nouns in this passage. (There are at least twenty.)*

C. *In the space provided, rewrite the paragraph, adding a minimum of <u>fifteen</u> adjectives in all. Not every noun needs to be described, and sometimes you may want to string two or three adjectives in front of one noun. Such variety in your adjective distribution will make your writing style more unpredictable and consequently, more interesting to read.*

If you want to save money on a car or truck, you will love this news. All cars and trucks on our lot are now available at discounts. Besides offering savings on models, we will add options such as radios, tires, and transmissions free of charge. What's more, all our vehicles come with a warranty. Discounts, options, and a warranty, what else could a buyer want?

_____

_____

_____

_____

_____

_____

_____

JOURNAL PROMPT

Write in your journal about a vehicle you would love to own—a car, a truck, a motorcycle, or even a boat. Describe it in detail. With what extras and special features would you want it to be equipped?

 ## NOTHER ADJECTIVE HANGOUT

So far the adjectives I've talked about live next door to nouns—usually right in front of them, sometimes directly behind. And, even though adjectives provide interesting and useful details about their noun neighbors, adjectives are dispensable. In other words, you can throw out adjectives without sacrificing the completeness of your sentence. For example, *"Many college students use pocket calculators for difficult math assignments,"* could be reduced to: *"Students use calculators for assignments."* The result is still a complete sentence; without adjectives, it merely lacks detail.

But some adjectives do play an *indispensable* role in establishing sentence completeness—when they are positioned *after being verbs:*

> *Wolfgang is <u>wonderful</u>.*

In the above sentence, the adjective *wonderful* is not in its usual location in front of a noun. Instead, it is behind the being verb <u>is</u>. But what's it doing back there? It's describing *Wolfgang,* the subject of the sentence. An adjective occurring after a being verb and describing the subject is called a *subject complement adjective.* (If you have learned about subject complement nouns [see Chapter 6], the subject complement adjectives may readily make sense to you.) Since subjects are nouns, and adjectives always describe nouns, adjectives make natural "completers" for subjects.

The following sentences all contain subject complement adjectives:

> *Michael is <u>brilliant</u>.*   *Michael looks <u>handsome</u>.*
> *Michael was <u>tired</u>.*   *Michael appeared <u>angry</u>.*

Do you see how the subject complement adjectives modify and complete the picture of the subject *Michael* and, at the same time, are *necessary* to make the above sentences complete?

You can use subject complement adjectives in your writing to emphasize noun qualities:

The spectators were <u>wild</u>. (one subject complement)

The spectators were <u>wild</u> and <u>unruly</u>. (two subject complements)

The spectators were <u>wild</u>, <u>unruly</u>, <u>angry</u>, and <u>rude</u>. (a string of subject complements)

DO IT YOURSELF! *Complement Sentences with Adjectives*

Directions

A. *The following verbs act as **being verbs** when followed by subject complement adjectives: looks, tastes, feels, sounds, smells, appears, seems, becomes, is, are, was, will be, has been.*

If you pick a verb from this list, then place a noun (person, place, or thing) in front of it and an adjective behind it, you can create this sentence pattern:

<u>noun</u> *subject + verb +* <u>adjective</u> *subject complement*

Write ten sentences that follow the above pattern. The first one is done for you as an example. To do the rest, select a verb (from the above list) and provide your own nouns and adjectives.

1. *The teacher is clever.* _____
2. _____
3. _____
4. _____
5. _____
6. _____
7. _____
8. _____
9. _____
10. _____

B. *Read the following paragraph. Write* <u>ADJ</u> *above any word you think is an adjective. In addition, draw a circle around any adjective that is doing the job of a* <u>subject complement</u>. *Remember, subject complements only occur after being verbs; and they always describe the subject of the sentence.*

The strange, ghostly figure entered the dark room. Its long, uncombed hair was white. Yet, its face was smooth and unwrinkled. The long arms were muscular. The legs and feet were delicate and bare. It wore a white tunic with a lustrous belt. The glow of the vision was beautiful.

Did you find a total of 25 adjectives? (Remember, articles are adjectives, too.) _____

How many were subject complement adjectives? _____

JOURNAL PROMPT

Do you believe in ghosts? Have you or someone you know ever had a supernatural experience? Describe the experience in detail. Do you believe that aliens have visited this planet? Why? Describe what you think visitors from outer space might look like.

OR THE BEST RESULTS: USE ONLY CAREFULLY PICKED, SELECT ADJECTIVES

When reading descriptive paragraphs like the one you just read about the ghost-like figure, have you noticed that some details are mentioned and others are left out? For example, in the above paragraph the writer tells us the room is dark, but not whether it is a big room or a little room, whether it is a bedroom or a living room. We learn that the figure's face is smooth and unwrinkled, but not whether it is pretty or ugly, whether its eyes are blue or brown, opened or closed, or whether the face even has eyes at all. Why have some details been included and others not?

Any noun worth writing about can conjure up countless descriptive details in a writer's mind. Yet, experienced writers work hard to select and use only those details which **directly support the impression they want to give their readers.**

For example, if you were to write a paragraph describing your bedroom, you would first decide what *impression* you want to give your reader. Then, you would summarize that impression in a single statement (a topic sentence). For example, *"My bedroom is comfortable."* If *comfortable* is what you want your reader to experience when he or she reads about your bedroom, you could describe the pillows on your bed with words like *soft, full, down-filled, and flannel.* Your comforter might be *warm, overstuffed, and engulfing.*

But, instead, you might decide to convey a different impression, like *"My bedroom is neat and tidy."* In that case, you would select different descriptive details. To describe your pillows, you might use adjectives like *clean, crisp, and orderly.* This, of course, doesn't mean your pillows are no longer *soft, full, down-filled, and flannel;* it just means you don't select those details for this particular description because they don't *directly support* the notion of "neat and tidy." In your neat and tidy description, you could characterize the comforter as *fitted, smooth, and wrinkle-free.* Again, it may be the same comforter that is *warm, overstuffed, and engulfing;* but you have selected the details that support "neat and tidy" instead. In other words, when writing description, the picture you create for your reader hinges on which details you select, *and* which details you leave out.

What?! You say you have a bedroom that is both comfortable *and* neat and tidy? Then write one paper that contains two paragraphs and select different details for each paragraph. Any more questions?

COLLABORATE!   *Selecting Details*

Directions

Create four different versions of the following paragraph. Fill in the spaces with carefully selected descriptive details that support the impression suggested in the statement written above each paragraph.

1. The manager in our office was CARING.

    The _____ manager seemed _____ as he greeted our staff every morning. He always responded to our _____ questions with _____ answers. It was obvious that he wanted his _____ employees to feel _____. The first order of business at the start of each week was always a _____ staff meeting which left everyone in a _____ mood.

2. The manager in our office was UNCARING and RUDE.

    The _____ manager seemed _____ as he greeted our staff every morning. He always responded to our _____ questions with _____ answers. It was obvious that he wanted his _____ employees to feel _____. The first order of business at the start of each week was always a _____ staff meeting which left everyone in a _____ mood.

3. The manager in our office was NEAT and PARTICULAR.

    The _____ manager seemed _____ as she greeted our staff every morning. She always responded to our _____ questions with _____ answers. It was obvious that she wanted her _____ employees to feel _____. The first order of business at the start of each week was always a _____ staff meeting which left everyone in a _____ mood.

4. The manager in our office was DISORGANIZED and SLOPPY.

    The _____ manager seemed _____ as she greeted our staff every morning. She always responded to our _____ questions with _____ answers. It was obvious that she wanted her _____ employees to feel _____. The first order of business at the start of each week was always a _____ staff meeting which left everyone in a _____ mood.

JOURNAL PROMPT

Write about a manager or supervisor you have worked for. Describe some of his or her traits. Select details for your description that support the traits you want to emphasize. Have you ever been a manager or supervisor? How do you think your subordinates would characterize you? Why? What kinds of traits would your ideal *manager or supervisor exhibit? Why?*

WHEN YOU DIG UP A THESAURUS, WHAT DO YOU FIND?

. . . words, words, and more words. Because the English language is rich in vocabulary, you have many words to choose from when selecting adjectives. For example, if you are describing a **small** noun, you could select from the adjectives *little, tiny, minute, microscopic, miniature, diminutive, petite, wee, puny,* and more. If you want to describe something **large**, your choices are *big, giant, enormous, oversized, gargantuan, immense, grand, and massive,* among others. And where can you find these long lists of choices? In a *thesaurus.*

When I was in college, I packed my thesaurus around with me everywhere. I never sat down to write a paper, or even a paragraph, without it.

A thesaurus is a book of synonyms. It lists words with similar meanings. Its purpose is not to provide definitions of words you have never heard before. But it can help you to start using words you may have heard and read but have not incorporated into your conversations and writing.

AN EASY WAY TO EXPAND YOUR VOCABULARY

You actually have *two* vocabularies. One is a **working vocabulary.** This includes the words you use (and overuse) in conversation and in writing assignments. But you also have another, much bigger, vocabulary—a **comprehension vocabulary**. This consists of the words you *understand* when you read textbooks or novels, the words you *understand* when your teacher speaks, the words you *recognize* when you listen to radio or television, the words you *recognize* when you read newspaper and magazine articles and textbooks. Your comprehension vocabulary is comprised of words you understand and recognize, the words you comprehend, but never think to use. Adjectives like *miniature, petite,* and *microscopic* may be in your comprehension vocabulary, but you might settle for *small* and *little* if they come to mind first. *Small* and *little* are popular choices in almost everyone's working vocabulary. They are also boring! You can make your writing more interesting by expanding your vocabulary; the easiest way to do this is to start moving words from your comprehension vocabulary into your working vocabulary. When you write, use *all* the words you *understand*. A **thesaurus** can help you think of them.

DOES YOUR WORD CHOICE INCLUDE THE CHOICEST WORD?

Dig up a thesaurus and unearth the riches of the English language. Next time you are tempted to use the word "happy" to describe a person or event, consult your thesaurus before you write the final draft. Here's what you will find:

. . . *joyous, joyful, merry, mirthful, glad, gleeful, delighted, cheerful, gay, laughing, genial, convivial, congenial, cheery, jolly, hilarious, sparkling, rejoicing, blissful, jovial, jocund, delirious, exhilarated, cloudless, pleased, intoxicated, pleasant, exultant, radiant, sunny, smiling, vivacious, content, good-humored, exuberant, rollicking, ecstatic, tickled . . .*

- In the above list, underline any words you would feel comfortable using in your writing.
- Which ones do you think are in your working vocabulary, and which ones are in your comprehension vocabulary?
- How can using a thesaurus improve your writing as well as your vocabulary?
- Isn't it time you had a thesaurus of your own?

Of course, not all synonyms of <u>happy</u> have exactly the same meaning. Each means a specific kind of happy. Happy can range from a calm "content" to a wild "ecstatic" feeling, from a noiseless "smiling" to a clamorous "laughing" response. There are many different kinds of happy. And finding the right adjective in a thesaurus can help you communicate the exact kind of happy you want to convey to your reader.

COLLABORATE!   *Playing with Word Choices*

Directions

A. *Together with a group (or on your own), read the following paragraph ALOUD. Pay special attention to the underlined adjectives.*

B. *Read the lists of suggested substitute adjectives taken from a thesaurus. Circle the word you like best in each list. As a group, discuss the reasons for your choices.*

C. *Revise the paragraph by inserting your final choices in the appropriate spots. Are you pleased with your product? Why or why not?*

The <u>big</u> apartment building was in an <u>old</u> part of town. The <u>loud</u> noises from the traffic on the <u>busy</u> street could be heard even from the top of the <u>long</u> flight of stairs. To Andy, however, his <u>little</u> fourth-floor bachelor apartment was a <u>good</u> place to escape from the outside world. Here he could transcend his problems as he looked out the window. He could see past the <u>shabby</u> dwellings below and focus on the <u>red</u> hills in the distance. This always helped him fall asleep peacefully.

Suggestions from a typical thesaurus:

1. the <u>big</u> apartment building

   massive   substantial

   sprawling   towering

   enormous   rambling

2. an <u>old</u> part of town

   historic   antiquated

aged   ancient

dilapidated

3. the <u>loud</u> noises

blaring   screaming

shrill   screeching

thunderous   deafening

4. the <u>busy</u> street

active   full

cluttered   congested

bustling   crowded

5. the <u>long</u> flight of stairs

endless   winding

lengthy   extended

unending

6. his <u>little</u> fourth-floor bachelor apartment

cramped   snug

cozy   tiny

secure

7. a <u>good</u> place

fitting   pleasant

safe   inviting

suitable

8. the <u>shabby</u> dwellings

ragged   crumbling

rundown   decaying

substandard

9. the <u>red</u> hills

crimson   blazing

scarlet   painted

sun-drenched

JOURNAL PROMPT

Write in your journal about the place where you live. What is the neighborhood like? What is the interior of your home like? Does your home ever serve as a retreat from out-side pressures? Explain.

WHAT'S A PARTICIPLE DOING IN AN ADJECTIVE CHAPTER?

When you revised the paragraph about Andy and the apartment building, did some of the adjectives you selected end in **"-ing"** or **"-ed"**? Aren't those *verb* endings? In fact, if you've already read Chapter 5 about verb tenses, you might recall that the two verb forms characterized by those endings were called the *present participle* and the *past participle.*

What in the world are participles doing in a chapter about adjectives? **They're acting as adjectives**, of course. So they *are* adjectives?? You know what they say, "If it walks like a duck, and quacks like a duck, then it just may be a duck." And participles sometimes act and sound like adjectives. Therefore, they may be adjectives in some sentences. The words, *painted, decaying, rambling, deafening,* and *bustling* are participles which, by the way, make wonderful adjectives—wonderful because readers love them!

You, too, were probably somewhat attracted to the participles on lists you just read, which only proves what I knew all along—that you're an animal. All living things (as your biology teacher will confirm) are attracted to three stimuli: light, sound, and movement. This is precisely why strong action words affect writing so profoundly and why human readers are naturally drawn to action *verb-based adjectives*: because they embody sound and movement.

The next time you write a paragraph, think of your reader as an animal. Use action-filled adjectives made from the participles of action verbs to energize your writing and attract attention. G-r-reat idea?!

DO IT YOURSELF!   *Use Verbs That Walk and Quack Like Adjectives*

Directions

A. *Verb-based adjectives, called participles, can inject energy and movement into your description. For example, you can replace <u>loud</u> cymbals with <u>crashing</u> cymbals to give your description more movement. You can replace <u>black</u> steak with charred steak and thereby suggest the action that made the steak turn black. Below are more examples. Fill in the empty spaces with your own participles and nouns:*

Participial Adjective	Noun
1. rushing	water
2. blaring	_____
3. _____	voices
4. calming	effect
5. barking	_____
6. well-known	_____
7. broken	_____
8. _____	snow

9. _____   fire

10. confused   _____

11. fried   _____

12. ruined   _____

13. _____   car

14. _____   child

15. used   _____

B. *Not only can you use certain VERB forms as adjectives, you can also use some NOUNS as adjectives. What happens when you put the noun <u>telephone</u> in front of the noun <u>book</u>. You get <u>telephone book</u>, of course. Telephone becomes an adjective telling <u>what kind</u> of book. The noun <u>orange</u> becomes an adjective in front of <u>juice</u>: <u>orange juice</u>. Then there's <u>baby</u> shower, <u>garbage</u> truck, <u>chicken</u> wings. . . . Nouns can become adjectives when you place them in front of other nouns. Remember, location is everything. (I say this so often you'd think I was selling real estate instead of teaching writing.) Try filling in the empty spaces with your own examples of this concept:*

Noun-Based Adjective   Noun

1. the car   door

2. the table   cloth

3. the hair   _____

4. the weather   _____

5. the motor   _____

6. the paper   _____

7. the clothes   _____

8. the medicine   _____

9. the record   _____

10. the vegetable   _____

C. *Create more verb-based adjectives and noun-based adjectives and incorporate them into an energetic paragraph that is both lively and descriptive. You may pick your own topic. Develop one of your journal prompts into a paragraph if you can't think of anything else to write about.*

WRITE RIGHT FOR THE JOB: Adjectives as Efficiency Experts

The uncanny ability of verbs and nouns to act as adjectives enables writers to substitute shorter sentences for longer, bulkier expressions. I have already mentioned, in previous chapters, the desire of business and industry to streamline writing to make it more efficient and economical. I call it "keystroke economics": every keystroke takes time, and time is money in the workplace.

If, up until now, you have thought the adjective only knew how to *add* bulk, see how it can work as an "efficiency expert" to reduce bulk:

1. The hinge of the *door* (noun) that *is squeaking* (verb) annoys me.
                      BECOMES . . .
    The squeaking door hinge annoys me. (*squeaking* and *door* become adjectives)

2. The receiver of the *telephone* (noun) that *was broken* (verb) does not work.
                      BECOMES . . .
    The *broken telephone* receiver does not work. (adjectives)

3. Yesterday I mailed the report of the *audit* that *was completed*.
                      BECOMES . . .
    Yesterday I mailed the *completed audit* report.

COLLABORATE!   *Putting the Efficiency Experts to Work*

Directions

Working together with in a group (or on your own), rewrite the following sentences into shorter versions by transforming verbs and nouns into adjectives.

1. The fee for the application is required and is due by January first.

    _____

2. The increase in tuition that has been legislated means fewer students will enroll.

    _____

3. The plants that are producing plywood are in Oregon and California.

    _____

4. Employees of the school who have retired serve on advisory committees.

    _____

5. Information about protection of the consumer is available through our office.

    _____

DO IT YOURSELF!   *Write with Adjectives*

Directions

In this chapter you have worked with many different aspects of adjectives. Using all your newly acquired expertise, insert adjectives into this passage from an adventure story.

A. First read the paragraph as it is written, trying to picture the scene. Notice the nouns are already underlined for you.

B. Expand the paragraph from its present length of 87 words to at least 100 words using well-chosen adjectives.

As you write with adjectives, bear in mind the following *guidelines for using adjectives* in your writing:

1. Avoid redundant adjectives that only repeat what the noun already says. Don't use "*long* sword," for example; "sword" already implies a long weapon.

2. Avoid lengthy strings of adjectives in front of one noun. Do not report that the main character's leg and foot were in "*a poor, rotten, awful, terrible* condition"; give your reader a break!

3. Select only those details that directly support the impression you want to communicate to your reader. Writing about "*big* feet" in an adventure story like this one probably would not do much to support the suspense the writer is trying to create; use "*bloody* feet" instead.

4. Use lively, verb-based adjectives when you can. For example, how about a "*crazed* glance," instead of a "mad glance"?

Have fun adding adjectives:

With the wound in my side, I could only lift my arm, and that with difficulty. My leg and foot were still in condition. I could hobble using the crutch. Calling out in a voice, I struggled to stand on my feet. Painfully balancing there, I waited while the monster crossed toward me again. There was an amusement in his glance that filled me with terror. Suddenly, he took steps forward; and before I could guess his intention, he put the end of his sword against my chest and pushed.

Expanded version:

_____

_____

_____

_____

_____

_____

_____

_____

_____

_____

_____

_____

JOURNAL PROMPT

In your own words, write about an exciting scene from a story you have read or seen on television or in a movie. Describe the details vividly. Or make up your own suspenseful incident and describe it. Or write about something suspenseful that has actually happened to you or someone you know. Describe, in detail, the events and the people involved.

THE READING CONNECTION

Have you ever found yourself groping for just the right word? Do some reading and expand your vocabulary!

1. One place to begin is a thesaurus. Locate a thesaurus and skim through it, looking up words of interest to you. Choose **three** different entries to bring back to class to share with your classmates.

2. Another place to find words is a special dictionary for description. One such book is *The Describer's Dictionary*, by David Grambs. It includes a collection of vivid words, mostly adjectives, that describe the physical world under headings such as "Patterns and Edges," "Light and Colors," "Terrain and Landscape," "Faces," and "Buildings and Dwellings." In addition this "dictionary" includes passages from well-known writers who have painted memorable pictures with words. If you are able to locate any special reference book for description, skim through it and explore its features. Share what you learn with your classmates.

3. Finally, literature of almost any kind will contain examples of interesting descriptions and skillfully used adjectives. Skim through books, short stories, poems, or nonfiction articles you already have in your possession or find at the library. These may include familiar works you have read before. Select several paragraphs to study carefully. Observe how the author uses selection of details to reinforce his or her descriptions and how the author uses **adjectives**. Bring your findings back to class.

THE WRITING CONNECTION

Practice using adjectives in your writing. Choose from the following topics:

1. Describe a place that has been important to you during your life. Include not only what it looks like, but describe the feelings you experience when you visit this place. If people or events are a part of the significance of this place in your life, include thoughts about them in the description of your feelings.

2. Visit a place you have never been before. Describe your reactions. Discuss how your first impression of the place is different from impressions you had about it before your actual visit. Speculate how the place might be different if you were to visit it at a different time of day or a different time of year.

3. From the perspective of someone who cannot see, describe something edible, like a piece of pizza. Focus on details such as tastes, textures, smells, and even the sounds you notice when handling or eating the food you are describing.

4. Describe an inanimate object, such a pencil, a sea shell, a pair of glasses, etc. When describing what it looks and feels like, pay attention to its dimensions and the materials it is made of. Perform tests with it (erase with the pencil, hold the sea shell up to your ear, put on the glasses, etc.) Describe the results of your actions.

5. Develop any one of the Journal Prompts in this chapter into a finished piece of writing to be turned in. Pay special attention to your use of adjectives.

SELF TEST FOR CHAPTER 7

1. Adjectives describe _____.

2. Adjectives are also called _____ because of their ability to change the words they describe.

3. Professional writer, William Zinsser, thinks adjectives are *unnecessary* if _____.

4. The three questions adjectives answer about nouns are (1) _____ (2) _____ and (3) _____.

5. The noun marker "the" is called the _____ article, and the noun markers "a" and "an" are _____ articles.

6. Adjectives that follow being verbs and describe the subject of the sentence are called _____.

7. Selection of details refers to choosing the adjectives that _____ the impression the writer wants give the reader.

8. A _____ is a book of synonyms.

9. Everyone has two vocabularies: a _____ vocabulary and a _____ vocabulary.

10. Verb-based adjectives that end in *-ed* and *-ing* are called _____.

FINAL JOURNAL WRITING

In your journal, write what you have learned about adjectives. Note the sections of the chapter you liked best and the ones from which you benefitted most. Reflect on how this chapter might affect your writing. Also, write about any concepts you found difficult to understand or apply. Try to be specific about any unanswered questions you still have about adjectives in your writing. Consider some ways you could obtain the answers to those questions.

CHAPTER 8

PRONOUNS FOR EVERY POINT OF VIEW

Pronouns and pronominal adjectives are tricky rather than difficult. Those who go wrong over them do so from heedlessness . . .

—H. W. FOWLER

QUESTIONS TO ASK YOURSELF WHILE READING CHAPTER 8:

1. How can being aware of antecedents enable me to use pronouns like a pro?
2. How can carelessly using the word "they" make my writing unclear?
3. How can starting a sentence with "It is . . ." make my writing unnecessarily wordy?
4. How can learning about pronouns help me avoid sexist language?
5. How can I use pronouns to create a specific point of view in my writing?

The Latin prefix *pro* means "for," so a pronoun is a word that stands *for* a noun. But why do we need words to stand for nouns? We don't need words to stand for verbs or for adjectives! Read the following paragraph written without using pronouns. Then answer the question for yourself—Why do we need pronouns?

> *The author has a friend named Barbara. Barbara is a college professor. Barbara is married to a man named Richard. Richard works for the State of Oregon. Barbara and Richard have a son named Thomas. Thomas is a tall young man; Thomas likes to play basketball. Together Barbara and Richard and Thomas often make trips to the Oregon coast because Barbara and Richard and Thomas have a cabin there. The cabin is a cozy place where Barbara and Richard and Thomas can retreat from work and school and spend quality time with Barbara and Richard and Thomas.*

Are you tired of reading *Barbara* and *Richard* and *Thomas*. Is the repetition distracting? Are the names so conspicuous they get in the way when you read the paragraph?

Here's what happens when we let *pronouns* write in place of nouns:

I have a friend named Barbara. She is a college professor. She is married to a man named Richard who works for the State of Oregon. Barbara and Richard have a son named Thomas. He is a tall young man who likes to play basketball. Together these three often make trips to the Oregon coast because they have a cabin there. It is a cozy place where they can retreat from work and school and spend quality time with one another.

Was my new version easier to read? Why? Compare the two paragraphs, sentence by sentence, and circle all the words I used in the place of nouns. These are PRONOUNS, words that make writing smoother and less repetitious.

JOURNAL PROMPT

Write about ways your family spends quality time together. Or come up with some new ideas for creating family time. Consider how you could arrange to set aside such time for your family members even if your schedules are busy and do not always coincide. How has spending time together been of value to your family? Write about memories of spending time with one or more members of your family when you were a child.

DO IT YOURSELF!   *Write Easier-to-Read Paragraphs with Pronouns*

When you write a paragraph about a certain noun (person, place, or thing), you may want to provide many details about that same noun, just as I did about Barbara. As you present those details to your reader, you can enlist pronouns to help you refer to the noun without being repetitious.

Directions
Revise the following paragraph about two researchers in Africa. Substitute a pronoun (he, him, she, her, they, them, it) for each noun in parentheses.

Dr. Craig Packer from the University of Minnesota does research on lions. _____ (Dr. Craig Packer) works together with his wife, Dr. Anne Pusey. _____ (Dr. Anne Pusey) accompanies _____ (Dr. Craig Packer) to Africa to study lions. Together _____ (Drs. Packer and Pusey) put radio collars on female lions. The females play an important role because _____ (the females) catch most of the prey. The collars help the research team know when the prey is scarce. What is the role of the male lion if _____ (the role) is not to hunt for food? Nature has given _____ (the male lion) the job of defending the female against other males.

Another researcher in Africa, Clare FitzGibbon from Cambridge University, studies cheetahs. Since _____ (the cheetahs) are animals that mostly sleep, Clare usually sits in a jeep and waits for two days before _____ (Clare) sees any action.

Unfortunately, sometimes _____ (Clare) falls asleep and misses _____ (the action).

Even with very little instruction about pronouns, you probably replaced the nouns in these paragraphs correctly. Have you ever before thought about how frequently and effortlessly you use pronouns in your everyday speech and writing?

JOURNAL PROMPT

Write about someone you know who has an interesting job. What makes the job so interesting? What enabled this person to acquire the job? Would you like to do the same job? What kind of job would you find interesting? Write about what you would need to do to prepare yourself for your dream job.

WHICH COMES FIRST, THE PRONOUN OR THE ANTECEDENT?

Just because you had no trouble popping a few pronouns into the paragraph in the previous exercise, don't let pronouns trick you into thinking they are always easy to work with. Remember Fowler's words, they "can be tricky at times." While English has only a handful of pronouns, it has over a hundred thousand nouns. This means each pronoun has an enormous job. One pronoun, alone, may be responsible for replacing thousands of nouns!

"He," for example, can stand for any singular male noun. (Think of how many of those there are!) That means "he" could replace either Richard or Thomas in my paragraph about Barbara's family. In that paragraph, I had to be very careful each time I used "he." It was important to me that you, the reader, always understood *which* male "he" referred to. For example, had I written, "Barbara has a husband named Rick and son named Thomas. He likes to play basketball," *who* would you think likes to play basketball? Thomas? Why? Isn't Richard just as capable of playing basketball? (Believe me—I know the man; and he is.)

If my intention is that Thomas likes to play basketball, I need to make sure that Thomas is the last noun I mention by name *before* I use the pronoun "he." This special relationship between the pronoun and the most recently mentioned noun is called "the pronoun and its antecedent." *Antecedent* means something that comes *before* something else. (If you have ever played poker and placed an "ante" into the pot, you did so before being dealt additional cards.) In my example, "he" is the pronoun and "Thomas" is the antecedent because Thomas is the most recent male noun mentioned *before* "he."

DO IT YOURSELF!   *Hunt for the Antecedents*

When you go hunting for pronouns and their antecedents, it would be handy to have eyes in the back of your head. Once you come upon a pronoun, you know the antecedent is somewhere behind you, lurking in that part of the writing you just passed through. In other words, if you see a pronoun up ahead, only by looking back will you find its antecedent.

Directions

In the following passage, the pronouns have been underlined. In the blank space provided, write the antecedent (the noun the pronoun refers to). The first one is done for you as an example.

Janell was lucky. Rolland Greene liked <u>her</u> (*Janell*). This was one of the reasons <u>he</u> (_____) tried to get <u>her</u> (_____) elected to replace <u>him</u> (_____) on the planning committee. <u>He</u> (_____) had explained to Janell that the committee members had decided <u>they</u> (_____) needed a woman. Now that the time had come for <u>him</u> (_____) to step down, Janell was the perfect choice. If <u>she</u> (_____) did not accept the position, the only other possible candidate would be Stephanie Parker; but the committee members knew <u>they</u> (_____) could not count on <u>her</u> (_____). Janell, however, had an outstanding record; and <u>that</u> (_____) clearly helped <u>them</u> (_____) decide <u>she</u> (_____) was the one <u>they</u> (_____) wanted for the position. After all, <u>it</u> (_____) was a very important job.

JOURNAL PROMPT

Write your observations about women or minorities in the workforce. Do you feel these groups are treated differently from white males? If so, how are they treated differently? If you do not feel different groups are treated differently in the workforce, explain why you feel the way you do. Write about any personal experiences that give you insights into this issue.

PRONOUNS WITH QUESTIONABLE REFERENCES

In the above paragraph, most pronouns clearly referred to their antecedents. Therefore, the paragraph was easy to read and understand. But not all pronoun references will be as obvious. Therefore, some sentences containing pronouns may be confusing to read and understand.

Think about this sentence, for example:

Julia told Gertrude <u>she</u> has a date to the prom.

Who has the date? Do you think it is Julia? But Julia is not the closest noun mentioned; Gertrude is. What if Julia had arranged a date for Gertrude? Considering that "she" could just as easily refer to Gertrude, and Gertrude is the closest female noun coming before "she," I think Gertrude would be justified in shopping for a prom dress. What do you think?

If you had written the sentence about Julia and Gertrude, you could change it to be clearer by writing either:

Julia said to Gertrude, "I have a date for the prom."
OR
Julia said to Gertrude, "You have a date for the prom."

Since one sentence often contains several nouns, making pronoun reference perfectly clear can be pretty tricky.

COLLABORATE!   *Clearing Up the Confusion*

The following paragraph illustrates what can happen when pronoun reference runs amuck.

Directions
Work as a group or on your own.
A. Read the following paragraph ALOUD and decide which noun is the antecedent for each underlined pronoun. (Remember it is the <u>closest</u> noun antecedent possibility.)
B. Then discuss what you think the writer <u>really</u> intended to say.
Have fun!

Today was a hectic day at the Smith residence. First, visiting Cousin George took the sheet off the hide-a-bed and then folded <u>it</u> up. Aunt Julia who was getting her coat on told Mom <u>she</u> had a hair appointment. Uncle Fred was busy reading a book about sex; <u>it</u> really interested him. My father reminded me I had a parking ticket on my car so I should pay for <u>it</u> immediately. In the middle of our discussion, Cousin George reappeared and started removing the drapes from the windows so he could clean <u>them</u>. I decided to leave this madhouse, but I couldn't because I had left my car key in a drawer and now I couldn't find <u>it</u>. My brother, Dustin, wouldn't let me use the phone because he was talking to his friend, Harvey; <u>he</u> told <u>him</u> <u>he</u> had a problem. His credit cards caused <u>him</u> to have too many bills so he burned <u>them</u>. Just then, the neighbors, Bill and Thelma, dropped by with their twin babies. Since <u>they</u> are both teachers, <u>they</u> always talk about how smart <u>they</u> are. Just then Thelma shrieked: a bee had landed on one twin, so I killed <u>it</u>.

C. Rewrite the above paragraph to make each pronoun clearly refer to the noun you think is the intended antecedent, or remove some pronouns and repeat nouns if necessary.

As you can see, pronouns can be pretty tricky. To ensure that you're not "tricked" into making silly (or serious) pronoun mistakes, take these three steps when you **proofread your writing:**

1.   Find *every* pronoun you have written.
2.   Locate the closest noun antecedent possibility.

3. Double check to see if the pronoun could be misunderstood to refer to another noun that you did not intend to be its antecedent. If so, replace the pronoun with an appropriate noun or rewrite the sentence so the pronoun indisputably refers to the intended antecedent.

HEN WRITERS DON'T TELL READERS WHAT "THEY" MEAN

In my experience, student writers often use the pronoun *they* without being clear about whom it references. For example, a student might write, *"Last time I signed up for classes, they had raised the tuition."* Who is *they*? "Classes" is a plural noun, so the reader could assume *they* stands for *classes* (the most recent plural mentioned). But you and I both can figure out that the classes didn't do their own tuition raising. Does the writer mean *the school* raised the tuition? But school is singular. Even if the school had been mentioned, the pronoun that would refer to *school* would be *it*, not *they*. Had school administrators raised the tuition? Had the voters raised the tuition? Had the school board members raised the tuition? Who had raised the tuition? Who does *they* stand for? The reader doesn't know. But then, maybe the writer doesn't know either. Do you really think the writer meant to say, *"The last time I signed up for classes, the school board members had raised the tuition"*? Maybe . . . maybe not. . . . maybe *who* raised the tuition is not even important. Maybe "they" is not the concern. Maybe the sentence should leave "they" out altogether:

> *The last time I signed up for classes, the tuition had been raised.*
>   OR
> *The last time I signed up for classes, I had to pay a higher tuition.*

Isn't this the real issue: the writer had to pay more money?!

Next time you use the pronoun *they* in your writing, think about whether or not *they* is really what you want to say. Think about what *they* means and to which noun it refers. Has the noun been recently mentioned so your reader clearly understands what *they* stands for?

COLLABORATE!   *Deciding Who "They" Are*

Directions

In the following selection, the pronoun "they" appears frequently.

A. Working with a group (or on your own), locate each "they."

B. Revise any sentences in which "they" does not make a clear reference to a specific noun antecedent.

Hint: Two (2) "they's" in this selection need NOT be changed. Can you find them <u>and their antecedents</u>?

Every time I go shopping for groceries, they seem to have raised the prices. Just yesterday, I was shopping for diet ice cream, and they had marked it up to twice what

I paid the last time I bought the same product. I always buy diet ice cream because they make it with less fat so it has fewer calories. That doesn't mean I lose weight, it just means I can eat more ice cream without feeling guilty. They say diet foods aren't as good for you as the real thing, but they are good for my conscience.

To go with my ice cream, I bought a fat-free pound cake. They make those in the bakery at the same store. The baked goods prices were higher, too. They were charging five dollars for a little pound cake that weighed only one-half pound. They had some cakes that weren't fat free, and they were cheaper. You would think they had to pay money to take the fat out. I think they just charge more because people are willing to pay money to lose weight.

JOURNAL PROMPT

Write about your own attempts to change your weight. Write about ways in which you have tried to make your diet more healthful. Comment on your attitude about diet foods. What is your attitude toward health foods? Where do you think exercise fits into the weight loss or weight gain picture?

WRITE RIGHT FOR THE JOB: "It Is," a Waste of Words

In nearly every chapter, I bring up the business world's aversion to extra words in letters and documents. While pronouns are actually designed to reduce bulk and repetition, they also can be guilty of creating bulky sentence structures with extra words. The most notorious offender is the pronoun *it*, an efficient little word by itself. But when you pair *it* with *is* and use this combination to begin sentences in business writing, you usually end up using more words than you need. For example in the sentence, "It is the new law that deserves careful review," just what does the *it* stand for? I will give you a clue: it has no antecedent. The noun that *it* stands for hasn't been mentioned earlier. So when the reader first encounters *it* at the start of the sentence, the pronoun communicates nothing but *neuter singular*. That means the reader doesn't know whether *it* stands for a rock, or an idea, or a neutered cat! Not until four words later, *"It is the new law . . ."* does the writer provide the answer to the riddle: *it* means the *law*. When writing on the job, you should not be creating riddles unless you work as a mystery writer ("It is a dark and stormy night . . .). In most cases, beginning sentences with "It is" interferes with clarity and conciseness.

Furthermore, writers who begin sentences with "It is," give up an important sentence position they could be using for emphasis. After all, the first word of the sentence is the most noticeable. Each sentence only has one first word, one word important enough to deserve an attention-arousing capital letter. *It is* placed at the start of a sentence steals the most precious position a writer has for creating emphasis. For writers to waste the opportunity to say something worth saying in that spot comes close to blasphemy in writing. Beginning a sentence with meaningless *"It is"* is a crime. Are you guilty?

COLLABORATE!   *Becoming an "It Is" Buster*

Directions

The following sentences are excerpts from actual business documents. Working with a group (or on your own), revise each sentence to eliminate "it is." Instead, place an idea you want to emphasize at the beginning. The first one is done for you as an example:

1. It is our opinion that the project you submitted does not meet the requirements outlined in our administrative policies.

   Our opinion is that the project you submitted does not meet the requirements outlined in our administrative policies.

2. It is the belief of this department that the legislation is essential.

   _____

3. It is unfortunate that some departments do receive more funding than others.

   _____

   _____

4. It is the business that is classified and not the individual employees within the business.

   _____

   _____

5. It is my understanding that this agreement will apply to all future requests.

   _____

   _____

6. It is their job to report newly acquired properties, and it is their job to report the deeds-in-lieu on the day the recording information is available.

   _____

   _____

7. It is also strongly recommended by the department that financial statements be obtained as soon as possible.

   _____

   _____

8. It is expected that implementing the proposed procedures will have a minimal effect on our company's profits.

   _____

   _____

ERSONAL PRONOUNS MAKE THE LIST

So far, the pronouns you have worked with in this chapter have been *personal pronouns.* Here's a chart of the whole family:

Personal Pronouns

	Singular	Plural
SUBJECTIVE CASE *(subjects and subject complements)*		
1ST PERSON	*I*	*we*
2ND PERSON	*you*	*you*
3RD PERSON	*he, she, it*	*they*
OBJECTIVE CASE *(direct objects, indirect objects, and objects of prepositions)*		
1ST PERSON	*me*	*us*
2ND PERSON	*you*	*you*
3RD PERSON	*him, her, it*	*them*

By looking at this list, you can see that any noun (whether it is a male or a female; a person, a place, or a thing; a singular or a plural) can be replaced by a pronoun. This also means that pronouns can do any *sentence jobs* nouns can do. For example, pronouns can be *subjects, subject complements, direct objects, indirect objects,* and *objects of prepositions.*

ICKING THE RIGHT PRONOUN FOR THE JOB

If pronouns can do all noun jobs, this must mean if I write, *"Mary loves John"* (a sentence with two nouns), I could replace it with a sentence containing two personal pronouns:

> <u>Mary</u> loves <u>John</u>.
>   . . . could instead be written . . .
> <u>Her</u> loves <u>he</u>. ????

What . . . You don't like *"Her loves he"*? Why not? Didn't I make the right choices? Can't *her* replace a female noun, like *Mary;* and can't *he* replace a male noun like *John*? Of course, they can! Then why doesn't my pronoun sentence "sound right"?

Even though I used pronouns of the correct sex (or "gender," as linguists call it), my sentence with the pronouns is not correct. Do you think it should read, *"He loves her"*? That does sound better. But it doesn't say what I wanted to say. *"He loves her"* would mean John loves Mary. And I happen to know that John can't stand Mary. (Isn't that always the way life is?)

If you had written, *"Mary loves John,"* using pronouns, you would probably have skipped all this nonsense and merely written, *"She loves him."* But why would you have done so? What makes *she* and *him* better choices than *her* and *he*? They do sound better, but can you explain why they are the correct choices?

HE CASE FOR THE "RIGHT-SOUNDING" PRONOUNS

The explanation for which pronouns to use has to do with *case*. Look again at the personal pronoun chart. Notice the two subheadings:

1. **Subjective Case Pronouns**—that means the pronouns under this heading can only be used to replace *subjects* and *subject complements*.

2. **Objective Case Pronouns**—that means the pronouns under this heading can only be used to replace *direct objects, indirect objects*, or *objects of prepositions*. (If you need to review the different jobs nouns can do in sentences, refer to Chapter 6, pages 143–154)

Since case can be a confusing concept, I've written the following story to explain it:

The SYNTAX COMPANY: *the CASE of the MISSING NOUN*

The SYNTAX COMPANY produces pre-fab sentence structures at its plant in Writingtown, USA. This means if you need to write a 500-word paper, you could just dial 1-800-SEN-TENCE, order 50 sentences over the phone, and you'd be done with it. You say you've never heard of such a place? Let's stop by for a visit . . .

Dee VERB is in charge of SYNTAX. She has more power and exerts more control than any one else at the plant. Ms. VERB is definitely the boss of SYNTAX.

Dee VERB's favorite employees are the NOUNS. She loves seeing NOUNS come to work because they are such hard workers. As far back as she can remember, no NOUN has ever come to work at SYNTAX and just hung out with nothing to do. NOUNS are always eager to start their day's assignment.

"What do you want me to do today?" they always say the minute they arrive at SYNTAX.

And Dee VERB gladly puts them to work.

"You can be the subject," she says to the first NOUN that comes in the door. "You can be the direct object," she says to the second NOUN, as she shifts into action.

Next, she hands out the assignment of indirect object. And, when SYNTAX quiets down a little, Dee VERB creates an environment where NOUNS can even work as subject complements. Dee VERB always makes sure those workaholic NOUNS are busy.

The best part is that NOUNS are not only hard workers, they are extremely flexible! NOUNS can change from doing one job in one sentence structure to doing a different job in the very next structure without ever having to stop to change uniforms. Even though a NOUN just finished being a subject in the last sentence, Dee can demand that it change to being a direct object in the very next sentence coming off the assembly line. The adaptable NOUN makes the move smoothly, without even having to put on a different apron or change its hat. The NOUN looks exactly the same, no matter what job it's doing.

As you might expect, as with most workaholics, NOUNS have one problem: they "burn out." Dee VERB does have a tendency to overwork them because they are so willing and so versatile. Ms. Verb knows she can put them up front where they'll initiate actions, or in back where they work in receiving, or in the other back area where they can perform modifications or identifications. NOUNS try to do it all—until, suddenly, they become exhausted and need time off.

It's not unusual for a NOUN to call in sick (or at least overworked) and tell Dee VERB, "I won't be showing up today. I've just been in too many sentence structures in a row, and I need a break. I'm staying home."

What does the boss do then? Dee VERB won't shut down the plant and stop SYNTAX from producing sentence structures just because an overworked NOUN refuses to make an appearance. So how does she cover the NOUN's job? You guessed it, she calls a PRONOUN. She can always depend on a PRONOUN to stand in for an absent NOUN.

But when she looks through her file where she keeps workers' phone numbers, she sees several different numbers listed under *personal pronouns*. One is labeled *subjective case pronouns* and another is labelled *objective case pronouns*.

"Now I've forgotten what I meant by that," she muses to herself as she debates which number to dial.

"Well, I'll just try the first one here," she mutters as she dials area code OBJ followed by the symbols JEC-TIVE on her phone.

"Ring, Ring."

"Objective case PRONOUNS, HER speaking," answers a very eager voice on the other end.

"Hello, HER. This is Dee VERB at SYNTAX, and I am trying to replace an overworked NOUN. Could you come in and do the job?" queries Ms. VERB.

"That depends," responds the PRONOUN, HER.

"That depends?? What do you mean *that depends*?" retorts a slightly agitated Dee VERB.

"I need to know which job your absent NOUN was scheduled for today. Was it supposed to be a subject or subject complement? Or was it scheduled as a direct object or indirect object or some other kind of object?" responds the PRONOUN politely.

"Well, let me check the schedule. Hmm. I have it down as a *subject*. That's right 'Mary' was scheduled to be the *subject* in the sentence structure we're producing today. We're working on 'Mary loves John'; but, then, 'Mary' called in sick."

"Sorry," replies the PRONOUN as her voice falls, "I can't do *subject* work. You see, I took the specialized two-year Objective Case Pronoun course at the local community college. That certifies me to do the job of any direct object, indirect object, or object of preposition. But it doesn't qualify me to replace a subject or subject complement. Even if I wanted to, I couldn't; my union wouldn't allow it. The number you need to call if you're looking for a PRONOUN to substitute for a NOUN subject is area code SUB and then JEC-TIVE. That will get you in touch with the subjective case PRONOUNS. One of them will have the training it takes to do Mary's subject job."

"Thanks, I should have remembered that," says Dee VERB. "Sorry I can't use you on this job, but there will be some objective work coming up soon. I'll be back in touch with you the next time an object takes time off."

Dee VERB lays down the receiver and picks it up again to call the subjective case pronoun number.

"RING! RING!"

Someone picks up the phone and says, "Hello. This is ___."

(Who do you think answers the phone?)

This is the moral of the story of CASE: certain pronouns, even though they may be the right number (singular or plural) or gender (male, female, or neuter), can *only be subjects or subject complements*; other pronouns can *only be objects*. That's why lists of personal pronouns in English handbooks are usually organized by case: **subjective** or **objective.** If you ever need to replace the subject of a sentence (or even a subject complement), you call in a *subjective case* pronoun. A personal pronoun chart such as the one on page 199 will tell you which pronoun can do the job. If you need to replace any kind of object (direct object, indirect object, object of preposition), the pronoun you need is one from the *objective case* category.

This pronoun concept points out, once more, the controlling personality of verbs. Verbs really do control much of what happens in the back of a sentence. When your sentences contain *action verbs,* the pronouns that follow them are in the *objective* case because action verbs are followed by direct objects and indirect objects. When your sentences contain *being verbs,* the pronouns that follow them are in the *subjective case* because being verbs are followed by subject complements.

COLLABORATE!   *Name the Case*

Directions

Work with a group or on your own.

A. In the following passage, identify pronoun cases by writing SUB (for subjective case) or OBJ (for objective case) ABOVE each underlined pronoun. Refer to the personal pronoun list on page 199 to determine the correct case for each pronoun function.

I will be taking a very difficult test in math tomorrow. Tom, the tutor, can help me. He explains things so well. Perhaps Tom will help me with the story problems. They are always the most difficult part. Tom always shows me the steps. Then I do them. Last time, I got an A on a test because of Tom's help. Afterwards, I thanked him. He simply replied, "I didn't make the A happen. It was you." I disagree. It was not I. It was he.

B. For an extra challenge, in the space provided below write the function of the pronouns used in the above paragraph. The first two are done as examples.

Pronoun 1: I = _____*subject*_____

Pronoun 2: me = _____*direct object*_____

Pronoun 3: He = _____

Pronoun 4: me = _____

Pronoun 5: They = _____

Pronoun 6: me = _____

Pronoun 7: I = _____

Pronoun 8: them = _____

Pronoun 9: I = _____

Pronoun 10: I = _____

Pronoun 11: him = _____

Pronoun 12: He = _____

Pronoun 13: I = _____

Pronoun 14: It = _____

Pronoun 15: you = _____

Pronoun 16: I = _____

Pronoun 17: It = _____

Pronoun 18: I = _____

Pronoun 19: It = _____

Pronoun 20: he = _____

JOURNAL PROMPT

Write about any experiences you have had relating to tutoring. Have you ever sought help from a tutor? If so, in which subject did you receive help? What did this experience enable you to accomplish that you may have found difficult to accomplish without tutorial help? Have you ever tutored anyone either formally or informally? Do you tutor your own family members when they need help with homework? Write about how both the tutors and the persons being tutored benefit from tutoring sessions.

1 N THAT CASE, IT SOUNDS STRANGE

Did some of the sentences in the paragraph about Tom, the tutor, sound strange to you? How about, *"It was not I"* and *"It was he"*? These are correct in written English because "I" and "he" follow a being verb which means they are subject complements; and subject complements are in the subjective case. (Check the chart of Personal Pronouns.) However, you will often hear different pronouns used in conversation. People may say, *"It was him,"* for example. Yet that is not the kind of standard English that would be acceptable in a formal document. Instead, *"It was he"* is correct because being verbs act as equal signs, so this sentence should say the same thing when you reverse it. The reversed, *"Him was it,"* certainly is not correct; but *"He was it"* is correct.

The other sentence, *"It was not I,"* is a sentence you may *never* hear said. Yet, this, too, is correct if we strictly apply *case* to syntax. Yet most people will say, *"It was me."* In fact, this misuse is so common that most English handbooks now accept expressions such as *"It was me"* and *"It is me,"* instead of *"It was I"* and *"It is I."* Even the plural *"It is us"* is accepted in the place of *"It is we."* Most sources now consider these objective pronoun choices acceptable in writing, even though *me* and *us* are in the wrong case to be acting as subject complements.

Since English is a "living" language, it can change if its speakers persist in the use of a certain form even though that form defies "the rules." That's how rules end up with exceptions. Exceptions aren't created by grammarians; they are created by people like you and me who misuse the language. Think about that the next time you hear someone complain that English has too many exceptions. Who is to blame? It is we (or us), not the language!

COLLABORATE!   *Deciding the Case*

Directions

A. *Working with a group or on your own, read the following passage and decide whether the underlined noun is a subject, subject complement, direct object, or indirect object.*

B. *Then choose the correct case of the pronoun that could replace the noun IF it were missing. Refer to the chart of Personal Pronouns on page 199 to verify your decisions. (Depending on the language environment you come from, what "sounds right" might not be the best choice for your writing.) The first one is done for you as an example.*

Hint: When replacing a noun in the back of a sentence, deciding whether you have an action or being verb will help you determine whether you need an objective or subjective case pronoun.

Marco the Magician (*subject/he*) ran five swords through a coffin-like box. <u>The box</u> (_____) was not empty. The box held <u>a woman</u> (_____). The woman was <u>the beautiful female assistant</u> (_____). <u>The woman</u> (_____) jumped out of the box. The crowd gave <u>the female assistant</u> (_____) a standing ovation. <u>The female assistant</u> (_____) bowed and curtsied. <u>The people</u> (_____) applauded Marco, too. The people loved both <u>Marco</u> (_____) and <u>the assistant</u> (_____). However, the real star was <u>Marco</u> (_____).

JOURNAL PROMPT

Write about a circus or magic show you have attended or watched on television. What were some of the acts or tricks you found particularly entertaining? Do you know how to perform any magic tricks? Explain. Write about any thoughts you have had about joining a circus, or becoming a performer, or merely attending a special performance.

WHEN "AND" AND "OR" CONFUSE THE CASE

Did you notice when nouns or pronouns are joined with *and* or *or*, it is harder to hear what is correct, such as in the second to the last sentence in the above passage: *"The people loved both <u>him</u> and <u>her</u>"*. An easy way to make the right pronoun decision without analyzing the entire sentence is to say the sentence with only one pronoun at a time. For example, to figure out whether the correct sentence should read *"The teacher watched <u>him</u> and <u>I</u>"* or *"The teacher watched <u>him</u> and <u>me</u>,"* merely try out each pronoun separately:

> *The teacher watched <u>him</u>.* YES!
> *The teacher watched <u>I</u>.* NO!!!
> *The teacher watched <u>me</u>.* YES!

Therefore, the correct version is, *"The teacher watched <u>him</u> and <u>me</u>."*

DO IT YOURSELF!   *Figure Out the Case in Spite of "And" and "Or"*

Directions

Circle the correct pronoun choice in each sentence. To improve your odds of making the right decision, try out each pronoun separately.

1. The teacher gave James and (I/me) two different tests.
2. The neighbors and (we/us) had a barbecue.
3. Will Jose or (he/him) give the speech?
4. Shannon and (I/me) attend this class together.

5. When will they give her and (I/me) a chance?

6. The choice was Nancy or (him/he).

7. (Her/She) and (me/I) love the Portland Trailblazers.

8. (Him/He) and Clyde Drexler watched the parade.

9. The audience watched Dan and (I/me).

10. The loud noise frightened you and (I/me).

HAT DO THE POSSESSIVE PRONOUNS POSSESS?

The possessive case is a third pronoun case, in addition to the subjective case and the objective case. Possessive case pronouns are words that not only take the place of nouns but also show ownership. The *possessive case personal pronouns* look like this:

Possessive Case Personal Pronouns

	Singular	**Plural**
POSSESSIVE CASE (*shows ownership*)		
1ST PERSON	mine	ours
2ND PERSON	yours	yours
3RD PERSON	his, hers, its	theirs

Except for the for word "mine," all the possessive case pronouns end in the letter "s." A sentence using a possessive case pronoun might read *"That car is <u>mine"</u>* (meaning *"That car is <u>my car</u>"*) or *"This baby is <u>theirs"</u>* (meaning *"This baby is <u>their baby</u>"*). So a single possessive case pronoun really stands for a two-word phrase; it stands for both the *noun and its owner.*

Many people confuse words such as *my* and *their* with possessive pronouns. They look and sound very much like possessive pronouns. But, strictly speaking, these possessive words really do ADJECTIVE jobs in sentences. Check your dictionary, and you will see they are designated as "possessive pronominal adjectives." Adjectives *describe* nouns; pronouns *replace* them. That means you will find adjectives *next to nouns* in sentences. But you will find pronouns only where *nouns have been omitted* from sentences (to replace the nouns that didn't show up for work).

Read the following sentence:

<u>Her</u> car is the blue car.

Here the word *Her* is an ADJECTIVE because, like all single-word adjectives it comes in front of the noun *car* and describes it by telling *which* car.

Compare the following sentence:

<u>Hers</u> is the blue car.

Here the word *Hers* is a PRONOUN. It is *taking the place of* the omitted phrase *her car* (a noun and its owner) and acting as the subject of the sentence. Both of the above sentences really have the same meaning, but the kinds of words used to communicate that meaning are different.

Because pronominal possessive adjectives are based on pronouns and look so much like the possessive pronouns, the two groups of words are often lumped together and called "pronouns." I prefer to make a distinction between these two possessive forms since one group *replaces* nouns (the job of a pronoun) and the other group *describes* nouns (the job of an adjective). Calling the descriptive words adjectives is not only accurate, it respects the logic of English and applies it consistently. Possessive pronominal forms include the following:

Possessive Adjectives	Possessive Pronouns
The house is *my* house.	The house is *mine*.
The house is *your* house.	The house is *yours*.
The house is *her* house.	The house is *hers*.
The house is *his* house.	The house is *his*.
The house is *its* house.	The house is *its*.
The house is *our* house.	The house is *ours*.
The house is *their* house.	The house is *theirs*.

Note: NONE of these possessive forms ever use apostrophes to help show possession.

COLLABORATE! *Who's a Possessive What?*

Directions

A. *Working with a group or on your own, READ the following paragraph. It contains some possessive forms that are <u>pronouns</u> and some that are <u>adjectives</u>.*

B. *Label each possessive by writing the word PRONOUN or ADJECTIVE above each underlined word. (Ask yourself, is the underlined word describing an existing noun or replacing a missing noun?)*

Hint: Refer to the chart of possessive pronouns and possessive adjectives to verify your answers.

<u>My</u> boyfriend, Mike, and I went to the state fair. <u>His</u> friend, Ray, was selling the tickets. Mike paid for <u>his</u>. But <u>mine</u> was free. We first headed for <u>our</u> favorite concession: Susie's family's "Rib City." <u>Her</u> family runs a barbecue stand. There they sell <u>their</u> famous ribs. <u>My</u> mom also makes good ribs. I prefer <u>hers</u>. But Mike loves <u>theirs</u>. Mike said, "<u>Your</u> barbecue ribs are even better, Honey."

"<u>Mine</u> aren't that good," I blushed.

"If I had to pick between <u>your</u> ribs, <u>your</u> mom's ribs, or Susie's family's ribs, I'd pick <u>yours</u>," he said with a twinkle in his eye.

I think he was just "ribbing" me.

JOURNAL PROMPT

Write about your favorite food. Where can you buy it? How is it prepared? Do you, or someone you know, do a particularly excellent job of preparing your favorite dish? What is it about this food that makes you like it so well? How often do you treat yourself to this taste experience?

WRITE RIGHT FOR THE JOB: Are Pronouns Sexist?

Pronouns are the most sexist words you use in your writing; but, at the same time, they are also the words you can call on to *eliminate sexism* from your writing. On the job, issues relating to equal opportunity and sexual harassment often stem from written statements that have been made in business documents. *The United States Code,* used as a guideline for writing in the legal profession, actually says that "words importing the masculine gender include the feminine as well." That means *mankind* includes *womankind; chairman* could also stand for *chairwoman;* and a *fireman* could be a *woman.* But today's women are demanding due recognition, and writers can no longer bury women's achievements under a man's title.

Pronouns and possessive adjectives come into the picture here, too. When the gender of a noun being referenced could either be male or female, traditionally the male pronoun has been used to stand for both genders. For example, "A *citizen* should fill out *his* voter's registration card in order to vote. If *he* has not done so, *he* cannot cast a vote in the upcoming election." Obviously females are also *citizens* with the same responsibilities. But the *male* pronoun is used for the sake of convenience, even though the writer intends to designate both sexes. Nowadays, this kind of pronoun use is considered sexist.

On the job, your supervisors will be wary of the slightest suggestion of sexism in any document, even an informal memo. This means your use of pronouns may become a major consideration when you write at work.

The obvious way to avoid sexist language is to always mention both sexes when a pronoun is used. For example, "A citizen should fill out *his or her* voter's registration card in order to vote. If *he or she* has not done so, *he or she* cannot cast a vote in the upcoming election." However, this often sounds clumsy and comes across as a contrived attempt to avoid sexism.

That's not very comforting, is it? If you use *he* and *him* and *his* to cover both males and females, you offend a large group of readers. Yet, if you try to avoid sexist language by conscientiously matching every reference to a *he* with *she, him* with *her,* and *his* with *hers,* you risk creating so many hurdles for your reader that *he/she* may try to avoid them by not reading what you have to say at all.

So what, then, are some sensible and acceptable solutions for handling sexist pronouns on the job?

1.   Be careful not to assume a certain sex in a pronoun if the noun it references could possibly be of the opposite sex. For example, don't refer to a doctor as "he" un-

less you know for sure the person really is a man. After all, there are many women doctors. Don't automatically refer to a nurse as "she"; a nurse could just as easily be a man. Don't assume that judges and lawyers are males and that secretaries and receptionists are always females. It ain't necessarily so. (Oops, did I say "ain't"? I meant "isn't.") Do your homework and find out the sex of the person about whom you are writing. Then use the appropriate pronoun.

2. When you receive correspondence regarding people with androgynous names, like Lynn Stevens, Tony Freeman, Kelly Walling, and Pat Smith, be careful about assuming their gender and referring to them in future correspondence as male or female unless you know for sure which they are. For example, if you know you are writing about a female, write:

   I heard from Kelly Walling. It appears <u>she</u> is dissatisfied with our services.

   If you know you are writing about a male, write:

   I heard from Kelly Walling. It appears <u>he</u> is dissatisfied with our services.

   But if you are not sure whether you are writing about a male or a female, write:

   I heard from Kelly Walling. It appears Kelly is dissatisfied with our services. (By the way, did you need to look up "androgynous"?)

3. Sometimes you can bypass the sexism issue by just leaving out pronouns or pronominal adjectives altogether. For example, the following sentence is sexist:

   The average worker takes <u>his</u> vacation in the summer.

   The following sentence is **not** sexist:

   The average workers takes <u>a</u> vacation in the summer.

   Sometimes articles *(a, an, the)* can replace possessives.

4. If appropriate, use the second person pronoun *(you)* instead of the third person *(he or she)*.

   Instead of writing:

   Remember, each applicant must type <u>his</u> application <u>himself</u>

   Address the reader directly, whenever possible:

   Remember, as the applicant, <u>you</u> must type <u>your</u> application <u>yourself</u>.

5. Use plural pronouns instead of singular whenever possible. Singular pronouns require that you specify a gender:

   <u>Each</u> political candidate thinks <u>he or she</u> has the best ideas and <u>his or her</u> solutions are the most practicable.

   Plural pronouns are the same for males and females:

   <u>All</u> political candidates think <u>they</u> have the best ideas and <u>their</u> solutions are the most practicable.

6. If nothing else works, repeat the noun instead of using a sexist pronoun or sexist pronominal adjectives.

   The sexist version:

   A <u>voter's</u> decision should reflect <u>his</u> own beliefs.

   The non-sexist version:

   A <u>voter's</u> decision should reflect <u>that voter's</u> own beliefs.

COLLABORATE!   *Stopping the Sexism*

Directions

Working with a group (or on your own) apply the above suggestions to eliminate sexism from the following complaint letter.

A. *Read each sentence carefully and decide whether any part of the sentence could be perceived as sexist.*

B. *Then determine the best way to eliminate the sexism.*

Note: Assume the writer of this letter does not know any of the parties mentioned in the letter. Therefore, any sexist references may be inaccurate.

Dear Dr. Mann:

Yesterday, we received a written complaint from a Pat Frazier about the deplorable treatment he received in your office.

Evidently he came to your office needing emergency care, and your receptionist was too busy with her personal phone call to notice his bleeding arm.

Then, when he finally managed to attract the attention of the your <u>nurse</u>, she proceeded to conduct an interview rather than treat his wound. First, she asked how the injury happened. Pat told her that a person on the subway accidentally poked the now bleeding arm with his broken umbrella. She unsympathetically remarked that every commuter seems to carry his broken umbrella back and forth to work.

Shortly after hearing that remark, Pat fainted from loss of blood and bumped his head; so now he also has a cut over one eye from hitting your nurse's file cabinet.

Our company will be investigating Pat Frazier's claims further. Meanwhile, I have written to him suggesting that he seek treatment from some other doctor the next time there is an emergency. I hope he will receive better treatment from him than the help you provided in your office.

Yours truly,

Shaw Vanlstikk

JOURNAL PROMPT

Write about a situation in which you sought medical care. Describe the kind of treatment you received. You need not necessarily dwell on negative experiences. Has the medical profession dramatically helped you or someone you know? Have you or someone you know ever worked in the medical profession? Comment on your perceptions of the medical field based on first-hand or second-hand knowledge. Imagine what the world would be like without hospitals and health professionals. Elaborate.

THE NOT-SO-PERSONAL PRONOUNS

So far this chapter has focused on the personal pronouns and their three cases, subjective, objective and possessive. These are not the only pronouns in English, however. Some other common categories of pronouns are *demonstrative pronouns, indefinite pronouns, numerical pronouns,* and *reflexive pronouns:*

Demonstrative Pronouns

Singular	Plural
this	these
that	those

"This" and "these" are used for things that are close by. "That" and "those" are for things that are farther away.

> *This* is here. AND *These* are here.
> *That* is over there. AND *Those* are over there.

Like some possessives, these forms may be used not only as PRONOUNS to *replace* nouns (*This* is an English textbook") but also as ADJECTIVES to *describe* nouns ["*This book* is an English textbook"].

Indefinite Pronouns

all	any	anything	both	each
either	everyone	everybody	everything	one
few	many	more	neither	none
somebody	someone	something		

These pronouns, as the name "indefinite" suggests, refer to things or people that are not definite, specific, or exact in meaning. Sometimes when we don't have a name for something or someone, the indefinite pronouns come in very handy.

(Indefinite pronouns may cause problems with agreement, however. The words "everyone," "everybody," and "everything"; "someone," "somebody," and "something" are singular even though you might think they sound like plurals. It is correct to write *"Everyone is here"* but not correct to write *"Everyone are here."*)

Numerical Pronouns

Numerical pronouns are *numbers*. They can be cardinal numbers like *one, two, three, four* (they go as high as you can count). Or they may be ordinal numbers like *first, second, third, fourth* (again, the sky's the limit).

As with possessive and demonstrative pronouns, numerical pronouns can be confused with adjectives. In the sentence, *"Three students were absent,"* the number "three" is an ADJECTIVE because it comes before the noun "students" and *describes* "students" (tells *how many*). But in the sentence, *"Three were absent,"* the number "three" is a PRONOUN because it *replaces* the omitted noun "students."

Reflexive Pronouns

	Singular	Plural
1ST PERSON	myself	ourselves
2ND PERSON	yourself	yourselves
3RD PERSON	himself, herself, itself	themselves

(Notice the correct forms are "themselves" and "himself" **not** "theirselves" or "hisself," which people sometimes say incorrectly.)

Reflexive pronouns reflect back to someone or something that has already been mentioned in the same sentence. For example, "Nathan, himself, made an appearance at the party." Here the reflexive pronoun "himself" is used to *emphasize* the noun "Nathan." In the sentence, "Nathan saw himself in the mirror," the reflexive pronoun is used to communicate that the subject of the sentence, Nathan, *did the action to himself.*

Using reflexive pronouns to reflect or refer back to an earlier noun in the same sentence is using reflexives as they were intended to be used. But writers use reflexives incorrectly if they use them in sentences where there are no nouns for the reflexive pronouns to "reflect." For example, it is incorrect to write: "Mr. Smith and myself will attend the meeting." Here the pronoun "myself" *does not reflect back to someone who has been mentioned earlier in the same sentence* because "Mr. Smith" and "myself" are not the same person. The correct version would be written: "Mr. Smith and I, myself, will attend the meeting."

DO IT YOURSELF!   *Be a Pronoun Sleuth*

Directions

The paragraph below contains many different kinds of pronouns.

A. Find one pronoun in <u>each sentence</u> and circle it.

B. Above each circled pronoun, write what kind of pronoun it is: <u>demonstrative, indefinite, numerical,</u> or <u>reflexive</u>. Use the lists on the previous pages to help you. The first one is done for you as an example:

demonstrative

(This) is Reggie Jackson. Reggie sees himself as a very private person. Reggie's friends and family know that. He owns several homes; at least three are in California. Many think of Reggie as a generous person. Reggie's sister is one. Reggie has helped everyone in the family. Reggie was married to someone in 1972. This ended in divorce. However, somebody special will surely come along again for a special man like Reggie Jackson.

JOURNAL PROMPT

Write about someone you know who is generous. Do you believe generosity is a learned trait or an innate one? Explain. Would you consider yourself generous or not generous? Why? Do you think people can sometimes be too generous? Explain.

OU ARE WRITING FROM WHICH PERSON'S POINT OF VIEW?

Have you ever heard of "the author's point of view"? Point of view is related to a pronoun concept called "person." Did you notice that the personal pronoun lists in this chapter contained the labels, *first person, second person,* and *third person*? What do these labels mean to you? At this point, you may want to review the lists of personal pronouns [subjective, objective, and possessive case] on pages 199 and 206.

The First Person

The first person pronouns are "I," "me," and "mine." In what kinds writing do you use these pronouns? How about your journal? Look through some of your previous journal entries. Did you use these first person pronouns frequently? Chances are, you did. This means you were writing from the first person "point of view." That is, you, the writer, were viewing the piece of writing as if it were happening to you, yourself. When you write letters, you also usually write from this point of view. Some authors of books and short stories purposely choose to write from the first person point of view to achieve a desired effect. If you have ever read "The Telltale Heart" by Edgar Allen Poe, you may recall that the first person is used to make the reader feel as if the events are really happening to the writer, minute by minute, paragraph by paragraph. The pronouns, "I," "me," and "mine" help Poe achieve that effect. Also, as you might expect, autobiographies are usually written in the first person.

The plural pronouns, "we," "us," and "ours" are also first person. These would be the pronouns to use when you write about experiences you have shared with others. If I were taking a trip with you and I decided to write a postcard to a mutual friend of ours, instead of saying, "*I am having a good time,*" I would write, "*We are having a good time.*" (That is, unless I was having a ball and you were miserable.) Notice I, the writer, am still writing about *my own* experience even though I am writing in the plural. So not only "I" and "me", but "we" and "us" can be used to create a first person point of view.

The Second Person

Who, then, is the second person? The second person is "you." The *reader* of a piece of writing is the second person. When I wrote, "*Have you ever heard of the author's point of view,*" I was writing in the second person because I was talking to you, the reader, directly. Have you ever written anything in the second person? Think about times when you've left someone a note: "*Call me when you get back to your office.*" That sentence is in the second person. The second person is entirely comprised of forms of "you." The most common writing done in the second person is instruction writing. After all, instructions are aimed at the reader: "*You must insert the answers here.*"

Sometimes when we read instructions, however, we don't see the word "you," even though we understand that "you" is implied. If you read "*Insert the answers here,*" you know who is supposed to insert the answers: You are! What the writer really means is, "*(You) Insert the answers here.*" The subject of such a sentence is called a "you understood" subject because "you" is understood even though the author may not have written it out. Instructions, such as recipes, are full of "you understood" sentences. In fact, most examples of second person point of view writing contain predominantly sentences with "you understood" subjects.

The Third Person

The third person point of view is someone else's point of view. It is not the writer's point of view or the reader's point of view. The pronouns used to create the third person point of view include the following: "he," "him," "his"; "she," "her," "hers"; "it," "its"; "they," "them," and "theirs." These all refer to *other* people, places, and things (other than the writer or the reader, that is). Most reports, and even most novels, are written in the third person: *"Susan raced into the room. Robert grabbed her passionately. They embraced."* So reads a typical romance novel written in the *third person*. The events are not happening to the writer (too bad for me) or to the reader (too bad for you, too); they are happening to others (Sigh!).

COLLABORATE!   *Reading for Point of View*

Directions

Together with a group of classmates (or on your own), analyze the following paragraphs for the author's point of view. Write the point of view in the space provided (First Person, Second Person, Third Person). Also discuss the author's use of pronouns other than personal pronouns.

1. Along the branch of the Seine was the Ile St.-Louis with the narrow streets and the old, tall, beautiful houses, and you could go over there or you could turn left and walk along the quais with the length of the Ile St.-Louis and then Notre-Dame and Ile de la Cité opposite as you walked.—Ernest Hemingway *(A Moveable Feast)* _____ point of view

2. . . . I stood in my PJs and looked out the window at the skyline, what I could see of it. There were so many lights and neon signs everywhere that it looked like daytime. I pulled down the shade and got into bed. I missed my old couch. In spite of the shade being down, I could still see everything in the room, clear as anything. A huge neon sign was winking, right at me. It might as well have been in the room. I shut my eyes tight and tried to go to sleep.—Carol Burnett *(A Memoir: One More Time)* _____ point of view

3. . . . Each child viewed the other with awe and envy, though Teresa never coveted Meggie's Calvinistic, stoic upbringing. Instead she pitied her. Not to be allowed to run to her mother with hugs and kisses? Poor Meggie!
    As for Meggie, she was incapable of equating Teresa's beaming, portly little mother with her own slender unsmiling mother, so she never thought: I wish Mum hugged and kissed me. What she did think was: I wish Teresa's mum hugged and kissed me.—Colleen McCullough *(The Thorn Birds)*
    _____ point of view

4. Outside, the fog had come down again. Kristin flew along, with head bent and hands clutched tight in the folds of her cloak. Her throat was bursting with tears—wildly she longed for some place where she could be alone, and sob and sob. The worst, the worst was still before her; but she had proved how it

felt to see the man to whom she had given herself humbled. —Sigrid Undset
(*Kristin Lavransdatter*) _____ point of view

5. . . . If you find that you've fallen head over heels for a woman born under the
sign of the Water Bearer, you'd better fasten your safety belt. It may take you
quite a while to actually discover what this girl is like—and even then, you
may have nothing to go on but a string of vague hunches. —*Aquarius 1994
Super Horoscope* _____ point of view

6. I would have done anything (and I mean anything) to look and feel better. To
be skinny. If someone had told me that cutting off my right arm would have
made me skinny forever, I would have severed the limb without anesthesia. If
there was a diet on earth that worked, I would have found it . . . we've all done
the same things. —Susan Powter (*Stop the Insanity!*) _____ point
of view

CONSISTENTLY, THE SAME POINT OF VIEW

When I correct a paper, I first look for point of view and then I look to see if the writer is
consistent about his or her use of point of view. Inconsistency can confuse or mislead the
reader. If I were to write, "*I love mystery movies.* [first person] *You can always count on them
to be exciting.* [second person]", the point of view would not be consistent. When I use "you"
here, who do you really think I mean? I really mean, "*I love mystery movies. I can always
count on them to be exciting.*" After all, I can be sure that I (the writer) will think they are
exciting, but it is pretty presumptuous of me to say that *you* (the reader) will feel that
way. For this reason, I always try to be careful not to use "you" in a piece of writing unless I mean to address my reader directly. Have you ever caught yourself unintention-
ally using "you" in your writing? Look over some of your past writing, such as your journal entries. You may be surprised at what you are doing with point of view.

COLLABORATE!   *Fixing Pointless Points of View*

Directions

*Working with a group or on your own, revise the following paragraph excerpts to make
the point of view in each consistently first person (either singular or plural). Be particularly watchful of the careless use of YOU.*

1. I think I could not find the perfect spouse because I would probably find
    something wrong with her. This is why I think no one can find their perfect
    mate. The only thing we can do is look for someone at least close to what we
    desire them to be.

2. I've brought girls home, and my parents didn't like the way she dressed. They
    didn't seem to realize that you can't control the way your date dresses.

3.   Everyone likes it when their partner does something special for them, just because. It makes you feel better.

4.   I would always tell my mate that they are the most wonderful person on the face of this earth or that they are beautiful. That is the way you can express your feelings for someone you love.

THE READING CONNECTION

Do some outside reading to find your own examples of different points of view:

1.   Bring to class something written in the first person (a letter from a friend, an excerpt from an autobiographical story, an excerpt from your journal). Look for frequent use of the pronouns "I," "me," "we," or "us."

2.   Also find something written in the second person (a recipe, a set of instructions that came with something you had to install or assemble, a note someone left you reminding you of something you needed to do, or even an advertisement from a magazine or a newspaper). Look for "you understood" sentences and the pronoun "you."

3.   Finally, find an example of third person writing (almost anything will do: a newspaper article, an excerpt from a novel or short story, a report you once wrote, a paragraph from an encyclopedia). Be sure third person pronouns are prevalent in the examples.

Share your samples with other students in class and discuss the advantages of using different points of view for different writing purposes.

THE WRITING CONNECTION

Select one or more of the following topics to write about. Pay special attention to point of view and use a consistent person throughout (either first person, second person, or third person).

1.   Write about an experience you once had at school, but describe it as if it happened to another student instead of you. That is, write about your own experience from a third person point of view.

2.   Write about a process that is very familiar to you, like washing your car, making a sandwich, ironing a shirt, etc. Write about it in the second person. In other words, make a set of instructions out of the process, instructions your reader will be able to follow easily.

3.   Write about one of the happiest moments in your life; describe what happened to you and how you felt. Use the first person point of view.

4.   Write an imaginary journal entry. Pretend you are someone else, living in a different place, at a different time. Let your imagination go: pretend you are an important person living in the future; or pretend you are a notorious character who lived in the past, etc. Write in your imaginary journal or diary using the first person point of view.

5. Develop one of your own journal entries into a finished piece of writing. Pay careful attention to your use of pronouns. Are all your references clear? Is your point of view consistent?

SELF TEST FOR CHAPTER 8

1. The word pronoun means _____.
2. Antecedents are nouns that are located _____ the pronouns that refer to them.
3. Beginning sentences with the two short words _____. _____ can cause sentences to be longer than they need to be.
4. The pronoun case used for subjects and subject complements is called the _____ case.
5. The pronoun case used for all kinds of objects is called the _____ case.
6. Possessive _____ *replace* nouns while possessive _____ *describe* nouns.
7. Sexist language uses _____ pronouns to refer to nouns that could be either male or female.
8. _____ pronouns demonstrate or point out the nouns they stand for.
9. _____ pronouns reflect back to or emphasize nouns already used in the same sentence.
10. "Someone" and "anybody" are examples of _____ pronouns.
11. Numbers can either be _____ or adjectives.
12. An author may write from the point of view of the _____ person, _____ person, or _____ person.

FINAL JOURNAL WRITING

In your journal, jot down interesting and important information you have learned about pronouns. Discuss which sections of the chapter you liked best. Write down any questions that are still unanswered in your mind. Reflect on the frustrations and successes you experienced while participating in in-class activities or working alone on homework assignments. Consider how this chapter may have helped you become a better writer and a more aware reader.

CHAPTER 9

Adverbs Helping Writers Make the Transition

I'm glad you like adverbs—I adore them; they are the only qualifications I really much respect.

—HENRY JAMES (IN A LETTER TO MISS M. BETHAM EDWARDS IN 1912)

QUESTIONS TO ASK YOURSELF WHILE READING CHAPTER 9:

1. What do adverbs add to my writing?
2. How can adverbs make my sentences more interesting and varied?
3. How can I use adverbs to change the emphasis in my sentences?
4. Which adverbs will help me make the transition from one idea to another?
5. Which adverbs could weaken my writing style rather than strengthen it?

ADVERBS: LOVE 'EM OR LEAVE 'EM?

While Henry James seems to have been as in love with adverbs as he was with Miss Edwards, many writers do not share his enthusiasm. It has been rumored that Mark Twain was of the opinion that writers should avoid adverbs. Yet, the other day, when leafing through a collection of Twain's works, I found numerous examples of Twain not following his own advice. In the following excerpt from "A Mysterious Stranger", I have underlined the adverbs:

> <u>There</u> was a question which we wanted to ask Father Peter, and <u>finally</u> we went <u>there</u> the second evening, a little <u>diffidently</u>, after drawing straws, and I asked it as <u>casually</u> as I could, though it did not sound as casual as I wanted, because I didn't know <u>how</u>: "What is the Moral sense sir?

William Zinsser is another adverb skeptic:

Most adverbs are unnecessary. You will clutter your sentence and annoy the reader if you choose a verb that has a precise meaning and then add an adverb that carries the same meaning. . . . Don't use adverbs unless they do some work.

Yet, even Zinsser seems to find adverbs "necessary" at times; for I stumble across them in nearly every paragraph of his writing. Take this sentence, in which he gives some important advice to writers: <u>*Ultimately* every writer must follow the path that feels *most* comfortable.</u> Here he uses two effectively placed adverbs. And the advice is useful besides: When you write, you must follow the path that feels most comfortable to you. It may well be that the most comfortable path includes an occasional well-chosen adverb.

What is this part of speech about which writers have such strong opposing opinions? What is an adverb? When will it help your writing, and when will it not help your writing? These are questions this chapter asks and intends to answer.

HAT DOES AN "AD"VERB ADD?

Just by looking at the label "adverb," you may already have assumed that adverbs add information to verbs. And you're right. **Adverbs describe verbs.**

DO IT YOURSELF!   *"Quickly" Locate the Adverb*

Directions
In the following paragraph, the verb in each sentence is written in upper case letters. <u>Underline</u> the word you think DESCRIBES the verb:

This summer's forest fires wildly RAGE throughout the Pacific Northwest. Hot shot crews bravely BATTLE the fierce flames. Some of these fire fighters will tragically LOSE their lives in these flames. Out-of-control fires quickly TRAVEL from wilderness areas to communities. Homeowners near forest lands anxiously WAIT for evacuation orders. They sadly WATCH the fiery destruction of their beautiful surroundings.

Check Yourself: Did you underline "wildly," "bravely," "tragically," "quickly," "anxiously," and "sadly"? If you did, you identified some adverbs.

UTTING ADVERBS IN ORDER

In the above paragraph about the forest fires, each adverb was located directly in front of the verb it described: "wildly" came before "RAGE," "bravely" before "BATTLED," and so on. That may lead you to assume that adverbs *always* come directly before the verbs they describe. After all, the other descriptive part of speech—the adjective (discussed in detail in Chapter 7)—was *always* next to the word it described. But that will *not* be true of adverbs that describe verbs. These adverbs are the "jumping beans" of the sentence; one minute you will find them by the verb; then suddenly they'll be the first word of the sentence; or they'll be waiting for you at the end of the sentence. Just see for yourself:

DO IT YOURSELF!　*Put the Move on Adverbs*

Directions

A. *Rewrite the above paragraph about the forest fires. However, instead of placing the adverbs you underlined directly in front of each verb, place them at the beginning of each sentence. To start you on the right track, the first sentence is done for you:*

Wildly this summer's forest fires rage throughout the Pacific Northwest.

_____

_____

_____

_____

_____

_____

_____

_____

_____

B. *Even though you have moved each adverb to the front of the sentence, you still have not explored all the placement possibilities. Rewrite the same paragraph again, but this time write the adverb as the last word in each sentence, following the example:*

This summer's forest fires rage throughout the Pacific Northwest wildly.

_____

_____

_____

_____

_____

_____

_____

_____

JOURNAL PROMPT

Have you ever been close to a forest fire or any other kind of fire? Explain the circumstances. Have you, or has someone you know, been a victim of fire? What did you learn from your experience? Have you ever participated in putting out a life-threatening fire or rescued someone from a fire? Discuss your participation in detail. Do you think about the threat of fire in certain situations? Why? How do you deal with those thoughts?

OU MAY TRAVEL FOR PLEASURE, BUT ADVERBS TRAVEL FOR EMPHASIS

As you can see, adverbs like to travel. They are the most nomadic of the English word classes. If you think back on what you have learned about word order earlier in this book, you will discover that the adverb is, in fact, the **only** part of speech that easily moves around in a sentence.

The adverb's *mobility* creates some wonderful options for you as a writer. Because adverbs are so willing to move, you can place an adverb at the beginning of your first sentence, but at the end of your next sentence, and right next to the verb in the sentence after that—if you choose to, that is. While these moves may not change the meaning of each sentence, they can dramatically change the *emphasis.*

Unlike oral communication in which you can make your voice louder or softer to create emphasis, written communication depends largely on word placement for emphasis. The word placed first in the sentence usually attracts the most attention. Sometimes the last word can attract attention, too, especially if it is the last word of the last sentence of a paragraph.

Look at what happens to the "forest fire" paragraph when I move the adverbs around to achieve different emphases:

> *This summer's forest fires <u>wildly</u> rage throughout the Pacific Northwest. Hot shot crews battle the fierce flames <u>bravely</u>. <u>Tragically</u> some of these fire fighters will lose their lives in these flames. Homeowners near forest lands <u>anxiously</u> wait for evacuation orders. <u>Sadly</u> they watch the fiery destruction of their beautiful surroundings.*

The decisions I made about where to place the adverbs reflect my personal preference. Maybe you would choose to place them elsewhere.

DO IT YOURSELF!   *Re-emphasize with Adverbs*

Directions
Write another version of the above paragraph by placing adverbs in locations <u>other than</u> the locations I picked.

_____

_____

_____

_____

_____

_____

_____

Of all the versions of the "forest fire" paragraph, which one do you like the best? Why?

_____

_____

The fact that adverbs modifying verbs easily move around in sentences could be a valuable piece of information for you as a writer. Once you begin to think of adverbs as movable parts, you can use their ability to move to help you create sentences with more interesting sound patterns and greater variety.

DVERB ANSWERS TO ADVERB QUESTIONS

Descriptive words typically answer questions about other words in the same sentence. So if the adverb "wildly" describes the verb "rage," what question does it answer about that verb?

Does it answer the question HOW? Does "wildly" tell HOW the fires "rage"? Yes! The following sentences refer to the "forest fire" paragraph. Fill in the word that answers the question.

1. HOW do the hot shot crews *battle*? _____

2. HOW will some fire fighters *lose* their lives? _____

3. HOW do the out-of-control fires *travel*? _____

4. HOW do the homeowners *wait* for evacuation orders? _____

5. HOW do they *watch* the destruction? _____

If you wrote the **adverbs** *bravely, tragically, quickly, anxiously, and sadly* as answers to the above questions, you answered them correctly—with adverbs! Adverbs answer the question, HOW?

But that isn't the only question adverbs answer. Some adverbs answer the question, WHEN? This makes good sense if you remember that verbs tell time. They tell time by changing from present tense to past tense to future tense. Upon reading the sentence "Jane *arrived*," for example, the reader knows that Jane arrived sometime in the past; but the reader doesn't know exactly *when* in the past. Did she arrive earlier or later or today or yesterday? With the help of adverbs, you, the writer, can set the time more precisely. You can, for example, write, "Jane arrived *yesterday*." The adverb "yesterday" describes the verb "arrived" by answering the question, WHEN did Jane arrive? (Of course, you could also write the sentence this way: *"Yesterday* Jane arrived"*—remember, adverbs are movable.)

A third question adverbs can answer is WHERE? WHERE did Jane arrive? Did she arrive *here*? Did she arrive *home*? Words like *here* and *home* can be used as adverbs:

> *Jane arrived <u>here</u>.*
> *Jane arrived <u>home</u>.*

DO IT YOURSELF!   *Ask the Adverb Questions*

Directions

The adverbs in the following selection have been underlined for you. Above each adverb write the word HOW or WHEN or WHERE to indicate which question the adverb answers:

<u>Yesterday</u> Jane arrived <u>home</u> from vacation and discovered something frightening. Her house had <u>just</u> been robbed! The thieves had <u>clearly</u> known about her vacation.

<u>Nowadays</u> most burglars <u>carefully</u> plan their burglaries. <u>First</u> they consider what kind of valuables could be in a home. <u>Then</u> they determine the house's accessibility. Can the house be entered <u>easily</u>? Can it be exited <u>hurriedly</u>? Most home burglaries are committed <u>quickly</u>: ten minutes is the average time.

<u>Fortunately</u>, you can <u>significantly</u> reduce your chance of becoming a victim of home burglars by taking some very simple precautions <u>here</u> and <u>now</u>.

JOURNAL PROMPT

Have you ever been the victim of a crime? What was the crime? How did you feel at the time it happened? How has this occurrence affected your life? What are your feelings about it now? What kind of precautions could you have taken that might have prevented the crime from being committed? If you have not been a victim, do you know people who have been victims? What have you learned from their experiences? Presently, what kind of precautions do you take to avoid becoming a crime victim?

ERBS LOOKING FOR A CHANGE? EMPLOY AN ADVERB . . .

Another word that explains what adverbs do is the word *modify. Adverbs modify verbs.* The word *modify* means to "change." Sometimes adverbs *change* verbs dramatically. The adverb most noted for changing verbs is NOT. *Not* is an adverb often found "smack dab" in the middle of a verb phrase.

> *John <u>will run</u> the marathon.*
> *John <u>will</u> NOT <u>run</u> the marathon.*

As soon as *not* is added to the verb phrase *will run*, the meaning of the verb changes one hundred and eighty degrees! Clearly, adverbs can **modify** verbs.

COLLABORATE!   *Using Adverbs to Make a Change*

Directions

The adverb <u>NOT</u> isn't the only adverb that can be placed in the <u>middle of a verb phrase</u>. Together with a group, or on your own, rewrite the paragraphs below by inserting adverbs from the following list into the middle of the underlined verb phrases. You may use some adverbs more than once.

Hint: Look for context clues in each sentence to help you determine the best adverb to modify each verb.

Adverbs:

1. finally
2. continually
3. completely
4. not *(you may use this one more than once; but look for obvious clues that it's the best choice for the sentence)*
5. secretly
6. carefully
7. originally
8. deliberately
9. previously
10. jokingly
11. painfully
12. only

Yesterday was Saturday, and I <u>was moving</u> into my new apartment. Unfortunately, the weather <u>was cooperating</u>. But that <u>did change</u> my plans. I <u>had reserved</u> a truck for Saturday, so my friends could help me on their day off. That wet morning, we all met for breakfast at our favorite diner. I <u>had promised</u> to feed everyone as payment for helping me move. At the diner, my friends <u>were talking</u> about dropping my furniture in the mud. I laughed at their silliness. But I <u>was worrying</u> about the rain ruining my belongings.

An hour later, we <u>were moving</u>. My friends <u>were carrying</u> my precious possessions up three flights of stairs. I <u>had asked</u> for a third floor apartment because of the view. Now I <u>was experiencing</u> the consequences of that decision. My friends, however, maintained a sense of humor. They <u>were making</u> wisecracks that relieved the stress of moving. By two in the afternoon, we <u>had finished</u> the task of moving all my furniture into the apartment. I was thrilled and relieved because we <u>had dropped</u> one piece of furniture into the mud—my bed! Oh well, at least my sheets are clean!

JOURNAL PROMPT

Have you ever moved? Describe the experience. What did you do to plan for the move? Did you move everything yourself? Did others help you? How did you reward them for their help? Was anything damaged during the move? What would you do differently next time you move?

LEASE DESCRIBE ME!!!

Words in every word class are aching to be described. Nouns and pronouns have a special word to describe them—the adjective. In this chapter so far, we have learned that verbs also have a special word to describe them—the adverb. But *everyone* wants to be described, not just nouns, pronouns, and verbs.

Adjectives themselves sometimes need a little tender loving description, and so do our new friends the adverbs. So who qualifies for the job of describing the describers? Who describes adjectives and adverbs? **Adverbs do!!** Yes, adverbs can describe adjectives. And adverbs can even describe their own; they can describe other adverbs.

DJECTIVES UNDERGOING A CHANGE

Let's look at some examples of **adjectives** being described by adverbs. Here's a sentence containing an adjective:

Philip is <u>athletic</u>. (The adjective "athletic" describes the noun "Philip.")

Add an *adverb,* and the sentence becomes:

Philip is <u>quite athletic</u>. (The adverb "quite" describes the adjective "athletic.")

DO IT YOURSELF!   *Describe the Describers—Describe Adjectives*

Directions

A. Write some sentences of your own describing just how athletic Philip is. In the place of "quite," experiment with the following adverbs: <u>extremely</u>, <u>very</u>, <u>rather</u>, <u>somewhat</u>, <u>truly</u>. Try putting each of these in front of the word athletic. Following the example, write the resulting sentences in the space provided:

1. extremely— *Philip is <u>extremely</u> athletic.*

2. very— _____

3. rather— _____

4. somewhat— _____

5. truly— _____

By comparing the above sentences, we can see how different adverbs can modify or change the meaning of one adjective.

B. *From the list of adverbs below select ones that will fit into the following paragraph to describe the underlined adjectives.*

CHOOSE FROM: extremely, excessively, very, inordinately, somewhat, fitfully, incredibly, quite, rather, fairly, truly, really, awfully, exceedingly, exceptionally, amazingly, remarkably, unbelievably, slightly, completely.

A(n) _____ lazy man is married to a(n) _____ ambitious woman. Fred is _____ lethargic. Wilma is _____ hyperactive. Fred never exercises and has developed a(n) _____ flabby body. Wilma never stops moving and has developed a(n) _____ annoying twitch. Fred lies on the couch all day and watches his _____ active wife. Wilma hustles and bustles and occasionally gives her _____ immobile husband a loving glance. Isn't their life _____ wonderful?

A DVERBS UNDERGOING A CHANGE

What if a sentence already contains an **adverb:**

> *Philip runs <u>quickly</u>. (The adverb "quickly" describes the verb "runs.")*

Add another adverb, and the sentence becomes:

> *Philip runs <u>fairly quickly.</u> (The adverb "fairly" describes the adverb "quickly.")*

DO IT YOURSELF! *Describe the Describers—Describe Adverbs*

Directions

A. *Write some sentences of your own to describe how quickly Philip runs. You may use the same adverbs you used in the previous exercise to describe how athletic Philip was, or you may come up with some other adverbs of your own. The first one is done for you as an example:*

1. *quite— Philip runs quite quickly.*

2. _____

3. _____

4. _____

5. _____

By comparing the above sentences, we can see how different adverbs can modify or change the meaning of another adverb.

B. *From the following list of adverbs, select ones that will fit into the paragraph below to describe the underlined adverbs.*
CHOOSE FROM: very, somewhat, quite, altogether, perhaps, rather, pretty, really, almost, incredibly, nearly.

An ambitious man _____ unpredictably married a lazy, but beautiful, woman. Barney exercises _____ regularly. _____ quickly, he has developed an athletic build. Betty watches soap operas _____ faithfully and _____ gradually has acquired a big tummy. Barney, however, watches television _____ rarely. He _____ always works around the house instead. On the other hand, Betty _____ never moves from the couch unless it is to drag herself to the kitchen to look for a snack. When she gets there, she sometimes finds her husband is working _____ busily preparing a gourmet dinner, since he loves to cook. Betty and Barney are living _____ happily, wouldn't you say?

JOURNAL PROMPT

Do you know any couples who seem to be mismatched? What do you think brought them together or keeps them together? Do you think that others have perceived you and your partner as a mismatch? Why? Do you believe you are well matched or not? Explain your answer. Should partners who are different try to be more alike, or is it more important that they respect each other's differences? Give reasons for your response.

WHO IS ON THE MOVE AND WHO ISN'T?

When adverbs describe adjectives and other adverbs, as in the previous paragraphs, are they *movable*? That is, could you place them elsewhere in the sentence and have the same meaning? If you answered NO, you are correct. When adverbs describe describers, they typically come right before the word they are describing. It is only when they describe verbs that adverbs are free to move around.

The following chart summarizes what adverbs do when you let them write:

Adverbs at Work

Adverbs modify—
   VERBS and . . .   ADJECTIVES AND ADVERBS

Adverbs answer questions—

About VERBS, they answer
HOW? WHEN? WHERE?

About ADJECTIVES and ADVERBS
they usually answer HOW?

Adverbs <u>Sometimes</u> move—

When describing VERBS,
they are often *moveable:*
they may be placed *in
front of the verb,* or they
may appear at the *beginning*
or the *end* of the sentence.

When describing ADJECTIVES and
ADVERBS, they are usually located *in
front of* the words they describe.

COLLABORATE!!   *Who Is the Adverb Telling about Now?*

Directions

*Work with a group (or on your own). In the following selection, the adverbs have been
underlined.*

A. Above each adverb, write the question the adverb answers.

*B. Then, discuss with your group which word or words you think each adverb describes.
Explain why you think so.*

<u>Recently</u> I broke my tooth. It happened <u>here</u> when I was eating my lunch on campus. <u>Quite</u> <u>unluckily</u>, I had ordered a hamburger. When I bit <u>down</u> on it, I felt an unusual crunch. It was my first bite. My tooth hit a rock and shattered <u>instantly</u>. Yes, a rock was <u>there</u> in my hamburger! I was <u>extremely</u> upset. After all, I had <u>not</u> ordered a rock in my hamburger! I <u>immediately</u> spit my mouthful of hamburger and broken tooth into my napkin. I was <u>so</u> embarrassed. I will <u>never</u> forget that moment. It will be an <u>awfully</u> long time before I <u>ever</u> order a hamburger <u>again</u>.

JOURNAL PROMPT

*Write about an accident you have had. Where and how did it occur? Were you injured?
Did you seek treatment for your injuries? Explain. Was the accident your own fault or
someone else's? Could anything have been done to prevent the accident? Have you become more cautious as a result of your accident? Explain.*

HAT'S THE TRUTH ABOUT THE ADVERB'S LY?

Look through the work you have done so far in this chapter, and re-read all the adverbs you have encountered. Do you notice a family resemblance among adverbs?
How about their tails? Words in the same word class often share the same *endings.*
For example, verb forms often end in *-ed* or *-ing.* Plural nouns end in *-s* or *-es.* What

have you noticed about the adverb endings? Does the ending -LY seem to dominate the list of adverbs? It does.

In fact, -LY is such a common adverb ending that adverbs are often thought of as the "-LY words." But be cautious about believing -LY's. Making any of the following assumptions about word endings can be dangerous:

DANGEROUS ASSUMPTION #1: All Adverbs Are -LY Words.

THE TRUTH: **Some** adverbs end in -LY (such as *finally, quickly,* and *gently*), but many adverbs do *not* (such as *very, quite, rather, here, tomorrow, almost,* and *not*).

DANGEROUS ASSUMPTION #2: All -LY Words Are Adverbs.

THE TRUTH: **Some** -LY words are adverbs; some are adjectives.

Let's look at this truth more closely to discover the difference between -LY words that become adverbs and -LY words that become adjectives. Read the following sentence:

> The <u>quiet</u> boy plays <u>quietly</u>.

In this sentence, the word *quiet* is an adjective because it describes the noun, *boy*. But look at what happens when I add an -LY to the adjective *quiet*: The <u>quiet</u> boy plays <u>quietly</u>. With the addition of an -LY, the adjective *quiet* turns into the adverb *quietly*. An adverb, of course, cannot describe a noun. I can't say "the *quietly* boy." Instead, the adverb *quietly* describes the **verb** *plays*. It tells HOW the boy *plays*.

DO IT YOURSELF!   *Create an Adverb with an "LY"*

Directions

A. *Complete the following sentences by adding the adverb that is suggested by the underlined adjective. (Create adverbs by adding "LY" to the underlined adjectives.) The first one is done for you as an example.*

1. The <u>quick</u> rabbit jumped *quickly.*

2. The <u>intense</u> politician spoke _____.

3. The <u>bad</u> singer sang the anthem _____.

4. The <u>safe</u> driver drove the car _____.

5. The <u>nervous</u>, expectant father paced the corridor _____.

6. The <u>excited</u> winner announced her victory _____.

7. The <u>slow</u> train rolled into town _____.

B. *Make up three sentences of your own using adjectives and -LY adverbs derived from them:*

1. _____

2. _____

3. _____

C. *Do you ever say "the singer sang **bad**" instead of "the singer sang **badly**"? ___ Or do you tell your friends to "drive **safe**" instead of "drive **safely**"? ___ If you do, you should incorporate some more -LY's into your sentences.*

The following formula expresses the concept you have just discovered:

$$\text{adjective} + LY = \text{adverb}$$

Therefore, -LY is a common adverb ending.

COLLABORATE! *Reveal the Source of the Adverb with the "LY"*

Directions

A. *In the following paragraph, underline the adverbs ending in -LY.*

B. *Above each adverb, write the adjective from which it was created. The first one is done for you as an example:*

My husband <u>*constant*ly</u> watches TV talk shows. To him, they are extremely interesting. My feelings are completely opposite. I find them incredibly dull. I definitely believe, however, that many more television viewers share my husband's feelings than share mine. Surely they do. After all, just look at the number of talk shows that air continually. Anyone who has access to cable television can habitually watch talk shows from early in the morning until the middle of the night. Generally these shows deal with problems and negative topics. I think this is a terribly sad comment on our society. If it were up to me, I would treat the positive aspects of life equally. If people mostly focus on the negative and just occasionally focus on the positive, our society will eventually feel the consequences.

JOURNAL PROMPT

How do you feel about talk shows? Do you like to watch them? Why or why not? Why do you think they are so popular? Have you or anyone you know ever been on a talk show? What was the topic of that show, and who was the host? Which talk show do you feel is the best one on television? Which is the worst? Explain your answers. Do you think talk shows are just a fad or do you feel that there will always be a place for them in our society? Why?

OES EVERY "LY" ACHIEVE THE SAME RESULT?

Since there are so many adverbs that end in -LY, does that mean you can use the -LY ending alone to help you spot an adverb? The answer is NO. Adverbs based on adjectives are not the only words that end in -LY. Look at the following list of -LY words that come from NOUNS:

the friend	becomes	friend*ly*
the state	becomes	state*ly*
the love	becomes	love*ly*
the brother	becomes	brother*ly*

Adding -LY to each of these words leaves readers wondering:

the friendly (what?)
the stately (what?)
the lovely (what?)
the brotherly (what?)

Perhaps these "LY words" would make more sense in complete sentences:

The <u>friendly</u> girl smiled at me.
The governor lived in the <u>stately</u> mansion.
We watched the <u>lovely</u> sunset.
The minister demonstrated <u>brotherly</u> love through his actions.

In these sentences, *friendly* describes the noun *girl; stately* describes the noun *mansion; lovely* describes the noun *sunset;* and *brotherly* describes the noun *love.* All these LY words describe nouns. That is the job of an adjective, not an adverb. So the conclusion we can draw is that sometimes LY can be an adjective ending as well. Adjectives seem to be created this way:

noun + LY = adjective

Y" OR NO "LY," HOW CAN I TELL AN ADVERB FROM AN ADJECTIVE?

By now you may be feeling a little confused about adverbs and adjectives, especially if it has been a long time since you've studied adjectives. So let's review the differences between these two word classes:

Comparing Adjectives to Adverbs

Adverbs	**Adjectives**
MODIFY—	MODIFY—
verbs, adjectives, and other adverbs	nouns and pronouns

Answer the Questions:	Answer the Questions:
How?	Which?
When?	What kind?
Where?	How many?

Ability to Move:	**Ability to Move:**
May move around in sentences when describing the verb; but do not move around when describing adjectives and adverbs.	Do not move around. Stay next to the noun/pronoun they describe.

Special Function:	**Special Function:**
None	May be subject complements or object complements.

TICKY STUFF

Coherence! Your paper lacks coherence! Coherence?? That sounds like something from a physics class. I remember having to learn the difference between cohesion and adhesion in ninth grade Physical Science. "Adhesion" meant that one thing stuck to another like an adhesive bandage sticking to my finger. "Cohesion" (which sounds like a close relative to *coherence*), meant "sticking together." But that was science. What does cohesion have to do with *writing*?

When writing has cohesion, ideas stick together. Do you realize that one of your responsibilities as a writer is to connect one idea to the next? Or have you never thought about gluing your ideas together?

In your writing, you are in charge. That also means your reader expects you to take charge. After all, your own ideas are familiar territory for you, but unfamiliar territory for your reader. When you decide to put a certain idea first and another idea next, you are laying out the route your reader will take through your writing. The reader depends on you for guidance and directions, depends on you to lead the way, depends on you to have an organized plan for moving through the ideas in your writing.

HE WRITER AS A BRIDGE BUILDER

And how do you live up to the responsibility of leading your reader smoothly through your writing? How do you create coherence? One way is by building bridges from one idea to the next. Typically, one piece of writing contains many different ideas. In the planning stages, for reasons known only to you, you decide which idea will come first in your writing and which will come second and so on. You may decide to group different ideas together for a variety of reasons.

But how often do you let your reader know *how* and *why* you have decided to organize your ideas the way you have? How often do you take time to explain your organization by using words like *first* and *second* and *finally?* How often do you describe scenes by hooking details together with the words *nearby, opposite,* and *behind?* How often do you draw conclusions from your ideas by saying to your reader, *therefore, thus,* or *consequently*—so the reader understands that the ideas you just presented are the ones that led to the conclusion you are about to express? How often do you use ADVERBS as bridges to create coherence in your writing?

Readers not only want to understand your ideas, but also *how* you arrived at those ideas. Readers want to understand the relationship of one idea to another, to understand which ideas are the most important and which are not so important. Therefore, you, the writer, need to build bridges—a variety of bridges to connect ideas in various ways. If you provide no connection from one idea to the next, your reader may not be able to make the giant leap necessary to move from one thought to another and may give up reading your writing altogether.

DVERB BRIDGES

While bridges used in writing come in several shapes and structures, an important single-word bridge is the ADVERB. Carefully study the following lists of adverbs that connect ideas:

1. If you simply want to add one idea to another, here are some ADVERBS that can accomplish that ADDITION:

again	then	besides	finally	further	next
furthermore	moreover	first	second	third	also

2. *Also* you might want to write about two contradictory ideas and point out differences. These ADVERBS can help you connect CONTRASTING ideas:

conversely	however	inversely	nevertheless	otherwise
still	yet	rather	instead	

3. *Instead* you may want to point out the similarities of several ideas. You may then use the following ADVERBS to prepare your reader for the upcoming COMPARISONS:

similarly	likewise

4. *Likewise* you may want to connect ideas in a strong argument to help the reader understand that your concerns have consequences. Then you can use these ADVERBS to point out the relationship of CAUSE and EFFECT:

accordingly	then	finally	later	thereafter
therefore	thus	hence	consequently	

5. *Consequently,* you may need to back up your conclusions with specific examples. Or you may want to emphasize an important detail. The following ADVERBS will help you build bridges to EXAMPLES and for EMPHASIS:

definitely   briefly   foremost   moreover   again

particularly   primarily   specifically   surely   especially

6. *Especially* when you are describing a location or a scene, you can take the reader with you if you employ these ADVERBS to establish LOCATION:

here   there   nearby   beside

opposite   behind   somewhere   anywhere

7. *Anywhere* you tell a story relating events in the order they occurred or give instructions step by step, sequencing is important. These ADVERBS will see to it that your reader doesn't become confused about TIME relationships:

soon	earlier	eventually	finally	hereafter
thereafter	immediately	initially	meanwhile	subsequently
afterward	since	first	second	third
last	lately	later	now	presently
previously	shortly	temporarily	already	formerly
always	whenever	instantaneously	often	usually

COLLABORATE!   *Inspect the Bridges*

Directions

A. *Bridges in writing are called* <u>transitions.</u> *In the following paragraphs circle the adverbs acting as transitions.*

B. *Above each adverb you circle, write what kind of bridge it is creating: addition, contrast, comparison, cause and effect, example-emphasis, location, or time. Use the list of adverbs you just studied to help you.*

1.   Narratives may be written primarily to recount events. Nevertheless, narration can also present a sequence of events to prove a point. Specifically, if you write about the first time you registered for classes, your purpose may be to prove to your readers that the registration process needs to be improved. Therefore, you do not simply tell the story of your registration experience. Rather you select and arrange the details of the experience that show the shortcomings of the present system.

2.   Narrative presents events in chronological order. Similarly, process writing also uses time sequencing. Unlike a narrative, however, a process essay details a series of events that produces the same outcome whenever it is dupli-

cated. Thus a reader may actually perform the process simply by reading about it. Therefore, the writer must not only provide clear, logical transitions between the steps in a process, but must also present the steps in a strict order.

3.   We often think of descriptive writing as telling about how something is perceived by the senses, specifically how something looks, smells, tastes, feels, and sounds. Yet, description may go further. Writers can also create vivid impressions from their own imaginations by effectively using language. When it comes to organization, we already know that a narrative always presents events in a time order; however, description usually presents things in spatial order instead.

4.   To compare or contrast two things, you must first determine the elements they have in common. However, a comparison should lead you, and thus your reader, beyond the obvious. Consequently, when two subjects are very similar, it is the contrast that is worth writing about; yet when two subjects are not very much alike, their similarities are worth discussing.

DO IT YOURSELF!   *Write . . . and Make Transitions along the Way*

Directions

A. *Study the information contained in the four paragraphs in the previous Collaborate exercise. Incorporate the suggestions for narrative writing, process writing, descriptive writing, and comparison–contrast writing into four paragraphs of your own written on the topics listed below.*

B. *After writing each paragraph, go back over it and circle all transitions you used. If a paragraph is lacking in transitions, add them and circle them.*

Topics:

1.   Write a paragraph that tells a story (a narrative).

2.   Write a paragraph that instructs—that tells someone how to do something (a process).

3.   Write a paragraph that describes a scene and how things in that scene are arranged spatially (a description).

4.   Write a paragraph that points out both similarities and differences between two things (comparison-contrast).

WRITE RIGHT FOR THE JOB: Very Is Very . . . Unnecessary?

Producing clean and concise writing on the job is important. Employers don't want you to waste words anymore than they want you to waste paper or supplies.

How can an awareness of adverbs make your writing more concise? At the beginning of this chapter, I quoted William Zinsser, the author of *On Writing Well.* You may recall that he warned, "Don't use adverbs unless they do some work." Is he implying that some adverbs in sentences aren't working—aren't making a contribution to the sentence? Yes, he is.

A notable example of an adverb whose contribution is sometimes questionable is the adverb *very*. *Very* is probably the most overused adverb in the English language. Unless you watch yourself VERY carefully, you may VERY easily find that you, too, are VERY prone to using "VERY" VERY often, at least VERY much more than is necessary.

Very is sometimes called "an intensifier." That is, it makes whatever it is describing more intense. Saying *"The weather is cold"* is less intense than saying *"The weather is <u>very</u> cold."*

But an intensifier is not always necessary to make a point strong. Compare *"The student is honest"* to *"The student is <u>very</u> honest."* If I have to put *very* in front of *honest* to make my point, what does that imply about just plain *honest*? Could it imply that the student who is just plain honest may sometimes tell lies? No. Honest students don't tell lies; honest is HONEST! And the word *very* cannot make it more so.

In many cases *very* cannot do any "work" in a sentence because the meaning is already, unquestionably, there to begin with.

DO IT YOURSELF!   . . . <u>Very</u> Carefully

Directions
A. *Rewrite the following sentences leaving out the word "very."*

1. Your comments are very true.

_____

2. I found a very unique vase at the auction.

_____

3. The climber reached the very top of the mountain.

_____

4. The blood-curdling scream was the very first sound I heard.

_____

5. Although I wrote as fast as I could, I was the very last person to finish my essay test.

_____

6. After being hit by a car, the cat was very dead.

_____

B. *Sometimes writers can accomplish the intensity they desire by selecting a more powerful word rather than modifying a less powerful word with <u>very</u>. For example, instead of saying, "The student who received the 'A' was <u>very happy</u>," I could say, "The student who received the 'A' was <u>elated</u>." Rewrite the following sentences and replace the un-*

derlined expressions with a single word that carries an equally strong meaning. You may want to consult a THESAURUS for ideas for replacement words:

1. The apartment building was <u>very big</u>.

_____

2. The city was <u>very old</u>.

_____

3. The molecule was <u>very small</u>.

_____

4. The steak was <u>very uncooked</u>.

_____

5. The scenery was <u>very pretty</u>.

_____

WRITE RIGHT FOR THE JOB: "There Is," Another Problem

Most writers who write on the job want readers to pay attention to every word in a document. That means writers need to work extra hard to make sure every word in a document has meaning.

Don't all words have meaning? You might think so. But what is the meaning of the word *there* in, *"<u>There</u> is a fly in my soup"*? Does *there* mean "far away" (as in "over *there*") instead of "nearby" (as in "right *here*")? NO! The simple fact is, *"A fly is in my soup!!"* I don't need *there* to help me say that. In fact, the word *there*, especially when used to **introduce** sentences, is often a wasted, meaningless word.

DO IT YOURSELF!   *Be a Word Conservationist: Eliminate "There" Waste*

Directions

Revise the following sentences to eliminate the meaningless use of <u>there</u>. The first one is done for you as an example:

1. There are many options available to employees.

   <u>Many options are available to employees</u>. OR *<u>Employees have many options</u>.*

2. There are certain issues that deserve comprehensive legislative review.

   _____

   _____

3. There is still a great deal unknown about this case.

   _____

   _____

4. There are some alternatives being proposed that also need to be reviewed.

_____

_____

5. There are a few issues we wish to respond to from the September meeting.

_____

_____

6. There are presently fifteen staff members who make up the fiscal division.

_____

_____

WRITE RIGHT FOR THE JOB: The "Only" Puzzle

Professional writing needs to be clear so that companies do not become embroiled in expensive legal battles over what an employee **meant** to say, but didn't. One adverb that often causes disputes over the meanings of sentences is the word *only*. *Only* is particularly difficult for writers to control because it is such a versatile word. *Only* is not just an adverb; it is also an adjective. That means it can, and will, describe any word you put it next to (sometimes whether you like it or not). Watch *only* at work in the following series of sentences:

> <u>Only</u> *he told me that she shot him.*
> He <u>**only**</u> told me that she shot him.
> He told <u>**only**</u> me that she shot him.
> He told me <u>**only**</u> that she shot him.
> He told me that <u>**only**</u> she shot him.
> He told me that she <u>**only**</u> shot him.
> He told me that she shot <u>**only**</u> him.
> He told me that she shot him <u>**only**</u>.

Think about **exactly** what each of the above sentences means. Explain why you should be careful when placing the word *only* into your sentences:

_____

_____

_____

In many sentences the word *only* could be applied to at least two different parts of the same sentence. The following sentence is an example:

> *The patient's pain can be reduced <u>only</u> by expensive therapy.*

- Does this sentence mean that the pain can be *reduced <u>only</u>*, but not eliminated altogether?

- Or does the sentence mean that the pain can be reduced *only by expensive therapy,* not inexpensive therapy?

Sentences with more than one meaning are said to be "ambiguous." On the job, ambiguous sentences are worthless because they do not communicate what the writer intended to say. Ambiguous sentences can also be costly. After all, companies are held liable for whatever their employees write—even when what they write is not what they meant to write. Adverbs are particularly good at creating ambiguous sentences. In fact, adverbs that cause double meanings even have a special name: *squinting adverbs.* In the sentence, *"The patient's pain can be reduced only by expensive therapy,"* ONLY is a squinting adverb. You can almost picture this fickle word closing one eye to focus on one part of the sentence and then arbitrarily switching to closing the other eye to focus on the other part of the sentence. That's a squinting adverb for you!

DO IT YOURSELF! *Close the Lid on Squinting Adverbs*

Directions

By MOVING the underlined **squinting adverb,** *create two <u>clear</u> sentences in place of each of the following <u>ambiguous</u> sentences. The first one is done for you as an example.*

1. Attorneys' fees <u>only</u> can be awarded when the claim is brought forth within two weeks.

   Version 1: *Only attorneys' fees can be awarded when the claim is brought forth within two weeks.*

   Version 2: *Attorneys' fees can be awarded only when the claim is brought within two weeks.*

2. My eyesight <u>only</u> is affected when I drink too much.

   Version 1:

   _____

   _____

   Version 2:

   _____

   _____

3. The student <u>only</u> can be absent two times during the term.

   Version 1:

   _____

   _____

   Version 2:

   _____

   _____

4. The cat <u>only</u> went outside after dark.

   Version 1:

   _____

   _____

   Version 2:

   _____

   _____

5. This program <u>only</u> is available when the cable is hooked up.

   Version 1:

   _____

   _____

   Version 2:

   _____

   _____

COLLABORATE!! *Do the Job on Adverbs*

Directions
Together with a group, or on your own, read the following selection.
A. Underline the unnecessary intensifying adverbs, meaningless adverbs, and squinting adverbs discussed in the Write Right for the Job sections of this chapter.
B. In the space provided, rewrite the selection to make it concise and clear.

There are many candidates running close races in the upcoming election. To be very honest, I am having a difficult time deciding whom to vote for. I know that I only have two weeks before I must cast my vote. There is much reading I have to do before then. After all, to make the very best decision, I must be well-informed about the candidates. But there are so many of the issues that confuse me. I cannot decide to vote for a certain candidate only by listening to the ads. I also need to read about the very most important issues in the voter's pamphlet. Personally, I will be very pleased when the election is over.

_____

_____

_____

_____

_____

_____
_____
_____
_____
_____
_____
_____
_____
_____

JOURNAL PROMPT

Are you a registered voter? If not, why not? If you are, are you registered with a specific party? Which one? Do you have strong political convictions? Which issues are the most important to you? For example, do you have a stand on abortion, capital punishment, gay rights, welfare, taxes, etc.? Elaborate on one of your convictions. Have you ever considered running for a public office? Explain.

THE READING CONNECTION

In your own reading, look for adverbs at work:

1. As you read a chapter from a textbook that you may have been assigned in one of your other classes, pay careful attention to the author's use of **transitions**. From your reading, make your own list of transition words and compare it to the list of adverb transitions discussed in this chapter. Tally how many times the author uses each transition word in the chapter you are reading. Bring your findings to class.

2. Read an article in a magazine, newspaper, or other publication. Pay close attention to adverbs including transition words. Experiment with substituting different adverbs or transitions with similar meanings for the ones the author has chosen. Reread the article with your own substitutions. How do your different word choices affect the overall impact of the piece of writing?

3. Read several pages from a book of your own choosing. Underline any adverbs you find. Draw arrows to other locations in the same sentence where the writer could have placed the same adverb. Bring your marked pages to class and discuss why you think the writer placed the adverbs where he or she placed them. Discuss how moving the adverbs around affects emphasis. If you prefer some of your own arrangements to the writer's original arrangement, be prepared to explain why.

THE WRITING CONNECTION

1. Write a narrative about an experience that taught you a lesson. When telling the story, pay special attention to your use of transitions. Underline any transitional adverbs you use in this narrative.

2. Write a set of instructions for others to follow in case they might sometime have to take over one of your chores or a task you frequently perform. For example, explain to someone how to do your laundry the way you would do it; or tell someone how to do an aspect of your job; or explain to someone how to complete one of your homework assignments like writing a speech, or preparing for a science lab. After writing your instructions, read them over and insert transition words where they could help your reader understand the sequencing of the steps involved in the process.

3. Write a physical description of an interesting cover of a book or magazine. Organize your description spatially: start at one corner of the cover and move around in a clockwise direction, or start in the middle and move out to the edges, etc. To help your reader follow the direction of your description, insert words and expressions that indicate location or spatial relationships. Circle any transition words that are adverbs.

4. Compare and contrast two people who have played significant roles in your life. Use transition words to point out specific areas of similarities and differences. Circle any adverbs you use in your writing—either for description or transition.

5. Go back over some of your journal entries from this chapter and from previous chapters. Check your entries for the use of adverbs, especially transition words. Experiment with moving some of your adverbs around. Insert transition words where they will enhance the coherence of your communication. Rewrite one or two of your entries to reflect these changes. Compare your rewritten entry to your original.

SELF TEST FOR CHAPTER 9

1. Adverbs describe or modify _____, _____, and

   _____.

2. In addition to being placed next to a verb, an adverb describing a verb can

   usually be placed at the _____ or _____ of a sentence.

3. The *meaning* of a sentence may not be affected if an adverb is moved, but the

   _____ may change.

4. Adverbs answer the questions _____, _____, or

   _____; adjectives answer the questions _____,

   _____, or _____.

5. Adding the ending "-LY" to an adjective usually results in a(n)

   _____; adding the ending "-LY" to a noun usually results in a(n)

   _____.

6. Adverbs sometimes interrupt the _____ phrases they modify.

7. Adverbs that describe verbs usually *cannot/can* (circle one) be moved around

   in a sentence. Adverbs that describe adjectives and other adverbs usually *cannot/can* (circle one) be moved around in a sentence.

8.   Transition words help a writer create _____ in a piece of writing.

9.   Since the word _____ can be both an adjective and an adverb, writers must be careful where they place it in sentences to avoid ambiguity.

10. When writers place the word _____ at the beginning of a sentence, they may be wasting a valuable sentence slot on a word that is virtually meaningless.

FINAL JOURNAL WRITING

What have you learned from this chapter that you can apply to your writing? What do you feel is the most important function of an adverb? Why? What adverb concepts are still unclear to you? How has learning about adverbs affected what you notice in your reading?

CHAPTER 10

PREPOSITIONS CREATING PHRASES
THAT POSITION

*The next grammar book I bring out I want to tell how to end a sentence with
five prepositions. A father of a little boy goes upstairs after supper to read to
his son, but he brings the wrong book. The boy says, "What did you bring that book
I don't want to be read to out of up for?"*

—E. B. WHITE

QUESTIONS TO ASK YOURSELF WHILE READING CHAPTER 10:

1. How do prepositions affect the way I see my world?
2. How can learning about prepositions make me more tolerant of people from other cultures?
3. What is a phrase?
4. Why should I be careful about where I place prepositional phrases?
5. How could prepositional phrases cause me to make mistakes in subject-verb agreement?
6. How can prepositional phrases help me create transitions in writing?
7. How can I streamline sentences that contain too many prepositional phrases?

 PREPOSITION PROPOSITION

*Would you consider it an imposition?
Would it adversely affect your disposition?
Or could I safely make the supposition
that I would not be met with opposition
if I offered you this proposition:
let's learn about the PREPOSITION . . .*

The root *position* appears in many English words. In this chapter, you will learn why
it appears in a word that is an important worker in your writing: the PREPOSITION.

Chapter 10   Prepositions Creating Phrases that Position

What do you already know about prepositions? For example, how would you define a preposition? Can you think of any examples of prepositions? Write what you know about prepositions:

_____

_____

_____

_____

_____

Did you come up with any of these responses:

- A preposition is a word like "on, at, by, with, for. . . ."
- A preposition is a "little word."
- A preposition is any word that can be followed by "the house" (*under* the house, *at* the house, *in* the house).
- A preposition is anything a squirrel can do to a tree; a squirrel can run "*around* the tree, *by* the tree, *into* the tree."
- A preposition is anything a rabbit can do to a log; a rabbit can jump "*over* the log, *alongside* the log, *on* the log."

Or were you able to recite from memory a list of over forty prepositions in alphabetical order? Some students have learned prepositions through rote memory.

USING THE TRADITIONAL APPROACH

I have no doubt that referring to the following list of prepositions will help you find prepositions in a piece of writing:

Commonly Used Prepositions

aboard	behind	in	regarding
about	below	inside	round
above	beneath	into	through
across	beside	like	throughout
after	between	near	to
against	beyond	of	toward
along	by	off	under
alongside	concerning	on	underneath
amid	despite	onto	until
among	down	out	up
around	during	outside	upon
at	for	over	with
before	from	since	within
			without

But how well does the preposition list actually fit our common perceptions of prepositions?

- For example, prepositions are "little" words. But how about *throughout, regarding*, and *concerning*? They are not little words, but they are prepositions. And where are the "little" words *a, an,* and *the*? They don't appear on the list because they are **not** prepositions.
- Can every word on the preposition list be followed by *"the house"*? We often say *"in* the house" and *"at* the house"; but when was the last time you said *"during* the house"? Would you have been able to identify "during" as a prepositions if you were using "the house" gimmick?
- The same applies to *"the squirrel and the tree"* or *"the rabbit and the log."* Can a squirrel run *during* the tree or a rabbit jump *during* the log?

If gimmicks are so unreliable, maybe *the memory method* is the best approach after all. But if your memory is like mine, it may be unreliable, too. So, referring to a list of prepositions might be the easiest way to identify prepositions, after all.

DO IT YOURSELF!   *Use the List Approach*

Directions

By referring to the list of Commonly Used Prepositions on page 245, identify the words you think are prepositions and circle them.

In today's American culture, adult children often move back to the family home. What are some typical reasons children return to the nest? Sometimes the reasons are emotional. An adult child will return home after a painful divorce. Such a situation often means grandchildren are brought into the grandparents' home to live. Sometimes the reasons adult children return are financial. They may move home if they are unemployed. Moving home may be a lifesaver for someone who is looking for work. Parents as well as children may benefit especially if parents enjoy having younger people in the household or need help with work around the house. In other words, when adult children return home, the experience can be positive. But to ensure that such an event turns into a positive experience, everyone involved, children and parents alike, should understand that the living arrangement is not permanent and that the adult child is expected to work towards emotional health and financial independence. Psychologists and family counselors recommend that this should be agreed upon before anyone moves in.

Count the number of words you circled. I found 13 prepositions in this selection. Did you find as many as six more?

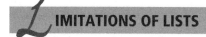

IMITATIONS OF LISTS

Did you know that the word *TO* in the fourth sentence (in *"to* live") is not a preposition? Likewise the *TO* in *"to* ensure" and the *TO* in *"to* work" (in the tenth sentence) are also not prepositions. Neither are "upon," "before," and "in" which occur in the last sentence.

How could that be? These words *are* on the preposition list!

But the list of prepositions only tells us which words are capable of being prepositions in sentences. That does **not** mean every word on the list will **always** be working as a preposition every time it appears in a sentence. Over and over, in our study of English sentences, we have seen the same word playing different roles as its location in a sentence changes and its relationship to nearby words changes. The same is true of prepositions. Compare the word *TO* used in the following sentence excerpts:

> *. . . return <u>to the family home</u>*
> *. . . return <u>to the nest</u>*

In both cases, <u>TO</u> shows **direction:** and it is followed by a <u>noun</u> *(<u>home</u>, <u>nest</u>)*, not a <u>verb</u>. But look at these uses of <u>TO</u>:

> *. . . <u>to live</u>*
> *. . . <u>to ensure</u> that such an event is a positive experience*
> *. . . the adult child is expected <u>to work</u>*

Here the word *TO* does not indicate direction or position; and it is followed by a VERB *(live, ensure, work)*, not a NOUN.

Of course, I don't expect you to understand the significance of prepositions being followed by nouns until you understand the role prepositions play in writing—what they accomplish in sentences and how they relate to neighboring words. That means learning about prepositions will require more than just looking at a list.

HE DEFINITION OF A PREPOSITION

Prepositions are exactly what their name implies. They are "positioners." They position things. In fact, they position people, places, and things. That means prepositions position nouns and pronouns. In the sentence, *"The baby is playing in the crib,"* the word "in" is a preposition because it positions the noun "crib" in relationship to the rest of the sentence: The baby was playing *"in* the crib." The preposition occurs "pre" or "in front of" the noun or pronoun it positions into the bigger sentence.

DO IT YOURSELF!   *Find the "Positioners"*

Directions

In the following paragraph, circle the words that are positioning. Use your list of prepositions to help you narrow down your choices.

As I walked into the room, I immediately noticed the open closet door on the wall to my left. Inside the closet hung a bright blue baseball cap. It hung above a soiled, gray duffel bag. By the bag on the floor of the closet, lay a catcher's mitt. The mitt would fit a left-handed catcher. As I turned my attention from the closet, I noticed an unmade single bed against the far opposite wall. On the bedspread was imprinted the name "Yankees" and the official Yankee emblem. A lamp shaped like a baseball bat rested on the nightstand by the bed. Above the desk across the room from the bed were three shiny trophies. As I turned and walked out of the room, I stumbled over a pair of muddy sneakers.

JOURNAL PROMPT

What does your room or where you live tell about you? Explain using descriptive details.

PREPOSITIONS ALWAYS SAY IT IN A PHRASE

Now that you have found the prepositions in the above paragraph, look carefully at the words that come *after* each preposition. In the first sentence, for example, "the room" comes after the preposition "into": *into the room*. The phrase *"into the room"* is called a PREPOSITIONAL PHRASE. **A prepositional phrase always begins with a preposition and ends with a noun or pronoun, which is called the object of the preposition.**

It makes sense that prepositions occur in phrases rather than alone. Since their function is to position nouns or pronouns, prepositions naturally appear in sentences together with the nouns and pronouns they position. There is no such thing as a *lonely* preposition; prepositions always have nouns to precede.

DO IT YOURSELF! *Become Better Acquainted with the Not-So-Lonely Prepositions*

Directions

A. *In the following paragraph, the prepositional phrases have been enclosed in brackets. Study the paragraph carefully and answer the questions that follow it:*

Everybody cheats. [In school] students cheat [on their homework]. They copy [off classmates' papers] and turn the assignments in [to the teacher] [with their own names] [on them]. [During tests], some cheating students bring tiny sheets [of paper] [with answers] written [on them]. Others sit [near their friends] who know the answers and copy [off their test papers]. Customers cheat [in stores]; they change price tags [on merchandise] so they pay less. Employees cheat [at work]; they take several breaks [in the place] [of one]. Taxpayers cheat [on their income taxes]. Is cheating just a part [of the American culture] or is it a human trait?

Questions:

1. List the <u>first</u> word in each phrase:

    _____

    _____

    _____

2. What kind of words are these words?

    _____

3. List the <u>last</u> word in each phrase:

    _____

    _____

    _____

4. What kinds of words are these words? (What parts of speech?)

    _____

    _____

5. Fill in the following definition for a prepositional phrase:

    A prepositional phrase begins with a _____ and ends with a

    _____ or _____.

B. Read the following paragraph in which you circled prepositions in the previous DO IT YOURSELF! This time underline all the <u>prepositional phrases</u>. Remember, each phrase will begin with a preposition and end with a noun or pronoun—the OBJECT OF THE PREPO-SITION.

As I walked into the room, I immediately noticed the open closet door on the wall to my left. Inside the closet hung a bright blue baseball cap. It hung above a soiled gray duffel bag. By the bag on the floor of the closet, lay a catcher's mitt. The mitt would fit a left-handed catcher. As I turned my attention from the closet, I noticed an unmade single bed against the far opposite wall. On the bedspread was imprinted the name "Yankees" and the official Yankee emblem. A lamp shaped like a baseball bat rested on the nightstand by the bed. Above the desk across the room from the bed were three shiny trophies. As I turned and walked out of the room, I stumbled over a pair of muddy sneakers.

C. In the following paragraph, the prepositions are followed by spaces. Create your own prepositional phrases by supplying your own noun or pronoun objects of prepositions and writing them in the spaces provided:

Yesterday I went on _____. I noticed a woman in _____. She smiled at _____ and waved at _____. I stopped at _____ and started a conversation with _____. We both sat down on _____ and looked at _____ and talked about _____. She had a tattoo on _____. I commented on _____. She responded to _____ with _____. I thought about _____ and asked her for _____. She said she would think about _____. I got up and walked towards _____. When I looked back at _____, the woman was gone.

JOURNAL PROMPT

Do you agree with the statement that everyone cheats? Why? Do you ever cheat? In which life situations do you cheat? If so, what goes through your mind as you are cheating?

$\mathcal{S}$OME VERY <u>SPATIAL</u> PREPOSITIONS

By reading the above paragraph about the room, you can see that prepositions position things in **space:** *into* the room, *by* the bag, *on* the floor, etc. Spatial positioning is the kind of preposition use that is suggested when someone tells you a preposition is anything that can be followed by "the house." The following prepositions position nouns in **space:**

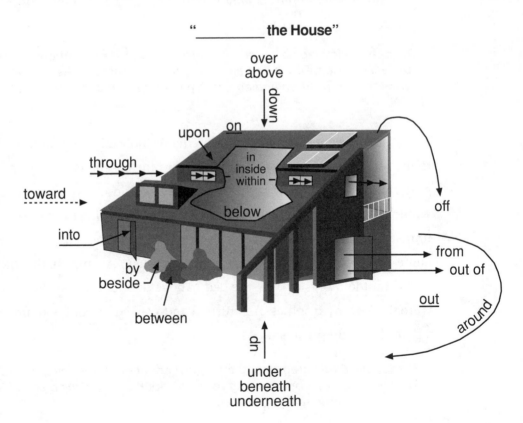

SOME VERY <u>TIMELY</u> PREPOSITIONS

Yet, prepositions can do more than position nouns and pronouns in space. Prepositions can also position nouns and pronouns in **time**. After all, a noun "thing" can be an event; and events can be characterized by time. For example, the noun "lunch," which is an event, may be positioned into a sentence in this way:

I have class <u>before lunch</u>.

The preposition *before* positions "lunch" in relationship to "class." I could just as easily say that I have class *"after* lunch" or *"during* lunch." Such prepositions position things in **time**.

COLLABORATE!   *Tell Time with Prepositions*

Directions

Together with a group or on your own, decide <u>which</u> prepositional phrases in the following paragraph indicate TIME relationships. Circle each "timely" preposition and underline the entire prepositional phrase it introduces.

Jorge and I became engaged at the end of August just before my twenty-third birthday. Two weeks later, he went away to college. His classes began on the day after Labor Day. We corresponded back and forth for three months. We talked on the phone on Sundays when the rates were cheaper. Throughout the semester, I spent hours thinking about Jorge. I could hardly wait until winter break when I would see him again. Finally, on December 15, I drove to the airport. Jorge's flight was due at 10 pm. I was there when he stepped off the plane. For three months I had awaited this day, and now he finally was home.

JOURNAL PROMPT

Write about a relationship with a friend, family member, or other loved one in which you experienced a lengthy separation. What did you do to stay connected during the separation? What were the circumstances that caused the separation? Describe the reunion. What changes took place during the separation?

SO WHAT'S THE GIMMICK?

Prepositions that communicate *time* relationships cannot be followed comfortably by "the house." Since a house is a place, it can be positioned in space but not in time. Therefore, "during the house" doesn't make much sense. If you want a gimmick for finding prepositions, "the circus" will work much better than "the house." You can say *in* the circus (space relationship); you can also say *during* the circus (time relationship). After all, a circus is not only a *place* (which can be positioned in a *space*) but, like "lunch," it is an *event* (which occurs at a certain *time*).

Reread the list of commonly used prepositions at the beginning of this chapter. Would each one make sense followed by "the circus"? Did you answer **yes?** That means we've just discovered our own new gimmick . . . based on our understanding of how prepositions work in sentences, of course!

WHAT DID E. B. WHITE MEAN?

What about prepositions occurring at the end of a sentence (see the quotation at the beginning of this chapter)? Can that really happen if prepositions are always positioning something that follows them? You will see words that look like prepositions placed at the ends of sentences. Sometimes, however, they are just preposition-looking adverbs: The doctor is *in*. (In is acting as an adverb telling *where* the doctor is.) Other times prepositions at the ends of sentences have objects that are located elsewhere in the sentence. These arrangements usually occur in idiomatic—or peculiar and unusual—expressions that have become popular in English. There is nothing wrong with such occasional placements; it is just one of the surprises that we speakers and writers of English have made a part of everyday usage.

Yet many students who come to my classes have been admonished *never* to end a sentence with a preposition—even though for decades respected grammarians have condoned the practice. This same controversy is what prompted Sir Winston Churchill to make his now famous tongue-in-cheek remark: *Ending a sentence with a preposition is something up with which I will not put.* How would you rewrite that remark to make it sound more natural?

Looking at the World through Preposition-Colored Glasses

Since prepositions position things in space and time, prepositions naturally affect how we see our world. How would you describe what the child in the picture on the following page is doing with his pencil?

One answer could be:

The child is holding the pencil <u>in his hand</u>.

But what do you think of this answer?

The child is holding his fingers <u>around the pencil</u>.

"Fingers <u>around a pencil</u>" does not sound as natural to native English speakers as "pencil in his hand." From the time children start school, they are instructed to hold pencils *"in their hands"* a certain way in order to write. And from that time on, they see themselves as holding pencils *"<u>in</u> their hands"* rather than as holding their fingers *"**around** their pencils".*

Here is another example. Which do you say?

The tree is <u>in the forest</u>.

OR

The forest is <u>around the tree</u>.??

Has the English language trained you to see the tree "in the forest" and not the forest "around the tree"? Does the way prepositions are used affect **your** perceptions of the world around you?

PREPOSITIONS WITH CULTURAL DIFFERENCES

Not all languages perceive relationships and positions the same way we do in English. For that reason, prepositions are difficult to translate. You may already have discovered that if you have ever studied a foreign language. For example, my friend Inge comes from Germany. Whenever she comes to visit and finds my front door unlocked, she lets herself in without knocking.

She usually hollers out, "Kris, your door was unlocked, so I just walked **into** the door."

I correct her, "Inge, you *didn't* walk *into* the door."

She says, "I didn't?"

"No." I respond, "You walked *through* the door."

And her amazed response is, "I did?"

Of course she's amazed. I just told her she walks through doors! (She thought only ghosts did that!!) Who has lost touch with reality here? I don't think it's my German-speaking friend, Inge.

Many other prepositional phrases, too, make people who are just learning English feel quite uncomfortable. For example, as a teenager I lived in a town called Lake Oswego; the community was built around a lake. One year, Cordula, an exchange student from Austria attended Lake Oswego High School. On her first day of school, my friends and I flocked around her; we quizzed her about her host family and where she was staying.

Her response was, "I am staying with a very nice family. They live *with* the lake."

We all giggled as we corrected her: her family lived "*on* the lake," not "*with* the lake"! Cordula was puzzled as she looked at her feet to confirm that they were not wet from walking out of the house that was positioned "*on* the lake."

Since we live in a global society where our future as students and workers will bring us in close contact with people from other cultures, realizing the ethnic uniqueness of prepositions is important. Otherwise, prepositions can easily cause cross-cultural misunderstandings. Picture this foreign visitor: a young man, Alex, who has studied English but has never been to the United States. He buys an airline ticket and sets out on his once-in-a-lifetime trip. His first stop is JFK airport, an overwhelming first impression. After a four-hour layover, Alex is finally in line to board the connecting flight. As he hands over the ticket he has been clutching in his hand for the last four hours, a smiling flight attendant tells him to get "*on* the plane." Alex's heart beats faster as he tries to picture how anyone could ride "*on* a plane." "Do you suppose Americans tie passengers to the wings? After all, I wasn't told to get *into* the plane." A simple prepositional phrase could frighten this foreign visitor enough to send him running the other way to catch a bus instead. But at the bus terminal, Alex will also be told to get "*on* the bus" rather than "*into* the bus." What a nightmare!

In our American culture, we teach our own children idiomatic meanings for certain prepositions. We warn, "Johnnie don't play *in* the street." What does that phrase mean? Is there a hole "*in* the street"—a hole Johnnie might fall *into*? Or do we fear a steamroller will pass by, roll over Johnnie, and embed his image "*in* the street"? Probably not. But then why do we holler at Johnnie to "Get *out of the street*" when we want him to come home?? Interestingly enough, years later, when Johnnie becomes a teenager, the prepositions will change. Then we'll tell him that we don't want him "***on*** the street" and to stay "*off* the street." No wonder foreign speakers have difficulty learning how to use our prepositions. It takes many years of living around English speakers to adjust to seeing the world through the unique prepositional lenses of the English language.

COLLABORATE!   *Fill in the Puzzling Prepositions*

Directions

All the answers to the following crossword puzzle are prepositions. Read each clue carefully and consider which preposition best fits into the puzzle. Refer to the list of commonly used prepositions on page 245, if necessary.

Across

1. Francis leaned _____ the left.

4. The groom stood _____ the bride during the wedding ceremony.

5. Children learn best _____ example.

6. _____ all the confusion, his voice could not be heard.

9. Terry's ideas are different _____ Debbie's ideas.

10. Have you ever read a book _____ dieting?

11. The student skipped _____ the difficult problems and did the easy ones first.

12. _____ my word, I promise not to tell your secret.

13. Do not shoot at the opossum until you are _____ range.

16. Sean always does well _____ math.

18. Bill read the instructions _____ operating the fire extinguisher.

19. Aaron has not called Jennifer _____ last Friday.

23. Sara knew nothing _____ the lost watch.

24. The policeman drove _____ the block.

25. Have you heard _____ the dancing bear?

26. You and I will divide the pie _____ us.

27. Janice Simms lives _____ the street from the college.

28. Jeremy and Justin never agree _____ any point.

29. We stopped at the new restaurant _____ the road.

31. The resort stayed open all _____ the year.

34. Joanie was happy when her husband walked _____ the doorway.

Down

2. _____ work, Maxine went to the health club.

3. The ground _____ the oak tree was covered with acorns.

5. Anyone with a score _____ fifty percent must retake the test.

6. Let us divide the money _____ the three of us.

7. _____ the movie the children ate popcorn.

8. Grandma walked _____ the stairs to the basement.

12. Citizens _____ the age of eighteen cannot vote.

14. The boy seemed uncomfortable _____ the entire discussion.

15. Since the weather was stormy, the family stayed _____ the house all day.

17. The passengers played shuffleboard _____ the ship.

20. Since James lives _____ the school, he walks home.

21. The supporters stood _____ their candidate with financial help.

22. Susan sat inside and listened to the rain beat _____ the window.

25. Stand _____ the scales quietly as the nurse weighs you.

26. _____ breakfast, Nancy likes to read the paper.

30. Don't be afraid to walk _____ a classroom full of strangers.

32. The outdoor enthusiast climbed _____ the mountainside.

33. Please wait _____ the corner of Fifth Street and Main Street.

Did some of the prepositions not sound quite right to you? If so, why do you think that is?

YOU MAY HAVE NO USE FOR ABSTRACT ART, BUT YOU CAN'T GET THROUGH LIFE WITHOUT ABSTRACT PREPOSITIONS . . .

So far we have learned that prepositions position nouns in space and time. But prepositions also position things **abstractly**; that is, they create abstract relationships in sentences. You may recall the term "abstract" from Chapter 6 in which *abstract nouns* were defined as something you could not physically touch or see. *Abstract relationships expressed by prepositions also are not physical.*

For example, the relationship of an author to his or her book is abstract. In English we express this relationship by saying, "The book is *by* the author." Here the preposition *BY* is being used abstractly to mean that the author wrote the book.

Therefore, I would say to a class full of students, "Go to the book store and pick up a book *by Charles Dickens.*"

But if my students interpret the preposition *BY* as **concrete** instead of **abstract,** they would think of a spatial relationship like "beside" or "next to."

In that case, they would return from the bookstore saying, "We didn't find Charles Dickens, so how could we pick up anything **by** him?" (. . . meaning next to him.)

But, remember, the word *BY* is abstract in the expression, "a book by Charles Dickens." It does not mean "next to"; it simply means Charles Dickens wrote the book!

Because abstract relationships are just that, **abstract**, the prepositions used to express these relationships often cause more confusion than the prepositions used to express the more concrete relationships of space and time.

And, as you might expect, abstract preposition uses are even more problematic for non-native speakers. As a Norwegian, I would say the book is **"off** (av) Charles Dickens." You see, Norwegians use the preposition for "off" to express the relationship between a book and its author. If I were speaking German, I would say the book is **"from** *(von)* Charles Dickens." And, if I were speaking Spanish, I would say the book is **"of** *(de)* Charles Dickens." It just happens, however, that the English language has chosen **by** to express this abstract relationship.

COLLABORATE!   *Making Difficult Preposition Choices (Some Abstract and Some Not)*

Directions

Even though you may have been an English speaker all your life, you may not be aware of all the preposition choices the English language prefers.

A. *Circle the preposition you would choose to use in each sentence:*

1. He went <u>in/into</u> the house.

2. I had never heard <u>about/of</u> him.

3. I had never heard <u>of/about</u> his famous rescue.

4. The ground was covered <u>by/with</u> snow.

5. He was bored <u>of/by</u> watching the movies.

6. All the attention was centered <u>around/on</u> the winning team.

7. Cruise ships are different <u>than/from</u> freighters.

8. I did that <u>on/by</u> accident.

9. The debate was <u>between/among</u> John and Harry.

10. The problem that occurred <u>between/among</u> the three students was discussed in the dean's office.

B. *How do your answers compare to these answers?*

1. into 2. of 3. about 4. with 5. by 6. on 7. from 8. by 9. between 10. among (<u>between</u> is used with two separate entities; among is with three or more)

- Look carefully at the ones you missed. Can you see any rationale that might be determining the language's choice of that particular preposition?
- Discuss your answers with your classmates and/or your teacher.
- A dictionary or an English handbook may be a useful resource for exploring preposition use further.

If the above exercise was difficult for you, you may have experienced in a small way the frustration second-language speakers feel when using prepositions.

PHRASE: MORE THAN JUST A GROUP OF WORDS

The term PHRASE becomes important as you grow in your understanding of sentences. What does *phrase* suggest to you—a group of words, perhaps? **A phrase is two or more words in a sentence.** But could a phrase be just *any* group of words? Read the following sentence and consider the questions:

Before the game, the lady in uniform will sing the national anthem.

1. Do you think the words "the lady in," which occur together, constitute a phrase?
2. Are the words "will sing" a phrase?
3. Is "in uniform" a phrase?
4. Do the three words "game, the lady" constitute a phrase?
5. Do you think "before the game" is a phrase?

I believe you probably answered these questions the same as I did: **1.** no **2.** yes **3.** yes **4.** no **5.** yes

But *why* did you answer the way you did?

_____

_____

A phrase is more than just any group of words in a given sentence. **A phrase is a word group that functions as a unit to do the job of one part of speech.** The parts of speech we have studied in this book are *verbs, nouns, adjectives,* and *adverbs.* In the above sentence, the phrase "will sing," for example, functions as the *verb.* But what kind of words do the prepositional phrases "in uniform" and "before the game" function as? If they truly are *phrases,* they, too, must each act as one part of speech.

Typically, prepositional phrases act as *modifiers* in sentences. That means they act either as *adjectives* or *adverbs.*

Let's explore how that works by comparing these two sentences:

Tonight the uniformed lady will sing the national anthem.

("Tonight" is an adverb telling *when;* "uniformed" is an adjective describing the noun "lady".)

Before the game, the lady in the uniform will sing the national anthem.

("Before the game" is an adverb prepositional phrase telling *when;* "in the uniform" is an adjective prepositional phrase describing the noun "lady".)

LET'S RUN THROUGH THAT ONE MORE TIME . . . SLOWLY

In the first sentence, the word "uniformed" modifies or describes the noun "lady." Therefore, "uniformed" is an ADJECTIVE. Like all adjectives it is stuck in position next to the word it describes. (Try to move it and you will end up with a "*uniformed* national anthem." Even I can't make sense of that one.)

In the second sentence, the same lady is described with a phrase: "the lady *in the uniform.*" These two words together do the same job as the single-word adjective "uniformed." Therefore, *"in the uniform"* is an ADJECTIVE prepositional phrase in this sentence. And being an adjective, it, too, is stuck in position next to the noun it describes. (Unless, of course, you can imagine "the national anthem in the uniform.") Note: an adjective phrase usually occurs immediately *after* the noun it describes while a single-word adjective usually occurs *before* the noun.

Now, focus your attention on the word "tonight." "Tonight" tells *when* the singing will take place; therefore, "tonight" is an adverb. Since adverbs can move around, this sentence could be written at least three ways:

Tonight the uniformed lady will sing the national anthem.

OR

The uniformed lady tonight will sing the national anthem.

OR

> *The uniformed lady will sing the national anthem <u>tonight</u>.*

Moving the *adverb* does not change the meaning of the sentence, but it does change the rhythm and the emphasis.

When the prepositional phrase "before the game" replaces "tonight," it also tells *when* the singing will take place. That means, this prepositional phrase is functioning as an ADVERB. It can also move just like a single-word adverb:

> <u>*Before the game*</u> *the uniformed lady will sing the national anthem.*

OR

> *The uniformed lady, <u>before the game</u>, will sing the national anthem.*

OR

> *The uniformed lady will sing the national anthem <u>before the game</u>.*

Moving the *adverb prepositional phrase* does not change the meaning of the sentence, but it does change the rhythm and the emphasis.

The conclusion is that **prepositional phrases act as modifiers in sentences: A prepositional phrase may function either as a single ADJECTIVE or a single ADVERB.**

To imagine a group of words acting as one kind of word is sometimes difficult for my students. They look at a phrase and question, "How can all those different words in "before the game" make one adverb? After all, *before* is a preposition; *the* is an adjective; and *game* is a noun object of a preposition. How do these three different words add up to one ADVERB?

I always answer by telling this story:

The Chocolate Cake Story

Pretend, it is the end of the month. As usual, there is not much left in the house to eat. Thank goodness my pay check comes tomorrow! I come home from a date feeling particularly hungry. So I look in the refrigerator. There I find two eggs and approximately one cup of milk left in the milk carton.

"Hmm," I say, "I think I'll boil some eggs and pour myself a cup of milk and call it breakfast."

So I open the cupboard where the pans are stored; and, as I pull out my pan for boiling eggs, I see a bottle of cooking oil with about two teaspoons of oil left at the bottom.

"Ha!" I exclaim, "I can have fried eggs for breakfast instead. That's a little tastier than boiled eggs."

I reach for the frying pan which is stored farther back in the same cupboard. As I pull out my skillet, I see the outline of a box pushed far into the recesses of the cupboard. With a little extra effort, I reach deep into the cupboard and pull out the box.

"It's a box of cake mix—chocolate cake, my favorite!!"

As I read the instructions on the box, I can't believe my good fortune: "Add two eggs, two teaspoons of oil, and one cup of milk. Stir the ingredients together until smooth and bake at 350 degrees."

Suddenly, I'm not having breakfast after all. Instead I'm going to have myself a birthday party, complete with cake! Of course, it isn't really my birthday. (I'm pretending about that too.)

My questions to you are these: once I bake my cake,
do I still have the eggs? _____
do I still have the milk? _____
do I still have the oil? _____

If you look carefully at the cholesterol content, the fat content, and the number of calories listed for the finished cake, you will discover that the eggs, oil, and milk have not disappeared. They are still very much there. But because the eggs are in the cake, I can no longer fry them as eggs and use them for breakfast; because the oil is in the cake, I can no longer use it to coat the pan; and because the milk is in the cake, I can no longer use it as a drink. Once baked in the cake, these foods will no longer function individually to do what they normally do. Instead, I have one new food with its own function—a cake that functions as dessert. And how did I create this food with this new function? Not by adding up a bunch of desserts. Eggs, and oil, and milk are not desserts. No, I added several different foods together to come up with one new food I could use in a new way.

Creating a prepositional phrase is like baking a cake. Here's the recipe for an adverb prepositional phrase:

Ingredients:
One preposition that shows relationships
One adjective that describes (optional)
One noun that names
Mix the above ingredients together until they read smoothly; and, PRESTO, you
    have created a phrase you can use as an adverb!
(The same recipe can be used to make adjective prepositional phrases too.)
Your original preposition, adjective, and noun are all still in the sentence. You just cannot use them in their traditional ways any more because you have chosen to bake them into your prepositional phrase cake to create the adverb you desire.

COLLABORATE!   *Which Flavor is the Prepositional Cake: Adverb or Adjective?*

Directions

Work with a group or on your own. In the following sentences the prepositional phrases are underlined. In the space provided, write whether each prepositional phrase is an ADJECTIVE or an ADVERB.

HINT: The easiest way to decide this is to determine which word in the sentence each phrase is describing:

If the prepositional phrase is describing a noun or pronoun, it is an <u>adjective phrase</u>.

If the prepositional phrase is describing a verb, or an adjective, or an adverb, it is an <u>adverb phrase</u>.

1. Frank's pressed clothes hung in the closet. _____

2. Today he dressed in a hurry. _____

3. Frank left home early in the morning. _____

4. After lunch he would attend an important meeting. _____

5. His promotion was the subject of the meeting. _____

6. I saw Frank with his briefcase as he entered the room. _____

7. One of the company managers followed him. _____

8. She closed the door to the conference room. _____

9. An hour later, Frank and the manager emerged from the conference room. _____

10. Frank smiled at me and winked and nodded. _____

Did you find four adjective phrases and six adverb phrases?

WRITE RIGHT FOR THE JOB: Prepositional Phrases Can't Hang Out Just Anywhere

Throughout this text, I have repeatedly emphasized that adjectives must be placed next to the nouns they describe. This is also true of adjective phrases. However, writers are often more careless about the placement of adjective prepositional phrases than of single-word adjectives. The result is often humorous and always misleading. A misplaced adjective phrase may create either

- a sentence with two possible meanings—an ambiguous sentence; or
- a sentence that clearly says something entirely different from what the writer intended.

In fact, both adjective and adverb prepositional phrases must be placed carefully to communicate clearly what the writer intends. Sometimes careless placement may actually cause a phrase intended to be an adjective to end up functioning as an adverb!

COLLABORATE! *Making Phrases Say What You Want Them to Say*

Directions

The following are actual sentences I have come across in my work with college and workplace writing. Work with a group or on your own

A. *Read each sentence—ALOUD.*

B. *Decide what you think the writer really intended to say.*

C. *Rewrite each sentence by moving the prepositional phrase to a location where it communicates more clearly. Some sentences may need to be completely rewritten or made into two sentences.*

1. Mr. Smith paid for the house with his wife Dorothy.

Rewrite: _____

_____

2. The president made the decision to fill the drainage ditch with his partners.

Rewrite: _____

_____

3. The legislation was designed to increase the production of cotton in the eyes of Congress.

Rewrite: _____

_____

4. In response to your questionnaire I have recently given birth to a male child in the enclosed envelope.

Rewrite: _____

_____

5. I removed the blouse for my favorite customer from the rack.

Rewrite: _____

_____

6. The man tripped over a wastebasket in a hurry.

Rewrite: _____

_____

7. Pushing on the gas pedal caused him to crash through the brick wall with his left foot.

Rewrite: _____

_____

8. Mike could now clearly see the woman on the bicycle with his new glasses.

Rewrite: _____

_____

9. Marilyn modeled the new pants she had bought with a seductive walk.

Rewrite: _____

_____

10. The man scratching his head with the big nose shrugged his shoulders.

Rewrite: _____

_____

_____

 HEN PREPOSITIONAL PHRASES KEEP SUBJECTS FROM AGREEING WITH VERBS

A prepositional phrase that immediately follows the subject of a sentence may interfere with your ability to select the correct form of the verb. Compare these two sentences:

> *One of the people <u>were waiting</u> for the northbound train.*
> *One of the people <u>was waiting</u> for the northbound train.*

Which sentence do you think is correct? Why?

If you picked the first sentence, you may have done so thinking that "people *were* waiting" sounded more correct than "people *was* waiting." The first sentence is not correct, however, because the subject of the sentence is "one"—**not** "people." After all, who was waiting for the northbound train? Only *one* was waiting for that train, not all the people. Therefore, the correct sentence is

> <u>One</u> of the people <u>was waiting</u> for the northbound train.

The subject of the sentence ("One") is singular, and the object of the preposition (people) is plural. Since a plural noun is located right next to a plural verb, the sentence actually "sounds" quite right even though it isn't. Remember, *verbs agree with subjects of sentences—not with objects of prepositions.*

DO IT YOURSELF!   *Spot the Interference*

Directions

Some of the following sentences are correct as written, but many are not.

A. To determine the correct form of the verb, first locate the prepositional phrase that separates the subject from the verb. Draw a line through the entire prepositional phrase.

B. Read the sentence without the prepositional phrase and change the verb if necessary.

(The first one is done for you as an example)

1. Each of the students have finished yesterday's assignment.

Each of the students has finished yesterday's assignment.

2. One of my friends live in Oak Knoll.

3. The members of the committee meets weekly at the capitol building.

4. The parents of the child was blamed for creating the problem.

5. Everyone of the boys were present.

6. Each one of the cats have been spayed.

7. Each of the children is present for the ceremony.

8. All of my friends are here for my birthday.

9. Only one of the boys are a licensed driver.

10. Mary and Jane from my class is absent.

Did you find two sentences that did not need to be changed?

(Note: Everyone is singular just like "one" because it refers to every person *one* at a time."

ADVERB PREPOSITIONAL PHRASES HELP CREATE SENTENCE VARIETY

Adverb prepositional phrases have much more mobility than adjective phrases. These phrases which often communicate time or place may occur next to the verb. But they often are just as effective placed at the beginnings or ends of sentences. Knowing that an adverbial phrase can easily be moved to the beginning of a sentence is a useful bit of information for writers striving for sentence variety. Instead of always starting sentences with subjects, writers can begin sentences with prepositional phrases.

DO IT YOURSELF!   *Shift Your "I's"*

Directions

In the following paragraph from a letter of application, the subject "I" begins every sentence.

A. *Read the sentences carefully and underline the prepositional phrases.*

I graduated from high school in 1964. I attended Portland State College after high school. I studied English there for four years. I graduated with a teaching certificate on June 13, 1968. I landed my first teaching job by the end of the summer. I have enjoyed teaching from the start. I still enjoy it to this day. I hope to make a significant contribution to education before my retirement.

B. *Rewrite each sentence in the above paragraph to begin with a prepositional phrase instead of the subject "I."*

_____

_____

_____

_____

_____

_____

_____

C. *Rewrite the paragraph once more. This time create more variety by beginning some sentences with prepositional phrases and other sentences with the subject "I." You decide how you want to arrange each sentence.*

_____

_____

_____

_____

_____
_____
_____
_____

D. *Which of the above paragraph versions do you like best?* _____
Why? _____
_____
_____

WRITE RIGHT FOR THE JOB: The *Passive* Role of Prepositions

One of the first requests I hear from employers for whom I conduct training is, "Please teach my staff **not** to use passive voice!" **Passive voice** is the opposite of **active voice. Voice** has to do with "direction" in a sentence; therefore, linguists often use arrows to indicate voice.

The most common voice we use in writing is active. An *active voice* sentence looks like this:

The dog bit Mary.

The same sentence expressed in the *passive voice* looks like this:

May was bitten by the dog.

By looking at the arrows I have added, you can see that, in the active voice sentence, the subject is doing the action of the verb: the "dog" does the "biting." The noun "Mary," which follows the verb, gets "bitten," or receives the action of the verb. The sentences we have studied so far in this book have contained these same relationships between nouns and verbs.

In the passive voice sentence, however, the subject "Mary" has the action of the verb done to her: "Mary was bitten." The "dog," who did the biting, enters the sentence this time as the object of the preposition BY. In other words the arrangement of the passive voice sentence is the reverse of the active voice sentence. The direction of the sentence (as marked by the arrows) is opposite.

Compare the above active and passive sentences yourself, and answer the following questions:

1. Which sentence is longer—the active voice sentence or the passive voice

   sentence? _____

2. Does one sentence contain more *information* than the other?

   _____

   _____

3. Why do you think a writer might choose to use the passive voice sentence instead of the active voice sentence?

_____

_____

Though the passive voice sentence contains more words, it does not give the reader more information than the active voice sentence containing fewer words. If people who write on the job are concerned with saving time and words, why would they ever use passive voice sentences at all?

WHEN WRITERS DESIRE A PASSIVE VOICE . . .

There are number of situations in which passive voice may be desirable for on-the-job writing:

1.   Writers choose the passive voice when the receiver of the action is more important than who did it:

The subpoena was served on February 27.

The above passive voice sentence is a better choice than the following active voice sentence:

The subpoena server served the subpoena on February 27.

2.   Writers choose the passive voice when they don't know who did the action, or when they don't want to admit who did the action:

The records were mysteriously destroyed.

Both of the above passive voice sentences are short because they have left something off; they have avoided telling who did the action. This is called a "truncated passive." Truncated comes from the same Latin word that gave us "tree trunk" and it means that an end has been cut off. In a truncated passive, the information behind the verb has been cut off. An example would be, "Mary was bitten." This is a truncated version of "Mary was bitten by the dog." The phrase "by the dog" has simply been cut off.

How does a truncated passive affect the reader? It leaves the reader in the dark! The reader knows what action happened but has no clue about who did it. For this reason the passive voice is especially useful to people in business who want to avoid "liability"—in other words, people who want to avoid being held responsible. When someone simply writes, *"The decision was made,"* no one has to take responsibility for making that decision! Compare that sentence to a passive voice sentence that is not truncated:

"The decision was made by the president."

Then compare both sentences to an active voice sentence:

"The president made the decision."

The active voice sentence says more with fewer words!

My suggestion to writers is to use the active voice whenever possible, for the following reasons:

1.   Active voice sentences convey the same information in fewer words; they are more efficient.
2.   Passive voice sentences that are truncated can be confusing and misleading.

If you ever use a computer grammar-check program to check your writing, you may come across a notation that tells you a sentence in your writing is passive voice. You now know what passive is; but how do you change *passive to active?*

- If your passive voice sentence is truncated, you may have to **add information**.
- If your passive voice sentence contains a prepositional phrase that tells who did the action, you may simply **reverse your sentence** and turn the object of the preposition into the subject of the sentence.

COLLABORATE!   *Don't Be Passive; Take Responsibility!*

Directions

Work with a group or on your own.

A. The following passive voice sentences are excerpts from business writing. Underline each prepositional phrase that tells who did the action.

Rewrite each sentence into the active voice, making the object of the prepositional phrase you underlined into the subject of the sentence. The result should be shorter than the original sentence.

Draw arrows to show the direction of the sentence.

(The first one is done for you as an example.)

1. Passive voice: The letter was mailed <u>by the secretary</u>.

   Active voice: *The secretary mailed the letter.*

2. Passive voice: Malpractice insurance is regarded as a necessity by most prudent

     doctors.

           Active voice: _____

           _____

3. Passive voice: The proposal for next year's budget has been submitted by the treasurer.

Active voice: _____

_____

_____

4. Passive voice: Experienced applicants will be given special consideration by this employer.

Active voice: _____

_____

5. Passive voice: The meeting concerning the new amendment was led by the chairperson of the committee.

Active voice: _____

_____

B. *The following passive voice sentences are* <u>truncated</u>. *Using a prepositional phrase,* **add your own information** *to account for who did the action. (The first one is done for you as an example.)*

1. The decision was made.

The decision was made by the manager.
_____

2. The difficult problem is being discussed.

_____

3. The verdict has finally been decided.

_____

_____

4. On July 15, the bill was paid.

_____

5. The suspect was taken into custody.

_____

C. *Now that you have made the above truncated sentences more complete, change them from passive voice to active voice by making the object of the preposition (in the phrase you added) into the subject of each sentence. The first one is done for you as an example.*

1. *The manager made the decision.* _____

2. _____

_____

3. _____

_____

4. _____

_____

5. _____

_____

_____

PREPOSITIONS FOR TRANSITIONS

Like single-word adverbs, adverb prepositional phrases can be used to build bridges between sentences; that is, they can act as transitions to make your writing more coherent. The following is a list of common prepositional phrases used as transitions:

Transitional Prepositional Phrases

Adding Information: in addition
Example: I washed the car. *In addition*, I polished the wheels.

Cause and Effect: for these reasons/for this reason
Example: I won the lottery. *For this reason* I was able to pay for my college education in cash.

Comparing/Pointing out similarities: in the same way
Example: I always plan my work day thoughtfully. *In the same way,* I plan my vacation time.

Concession/Agreeing with Other Points of View: of course/at the same time
Example: *Of course* you are right when you say that good grades are important. *At the same time,* being able to apply what you have learned is just as important.

Conclusion: after all/in a word/in essence/in conclusion/in general/in short/in the end/in summary/on the whole
Example: I have listed my qualifications and described my experience. *On the whole,* I believe I am qualified for the job.

Contrasting/Pointing Out Differences: after all/in spite of/on the contrary/on the other hand/in contrast
Example: *In contrast* to city living, country living is much slower paced.

Emphasizing: in other words/in fact/in particular/above all
Example: I believe a good mother must possess many qualities. *Above all,* she must be patient.

Illustration: for instance/in this way/for example
Example: I enjoy many activities. *For example,* I find bird watching especially rewarding.

Parenthetical Information: by the way
Example: I saw John at the committee meeting on Wednesday. *By the way*, did you know his wife just had a baby?

Place: at a distance/on the same side/on the opposite side/on the near side/on the far side/in the vicinity/to the left/to the right/in the distance
Example: *In the distance*, we could see the riders approaching.

Purpose: for this purpose/for this reason
Example: I know you would like to break into the hotel business. *For this reason*, I am offering you a part-time job working at the front desk.

Repetition: in brief/in short/in other words
Example: I have listened to your remarks and am willing to stand behind you. *In other words*, I will support you.

Result: after all/at last/in conclusion/in consequence/for that reason/as a result
Example: The owner closed the plant down for repairs during July. *As a result*, we all had an unexpected summer vacation.

Succession in Time: after this/at last/from the start/until now/after that
Example: She read several chapters in the novel. *After that*, she fell asleep.

Time: at length/at the beginning/at the outset/at the start/from now (on)/until now/in the meantime/at last
Example: We worked hard all day. *At last*, we finished building the fence.

COLLABORATE!   *Making the Transition with a Preposition*

Directions

Work with a group or on your own. In the following paragraphs, suggestions for certain kinds of transitions are indicated in parentheses. Insert a prepositional phrase to effect the transition called for. Refer to the above list of TRANSITIONAL PREPOSITIONAL PHRASES, as necessary.

Today, television dominates family life in the American culture. (illustration), Dad comes home after work and watches television instead of engaging in a conversation with his children about their school day. Today's children do not find this unusual. (concession) they would undoubtedly benefit from interacting with their father or mother, but they have learned not to expect such interaction, thanks to the TV. Since they were babies, the television has been a significant family member. (result), they accept its presence without question. (result), family relationships are not as strong as they used to be before the advent of the "tube."

Many sociologists believe the decline of family values during the last forty years can be directly attributed to television watching. (succession in time), when television was first introduced into homes, promoters argued that the television would bring families together. (conclusion), the family would be gathered in one room together enjoying television programs. Yet in today's homes, Mom is fixing dinner in the kitchen where there may or may not be a TV. (place) in the living room, Dad is watching the news. (addition), little Josh is being entertained by cartoons in his bedroom while his sister Jennifer is being taught the alphabet by puppets on another channel in her bedroom. (Repetition), everyone is watching television, but no one is enjoying time together as a family.

JOURNAL PROMPT

How has television affected your family and your relationships with various family members? What are some of the benefits of television viewing? In your own experience, do you have any regrets about the time you have invested watching television? Explain.

WRITE RIGHT FOR THE JOB: Excess Prepositional Phrases

In my work with people who write on the job, the overuse of prepositional phrases often becomes an issue. Phrases have a profound effect on rhythm in sentences. Too many prepositional phrases may lull a reader to sleep:

> *Yea, though I walk <u>through the valley</u> <u>of the shadow</u> <u>of death</u>, I fear no evil.*
> *(3 phrases)*

Their rhythmic effect often makes sentences "sing-songy":

> <u>*Over the river*</u> *and* <u>*through the woods*</u> <u>*to grandmother's house*</u>*, we go.*
> *(3 phrases)*

Too many prepositional phrases can make a piece of business writing sound like a ride on a bumpy road:

> *I work <u>for the Department</u> <u>of the Interior</u> <u>of the Federal Government</u> <u>of the United States</u> <u>of America</u>. (5 phrases!!)*

As you can see, the preposition *OF*, which shows possession, is a particular nuisance in business writing.

In order to streamline documents, then, some employers are on the lookout for ways to reduce the number of prepositional phrases. Of course, not all prepositional phrases can or should be eliminated. But as we have seen, a single adjective or adverb can sometimes accomplish the job of an entire phrase.

The following is a list of phrases commonly used in business writing. They can all be replaced by the suggested shorter expressions:

Phrases that Can Be Replaced by Single-Word Adverbs or Single Prepositions

in the course of	during
in the neighborhood of	about
during the time that	while
most of the time	frequently
on the occasion of	on
under separate cover	separately
at a later date	later
at an earlier date	earlier
with regard to	about

Phrases that Can Be Replaced by Adjectives or Nouns (and Even a Verb)

green in color	green
neat in appearance	neat
controversial in nature	controversial
a charge in the amount of three dollars	a three dollar charge
winter of the year	winter
the month of February	February
some of the members	some members
of the opinion	believe
pursuant to your request	as you requested

Phrases that Can Be Replaced by "Because"

due to the fact that	because
for the reason that	because
in view of the fact that	because
owing to the fact that	because
on the grounds that	because
on account of the fact that	because

COLLABORATE!   *Saying It in a Word, Not a Phrase*

Directions

The following document contains sentences from actual letters and memos. Working with a group or on your own, rewrite the document to reduce the number of prepositional phrases. For example, the first sentence may be rewritten in this way: "In February our company sent you a letter because your payment was overdue." Notice, not __all__ of the phrases are eliminated; but the result is shorter and reads more smoothly.

Hint: Use the suggestions in the previous section to help you replace phrases with shorter expressions.

Dear Ms. Dee Lynn Quint,

In the month of February, our company sent you a letter on account of the fact that your payment was overdue. On the occasion of January 1, 1996, you purchased a computer program and promised to pay a charge in the amount of $300 for an operating license. In view of the fact that this program will save your company in the neighborhood of $1500 in the winter of each year, I do not understand your refusal to pay the one-time charge in the amount of $300. At an earlier date, you said you refused to pay on the grounds that you wanted some free computer training for some of the members of your staff. Pursuant to your request, we provided a trainer to work with your staff during the time that they were learning the new program. At a later date, you again refused to pay for the operating license for the reason that your business had lost a contract that was controversial in nature. We are of the opinion that your business dealings that are controversial in nature are not our responsibility. Therefore, we will be sending you a legal notification under separate cover. It will arrive in an envelope that is green in color. Please do not ignore this notification.

Sincerely,

Ward D. Mann

THE READING CONNECTION

1. Read several pages of a textbook or newspaper or magazine. Underline every prepositional phrase you find. Also circle the preposition in each phrase. When you are finished reading, look back over the pages you have marked and create a list of the prepositions you encountered, keeping track of how many times you came across each preposition. Circle the five most frequently occurring prepositions on your list. Bring your findings to class and compare them with your classmates' findings.

2. Read several pages of a book or magazine article paying careful attention to the author's use of prepositions.

    a. Select some sentences in which the prepositional phrases could be moved around to create different emphases.

    b. Pay special attention to prepositional phrases used as transitions. What kinds of transitional phrases does the author use?

    c. How frequently does he or she use them?

    d. Be prepared to discuss your findings in class.

THE WRITING CONNECTION

You may already have discovered that you use prepositional phrases frequently in your own writing. Write on one or several of the topics listed below. During the revision step in your writing, check your sentences for prepositional phrases. How often have you started sentences with prepositional phrases? How often have you used prepositional phrases for transitions? Strengthen your original draft by thoughtfully placing prepositional phrases where they will enhance your finished piece of writing.

1. Write a detailed description of a simple object you value. Perhaps it is your favorite pen, your toothbrush, your wedding ring, or a teddy bear you have not been able to part with. Using spatial organization, describe your object in scrupulous detail. Pay special attention to your use of *spatial prepositions*. Consider varying the locations of your prepositional phrases, sometimes placing them at the beginnings as well as the endings of sentences.

2. Write a narrative in which you tell about an interesting, humorous, or exciting experience you have had. Perhaps you once met a celebrity, or competed in a challenging athletic competition, or helped deliver a baby, or saved someone's life. Organize your story chronologically; sequence the events carefully in time. Pay special attention to your use of prepositional phrases that express *time relationships*. Experiment with placing prepositional phrases in different locations in your sentences to create sentence variety.

3. Compare and contrast two of your favorite activities, or two of your least favorite activities, or compare your favorite activity to your least favorite activity. Discuss how the two activities you have chosen are alike and how they are different. Discuss *why* you like one activity more or less than the other. As you revise your writing, pay close attention to the use of transitions to make your writing coherent. Add transitions, including *transitional prepositional phrases*, if you think they will enhance your finished product.

4. Write about a process you have performed at work. Perhaps you drove a truck, operated a cash register, prepared meals, developed X-ray film, or operated equipment. Explain the process you performed in the form of instructions so a reader could easily duplicate the process. Pay close attention to your use of all kinds of prepositional phrases, especially those that express time and space relationships. Also read carefully for transitions.

5. Develop one of your journal prompts into a finished piece of writing. Be aware of your use of prepositional phrases and their location.

SELF TEST FOR CHAPTER 10

1. Preposition are used to _____ people, places, and things into sentences.

2. A prepositional phrase begins with a _____ and ends with a _____ or _____ which is called the object of the preposition.

3. Some prepositions express spatial relationships while others express _____ or _____ relationships.

4. In the phrase "by the author," the preposition BY does not mean "next to" be-cause it is being used to express an _____ relationship.

5. A phrase is a group of words that functions as _____ in a sentence.

6. Prepositional *phrases* function as _____ and _____ in sentences.

7. Prepositional phrases placed between subjects and verbs may cause a writer to experience problems with _____.

8. Because adverb prepositional phrases can move around, they can help a writer create sentence _____.

9. In a passive voice sentence, the doer of the action is usually the _____.

10. Prepositional phrases that act as _____ can help writers move smoothly from one idea to another.

FINAL JOURNAL WRITING

Write about what you have learned in this chapter. In what way has your concept of the term "phrase" changed? How has learning about prepositions changed what you notice in a piece of writing? What tools have you acquired to help you organize writing according to space and time? What was the most interesting information you learned about prepositions? What was the most useful information you gained from this chapter? How do you think learning about prepositions will affect your reading and writing? Which concepts were most difficult for you? Why?

CHAPTER 11

VERBALS BRINGING MORE LIFE TO SENTENCES

> *To be, or not to be: that is the question:*
> *Whether 'tis nobler in the mind to suffer*
> *The slings and arrows of outrageous fortune,*
> *Or to take arms against a sea of troubles,*
> *And by opposing end them? . . . To die, to sleep;*
> *To sleep; perchance to dream . . .*
>
> —WILLIAM SHAKESPEARE, HAMLET

QUESTIONS TO ASK YOURSELF WHILE READING CHAPTER 11:

1. How can verbals make my writing more energetic and more interesting to read?
2. How can my knowledge of verbal phrases help me eliminate sentence fragments from my writing?
3. How can knowing about misplaced and dangling participles help me write clearer sentences?
4. How can my understanding of verbal phrases improve my ability to use commas when punctuating my sentences?
8. How can my knowledge of verbal phrases contribute to my ability to create easier-to-read lists in my writing?

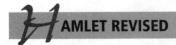

HAMLET REVISED

> *To teach verbals or not to teach verbals: that is the question:*
> *Whether it's nobler to suffer the slings and arrows of outrageous critics*
> *(who say, "Don't teach verbals");*
> *Or to take arms against a sea of verbal troubles*
> *And finally end them? . . . To explain verbals,*
> *Perchance to succeed, is that to dream?*
>
> —*Eide*, Writing with the Lights On

Just last week I attended a staff gathering where I ran into a colleague who had been teaching a basic writing class like mine. She remarked in a frustrated tone, "I enjoy teaching writing, but I feel guilty about exposing students to verbals. They become so confused." This isn't the first time a colleague has expressed reservations about teaching *gerunds, participles,* and *infinitives.*

"GER" what? I said, "GER*UND.*" Mr. Gerund and the others are easier to become acquainted with if you start out on a first-name basis. So, let me introduce you to **George Gerund, Picturesque Participle**, and **Infinite Infinitive**. All three are busy workers in sentences.

USY DOING WHAT?

George Gerund has a job working as a NOUN. What else would a guy named George do? Picturesque Participle works as an ADJECTIVE. After all, what's more picturesque than an adjective? And Infinite Infinitive fills in for three different jobs. He sometimes works as a NOUN, sometimes as an ADJECTIVE, and sometimes even as an ADVERB. He's nicknamed "infinite" because he never has a clue about time.

Even though George Gerund and Picturesque Participle and Infinite Infinitive act— and sometimes look—different, they are all part of the same family—the *Verbal* family.

HE FAMILY "THREE"

Where do you suppose they got a last name like that—*verbal*??? Their parents were *verbs,* of course. But George Gerund is a noun. How could he have come from a verb? And Picturesque Participle is an adjective because she describes or pictures things. How could she have been produced by verbs? And Infinite Infinitive is clueless about time? That's hardly a verb trait; verbs always tell time in sentences. How can these three very different sentence parts all be related to verbs?

Take a look at them, and maybe you can tell me why they're called *verbals.*

> Here's George Gerund: <u>Running</u> *energizes me.*
> And Picturesque Participle: *The* <u>running</u> *water fills the bucket.*
> And, finally, Infinite Infinitive: *I like* <u>to run</u>.

Do you see the family resemblance? Why do *you* think these words are called VERBals? Write your answer here:

_____

_____

Verbals clearly look like verbs and are obviously derived from verbs, but they don't do verb jobs in sentences. **Neither a gerund, nor a participle, nor an infinitive can ever function as the verb of a sentence!**

CLOSER LOOK: THE INFINITIVE

To understand all three "verbals" better, let's get to know them one at a time. The first problem is to tell them apart. That may be easy enough with Infinite Infinitive. He looks different from the others: "to run" looks different from "running." All infinitives start with "to." Therefore, the word "to" when used together with a *verb stem* (a verb without an ending) is called an *infinitive marker*. Other examples of infinitives would be

> to go
> to be
> to sit
> to stand

DO IT YOURSELF!   *Write Infinitive Possibilities*

Directions

Following the above examples, write ten more infinitives of your own:

1.

2.

3.

4.

5.

6.

7.

8.

9.

10.

There, wasn't that easy? But in addition to beginning with "to," what else is different about how Infinite Infinitive looks? How else does he differ from George Gerund and Picturesque Participle? Did you notice that he has no "tail," no ending? Infinitives have no -ING . . . ever!! The absence of endings, in fact, is exactly what makes infinitives so infinite. After all, endings are the parts that give us clues to the *time* verbs express. Infinitives have no endings. Therefore, they're timeless—or infinite.

DO IT YOURSELF: *Revisit Shakespeare*

Directions

A. *Now that you know how to spot infinitives, <u>underline</u> all the infinitives you find in the Shakespeare quote that comes at the beginning of this chapter on page 278.*

B. *Also underline the infinitives in the section headed "Hamlet Revised" on page 278. List all the different infinitives you found:*

1. _____

2. _____

3. _____

4. _____

5. _____

6. _____

7. _____

8. _____

9. _____

HE TWINS

Let's return to George Gerund and Picturesque Participle. They look like twins in the following sentences:

> <u>Running</u> *energizes me.* (George Gerund)
> *The* <u>running</u> *water fills the bucket.* (Picturesque Participle)

Sometimes you can't tell gerunds and participles apart by the way they *look*; so you have to observe how they *act*. It's like that with twins, you know. When you first see them, you may not be able to tell them apart because they look so much alike; but when you get to know them better, their *actions* can help you figure out which is which.

CLOSER LOOK: CATCHING THE GERUND IN THE ACT

Let's observe how George Gerund and Picturesque Participle *act* in sentences. Here's the gerund again:

> <u>Running</u> *energizes me.*

What is the word "running" acting as in this sentence? It sure *looks* like a verb, but is it *acting* as a verb? What is the verb in this sentence? The verb is "energizes," isn't it? What, then, is "running"?

Did you answer that "running" is the subject? After all, what is it that "energizes me"? The "running" does. Did I say *"the* running"? Isn't "THE" a noun marker—something I can put in front of nouns like *"the* car" and *"the* tree" and *"the* house"?

Yet, I just put that same noun marker in front of "running!" Then "running" must be a noun in this sentence. In fact, it is the noun subject of the sentence. Test it out: If you take "running" out of the sentence, what do you end up with? "___ energizes me." Is that a complete sentence? Of course not. It's missing its noun subject.

The gerund **always** acts as a noun in a sentence. That's why I've nicknamed it George Gerund—to remind me that just like the name George, **gerunds are always nouns.** Like other nouns, gerunds act not only as subjects; they may also be direct objects, indirect objects, subject complements, and even objects of prepositions. (For a review of all the different ways nouns function in sentences, see Chapter 6).

COLLABORATE!   *When George Nouns Around . . .*

Directions

Work with a group or on your own.

A. In the following paragraph, I have used the noun George to perform a variety of sentence functions. Decide which noun job George is doing in each sentence: above the word George, write subject (S), direct object (DO), indirect object (IO), object of preposition (OP), or subject complement (SC).

George is my favorite pastime. I enjoy George. I get my exercise by George. Why don't you give George a try? Then maybe your favorite pastime will become George, too.

B. In place of George, insert a gerund like running, dancing, or even something silly like sneezing! Read the resulting paragraph aloud. Write one of your versions in the space provided:

_____ is my favorite pastime. I enjoy _____. I get my exercise by _____. Why don't you give _____ a try? Then maybe your favorite pastime will become _____, too.

DO IT YOURSELF!   *Look for George in Disguise*

Directions

In the following paragraphs locate all the GERUNDS and circle them. Remember, you are looking for nouns that end in -ING which are derived from verbs.

In many families, drinking has become a problem. Excessive drinking is often a sign of alcoholism. Most people who live with alcoholics try to persuade drinkers to give up their addiction by pleading with them. Usually these efforts are labeled "nagging." Such accusations cause quarreling to erupt. Fighting often follows. Clearly, the answer is not blaming. After all, drinking is a disease. For the drinker, stopping is difficult. Unfortunately, for the drinker's family, worrying is a part of everyday life.

Questions to Think About

- Which of the gerunds you circled are acting as subjects?
- Which are acting as direct objects? As subject complements? As objects of prepositions?

JOURNAL PROMPT

Has your life been affected by drinking? What kinds of problems ensued? How did you deal with these problems? What are some positive and negative results of drinking? What advice would you give someone who is dealing with a drinking problem or who is dealing with a loved one who has a drinking problem?

CLOSER LOOK: THE PARTICIPLE PLAYS ITS PART

Finally, let's look closely at Picturesque Participle. Participles, too, can end in -ING. This "tail" makes them look just like gerunds. But unlike gerunds, participles do not always end in -ing. Participles may also end in *-ed* or be irregular like the participles *sung, brought,* and *given.* (For a more complete list of participles, refer to Chapter 5.)

The main difference between gerunds and participles, however, is not how they look, it is how they function in sentences: Participles **never** act as NOUNS. Instead Picturesque Participles **always** act as ADJECTIVES. They make things more picturesque. In fact, they help writers portray not only things, but also people and places, in more picturesque detail.

R—ING IN THE PRESENT PARTICIPLES

We usually think of adjectives as describing nouns by telling how they look: *old, young, pretty, ugly,* etc. Participles are special adjectives that describe nouns by telling what they are *doing* rather than how they look. For example:

Adjectives	Participles As Adjectives
the *happy* child	the *laughing* child
the *old* man	the *aging* man
the *active* woman	the *running* woman
the *sad* actress	the *sobbing* actress
the *swift* river	the *rushing* river

These participles that end in -ING are called *present participles.* They look just like gerunds. But, remember, gerunds act as nouns and participles act as adjectives.

PAST PARTICIPLES GET AN -ED . . . SOMETIMES

There are also *past participles* that act as adjectives in sentences. Past participles are those verb parts we normally use to make the perfect tenses:

> *The convict **has** <u>escaped</u> from prison.*
> *The police **had** <u>known</u> some facts about the escape plans.*
> *This fact **has** <u>troubled</u> the key witness in the case.*

The underlined words in the above sentences are past participles. When acting as verbs in verb phrases, they always occur together with *has, have, or had* as a helper. However, if you wanted to use the actions in the above sentences as adjectives to DE-SCRIBE nouns, you could use them in this way:

> *The <u>escaped</u> convict now roams the streets.* ("escaped" describes the convict)
> *The <u>known</u> facts did not prevent the success of the breakout.* ("known" describes the facts)
> *The <u>troubled</u> witness fears for her life.* ("troubled" describes the witness)

Here the participles act as ADJECTIVES instead of verbs. Do you see how Picturesque Participles help writers and readers picture nouns in more detail? Because participles are based on verbs, they are more energetic than regular adjectives.

DO IT YOURSELF!   *Put Picturesque Participles into the Paragraph*

Directions
A. *First, read the entire selection.*

B. *Then, go back and replace the adjective "picturesque" with a participle from the list on the following page. If you pick the participles in the order they are listed, the paragraph will say what I intended it to say. If you would rather mix up the participles or make up participles of your own, you may write a more creative version. Do as you like, but remember to use only participles to replace the adjective "picturesque."*

My favorite uncle is named Denis with one "N." He's a <u>picturesque</u> fanatic. Every year this <u>picturesque</u> man travels from Norway to Oregon just to go to <u>picturesque</u> dance halls. He is always a <u>picturesque</u> addition to the dance floor. The <u>picturesque</u> ladies flock around him and vie for his attentions. They all want to dance with <u>picturesque</u> Uncle Denis. His <u>picturesque</u> smile and <u>picturesque</u> eyes make him popular, even with the most <u>picturesque</u> women. Even <u>picturesque</u> women keep their eye on Uncle Denis, much to their <u>picturesque</u> husbands' chagrin. <u>Picturesque</u> Uncle Denis always brings his video camera when he comes to the United States. He asks me to film his smooth actions as he moves the <u>picturesque</u> ladies across the dance floor in his <u>picturesque</u> arms. The video tapes become <u>picturesque</u> souvenirs that he takes home to show to

<u>picturesque</u> audiences: his string of Norwegian <u>picturesque</u> partners. I just drove Uncle Denis to the airport last week. He was heading back to Norway to celebrate his eighty-first birthday!

List of Picturesque Participles for You to Insert

1.	dancing	10.	married
2.	aging	11.	pouting
3.	overflowing	12.	visiting
4.	welcomed	13.	captivated
5.	enamored	14.	guiding
6.	swinging	15.	treasured
7.	winning	16.	enchanted
8.	laughing	17.	dancing
9.	discriminating		

C. *In the space provided, write a paragraph containing the following expressions which are nouns described by participles:*

the <u>chained</u> animal/ the <u>barking</u> dog/ the <u>crumbling</u> building/ the <u>condemned</u> apartment/ the <u>blaring</u> noises/ the <u>screaming</u> sirens/ the <u>annoyed</u> neighbors/ the <u>sleeping</u> children

_____

_____

_____

_____

_____

_____

_____

_____

_____

_____

JOURNAL PROMPT

Do you have a favorite relative or friend who is an unusual character? How old is this person? What is unusual about him or her? Do you have the opportunity to spend time with this person? Have you learned anything that you can apply to your own life by observing how this person lives his or her life?

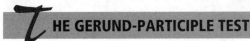

THE GERUND-PARTICIPLE TEST

If you are still a little unsure about your ability to distinguish gerunds from participles, try the **Gerund-Participle Test**. Gerunds, remember, are nouns. Nouns are *necessary* parts of a sentence that help determine its structure. If you remove a noun, you will notice a discomforting gap in your sentence. Often, the sentence will even become an incomplete idea or a fragment. Look at the following examples:

Sentence *With* Gerund:	Sentence *Without* Gerund:
Traveling is my hobby.	. . . is my hobby.
I enjoy **traveling**.	I enjoy . . . .
My greatest pleasure is **traveling**.	My greatest pleasure is. . . .
By **traveling** I learn about the world.	By . . . I learn about the world.

If you carefully read the sentences *without* the gerunds, you will see what I mean about the discomforting gaps left behind when gerunds are removed.

But participles, since they are adjectives rather than nouns, play a less significant role in sentence structure. Therefore, they *can* be removed from sentences without causing a stir. Compare the following sentences:

Sentence *With* Participle:	Sentence *Without* Participle:
The **purring** cat lay by the fire.	The . . . cat lay by the fire.
The **screeching** noises hurt my ears.	The . . . noises hurt my ears.
The **excited** winner jumped up and down.	The . . . winner jumped up and down.

Read the above sentences without the participles. Are the sentences still complete? Of course they lack some descriptive detail, but they are still normal-sounding, complete sentences.

To conduct the Gerund-Participle Test, then, all you do is simply *remove* the word in question. If the resulting sentence has an uncomfortable gap, the word in question is a gerund. But if the resulting sentence is a normal-sounding complete sentence, the word in question is a participle.

DO IT YOURSELF! *Conduct the Gerund-Participle Test*

Directions

Apply the information you gained from the previous examples.

A. Read the following paragraph which contains some sentences with participles and some with gerunds.

B. Decide which underlined verbal is a gerund and which is a participle on the basis of the GERUND-PARTICIPLE TEST. Then write the word "gerund" or "participle" above each underlined verbal.

Jogging is my addiction. For me, it is an <u>invigorating</u> activity. My neighbor does not enjoy <u>jogging</u>. She prefers <u>walking</u>. She buys <u>walking</u> shoes; I buy <u>jogging</u> shoes. She calls me a <u>jogging</u> junkie. I call her a <u>walking</u> wonder. <u>Jogging</u> and <u>walking</u> are two excellent forms of exercise. But, personally, I prefer <u>jogging</u>.

JOURNAL PROMPT

Have you ever tried jogging or walking for exercise? Which do you prefer? Why? Do you have friends who jog or walk? Why do you think they prefer one activity over the other? Have you, instead, just thought about taking up jogging or walking? If so, when do you intend to start? If you would like to start but have not, what is keeping you from beginning an exercise regimen?

COLLABORATE!!   *Keep All Three Verbals in the Air at One Time*

Directions

To review your ability to distinguish infinitives from gerunds from participles, find the verbals in the following paragraph and <u>label them accordingly</u>. Remember, infinitives always begin with the word "to." Gerunds always end in -ING. Participles may end in -ING, or -ED, or be IRREGULAR. To distinguish gerunds from similar-looking participles, you may need to apply the GERUND-PARTICIPLE TEST.

Studying is not always fun. Sometimes it's a dreaded chore. Thinking is hard work. I like to read, but writing is difficult. Revising, especially, is consuming work. I love to relax, however. I am one overworked student who would rather indulge in a relaxing bath instead of studying. Sleeping is also high on my list.

RE VERBALS JUST GOING THROUGH A PHRASE?

So far in this chapter you have been just introduced to the exciting world of verbals. The potential of what verbals can do in writing is beyond exciting, however! Verbals can enable you and me to **energize** our writing because verbals create opportunities for us to introduce action into our sentences over and over and over.

DO IT YOURSELF!   *Discover the Bigger Verbal World*

Directions
A. *Read and compare the following paragraphs:*

Paragraph #1:

My teammates and I had our minds set on <u>a win</u>. <u>A loss</u> was out of the question. For weeks ahead of time we worked on <u>plays</u>. We built our confidence and teamwork by <u>such practice</u>. Saturday morning came, and we definitely anticipated <u>a victory</u>. As we marched onto the field, the <u>noise</u> from the crowd inspired us. We heard the familiar <u>chant</u>: "Go Cougars Go." From that point on, we knew that our coaches' words would come true: "<u>Dedication</u> pays off in the end."

Paragraph #2:

My teammates and I had our minds set on <u>winning the big game</u>. <u>Losing the championship</u> was out of the question. For weeks ahead of time we worked on <u>passing the ball and running with it</u>. We built our confidence and teamwork by <u>going over and over the plays</u>. Saturday morning came, and we definitely anticipated <u>bringing home the state championship</u>. As we marched onto the field, the <u>cheering of spectators in the stands</u> inspired us. We heard the familiar <u>chanting of the hometown fans</u>: "Go Cougars Go." From that point, we knew that our coaches' words would come true: "<u>Giving your all</u> pays off in the end."

B. *Write the expressions from Paragraph #2 that were used to replace the following nouns in Paragraph #1:*

Noun—	Replaced by the Phrase—

1. a win: _____
2. a loss: _____
3. plays: _____
4. such practice: _____
5. a victory: _____
6. noise: _____
7. chant: _____
8. dedication: _____

What kinds of words do all these phrases begin with?

_____

C. *Read both of the preceding paragraphs aloud, carefully.*

As a reader, do you respond differently to each paragraph? _____

What do you like or dislike about the way the writer tells the story in each paragraph? _____

_____

_____

JOURNAL PROMPT

Have you ever played on a championship team? What kind of team was it? Which championship did you win? What kind of contribution did you make to your team? What did this experience teach you? Have you ever attended a school or lived in an area where the home team has won a championship? Describe the effects the championship team had on the fans? If you were a fan, how did the experience affect your life?

THE GERUND PHRASE AND OTHERS

In Paragraph #2 about winning the big game, you have just observed *gerund phrases* at work. All verbals are capable of attracting strings of words that resemble "back halves" of sentences. Because verbals are related to verbs, they naturally attract objects, complements, and adverbial phrases. Together, a verbal plus the words that naturally follow it are called a *verbal phrase.* All verbals can introduce verbal phrases. That means there are not only gerund phrases, but also participial phrases and infinitive phrases. The gerund phrases function as nouns while participial phrases function as adjectives, and infinitive phrases function either as nouns or adjectives or adverbs in sentences.

GERUND "MAGIC"

The magic of gerund phrases is that, while they are *nouns,* they can have the *verb* quality of ACTION. That makes them vital and energetic nouns that can help us writers bring our writing to life.

COLLABORATE!   *Phrase Out the Noun; Phrase in the <u>Action</u> . . .*

Directions
Work with a group or on your own.

A. Read the following paragraph carefully. Pay close attention to the underlined noun expressions.

B. Read through the list of gerund phrases that follow the paragraph. Decide which phrase best replaces each noun expression.

C. In the space provided, write your new version of the paragraph substituting gerund phrases for ordinary nouns and their modifiers.

The Paragraph:

<u>The fry cook position</u> was my first real job. Shortly after <u>my sixteenth birthday,</u> I was hired by Bob's Fast Foods in the Millmore Mall. I liked <u>the location.</u> The Millmore Mall had always been the best place in town for <u>a good time.</u> But <u>this job</u> was another story. <u>The unpleasant work</u> was not my idea of a good time. I liked <u>the pay,</u>

though. Of course, <u>the money</u> wasn't exactly like <u>a lottery win</u>. But even <u>a small salary</u> was better than <u>no salary</u>.

Gerund Phrases:

1. taking home a paycheck
2. flipping hamburgers
3. winning the lottery
4. turning sixteen
5. cooking fast food
6. standing over vats of hot grease
7. cashing my check
8. earning minimum wage
9. hanging out and having fun
10. working at the mall
11. earning nothing at all

Revised Version of the Paragraph Containing Gerund Phrases:

_____

_____

_____

_____

_____

_____

_____

_____

_____

_____

JOURNAL PROMPT

What was your first job? How much were you paid? What did you learn from your first job? What did you like about the job? What did you dislike? Did your first work experience affect decisions you made about future work choices? Explain.

THERE'S NO END TO GERUND PHRASES

Gerund phrases are simply any group of words that sound reasonable to you following a gerund. For example, if the gerund were "dancing," some possible gerund phrases could be:

dancing the polka . . .
dancing to the sound of the music . . .
dancing with Fred and then with Joe . . .
dancing alone on the massive stage while the entire audience cheered . . .
dancing slowly . . .

As you can see, the possibilities of words you can add to a gerund to make a gerund phrase are limited only by your imagination.

DO IT YOURSELF!   *Stretch Your Imagination*

Directions

Create at least three different gerund phrases that begin with each of the following gerunds:

Gerund #1

washing_____

washing_____

washing_____

Gerund #2

taking_____

taking_____

taking_____

Gerund #3

wearing_____

wearing_____

wearing_____

ERUND PHRASES EVERYWHERE

Since gerund phrases are used as nouns, that means gerund phrases must be versatile. After all, nouns work not only as subjects, but objects and complements as well.

COLLABORATE!!   *Gerund Phrases Everywhere*

Directions

A. *Working with a group or on your own, complete the following sentences by filling in gerund phrases where normally nouns would do the different noun jobs. In each set the first one is done for you as an example. Remember, any of the thousands of verbs in English can add an -ING ending to create a gerund. So use a different gerund to start each gerund phrase you write.*

1. Gerund phrases as SUBJECTS of sentences:

    a. *Dancing the polka* is fun.

    b. _____ is fun.

    c. _____ makes life interesting.

      d. _____ is my least favorite activity.

      e. _____ upsets my stomach.

2. Gerund phrases as DIRECT OBJECTS:

    a. I love *going on long walks with my husband*.

    b. My mother enjoys _____.

    c. My best friend has never liked _____.

    d. After a long trip away from home, I anticipate _____.

    e. Finishing my homework requires _____.

3. Gerund phrases as OBJECTS OF PREPOSITIONS:

    a. I relax BY *taking a hot bath*.

    b. I always start my day BY _____.

    c. I need money FOR _____.

    d. We had an argument ABOUT _____.

    e. My toddler drives me crazy BY _____.

4. Gerund phrases as SUBJECT COMPLEMENTS:

    a. Living right is *finding a parking space by the front door*.

    b. Success is _____.

    c. Love is _____.

    d. My favorite entertainment is _____.

    e. My least favorite pastime is _____.

B. *Write a paragraph using at least five sentences with gerund phrases; you may incorporate some of the sentences you completed above or invent others.*

THE PARTICIPIAL PHRASE

You have already seen the gerund phrase at work in writing. Now let's turn to the picturesque participles and observe how they affect a piece of writing when they bring phrases along.

DO IT YOURSELF!   *Get the Picture with Participial Phrases*

Directions

A. *Read and compare the following paragraphs.*

Paragraph #1:

    <u>Happy</u> Sara raced to the <u>moored</u> red canoe. Her <u>prepared</u> father followed her. It was a <u>perfect</u> day. The <u>bright</u> sun warmed the water. The <u>gentle</u> breeze provided just enough air to keep the canoers refreshed. What a wonderful way to spend Father's Day!

Paragraph #2:

Wearing a smile on her face, Sara raced to the red canoe tied to the dock with a ragged ski rope. Her father, carrying two paddles and several life jackets over his shoulder, followed her. It was a day made just for canoeing. The sun reflecting off the still lake warmed the water. Blowing gently through the soft spring leaves, the breeze provided just enough air to keep the canoers refreshed. What a wonderful way to spend Father's Day!

Which paragraph do you prefer? Why?

B. *Write the PARTICIPIAL PHRASES from Paragraph #2 that were used to replace the following ADJECTIVES in Paragraph #1:*

Single-Word Adjective   **Participial-Phrase Adjective**

1. happy— _____

2. moored— _____

3. prepared— _____

4. perfect— _____

5. bright— _____

6. gentle— _____

JOURNAL PROMPT

Have you ever celebrated a memorable Father's Day or Mother's Day? Or are those occasions not events you celebrate? Explain. What would be your ideal way to spend a day with your parent or your child?

COLLABORATE!   *Picking the Participial Phrase*

Directions

Work with a group or on your own.

A. *Insert the participial phrases that describe the underlined nouns or pronouns. I have listed the phrases in the order that they should occur in the paragraph. (Note that sometimes the phrases are located immediately in front of the word they describe; other times these phrases are located immediately behind the word they describe.)*

Yesterday, my son visited his grandparents. _____, Nick greeted the old man with a warm, "Hi Papa!" _____, Grandpa replied, "Welcome, Nick." Then Nick spotted Grandma _____. _____ _____, he called to her, "Grandma, I come to your house." "How wonderful!" replied Grandma, _____. _____,

Little Nick eyed the cat _____ "I want down," cried Nick,

_____ . _____, he raced across the room.

But the cat, _____, ran away and never reappeared.

1. jumping up into Grandpa's lap

2. beaming proudly

3. coming down the stairs

4. waving both hands in the air

5. taking him in her arms

6. looking over Grandma's shoulder

7. hiding under the rocking chair

8. squirming out of the old woman's embrace

9. fueled by excitement

10. frightened by the invasion of a stranger

B. *To have some fun with participial phrases, insert the above phrases into different blanks from the ones they were written for. Write your resulting paragraph here:*

_____

_____

_____

_____

_____

_____

_____

_____

_____

_____

JOURNAL PROMPT

Reflect on the roles of grandparents in your life or in today's society overall. Have you or your children had a strong grandparent figure? What influence has this person had on your family? Are you, yourself, a grandparent? How is the experience different from being a parent? If you are not yet a grandparent, what kind of grandparent would you like to be someday?

DO IT YOURSELF!   *Create Participial Phrases*

Directions

A. *In the space suggested, write some of your own participial phrases to replace the following adjectives. Remember, you can begin a participial phrase with any present or past participle. The first one is done for you as an example:*

1. The <u>flashy</u> man entered the room.

    The man <u>wearing a red plaid suit</u> entered the room.

2. The <u>sad</u> woman could hardly speak.

    The woman _____ could hardly speak.

3. The father watched his <u>joyful</u> children.

    The father watched his children _____.

4. The <u>busy</u> teacher did not answer my question.

    The teacher _____ did not answer my question.

5. The <u>angry</u> customer demanded her money back.

    _____ the customer demanded her money back.

6. My <u>delighted</u> daughter thanked me for the present.

    _____ my daughter thanked me for the present.

B. *In the space provided, write a paragraph in which you use verbal phrases (both gerund and participial, if you can); use some of the phrases from this exercise and add more of your own.*

_____

_____

_____

_____

_____

_____

_____

_____

_____

COLLABORATE!   *Distinguishing Gerund Phrases from Participial Phrases*

Directions:

Work with a group or on your own. In the following paragraphs, identify which under-lined phrases are gerund phrases and which are participial. If necessary, review the GERUND-PARTICIPLE TEST: Gerund phrases are always nouns and cannot be removed from sentences without dramatically affecting the structure of the sentence. Participial phrases are always adjectives, so they may be removed without affecting sentence structure.

By <u>digging through garbage</u>, researchers have discovered that we Americans throw away about 15 percent of the food we buy. <u>Wasting food</u> is common. Cheese <u>covered with mold</u>, meat <u>discolored from age</u>, and apples <u>bitten into only once</u> find their way into city dumps. Food <u>left in the refrigerator too long</u> becomes garbage. <u>Throwing away food</u> is a common practice. Yet, in our culture, <u>shopping for food</u> continues.

At holiday time, especially, <u>filling the grocery basket</u> is a ritual. That ritual also includes <u>buying foods we may never eat</u>. How much of the 23-pound Thanksgiving Day turkey becomes garbage? Five pounds? A week after a holiday, how many containers of chip dip <u>laced with mold</u> are thrown into the garbage? <u>Returning from a Fourth of July camping trip</u>, do you discard half-full bags of chips and stale hamburger buns <u>untouched by human lips</u>?

JOURNAL PROMPT

Do you or your family waste food? What kinds of food are you most likely to discard? What do you do with leftovers? Do you buy and prepare more than you can consume during the holidays? What can you do to reduce the amount of food you waste? How will you benefit personally from reducing food waste?

INFINITIVE PHRASES

Infinitives are phrases from the start. After all, it takes two words to make an infinitive: *to go, to sit, to talk,* and so on. But infinitives, too, can be expanded. They, too, attract just about anything that walks by. Look at these expanded infinitive phrases:

> *to dance with my Uncle Denis*
> *to dance the waltz*
> *to dance slowly*
> *to dance on the stage with all the other ballerinas in the "Nutcracker"*

Again, as with gerund phrases and participial phrases, the extent of the infinitive phrase is limited only by your imagination.

Obviously, you will not easily confuse infinitive phrases with gerund and participial phrases because they begin with very different words. But you might confuse infinitive phrases with prepositional phrases. After all, isn't the word "to" a preposition as well as an infinitive marker? So whether or not you have studied prepositions, you may feel some confusion when you encounter a phrase that begins with "to."

Prepositions, however, are followed by *noun* or *pronoun* objects. Infinitives, on the other hand, are followed by *verb stems*. In addition, prepositions indicate direction *(to the store);* infinitives do not indicate direction *(to sing* does not tell **where**). Study the following lists carefully:

Prepositional Phrase *(Followed by Noun; Directional)*	**Infinitive Phrase** *(Followed by Verb Stem; Not Directional)*
to **school**	to **study**
to the big **school**	to **study** math
to the very big **school**	to **study** for my math test

After studying the previous examples, in your own words summarize the difference between prepositional phrases and infinitive phrases:

_____

_____

_____

DO IT YOURSELF!   *Watch Your P's and I's (Prepositions and Infinitives)*

Directions

In the following paragraph, indicate whether the underlined elements are prepositional phrases or infinitive phrases by labeling each phrase as PREP (PREPOSITIONAL) or INF (INFINITIVE):

To fear something unnaturally is a phobia. I am afraid to fly. You could say, I have a phobia about flying. But I have family and friends who live far from me. To visit them, I need to take a plane. Every time I go to the airport, I deal with my fear of flying. I once loved to fly. But I made a long trip to Norway one winter that changed my feelings about flying. On that trip, I missed a connection because of snowy weather. Consequently, I was forced to fly a route different from the one I had originally planned. First my plane went to England. Once there, I boarded a carrier to Holland. Then I continued to Denmark. Finally, I boarded my last plane and headed to Norway. I was so happy to be there at last. I ran straight to the phone to let my relatives know I had arrived in my homeland safely.

JOURNAL PROMPT

Do you have any phobias? For example, are you afraid of speaking in front of a group, being enclosed in a small space, traveling too far from home, or going to the dentist or the hospital? What is your phobia? How do you deal with it? Where do you think it came from? What happens to you when you have to face something you are phobic about? Does your phobia limit the choices you make in your life? Have you become better or worse about your phobia as you've grown older? What, if anything, have you done or do you plan to do to help eliminate your phobia?

*I*NFINITELY MORE ABOUT INFINITIVES

Once we can clearly identify infinitives, the next question is, what are they doing in sentences? Their relatives George Gerund and Picturesque Participles are employed in sentences in dependable positions: gerunds always perform noun jobs, and participles always work hard as adjectives. But what about that Infinite Infinitive?

Well, infinite is as infinite does! The infinitive has infinitely more job opportunities than the two other verbals. Infinitives can do the job of nouns, AND adjectives, AND even adverbs! They can replace both of their relatives and do more besides!

Infinitives as Nouns

For example, instead of using a noun *gerund:*

Running ten laps energizes me.

I can use a noun *infinitive:*

To run ten laps energizes me

In the above sentences both verbal phrases are acting as noun subjects. I can also use the noun gerund as a direct object and write:

I like running ten laps.

An infinitive can be a direct object, too:

I like to run ten laps.

In other words, both gerunds and infinitives can do noun jobs in sentences.

Infinitives as Adjectives

Used as an adjective, the infinitive competes with the *participial phrase.* For example, I can choose to describe the noun "road" using a participial phrase:

The road going to grandmother's house is the unpaved country road.

Or I can use an infinitive phrase to describe "road":

The road to take to grandmother's house is the unpaved country road.

While the meaning may be slightly different in each phrase, both phrases do describe the noun "road" and, therefore, act as *adjectives.*

You may have noticed that infinitives describe nouns by telling what someone can do to them. Which "road" is being described? It is not the *long* "road" (adjective that tells *what kind*); nor is it the road *going to grandmother's house* (participial phrase tells what the "road" is doing); but it is the "road" *to take to grandmother's house* (infinitive phrase tells what someone can do to the "road"). This is the unique way in which infinitives describe nouns.

Infinitives as Adverbs

Finally, infinitives may also act as ADVERBS. You may remember that adverbs describe not only verbs but other describers as well:
Infinitive phrase describing a VERB:

Wally stayed <u>to watch the movie</u>. (The infinitive phrase tells why "He stayed.")

Infinitive phrase describing a DESCRIPTIVE WORD:

Wally was happy <u>to watch the movie</u>. (The infinitive phrase describes the descriptive word "happy" by telling what action made Wally happy.)

Compared to the dependable gerund and participle, each of whom always stick with the same job, the infinitive seems to have infinitely more job possibilities in sentences. It truly is the Infinite Infinitive!
The following chart summarizes what you have learned about verbals:

Verbal Chart

Name of Verbal	How It Looks	How It Acts
GERUND	ENDS IN *-ing*	NOUN—subject, direct object, indirect object, subject complement, object of preposition
PARTICIPLE	ENDS IN *-ing* or ENDS IN *-ed* or IS AN IRREGULAR PAST PARTICIPLE (such as *sung, brought, given,* etc.)	ADJECTIVE—modifies *nouns* and *pronouns.*
INFINITIVE	TO + A VERB STEM (such as *to go, to play, to be,* etc.)	NOUN—subject, direct object, indirect object, and subject complement OR ADJECTIVE—modifies *nouns* and *pronouns* OR ADVERB—modifies all sentence parts except nouns or pronouns

PHRASES CAUSE "PHRAGMENTS"

Verbal phrases are always an interesting and lively addition to simple sentences. But when you use them in your writing, beware of the **danger** they pose! What danger lurks nearby when writers use verbal phrases? The danger is *the danger of writing SEN-TENCE FRAGMENTS.*

As you know, complete sentences require subjects and verbs. Simply put, that means, as a writer, you name *doers* and then tell *what they're doing.* For example, in the sentence "The man is painting the house," the *man* is the doer or *subject* of the sentence; and *is painting* tells what he's doing—the *verb* of the sentence.

Verbals, as we know, *never* function as verbs, but they sometimes look exactly like verbs. Therein lies the DANGER. Student writers often think they have written verbs when they have actually written verbals. That means they think they have fulfilled the verb requirement of a sentence when in reality they have only added something like a participial adjective to their writing.

Compare these word groups:

> *The house painted by the man.*
> *The house was painted by the man.*

One of these expressions is a complete sentence, and one is a FRAGMENT, or an incomplete sentence. Which is which? _____

Did you identify the first group of words as a fragment because it is simply the noun "house" with an adjective participial phrase describing it? To repair this fragment, I simply added the verb of being "was;" and then "painted" became part of a verb phrase instead of acting as a participial adjective.

DO IT YOURSELF!   *PHIX THE PHRAGMENTS (Just Testing My Spell-checker)*

Directions

A few of the following items are complete sentences, but most of them are fragments created by some type of verbal. Repair the fragments by rewriting them as complete sentences. You may add words, if you like. Often the easiest repair is to add a being verb such as IS, WAS, ARE, WERE, WILL BE, HAS BEEN or HAD BEEN. Write your repaired version in the space provided. If the sentence is already complete, merely write the word COMPLETE in the space provided.

1. The road paved by the county.

_____

2. The man painting the house.

_____

_____

3. The way to run the business during the holidays.

_____

_____

4. Joan was earning a high wage.

_____

_____

5. Getting high grades in all my classes.

_____

_____

6. Losing the game after working so hard.

_____

_____

7. The old trunk containing a beehive.

_____

_____

8. The hot water heater replaced by the plumber.

_____

_____

9. The Oregon Ducks had played a great game.

_____

_____

10. The ground covered with snow.

_____

_____

11. The police officer directing the traffic.

_____

_____

12. To join the army during a time of national emergency.

_____

_____

_____

PARTICIPLES THAT LOSE THEIR PLACE

Participles are particularly problematic. They must be placed in precise positions or they puzzle and perplex us. (I think the "P" is stuck on my keyboard.)

Participles are adjectives that describe nouns. (I think I've already said that a few times in this chapter.) And adjectives are very fussy about their location in sentences. Since their job is to describe nouns, they feel they should have the privilege of sitting next to nouns in sentences—on one side or the other. If they can't be next to "their" noun, they simply won't do their job—they won't describe their noun at all. Read the following sentence carefully:

The doctor delivered the baby underline{wearing jeans and a sweatshirt}.

What is wrong with this picture? Do you get the impression that the baby was born dressed in casual clothing? If you do, it is because I placed the adjective participial phrase "wearing jeans and a sweatshirt" next to the noun "baby." In this location the phrase does the only thing it is capable of doing: it describes the noun it is sitting next to. I could make this sentence say what it really should say simply by moving the participial phrase next to the noun it was intended to describe. It would then read like this:

The doctor <u>wearing jeans and a sweatshirt</u> delivered the baby.

OR

<u>*Wearing jeans and a sweatshirt*</u>*, the doctor delivered the baby.*

Adjectives, whether they are single words or phrases, belong **next to** (before or after) the nouns they describe!!

DO IT YOURSELF!   *Help Misplaced Participles Find Their Nouns*

Directions
In the following sentences, the participial phrases have been misplaced.
A. Underline the participial phrase.
B. Circle the noun the phrase is intended to describe and write it in the space provided.
C. Rewrite the sentence by moving the phrase next to (either in front of or behind) the noun it is intended to describe. Write your revised version in the space provided. The first one is done for you as an example.

1.   Underline the misplaced participial phrase:

     <u>Piled high with papers and trash</u>, the professor avoided his (office.)

     Which noun is the phrase intended to describe? *office*

     Revised version: *The professor avoided his office piled high with papers and trash.*

2.   Underline misplaced participial phrase:

     Suffering from a severe diaper rash, the concerned mother went to the emergency room with her baby.

     Which noun is the phrase intended to describe? _____

     Revised version: _____

     _____

3.   Underline the misplaced participial phrase:

     Wearing a short skirt, Frank noticed the attractive woman.

     Which noun is the phrase intended to describe? _____

     Revised version: _____

4. Underline the misplaced participial phrase:

   Covered with greasy gravy, I thought the steak would be very fattening.

   Which noun is the phrase intended to describe?_____

   Revised version:_____

   _____

5. Underline the misplaced participial phrase:

   Making the winning basket, Susan watched her hero during the final minutes of the ball game.

   Which noun is the phrase intended to describe?_____

   Revised version:_____

   _____

6. Underline the misplaced participial phrase:

   Buried under a pile of dust, the historian had a difficult time finding the ancient records.

   Which noun is the phrase intended to describe?

   Revised version:_____

   _____

7. Underline the misplaced participial phrase:

   Covered with frosting, John could not tell whether his birthday cake was chocolate or white.

   Which noun is the phrase intended to describe?_____

   Revised version:_____

   _____

8. Underline the misplaced participial phrase:

   Flying to California, the Grand Canyon was seen by the passengers.

   Which noun is the phrase intended to describe?_____

   Revised version:_____

   _____

9. Underline the misplaced participial phrase:

   My friends saw the Grand Canyon flying to California.

   Which noun is the phrase intended to describe?_____

   Revised version:_____

   _____

10. Underline the misplaced participial phrase:

    Sam heard the wind lying in his bed.

    Which noun is the phrase intended to describe?_____

Revised version:_____

_____

BONUS: Here's one with a slightly different pattern. Can you fix it?

Turkey being a tradition at our house, we had my mother-in-law for dinner.

_____

_____

____(This may require more than one sentence.) _____

O DANGLING PARTICIPLES REALLY DANGLE?

No, "dangling participles" don't really "dangle," but people like to say they do. Have you ever heard of a dangling participle? If you check the index of any reputable English handbook, you are likely to find an entry for "Dangling Participles." What are these suspended parts that receive so much attention? Here's an example:

Rushing out the door, the wastebasket tipped over.

The underlined participial phrase in this sentence is called a dangling participle. As you can see, the phrase "rushing out the door" clearly describes a noun that is moving in a hurry. Yet the only noun in this sentence is "the wastebasket"! I guess it is possible for wastebaskets to rush out doors if they have feet—and sometimes, in cartoons, they do.

But in real life, this sentence leaves a big question unanswered. Who is really rushing out the door? If we presume that it cannot be the wastebasket, who is it? It is probably a person, but the person described by "rushing out the door" is not mentioned in this sentence. Therefore, the adjective participial phrase "rushing out the door" is hanging out in a sentence where it has nothing to describe. For that reason this participle is said to "dangle."

Personally, I can't see the logic of that label. After all, everything I've ever observed dangling has always been attached to something, something that it hangs from when it dangles. But "dangling" participles are attached to nothing in the sentence, so how can they "dangle"? I really think the term should be "detached participles" instead of "dangling participles." But I haven't met anyone yet who is inclined to change to my way of thinking, so I shall probably go through the rest of my life teaching about "dangling participles," which, in my heart, I know don't really dangle at all.

How do we repair sentences with "dangling" participles? We simply *insert* nouns or pronouns that these lonely, detached phrases can attach themselves to:

Rushing out the door, the wastebasket tipped over.

becomes instead:

Rushing out the door, <u>Jerry</u> tipped the wastebasket over.

COLLABORATE!   *Attaching Detached Participles*

Directions:

The following sentences all contain "dangling" participial phrases.

A. *Working with a group or on your own, underline the participial phrase in each sentence.*

B. *Then make up your own nouns (or pronouns) for the phrases to describe.*

C. *Rewrite the sentence to include your nouns or pronouns. Rewriting may take some thought since each sentence is different. Be sure, however, that, in every case, your participial phrase ends up NEXT TO the noun you have provided for it to describe. Note: In the first two items, clues are included to help you get started.*

1. Looking down from the forty-fifth floor, the cars seemed like toys.

   (Clue: Who was looking down from the forty-fifth floor?)

   _____

   _____

2. Driving home, a deer was seen. (Clue: Who was driving home?)

   _____

   _____

3. Turning the corner, a beautiful mountain appeared in our view.

   _____

   _____

4. Flying low, a herd of elk could be seen.

   _____

   _____

5. Walking over to the edge of the canyon, the golf course suddenly appeared.

   _____

   _____

6. Calling for an ambulance, the corpse was delivered to the morgue.

   _____

   _____

7. Born and raised in the city, farms were always amazing to me.

   _____

   _____

8. Speaking as an old friend, this purchase should not be considered.

   _____

   _____

9. Driving down the street, a shot was fired.

   _____

   _____

10.   Putting out the fire, the entire house became wet.

_____

_____

COLLABORATE!   *Participle Pandemonium*

Directions

Work together with a group or on your own. The following passage is full of misplaced and "dangling" participles.

A. Read the passage, carefully noting the misplaced and dangling participial phrases that have been underlined for you.

B. Decide whether

—the phrase is misplaced and needs to be <u>moved</u> next to the noun it is intended to describe,
OR
—the phrase is dangling and the sentence needs <u>more information</u>.

C. Then <u>rewrite</u> each sentence to say what you believe the writer intended to communicate. You may sometimes need to change one sentence into two different sentences to make the writing clear.

<u>Ringing loudly</u>, I turned off my alarm and got out of bed. <u>Needing to be at school early</u>, skipping my morning shower was my only choice. But <u>tempted by the thought of raisin bread</u>, a quick breakfast was something I considered. <u>Having become moldy however</u>, I could not eat the bread. <u>Rushing hurriedly out of the house</u>, the garage door opener would not work for me. <u>Making several attempts</u>, the garage door finally responded <u>straining my back</u>. The expressway was the best route <u>trying to arrive on time</u>. Unfortunately, <u>looking out my car window</u>, the traffic was heavy. <u>Arriving at the college parking lot</u>, every space was full. <u>Frustrated by the lack of parking</u>, getting to class on time seemed impossible. <u>Driving around for ten minutes</u>, a space finally opened up. <u>Running up the stairs</u>, the classroom was just around the corner. <u>Looking at my watch</u>, the time was exactly eight o'clock. But what was this??? <u>Reading the sign posted on the door</u>, the class was canceled because of instructor illness!!!

JOURNAL PROMPT

Discuss your attitude toward being late. Are you a person who is constantly late? Or are you always on time or early? How does the way you treat time affect other people around you? How do you feel about the way your friends and family treat time? Are some people always late when you are on time or early? Or is it the other way around? What kind of adjustments do you make to enable yourself to get along with people who treat time differently from the way you treat time?

*P*UNCTUATION PITFALLS CAUSED BY VERBAL PHRASES

Punctuation is a subject we haven't discussed much in this book so far. But now, as the sentences we encounter become more sophisticated, punctuation (especially commas) becomes an integral part of our writing.

One instance in which writers use commas together with verbal phrases is when the phrases *introduce* sentences. In the exercise you just completed called "Participle Pandemonium," you will notice, if you look carefully, that commas come after *introductory* participial phrases. In a later chapter on commas, you will discover the reason for that is a part of a comma rule about introductory information. Participial phrases often begin sentences, and so do infinitive phrases and gerund phrases. Does this mean that *any* verbal phrase appearing at the beginning of a sentence must be followed by a comma? NO! It means that any verbal phrase *that is introductory to a sentence* must be followed by a comma.

Wait a minute . . . Isn't "beginning a sentence" the same as "introductory to a sentence"? **Absolutely Not.** Something beginning a sentence could merely be the first part of a sentence such as the subject. Subjects often begin sentences, but they are not followed by commas. Since gerund phrases are nouns, they can be subjects, too. When a sentence begins with a gerund phrase subject, that subject is not followed by a comma. After all, that subject is a *part* of the main idea of the sentence rather than *introductory* to the sentence.
Compare the following sentences:

> *Listening to the music made Tom sleepy.*
> (Gerund phrase subject; NOT introductory information)

> *Listening to the music, Tom fell asleep.*
> (Participial phrase; introductory information)

Both of the above sentences are punctuated correctly. The first sentence contains no comma because the underlined phrase is a gerund that acts as the subject—a necessary part of the sentence. The second sentence contains a comma because the underlined phrase is participial: it only *describes* the subject and, therefore, is not a necessary part of the sentence's structure.

Since participial phrases always describe, they are always set off by commas when they introduce sentences. Since gerunds are nouns, they are normally functioning as subjects when they occur at the beginning of sentences. Therefore, beginning gerund phrases are typically not followed by commas.

Infinitive phrases are more complex. Since they sometimes functions as nouns, they can be subjects. In that event, they are not followed by a comma. Yet, they can also function as adjectives *describing* the subject of the sentence. In that case, they will be followed by a comma. Compare the following sentences:

> <u>*To practice the piano*</u> *is a daily routine for Tom.*
> (The infinitive phrase is the subject; not introductory material.)

> <u>*To practice the piano*</u>*, Tom needs self-discipline.*
> (The infinitive phrase is introductory material)

An easy way to tell whether you should place a comma after a verbal phrase appearing at the start of a sentence is to ask yourself whether the sentence would be complete without the phrase. If it would, a comma should follow the phrase because it is introductory to the sentence rather than a necessary structural part of the sentence. If the sentence *would not* be complete without the beginning verbal phrase, no comma should follow the phrase because it is a necessary part of the sentence rather than an introductory part. Which sentence still sounds complete without the infinitive phrase?

_____ is a daily routine for Tom.

_____, Tom needs self-discipline.

DO IT YOURSELF!   *Consider Calling on a Comma*

Directions

Read the following sentences carefully and decide for yourself whether the underlined verbal phrase is a necessary part of each sentence or not. If the phrase is merely descriptive and introductory to the sentence, insert a comma following it. If the phrase is part of the sentence that cannot be dropped, do not insert a comma. Circle any commas you insert, so your answers are easy to see.

1. <u>Wearing a flowing gown</u> the woman entered the room gracefully.
2. <u>Wearing a flowing gown</u> makes walking up stairs awkward.
3. <u>To help his charity</u> he worked many long hours on the telethon.
4. <u>To help his charity</u> was his goal.
5. <u>Being late to class</u> will hurt my grade.
6. <u>Being late to class</u> I could not stop for coffee.
7. <u>To lock the door</u> Mark used two different keys.
8. <u>To lock the door</u> required two different keys.
9. <u>To finish her work early</u> Anita had to give up her lunch hour.
10. <u>To finish her work early</u> was Anita's goal.

WRITE RIGHT FOR THE JOB: Parallel Job "List"ings

All the sentence issues we have discussed in this chapter apply just as much to on-the-job writing as they do to academic writing or creative writing. Since employers value clear communication, avoiding misplaced and dangling participles is particularly important to writers in the workplace. Punctuation decisions, too, often become critical in the production of a professional document.

On the job, lists are often used in letters and reports. While lists may appear in academic and creative writing, they appear more often in business documents. A list can occur quite informally, imbedded in a sentence:

In your letter of application, please include <u>experience, education, and references.</u>

A list can also <u>look</u> like a list:

> *In your letter of application, please include the following:*
>
> 1. *Experience*
> 2. *Education*
> 3. *References*

Employees are often encouraged to write such formal-looking lists because they are easier to read at a glance. A busy reader can more easily skim a list when it is set up in a column instead of imbedded in a sentence. Also, a reader can more easily use a formal list as a checklist when responding to requests for information.

Regardless of how lists physically look in a document, the items on the lists should be structured in a *parallel* way. To begin to understand the notion of parallel structures, compare the following examples:

> *I prefer the following jobs: typing documents, to take notes at meetings, and answer the telephone.*

What are the three items on this list? Copy them into the spaces below using *the exact words* that were used in the above sentence:
I prefer the following jobs:

1. _____

2. _____

3. _____

Now look at this version:

> *I prefer the following jobs: typing documents, taking notes at meetings, and answering the telephone.*

Copy the list in this sentence using *the exact words:*
I prefer the following jobs:

1. _____

2. _____

3. _____

Which of the previous lists that you copied is easiest to read? _____

_____

Why? _____

_____

Did you select the second list? The second list reads more smoothly because the items on the list have parallel structure.

ISTS AND COMMON DENOMINATORS

Parallel structure in writing is similar to common denominators in math.

How good are you at math? Do you remember how to add fractions? If so, solve this problem:

$$
\begin{array}{r}
1/2 \\
1/3 \\
+\ 1/4 \\
\hline
\end{array}
$$

THE ANSWER:_____

Is you answer 1-1/12? Then I presume that to arrive at this correct answer, you first found a common denominator:

$$
\begin{array}{r}
1/2 = 6/12 \\
1/3 = 4/12 \\
+\ 1/4 = 3/12 \\
\hline
\text{THE ANSWER: } \underline{13/12 = 1\text{-}1/12}
\end{array}
$$

By converting all the fractions in the problem into twelfths, did you *change* their value? No. You simply made the fractions easier to add and subtract, *easier to compare and contrast*. Isn't a list in writing just a kind of verbal addition problem with the word "and" taking the place of the plus (+) sign? Just as in math, in writing—if your *verbal* addition problems have items that are expressed in different forms (like a gerund phrase, an infinitive phrase, and a verb stem), they will be difficult to read, difficult to compare and contrast. Therefore, you need to convert every item on your written list to a common denominator.

When I was writing the above list about the jobs I prefer, I initially paid no attention to a common denominator—one item began with a gerund, another began with an infinitive, and still another began with a verb stem. I did not put the items into the same form before asking my reader to add them together. So when I revised my sentence, I corrected my list by giving all the items the same common denominator. My common denominator became *-ing*. In other words I made all the items on my list begin with **gerunds:**

typing documents = **typ*ing*** documents
to take notes at meetings = **tak*ing*** notes at meetings
answer the telephone = **answer*ing*** the telephone

I could, instead, have chosen a different common denominator. I could have made all the items into **infinitives:**

typing documents = **to type** documents
to take notes at meetings = **to take** notes at meetings
answer the telephone = **to answer** the telephone

Still another option would have been to **introduce my list differently.** If I had simply said, "I like to *type* documents, *take* notes at meetings, and *answer* the telephone," the word "to" at the start of my list could have acted as an infinitive marker shared by all three items on the list.

The above choices all involve using verbals in lists. While verbals are often troublemakers in lists, they are not the only structures that can make lists parallel. **Lists are PARALLEL when every item on the list is in the same form.** For example, a list might be all nouns or all verbs. You wouldn't put *worked, played, and apples* on the same list. But you might put *worked, played, and picked apples* on the same list.

COLLABORATE!   *Finding the Common Denominators*

Directions

Work with a group or on your own.

A. The following examples contain lists that are not parallel. Decide upon a common denominator that will convert all items on the list into the same form. Write your parallel version in the space provided. If necessary, you may divide or combine different items on the list, making your finished list longer or shorter than the original.

1.   In your report, please provide the following information:

   • Time of injury
   • Date of injury
   • Giving the location where the injury occurred

   _____

   _____

   _____

   _____

2.   Please follow these steps when using the copy machine:

   A. After lifting the cover, place the original on the glass.
   B. You must select the number of copies you desire.
   C. Close the cover and press the START button.
   D. Removing the original after closing the cover again.

   _____

   _____

   _____

   _____

   _____

   _____

   _____

3. A positive recommendation will be made if you can ensure your company will be doing the following:

    - Providing security for all major events
    - An improvement in the level of service
    - Compute the costs each month

    _____

    _____

    _____

    _____

4. The skills I have to offer my future employer are as follows:

    - Communicating well in writing
    - Deal positively with stressful situations
    - To work as a team member

    _____

    _____

    _____

    _____

5. Our mission is to respect the contributions of all employees, acknowledging that every worker has value, placing the customer first in all business transactions, and to work towards the goals of the company.

    _____

    _____

    _____

    _____

B. *The following are non-parallel lists adapted from student papers. Revise them to be parallel. Use verbals to help you create an effective finished product.*

1. I would like a woman to be capable of supporting herself, having her own job, maybe her own apartment, also to make her own decisions without needing the opinion of others.

    _____

    _____

    _____

2.   The things I look for in an ideal spouse are one same religion, two common in-
     terests and third someone that I can bring home and introduce to my parents
     without being embarrassed.

     _____

     _____

     _____

3.   Other men may not agree, but I think that a woman who isn't moody, some-
     one he has something in common with, and easy to talk to are the three most
     desirable characteristics of ideal mates.

     _____

     _____

     _____

THE READING CONNECTION

Spend some time looking for the following in your reading:

1.   Look for -ING forms and -ED forms and irregular past participles that are **not**
     accompanied by verb helpers. In other words, look for gerunds and participles
     at work in the writing of others. Also look for infinitives (to + a verb stem). Bring
     back sentences or paragraphs from your reading that illustrate the use of verbals;
     share these with your classmates.

2.   Compare several different authors and their styles. Do some authors use verbals
     more than others? Explain. How does the presence or lack of verbals affect your
     reaction to a piece of writing?

3.   Look for written material that contains lists. For example, instructions for as-
     sembling something typically contain lists. You may also find lists in business
     letters or memos. Newspapers or magazines, too, may contain articles that in-
     corporate lists. Bring samples of lists you have found to class. Discuss whether
     or not the writer of each list was careful to use parallel structure. Identify the
     "common denominators" in the lists you have gathered.

THE WRITING CONNECTION

Choose one the following topics to write about. As you revise what you have written,
pay special attention to effective incorporation of verbals into your finished product.

1.   Use a gerund as a stimulus for a piece of writing. For example, write about *sail-
     ing, coping, dying, working, avoiding, believing, succeeding, fishing, needing* or any
     other -ING word that sparks ideas for you. Before you begin your first draft,
     spend some time free writing, brainstorming, or mind-mapping your thoughts.

2. Write a description of an **event.** For example, describe a wedding you attended, or a funeral; or describe a certain kind of ceremony, an important ball game, or a performance of some sort. Use verbals and verbal phrases to describe what people do and the things that happen during the event. Be careful to place descriptive verbal phrases next to the people and things they describe.

3. Create a piece of writing in which you incorporate a list of some kind. For example, you could write about several different ways you save money; several favorite movies, including a number of reasons that you like each one; several places you would like to visit someday, including several reasons for wanting to visit each place; or several reasons for believing strongly about something you believe in. As you revise your first draft, pay careful attention to any items that should be parallel in structure. Choose the "common denominator" that you feel works best for listing your ideas in a parallel way.

4. Develop any one of your journal entries from this chapter (or from previous chapters) into a finished piece of writing. Be conscious of effectively using verbals and incorporating lists into your writing when appropriate.

SELF-TEST FOR CHAPTER 11

1. Three kinds of verbals in English are _____, _____, and _____.

2. Verbals that always function as nouns in sentences are called _____.

3. Verbals that always function as adjectives in sentences are called _____.

4. Verbals that may function either as nouns, adjectives, or adverbs are called _____.

5. Participles may end in _____ or _____ or they may be irregular past participle forms.

6. In the **Gerund-Participle Test,** _____ can be dropped from a sentence without creating an incomplete sentence.

7. _____ phrases, which act as adjectives, should be located next to the noun they describe.

8. To repair a _____ participle, the writer must add information to the sentence containing the participle.

9. When beginning a sentence with a verbal phrase acting as a subject, the phrase *should/should not* (circle one) be set off with a comma.

10. When a list has _____, its items are all expressed in the same form.

FINAL JOURNAL WRITING

Write in your journal about what you learned in this chapter. How have your thoughts about verbs changed after learning about verbals? Do you feel more confident that you can now make your writing sound lively and energetic? Explain. Was the concept of verbal phrases difficult to grasp? Why? Do you think you misplace phrases in your writing? What can you do to avoid this in the future? How will you handle the writing of lists differently in your future writing? In what way was the chapter useful or not useful for you?

CHAPTER 12

CLAUSES—SENTENCES INSIDE SENTENCES WITH COMPLEX IDEAS

Have you heard the one about the English teacher who took her young daughter to see Santa Claus? They went to a large department store that featured a convincing Santa who was assisted by helpers also dressed in red suits. The child bravely climbed onto Santa's lap and whispered everything she wanted for Christmas. But, on the way home, she asked her mom some unsettling questions: "Mom, I know that man in the red suit was really Santa Claus. But who were the other people dressed in red suits—the people who told us to stay in line, took our pictures, and handed out the candy canes—who were they? Were they Santas too?" Mom replied, "No, Honey. Those were the <u>subordinate clauses</u>."

—*AUTHOR UNKNOWN*

QUESTIONS TO ASK YOURSELF WHILE READING CHAPTER 12:

1. How will learning about clauses help me make my writing more interesting and varied?
2. How can knowing the difference between an independent clause and a dependent clause reduce my chances of writing sentence fragments and run-on sentences?
3. How can complex sentences help me write more detailed explanations?
4. How can I use compound sentences to compare and contrast ideas in writing?
5. How can my awareness of different kinds of clauses improve my ability to use commas and semicolons effectively?

Did you miss the point of the Santa Claus joke? You may have if you've never heard of **subordinate clauses**. Subordinate clauses are not Santa's helpers; they are important players in sentences. All sentences are comprised of **clauses**—some of them subordinate, and some not.

ECOMING ACQUAINTED WITH CLAUSES THAT DON'T WEAR RED SUITS

What is a *clause*? The word clause refers to a group of words. It originally meant "close" in Latin and referred to a word group that occurred at the close of a rhetorical statement or legal argument. Today "clause" is still used to talk about sections of laws. But, in the study of sentences, it has come to have a more specific definition that lies somewhere between a *phrase* and a *sentence*. In fact clauses, phrases, and simple sentences are often confused. By studying the following chart, you may discover why:

Simple Sentence	Clause	Phrase
A group of words that **always** contains a subject and a verb and expresses a complete idea	A group of words that **always** contains a subject and a verb and **may sometimes** express a complete idea OR **may sometimes** act act as one part of speech (for example, clauses may act as nouns, adjectives, or adverbs)	A group of words that acts as one part of speech (for example, phrases may act as nouns, adjectives, or adverbs)

DO IT YOURSELF!   *Test Yourself on the Definitions*

Directions

A. *Refer to the above chart to complete the statements below with <u>one or more</u> of the following terms: PHRASE, CLAUSE, SIMPLE SENTENCE*

1. A group of words could be

   _____.

2. A group of words acting as one part of speech (noun, adjective, or adverb) could be

   _____.

3. A group of words containing a subject and a verb could be

   _____

4. A group of words expressing a complete idea could be

   _____

B. *Write out the definitions, as you understand them, for the following:*

1. A **simple sentence** is

    _____

    _____

    _____

2. A **phrase** is

    _____

    _____

    _____

3. A **clause** is

    _____

    _____

    _____

—Does your last definition look something like this: *A clause is a group of words that* **always** *contains a subject and a verb. A clause* **may sometimes** *express a complete idea, OR a clause* **may sometimes** *act as one part of speech (noun, adjective, or adverb)?*

MAKING TWO DEFINITIONS OUT OF ONE

The clause definition is quite complicated because it contains one **always** statement and two different **sometimes** statements:

1. a clause **always** contains subject and a verb;	a clause **may sometimes** express a complete idea
OR	
2. A clause **always** contains a subject and a verb;	a clause **may sometimes** act as one part of speech (noun, adjective, or adverb)

If we break the definition up in this way, we can see that there must be at least <u>two</u> different kinds of clauses:

1. A clause that contains a subject and a verb and expresses a complete idea.

   _____

2. A clause that contains a subject and a verb and acts as one part of speech (noun adjective, or adverb). _____

If I tell you that definition #1 identifies a clause called an INDEPENDENT CLAUSE, what would you guess the clause identified by definition #2 is called?

Did you guess "dependent clause"? If you did, you're exactly right! After the preceding definitions, write the words "Independent Clause" and "Dependent Clause" in the appropriate places. Clearly the independent clause is the one that most resembles a sentence, and the dependent clause is the one that most resembles a phrase.

JUST HOW INDEPENDENT IS AN INDEPENDENT CLAUSE?

An independent clause is also called a MAIN CLAUSE. Both terms have the same meaning. Some teachers just prefer the term "independent" while others prefer the shorter term "main."

Isn't the definition of an independent clause exactly like the definition of a simple sentence? Yes, it is. Then why don't we just call independent clauses "sentences"? Some experts do. But we can make a distinction. In fact, you can probably explain the difference between a sentence and an independent clause yourself simply by studying the following example:

My brother went to the store, and he bought some groceries.

1. How many sentences did I just write? _____

2. Did you answer ONE, or did you answer TWO? _____

3. Look at the example again. How many subject-verb combinations are there in

   the example? _____

4. Did you find TWO? _____

Be careful, however, before you jump to the conclusion that there are two sentences; for you see, there is one part of the definition of a sentence that we have been assuming because it seems so obvious: *A sentence begins with a capital letter and ends with an end mark, such as a period or a question mark.* If we keep this in mind, we immediately see that the statement about my brother going to the store is only one sentence. After all it has only one capital letter and one period.

However, even though the above example is only one sentence, it does contain two independent clauses. Remember your definition: An independent clause is a group of words that contains a subject and a verb and expresses a complete idea.

So the sentence about my brother contains *two sets of subjects and verbs and two complete ideas*; therefore, it contains two independent clauses:

Idea #1: My brother went to the store
Idea #2: he bought some groceries

These two clauses could easily be written as two separate sentences:

My brother went to the store.
He bought some milk.

Instead, however, I chose to write the two ideas as one sentence joining them with the word "and." A sentence, like this one, containing two independent clauses is called a *compound sentence* because it contains two "sentences"—or at least two structures which *could* be written as two simple sentences *if* I put a period after each complete idea.

AND WHAT ABOUT "AND"?

The independent clauses in compound sentences are typically connected with a word like "and." In earlier chapters we have seen "and" connecting two identical sentence parts—like two verbs or two subjects or two phrases. Now we see this same "and" connecting two independent clauses that are each capable of being sentences.

The word "and" is a **coordinating conjunction.** That's quite a mouthful! But it's a label you can easily remember if you learn a little more Latin:

- The word "conjunction" contains the word "junction." What do you think of when you see a road sign telling you a junction is coming up ahead? Do you think of two roads coming together? Also, if you've ever worked with electricity, you may be familiar with a junction box where circuits come together. So a junction is simply a place where things come together or <u>join</u>. "Junction," in Latin, means "join or connect."

- The prefix "con" in "*con*junction" is Latin for "with." The word "conjunction," then, is a logical label to give to words used "with a joining" of two sentences or two sentence parts.

- And what about the "coordinating" part of "**coordinating** conjunction"? "Coordinating" means "matching." When you coordinate your wardrobe, you make sure your clothes match, don't you? **A coordinating conjunction, then, marks the place where matching** parts join together. (Matching parts could be two simple sentences, two independent clauses, two nouns, two verbs—in other words, two of the *same kinds* of structures.)

THE "BOYFANS" FAMILY

"AND" is not the only coordinating conjunction in English. It's just the most frequently used member of a bigger family: the BOYFANS family. Here's a complete list of all the **BOYFANS words:**

<u>But</u>   <u>Or</u>   <u>Yet</u>   <u>For</u>   <u>And</u>   <u>Nor</u>   <u>So</u>

Do you see why I call them the BOYFANS words? BOYFANS is a term worth remembering because it can help you recall the list of coordinating conjunctions in English.

Why would it be important for you to recall this list? When you study punctuation and punctuation rules, you will discover that the BOYFANS words are treated differently from other connecting words in sentences.

Study the following examples of BOYFANS words (or coordinating conjunctions) and how they are punctuated when joining matching structures:

In Simple Sentences . . .

John <u>and</u> Katie love baseball.
(**and** connects two subjects—"John" and "Katie")

John plays <u>and</u> officiates baseball.
(**and** connects two verbs—"plays" and "officiates")

Katie's team plays at home <u>and</u> on the road.
(**and** connects two phrases—"at home" and "on the road")

In Compound Sentences . . .

*John is a catcher, **and** Katie is a pitcher.*
(**and** connects two independent clauses—"John is a catcher" and "Katie is a pitcher")

*John **and** Katie both play baseball, **and** their friends attend the games **and** cheer for them.*
(Can you explain the three different uses of **and** in this compound sentence?)

DO IT YOURSELF!   *Take the "BOYFANS" Test*

Directions

Based on what you observe in the above examples, respond to the following statements by writing the words TRUE or FALSE in the space provided:

_____ 1. BOYFANS words always connect two structures that are the same.

_____ 2. BOYFANS words are always preceded by a comma.

_____ 3. Every sentence containing a BOYFANS word is a compound sentence.

_____ 4. One simple sentence may contain two verbs or two subjects.

_____ 5. A compound sentence contains at least two sets of subjects and verbs.

_____ 6. You should place a comma before a BOYFANS word that connects two independent clauses.

(Check your answers at the end of this chapter on page 344.)

NOTHER PUNCTUATION OPTION

If independent clauses are not connected with one of the BOYFANS words, they are often simply brought together in the same sentence with a semicolon (;):

John is a catcher; Katie is a pitcher.
John and Katie both play baseball; their friends attend the games and cheer for them.

DO IT YOURSELF!   *Distinguish Simple from Compound*

Directions

Read the following sentences carefully.

A. Draw a slash (/) in front of each BOYFANS word (but, or, yet, for, and, nor, so).

B. Insert a comma (,) in front of the BOYFANS word (coordinating conjunction) only when it connects two complete ideas. CIRCLE any commas you insert.

C. Insert a semicolon (;) if two complete ideas occur together in a sentence without a BOY-FANS word to connect them. CIRCLE any semicolons you insert.

D. Label each sentence as <u>simple</u> or <u>compound</u> in the space provided.

SIMPLE or COMPOUND?

_____   **1.** In English class we learn about sentence structure and write in journals.

_____   **2.** The teacher and the students read and critique the written work.

_____   **3.** I always read my critiqued papers carefully and afterwards I rewrite them.

_____   **4.** I enjoy reading my classmates' papers for they give me ideas to use in my own writing.

_____   **5.** The teacher does not write a grade on our papers but he writes many comments.

_____   **6.** I will receive a grade at the end of the term based on attendance and the quality of my written work.

_____   **7.** I do not always like to see errors marked on my papers yet I benefit from the corrections.

_____   **8.** We all write rough drafts and then we revise them.

_____   **9.** My best friend wrote about her pet bird I wrote about my pet snake.

_____   **10.** My teacher had never owned a bird or snake nor had anyone else in class.

COLLABORATE! *Simple and Compound Sentences Working Together in Paragraphs*

Directions

Read the following paragraphs carefully.

A. Draw a slash in front of each coordinating conjunction (BOYFANS word).

B. If there is a complete idea containing a subject and a verb on each side of the slash you have drawn, the sentence is compound. If not, the sentence is simple. Write "compound" or "simple" in the space provided following each sentence.

C. Insert a comma (,) in front of the coordinating conjunctions—only IF they are connecting two complete ideas. CIRCLE any commas you insert.

D. Insert a semicolon (;) if two complete ideas occur together without a BOYFANS word to connect them. CIRCLE any semicolons you insert.

Anita's family went to the Humane Society to find a cat or a dog. _____ The boys in the family wanted a cat but the girls wanted a dog. _____ Mom and Dad decided the children could look at both kinds of animals. _____ They first looked at cats for the cats were kept in the nearest kennel. _____ The kennel was full of adult cats and newborn kittens. _____ The boys couldn't decide whether they wanted a full grown adult cat or a kitten. _____ They started to argue so the girls went on to the dog kennel without them. _____ The dog kennel was noisy and smelly but the girls loved it. _____ The pens were filled with dogs of all sizes and shapes._____ Anita and her sisters didn't want a big dog nor did they want a little dog. _____ Finally they found the perfect mutt and they went back to show the boys. _____ The boys liked the dog yet they had found an adorable cat. _____ The decision between the two pets was impossible Anita's family ended up adopting both a cat and a dog. _____

JOURNAL PROMPT

Are you an animal lover? If so, what is your favorite kind of pet? Do you favor a particular breed of animal? Why? Have you ever visited the Humane Society or Animal Shelter in your area? Describe your experience. Have you ever taken an animal to the Humane Society? Explain. Have you ever adopted a pet? Were you pleased with your choice? Why or why not?

HEN SENTENCES RUN INTO EACH OTHER

A common problem found in student papers is something called a *run-on sentence*. A run-on sentence is created when a writer simply runs one complete idea into another without using the necessary punctuation. Here is an example of a run-on sentence:

Damon went to Las Vegas he stayed at the Mirage Hotel.

Can you tell where one sentence ends and the other begins? Write the two sentences that you think make up the above run-on:

1._____

2._____

As a writer, you need to be able to spot run-ons in your own writing and repair them. You have several different options for repairing the above run-on sentence:

Option 1: Divide the run-on sentence into simple sentences.

Damon went to Las Vegas.
He stayed at the Mirage Hotel.

Option 2: Write the run-on as a compound sentence using a BOYFANS word as a connector. Remember to put a comma *in front of* the BOYFANS word.

Damon went to Las Vegas, <u>and</u> he stayed at the Mirage Hotel.

Option 3: Write the run-on as a compound sentence punctuated with a semicolon.

Damon went to Las Vegas; he stayed at the Mirage Hotel.

DO IT YOURSELF!   *Repair the Run-ons*

Directions
Repair the following run-on sentences.
A. First draw a slash (I) between the complete ideas.
B. Then rewrite each run-on using all three options suggested above.

1. Damon doesn't like to gamble he likes to go to shows.

    Option #1:   (Break into a simple sentence.)

    _____

    _____

    _____

    Option #2:   (Insert BOYFANS word and comma—remember, you can use <u>any</u>
    BOYFANS word: but, or, yet, for, and, nor, so.)

    _____

    _____

    _____

Option #3:   (Separate using a semicolon.)

_____

_____

_____

2. Nowadays many hotels have theme parks even children enjoy vacationing in Las Vegas.

Option #1:   _____

_____

_____

Option #2:   _____

_____

_____

Option #3:   _____

_____

_____

3. My favorite theme park is the one at the MGM Grand Hotel I always spend an entire day there during my vacation.

Option #1:   _____

_____

_____

Option #2:   _____

_____

_____

Option #3:   _____

_____

_____

4. Many attractions in Las Vegas are very expensive I cannot afford to take them all in.

Option #1:   _____

_____

_____

Option #2:   _____

_____

_____

Option #3:   _____

_____

_____

5. Other attractions are free people can enjoy them over and over.

    Option #1: _____

    _____

    _____

    Option #2: _____

    _____

    _____

    Option #3: _____

    _____

6. The battle of the pirate ships at the Treasure Island Hotel is one exciting free attraction it is always well attended.

    Option #1: _____

    _____

    _____

    Option #2: _____

    _____

    _____

    Option #3: _____

    _____

7. Another enjoyable aspect of visiting Las Vegas is going out to eat the city has hundreds of excellent restaurants.

    Option #1: _____

    _____

    _____

    Option #2: _____

    _____

    _____

    Option #3: _____

    _____

8. Many of the restaurants offer elegant buffets the prices are usually very reasonable.

    Option #1: _____

    _____

    _____

Option #2: _____

_____

_____

Option #3: _____

_____

_____

9. The cost of visiting Las Vegas is usually less in the winter the hotels are not very crowded then.

Option #1: _____

_____

_____

Option #2: _____

_____

_____

Option #3: _____

_____

_____

10. Las Vegas is a rapidly growing resort city new hotels and attractions welcome me on every visit.

Option #1: _____

_____

_____

Option #2: _____

_____

_____

Option #3: _____

_____

_____

SHOULD INDEPENDENT CLAUSES BE SENTENCED?

Independent clauses and compound sentences are not difficult concepts for most students. After all, an independent clause closely resembles a simple sentence. In fact, some authorities think that independent clauses should just simply be called "sentences."

Then if we write a compound sentence, we could simply say we have written a sentence that contains two sentences—just as when we write a compound word like "fingerprint," we say we have written a word that contains two words: "finger" and "print." What is your opinion? Should we rid the English language of "independent" clauses forever by *sentencing* them?

HOULD DEPENDENT CLAUSES RECEIVE ALL THE ATTENTION?

Most experts agree that the **dependent clause** is the one that should receive the most attention in a discussion of clauses. In fact, some believe dependent clauses are the <u>only</u> structures we should even call "clauses."

A dependent clause is a group of words with a subject and a verb that *does not* express a complete idea. Dependent clauses, like phrases, act as a single part of speech in a sentence. They are typically adverbs, adjectives, or nouns.

The word *dependent* implies that something cannot stand alone because it relies on something else to prop it up. And this is true of dependent clauses. Dependent clauses rely on simple sentences (or independent clauses) to prop them up and make their ideas complete.

There are two major categories of dependent clauses. One category is **subordinate clauses**, and the other is **relative clauses**. Let's begin with the subordinate clauses. The term "subordinate" is a less familiar word than "dependent." In the joke about the child visiting Santa Claus, the "subordinate clauses" were the clauses that worked for Santa Claus. If you have ever been in the military, you may be familiar with the word *subordinate* in a professional context. Military personnel with lesser ranks are often called "subordinates." So we can conclude that whether we're talking about elves or privates, the term subordinate means "less than." Therefore, in our writing, *subordinate clauses are <u>less than</u> complete sentences—less than independent clauses.*

OW SUBORDINATE CLAUSES LOSE THEIR INDEPENDENCE

When studying phrases, we encountered word groups that were less than complete sentences. But how are dependent subordinate clauses different from phrases? The difference is that *every* clause must contain a subject and a verb. Even a dependent clause must contain a subject and a verb.

But how can a group of words with a subject and a verb ever be *less than* a sentence? After all, doesn't the presence of a subject and a verb automatically make a complete sentence? Don't the following *two words* constitute a complete sentence?

Susan snores.

This is a two-word sentence, a two-word independent clause. That *proves* that all I need for a complete idea is two words! (Or does it?)

The next logical question is: How could I possibly write a group of words that contains a subject and a verb and yet <u>not</u> have a complete idea? How could I write a dependent clause? My best explanation is in the form of a math analogy. Comparing English to math always works well because both subjects are based on a system of logic. Consider this *addition problem:*

$$\text{Susan} + \text{snores} = \text{a complete idea}$$

Because

$$\text{subject} + \text{verb} = \text{a complete idea}$$

Now, let's give the subject "Susan" a number value of 2; and let's give the verb "snores" a number value of 3. (After all, verbs are more valuable than subjects in sentences.) Our comparison now looks like this:

$$\text{Susan} + \text{snores} = \text{a complete idea}$$

compares to

$$\text{Subject} + \text{verb} = \text{a complete idea}$$

compares to

$$2 + 3 = 5$$

Once we plug in all the numbers, a complete idea is worth **5.** Are you still with me? If not, reread all the above addition problems.

But what happens to the math problem if the *subject* and *verb* in the statement must somehow equal *less than* a complete idea? (After all, dependent subordinate clauses do contain *less than* a complete idea.) In math, we could simply change the **5** to a **4** to end up with something "less than." So my addition problem and its counterpart clause would look like this:

$$2 + 3 = 4$$

$$\text{Susan} + \text{snores} = \underline{\text{less than}} \text{ a complete idea}$$

The problem now is that neither one of the above statements is accurate any more. Is it possible to make the math problem equal **4** without getting rid of the **2** or the **3**? It is if you know how to use negative numbers! What happens if you add a negative one *(−1)* to **2** and **3**?

$$-1 + 2 + 3 = 4$$

Now the statement is accurate! *Adding* negative numbers is one way to make something "less than" in math without getting rid of the numbers you started with—you simply ADD negative one! And that is exactly how to make a complete idea with a subject and verb into incomplete idea without getting rid of the subject and the verb you started—you simply ADD a negative-one! But the negative-one in a sentence needs to be a *word* instead of a number because sentences are verbal statements instead of numerical statements. Here's a word in English that has a negative value: IF. What happens to your complete sentence, "Susan snores," when you add the word IF:

If Susan snores . . .

The above statement no longer expresses a complete idea even though it still contains a subject and a verb! The word "IF" has the negative effect of making "Susan snores" unable to stand alone; "If Susan snores . . ." has become dependent on something else in the sentence for its completion.

Would you be comfortable putting a period after "If Susan snores" just because it contains a subject and a verb? I wouldn't. But I would be comfortable finishing the sentence this way:

If Susan snores, Fred cannot sleep.

What did I add to create a complete sentence? I added an independent clause. Certainly the clause, "Fred cannot sleep," expresses a complete idea. It makes sense that the only way to make a complete sentence out of a dependent clause that cannot stand alone is to ADD an independent clause that expresses a complete idea. After all, every sentence, no matter how simple or complex, needs *at least one complete idea.* That is the same as saying every sentence, no matter how simple or complex, needs *at least one independent clause.*

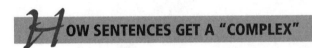

OW SENTENCES GET A "COMPLEX"

A sentence with one dependent clause and one independent clause is certainly not simple. In fact, it is called a **complex sentence.** A complex sentence is like a complex vitamin capsule. **It contains at least two different kinds of clauses** just like a complex vitamin contains two or more different kinds of vitamins. The complex sentence, not the simple sentence, is the most common sentence you and I write. That must mean we are complex thinkers. At least we spend much time and energy placing conditions on our sentences. Since complex sentences are such a significant part of writing, they are worth some careful study.

DO IT YOURSELF!   *Dissect a Complex Sentence*

Directions
To better understand the anatomy of a complex sentence, read the following sentence and answer the questions that follow:

If Susan snores, Fred cannot sleep.

1. How many subject-verb combinations do you find in the above sentence?

   _____

2. How many clauses are in the above sentence? _____

3. Which clause is an independent clause that expresses a complete idea and could

   stand alone as a sentence? (Write it out.)

   _____

4. Which clause is dependent and cannot stand alone? (Write it out.)

_____

5. Which word makes the dependent clause unable to stand alone as a complete sentence?

_____

_____

ONJUNCTIONS THAT SUBORDINATE THEIR CLAUSES

To make a complete sentence incomplete without removing the subject and the verb, writers ADD to the sentence. IF is only one of the words in English that has a negative effect when added to complete ideas. English has a collection of words that can make a sentence become **dependent or subordinate** (less than a sentence). These words are called **subordinating conjunctions**, and they include the following familiar expressions:

The Subordinating Conjunctions

after	before	unless
although	if	until
as	since	when
as if	so that	whenever
as long as	than	while
because	though	

To create a dependent subordinate clause, you can simply place any one of these words in front of a complete sentence.

DO IT YOURSELF! *Make Any Sentence Into a Subordinate Clause*

Directions

A. Place a different subordinating conjunction from the above list in front of each of the following sentences to create a subordinate clause. Notice, it doesn't matter how long or complicated a sentence is, it can still become a subordinate clause.

B. Change the period at the end of each sentence to a comma to remind yourself that you have created a dependent subordinate clause that is no longer a complete sentence. The first one is done for you as an example:

1. I heard a sudden cry of pain.
    Until I heard a sudden cry of pain,

2. Women are wiser than men.

    _____

3. I pursued an education and earned a degree.

    _____

4.   Frank had chip on his shoulder after winning the award.

   _____

5.   Water and oil do not mix.

   _____

6.   Everything I touch seems to turn to mold.

   _____

7.   George is over the hill.

   _____

8.   The ghosts were invisible.

   _____

9.   All men desire knowledge.

   _____

10.   The teacher called on the boy sitting in the back row wearing a baseball cap.

   _____

B. *Write complete sentences beginning with the above clauses. Insert a comma after the subordinate clause before you add the words that complete the idea. The first one is done for you as an example:*

1.   *Until I heard a sudden cry of pain, I did not notice the child's injury.*

2.   _____

   _____

   _____

3.   _____

   _____

   _____

4.   _____

   _____

   _____

5.   _____

   _____

   _____

6.   _____

   _____

   _____

7.   _____

   _____

   _____

8. _____

_____

_____

9. _____

_____

_____

10. _____

_____

_____

C. Write a paragraph using as a topic sentence one of the sentences you just created above. In your paragraph try to include at least three other sentences that begin with subordinate clauses.

_____

_____

_____

_____

_____

_____

_____

_____

_____

_____

_____

_____

SUBORDINATING CONJUNCTIONS AT THE JUNCTION

Why would words like *IF* and the others be called "conjunctions" if they do not occur at the junction where the dependent clause meets the independent clause?

Subordinating conjunctions may not always occur at the junction. But they *can*! Instead of writing

> **I͟f** Susan snores, Fred cannot sleep.

I could write . . .

> Fred cannot sleep **i͟f** Susan snores.

Notice the second version has no comma. The subordinating conjunction *IF* acts as a divider between the two clauses when the subordinate clause comes after the independent clause; therefore, no comma is needed. Because subordinating conjunctions **can** occur "at the junction" of two clauses, they are legitimately part of the conjunction family. They are, however, not coordinating conjunctions like the BOYFANS words because they do not connect *matching parts*. Instead, subordinating conjunctions connect *different parts*: they connect dependent subordinate clauses to independent clauses in complex sentences.

Both of the above example sentences about Susan and Fred communicate the same information. The only difference is how I have chosen to arrange the information. If I wanted to, I could even arrange the sentence in a third configuration:

*Fred, **if** Susan snores, cannot sleep.*

In this arrangement the dependent subordinate clause actually *interrupts* the main sentence (or independent clause); therefore, commas *surround* the interrupting clause. This kind of arrangement may seem awkward, but at times it can be useful for emphasis.

DO IT YOURSELF!   *Reverse the Clauses*

Directions: *In the following sentences, reverse the clauses. Be sure to insert commas only when the dependent clause comes at the beginning of the sentence. CIRCLE the commas you insert. The first one was done for you as an example.*

1. The dog slept after he ate.
    After he ate, the dog slept.

2. The race will be more challenging because Tom is running.
    _____

3. The dance was still not well attended although Thanh sang with the band.
    _____

4. Since John is always late, I will ask Karen to take me to the airport.
    _____

5. I will surely get an "A" in this class unless I flunk the final exam.
    _____

6. She will continue to work as long as she is healthy.
    _____

7. Before I go to bed, I always take my medicine.
    _____

8. As Alice entered the room, all heads turned.
    _____

9. Whenever it snows, Shannon avoids driving to work.
    _____

10. I will buy a house at the beach if I win the lottery.

_____

B. *The following paragraph contains numerous sentences containing subordinate clauses. Underline all the subordinate clauses and ADD any necessary COMMAS. CIRCLE all the commas you insert.*

Whenever I go to a video rental store I find at least a dozen interesting movies. I always rent only two movies on each visit although I want to rent more. Since I can't rent too many movies at once I try to diversify my choices. Because I like comedies best I always pick out at least one comedy. I often try to find a foreign film as long as the store has a sizeable foreign film section. I almost never rent action thrillers unless the films have received excellent reviews. Since there are so many movies available for rent limiting my choices is difficult. Until there are fifty hours in a day I will continue to rent only two movies at a time.

JOURNAL PROMPT

How frequently do you watch movies? Do you usually rent them for home viewing, or do you go out to theaters? What kinds of movies do you prefer? Why? What is one of your all-time favorite movies? Why do you think you like it so much?

WHAT IS A SUBORDINATE CLAUSE . . . REALLY?

Before we proceed any further, let's look at our original definition of clauses. It included the statement, *"a clause may act as one part of speech."*

So far we have seen one kind of clause, the independent clause, that can act as a complete sentence. That certainly is not *one part of speech.* We have seen another kind of clause, the dependent clause, that is less than a sentence. Does it act as one part of speech? Yes, it does.

All the other structures we have studied so far that have been less than sentences have acted as one part of speech. Prepositional phrases and verbal phrases in sentences acted as single parts of speech; they were either adverbs, adjectives, or nouns.

Dependent subordinate clauses also act as one part of speech. In fact, they act as *adverbs* in sentences. No wonder they're so easy to move around, from the front to the back to the middle of the sentence. Adverbs, after all, are the most moveable parts in sentences. For that reason, adverbs help writers create sentence variety. Subordinate clauses are just gigantic adverbs. And, because they too are movable, they too can be used to create more varied and interesting sentences.

Do you also remember that adverbs answer the questions "when," "where," and "how"? The question "how" is extended to "under what condition" when we include subordinate clauses as adverbs.

COLLABORATE!   *Decide the Adverb Question*

Directions

Work together with a group or on your own.

A. The following paragraph contains eight sentences with dependent subordinate clauses. Underline these subordinate clauses. They may be located in the front or in the back of the sentence.

B. Above each subordinate clause, write which question you think the clause answers: When? Where? How? or Under what condition?

So that I can help prevent pollution, I use the city bus system. The bus is easy to take since there are bus stops every few blocks throughout the city. Because the public transportation system is very popular, buses go everywhere in town. Although I own a car, I find the bus system more convenient for my downtown errands. I never have to worry about parking when I take the bus. I also never worry about needing exact change as long as I buy a bus pass every month. While many people simply pay for each bus ride, I always buy a bus pass and receive a discount. Until I become rich enough to have my own limousine, I will continue to ride the bus around town.

Did you find that most subordinate clauses answered the question, "Under what condition?"

JOURNAL PROMPT

Do you own a car? Do you ever use public transportation? What are some of the advantages of public transportation over driving your own vehicle? What are some of the disadvantages of public transportation? Have you ever rented a limousine or ridden in one? Tell about your experience.

EPENDENT CLAUSES THAT RELATE

The dependent subordinate clause introduced by a subordinating conjunction is not the only kind of dependent clause. A second kind of dependent clause is called a **relative clause.**

Instead of being introduced by subordinating conjunctions, dependent relative clauses are introduced by **relative pronouns**. Yes, I said pronouns—those words that stand for people, places, and things! When pronouns introduce dependent clauses, they are called "relative" because they often relate the information in the clause directly to a noun in the main sentence.

The following words are relative pronouns. All but one begin with the letter "W":

The Relative Pronouns

who	whose	what	whoever	whichever
whom	which	that	whomever	whatever

You can also find nearly all of these same words at the beginning of questions:

Who is my friend? What is your name? Whose idea was this?

When they appear in *questions,* these pronouns are called "interrogative pronouns" that introduce complete ideas or independent clauses. But in *statements,* they do not introduce complete ideas. In statements, they usually occur next to a noun:

The man who is my friend . . .

Does this sound like a complete idea to you. Or do you want more information about "the man who is my friend"? For example:

The man who is my friend smiled at me.

Now, there's a sentence!! If you look at this sentence carefully, you will discover it contains two clauses:

1.   *The man _____ smiled at me.*   (subject=man; verb=smiled)
2.   *who is my friend*   (subject=who; verb=is)

The first clause is an independent clause and can stand alone as a complete sentence. The second clause, however, is a dependent clause; its subject "who" relates to "the man." That means the example sentence is a *complex sentence:* it contains *one independent clause* (The man . . . smiled at me) and *one dependent relative clause* (who is my friend).

DO IT YOURSELF!   *Find the Relative Clauses*

Directions

A. *In the following sentences, circle each relative pronoun and underline the clause it introduces.*

B. *Once you have found them, cross out all the relative clauses and rewrite the paragraph without them. Use the space provided for your rewrite.*

Carol, who is my daughter-in-law, flew to Mississippi for Christmas. She traveled with her son, who is only two years old. They took a flight that departed late at night, and they arrived in Mississippi in the morning. When she arrived there, she was greeted by relatives whom she had never met before. They carried signs that said, "Welcome Carol!!" They also brought her a special gift, which they had made just for her. It was a photo album that contained pictures of all the family members who lived in Mississippi. This was the best gift that anyone could have given her. Carol will always remember her Christmas in Mississippi.

REWRITE of paragraph without relative clauses

_____

_____

_____

_____

_____

_____

_____

_____

_____

_____

_____

After eliminating all the relative clauses, does the above paragraph still make sense? What kind of information seems to be lacking?

WHO'S RELATED TO THE RELATIVE CLAUSE?

Earlier you learned that all *dependent* clauses function as some part of speech and that subordinate clauses are giant adverbs. Since relative clauses are also dependent clauses, they too act as a part of speech. The ones in the previous paragraph about Carol's trip were all *adjectives.* That's why you were able to eliminate them and still have sentences that made sense. After all, adjectives are descriptive words that writers can put into sentences or take out of sentences at will.

Adjectives, of course, describe nouns, and they are always located next to the nouns they describe. Look back at the paragraph about Carol and make a list of all the nouns that are described by adjective relative clauses. The first one is done for you as an example:

Noun	The Describing Adjective Relative Clause
Carol	*who is my daughter-in-law*

RELATIVE CLAUSES TAKING OVER FOR NOUNS

Relative clauses can also act as another part of speech; they can actually be <u>nouns</u>. In the following sets of sentences, different nouns have been replaced by relative clauses.

1. The prize will be awarded to the *winner*.
    The prize will be awarded to *whoever writes the best essay*.
2. Columbus believed the *theory*.
    Columbus believed *that he might find a shorter route to the Indies*.
3. I know my *limitations*.
    I know *what I am not capable of doing*.
4. Did the detective discover her *identity*?
    Did the detective discover *who was the victim of the crime*?
5. His *speech* was worth hearing.
    What he said was worth hearing.

When relative clauses act as nouns, they become important, indispensable parts of the main sentence. Unlike adjective relative clauses, noun relative clauses cannot be removed without destroying the completeness of the sentence. Try reading the above sentences leaving out the underlined noun relative clauses. What happens to the sentences?

WHEN DEPENDENT CLAUSES MASQUERADE AS SENTENCES

Recognizing dependent clauses, whether they are subordinate clauses or relative clauses, is important for you as a writer. Since dependent clauses contain subjects and verbs, they can easily be mistaken for complete sentences. But remember, a dependent clause does not contain a complete idea; therefore, if you try to punctuate one as a complete sentence, you have written a *fragment*.

COLLABORATE!   *Find the Fragments*

Directions

*Work with a group or on your own. Using what you have learned in this chapter, label each of the following word groups as a COMPLETE SENTENCE or a FRAGMENT. To be complete, a sentence needs at least one independent clause (a clause that **does NOT begin with a subordinating conjunction or a relative pronoun**). Refer to the list of SUBORDINATING CONJUNCTIONS (page 331) and the list of THE RELATIVE PRONOUNS (page 337) to ensure your answers are correct.*

1. While Alex was walking down the street to his house._____
2. The car stopped suddenly._____
3. That the man asked for directions._____
4. Because he lived here, Alex knew the names of the streets._____

5. While the stranger appreciated the advice._____

6. Alex turned away._____

7. Not that the street was hard to find._____

8. It was unknown._____

9. Not very many people lived there._____

10. Since the street was new and the houses had no numbers._____

WRITE RIGHT FOR THE JOB: Are You a "That"-A-Holic?

In earlier chapters of this book, I have repeatedly emphasized the importance of conciseness in workplace writing. Relative clauses are often introduced by a word considered unnecessary by efficient employers. The word is *that*. Some employers want their employees to stop using *that* as a relative pronoun altogether. Instead of

> *This is in response to the letter <u>that</u> I received yesterday.*

most employers, nowadays, favor

> *This is in response to the letter I received yesterday.*

In the above sentence, the second clause "I received yesterday" is still considered a dependent relative clause because the reader assumes the word "that" is *implied*. For some people, like me, the word *that* seems to want to pop up in every sentence I write. In fact, I consider myself a "THAT-A-HOLIC." I don't mean to do it, I just can't help myself! I even use **that** when I am not aware of it!! I don't notice all the **that**'s in my writing until I proofread my work. It sometimes takes me five readings to spot them all. I am a notorious **that** user.

Yet, when I conduct seminars for workers who write, I emphasize how eliminating **that** can help streamline sentences.

COLLABORATE!   *Taking the First Step to Wiping Out "That"*

Directions
Working with a group or on your own, revise the following paragraph, eliminating THAT whenever possible. You will notice other words (like "has been" or "they") also falling by the wayside as you drop the word THAT from your writing.

From the information that has been provided and the analytical results of the samples that have been obtained, it appears that the source of the bacteria that has been detected is from the application that has been performed by Greenhouse Spraying Company. This means that many farmers that are cultivating wheat will have to burn their crops. Sam and I both agree on several of the solutions that have been designed to solve this problem. We feel that the members of the hazardous material team are experts and that they can offer the assistance that you need. They have agreed that they will identify the areas that are at risk in your communities. Please contact us if you feel that they can help you.

THE READING CONNECTION

1. Choose three different books or magazines or newspapers. Select several paragraphs from each work you choose. Copy down all the sentences containing dependent subordinate clauses or relative clauses. Does one author seem to use more of these complex structures than the others? How does the presence of dependent clauses or the lack of dependent clauses in a piece of writing affect how simple or complicated the writing seems?

2. Select a page from two different textbooks. Circle BOYFANS words every time you come across them. Carefully reread the sentences that contain the BOYFANS words. Are any of these sentences compound sentences? If so, write the compound sentences in the space provided, and bring them back to class:

_____

_____

_____

_____

_____

_____

_____

_____

_____

_____

3. Read over some of the journal entries you have written for this class. Pay special attention to any sentences beginning with subordinating conjunctions. Have you placed a comma after the introductory dependent clauses? If not, correct the punctuation in those sentences and rewrite the sentences in the space provided. Circle the commas you insert:

_____

_____

_____

_____

_____

_____

_____

_____

_____

4. After completing one or several of the above reading connections, make your own list of the most commonly used BOYFANS words, subordinating conjunctions, and relative pronouns you have come across in your reading and your own writing:

BOYFANS Words (Coordinating conjunctions)	Subordinating Conjunctions	Relative Pronouns
_____	_____	_____
_____	_____	_____
_____	_____	_____
_____	_____	_____
_____	_____	_____
_____	_____	_____
_____	_____	_____
_____	_____	_____
_____	_____	_____
_____	_____	_____
_____	_____	_____
_____	_____	_____
_____	_____	_____
_____	_____	_____
_____	_____	_____
_____	_____	_____
_____	_____	_____

THE WRITING CONNECTION

For writers, the different types of sentences are important. Paragraphs that contain different kinds of sentences (simple, compound, and complex) are more interesting to read than paragraphs made up of only simple sentences—or worse yet, paragraphs made up of only complex sentences.

Writers use different kinds of sentences for different purposes. Simple sentences are effective as introductory and concluding sentences. The fact that they are often short, or at least contain only one idea, makes them powerful. Sometimes, instead of using a transitional word or phrase, a writer can use a short, simple sentence to make the transition from one idea to the next. At times, if your writing becomes overburdened with long explanations, simple sentences are necessary just to give your reader a break.

Compound sentences are exceptionally well suited for comparison-contrast writing in which similar or disparate ideas are presented side by side.

Complex sentences, which are the ones we all write most often, help writers explain ideas complete with cautions, conditions, and extenuating circumstances. They are particularly useful in "cause and effect" writing. Complex sentences also help writers *level* their ideas. When several ideas are presented in one sentence, the lesser one can be expressed by the dependent clause, while the main idea of the sentence can be expressed by the independent clause. Such leveling helps readers appreciate how different ideas relate to one another.

Keep in mind the above discussion of the different ways to incorporate simple, compound, and complex sentences into your writing as you write on one or several of the following topics. From now on, make checking for *variety in sentence structure* a part of revision work.

1. Write about a problem you are presently trying to deal with. Explore some of your possible solutions and weigh their implications. Compare several different solutions and decide on which one is the best. Gives reasons for your final decision.

2. Consider what you would change about yourself if you had the power to do so. Consider *why* you would make the changes and *how* you might go about accomplishing the changes. Project how your life would be different if you were able to make the changes you would like to make.

3. Begin a piece of writing with the subordinate clause, "If I could go back in time . . . ." You may choose to go back to a time and place in your own life and perhaps change something you did or didn't do. Then project how your actions would affect your present life. Or you may instead go back in time into a historical period and imagine yourself as a participant in a particular historical event. Let yourself go with this one!

4. Describe your ideal vacation. Where would you go? What would you see? Who would you take with you? How long would you be gone? During which time of year would you take this vacation? Why?

5. Develop one or several of your journal entries into a finished piece of writing. Or take two journal entries on two topics that would lend themselves to being compared and contrasted. Examine, in detail, the similarities and differences between the topics you chose.

SELF TEST FOR CHAPTER 12

1. Like a sentence, every clause contains both a _____ and a _____.

2. Like a phrase, some clauses act as _____.

3. A compound sentence consists of at least two _____ _____

4. The BOYFANS words are really _____ _____.

5. The BOYFANS words included the following: _____, _____, _____, _____, _____, _____, _____.

6. The words that introduce dependent subordinate clauses are called _____ _____.

7. Subordinate clauses are quite moveable in sentences because they are actually gigantic _____.

8. Relative clauses may act either as _____ or _____ in sentences.

9. Every sentence you write should have at least one _____ clause.

10. A complex sentence contains at least one _____ clause and at least one _____ clause.

FINAL JOURNAL WRITING

What new concepts did you learn in this chapter? Which concepts were already familiar to you? Which part of this chapter do you think was the most valuable? Which was the least valuable? Why? How do you think knowing about different kinds of clauses can help you improve your writing? What are some of your unanswered questions about concepts that were touched upon in this chapter?

Answers to "True and False Test over BOYFANS Words" on page 321: 1. true; 2. false; 3. false; 4. true; 5. true; 6. true.

Points—Punctuation
Points that Mark the Way for Readers

COMMAS MARKING MORE THAN PAUSES

Have you finally COMMA to the conclusion that you make COMMAn mistakes in punctuation?

Has your teacher said to you, "Please COMMA here: You need a punctuation mark in this spot where you have—nothing!"??

Have you COMMA to the end of your rope when it COMMAs to punctuation? In fact, have you beCOMMA so frustrated that you've started biting your fingernails just to COMMA down?

Now you can COMMA down the WRITE way instead . . .

COMMA one, COMMA all, COMMA on and learn about, you guessed it, COMMAS!

—Advertisement for a punctuation workshop

QUESTIONS TO ASK YOURSELF WHILE READING CHAPTER 13:

1. Why are commas so difficult to master?
2. Will just reading my writing aloud while I listen for pauses enable me to place commas correctly?
3. What do I need to know about punctuation to make the right decisions about where to place commas?
4. Should a comma always come before the "and" in a list?
5. How should I use commas when I am punctuating dates in business letters?

Punctuation, which comes from the Latin word *punctus* meaning "point," is literally the placing of points into your writing. Points didn't begin to appear in written English until the late fifteenth century when William Caxton started printing books using the newly invented printing press. Before printing, all the writing in hand-copied manuscripts ran together. Words were not divided by spaces, punctuation marks, or even indentations for paragraphs.

The first marks suggesting anything like punctuation actually did appear in texts earlier than the time of the printing press, but these marks were not designed to be used as readers use them today—to help group words that belong together to discern the meaning the writer intended. Rather, the first marks appearing in texts were signals for readers who read aloud to non-readers. Slash marks (/) were inserted to mark where the readers should "pause" when reading orally. These slashes were, in fact, the great-grandparents of commas. Curve the slash just a little, make it smaller, and drop it down to touch the line that supports the writing, and there you have it—a comma (,) evolved from a slash (/)!

Not only has the physical appearance of the comma changed, but its reason for appearing in sentences has also changed. The comma ceased to stand for "pauses" way back in 1640 when Ben Jonson proposed an approach to punctuation based on *syntax,* or sentence structure, rather than pauses. Jonson's book *English Grammar,* published in 1640 after his death, provides the foundation for the modern system of punctuation rules we use today in English.

As you and I know, maybe all too well, in today's world punctuation is an integral part of writing. Even the most occasional writers are faced with punctuation decisions every time they put pen to paper (or finger to computer keyboard).

TO PUNCTUATE OR NOT TO PUNCTUATE . . . THAT IS THE QUESTION

Sometimes when you write, you write just for yourself. If you write a journal entry or keep a diary, you may not need punctuation; you may plan on being the only person ever to read those private thoughts. But other times you write to share your ideas with someone else: the reader. The reader of a piece of writing is also called the "audience." One purpose for punctuating is to make your writing easier for your audience to read.

A significant difference between a writer and a reader is that a writer begins with an idea or image, and then picks the appropriate words to convey that image to the reader; the reader, however, begins with no image at all, but must use the sequence of words he or she is given to create some sort of meaningful image or idea in the end. To accomplish this, the reader needs all the guidance the writer can provide.

TAKING YOUR READER ON A TRIP

Think of your writing as a journey, a journey on which you, the writer, are the guide. You lead your readers down a one-way street, for writing is a linear medium; your readers follow you from the first word on the first line and move only in one direction—from left to right. Readers are strangers traveling through new territory as they follow you on your writing journey. Coming across one word after another, readers discover ideas at every turn; the ideas are already familiar to you, but they are new to your readers. Every step along the way offers surprises for readers who may have started the journey with no preconceptions about what you, the writer, have in store for them. The images that flash into their minds as they follow you come chiefly from your words and how you have arranged them. You are responsible for the word choices and the syntax that makes your sentences say what they say.

You are also responsible for making the journey through your writing as smooth as possible. It is your job to see to it that your readers can move through your entire piece of writing without having to backtrack, reread, or pass over the same spot more than once.

Therefore, knowing that anyone who is in a new territory depends heavily on traffic signs, you place signs along the road of your writing journey. Some signs say, "Come to a full stop.... Some say stop abruptly and dramatically!!!! Some say stop, but don't linger,,,, Some say YIELD because an explanation is coming up ahead : : : : Some say stop but don't get off the subject ;;;; Punctuation marks are the traffic signs you insert to make your writing easy to follow.

It is hoped that the readers will have studied the rules of the road well enough to understand what each sign is telling them. But even more important is that you, the writer, have studied the rules well enough to place the appropriate signs in the necessary places to prevent accidents—such as accidental misreading of your ideas. When writing for an audience, you become the traffic sign engineer who marks the writing journey with punctuation marks. To fulfill this important writer's role, you may need some specific training in the rules of punctuation.

ECOMING A PUNCTUATION ENGINEER WITH STYLE

Punctuation is a system of rules designed to group words in meaningful ways. From one generation to another and from one subject area to another, these rules change slightly. Therefore, I prefer to think of them as *guidelines* rather than rules. As a punctuation engineer, you may need to keep up with the latest conventions as well as be well informed about the punctuation practices in your particular field. Journalists, for example, follow slightly different conventions from secretaries; and students may be given still another set of punctuation guidelines to write by.

While English spelling is governed by an elaborate and ridiculous system that seems to have as many exceptions as it has rules, this is not true of punctuation. Punctuation "rules," while they may not be as universal as the *logic* that governs syntax, are much more dependable than spelling rules.

In punctuation, rather than finding rules and exceptions to rules, you are more likely to find guidelines that offer you *choices*. To punctuate one group of words, you, as a writer may have several options from which to choose. For example, if you desire to punctuate

I am taking a writing class my sister is taking math

your choices include the following:

1. Two *periods* (or "full stops," as the British call them):
    I am taking a writing class. My sister is taking math.
2. Or a *semicolon* and a period:
    I am taking a writing class; my sister is taking math.
3. Or a *comma* in place of the semicolon—but only *if you insert a coordinating conjunction:*
    I am taking a writing class, *and* my sister is taking math

All the above options are "correct." *You* decide which one to use. And *how* do you decide? You may decide by process of elimination:

- If I use a period, my sentences will sound short and choppy.
- But if I use a comma, I'll have to use an "and"; I have too many of those in this paragraph already.
- Therefore, I think I'll decide on a semicolon. That way the reader can see that my two sentences are so closely related they can be put into one sentence. At the same time, I have made it clear that they are two complete ideas.

Since punctuation is often a choice, it can become a part of a writer's style. Some writers never use semicolons; some use them constantly. That is a stylistic choice. If, however, you avoid using semicolons because you don't know anything about them, that is not a stylistic choice. In fact, by limiting your knowledge of punctuation, you limit your choices as a writer. By learning some simple punctuation guidelines, you can change that.

DO IT YOURSELF!   *How Limited Are Your Choices?*

Directions
In the space provided, reflect on what you know about punctuation.

- What classes have you taken in which you learned about punctuation?
- Which marks are you comfortable using and which marks are you not comfortable using?
- When you write a paper, how do you decide where to punctuate and which marks to use?
- Do teachers often correct your punctuation?
- Which marks are corrected most often on your papers?
- If you could master punctuation, how do you think your feelings toward writing would be affected?

_____

_____

_____

_____

_____

_____

_____

_____

_____

_____

HE COMMA AND BAD INFORMATION

The most common mark made *inside* a sentence is the comma. All the students I've ever known use the comma; but, too often, they also *misuse* the comma.

The first cause of comma misuse is simply **bad information**. A common bit of bad information that many student writers cling to is

> *Read your writing aloud. Every time you hear yourself pause, place a comma in that spot.*

That's not only bad advice, it suggests a practice that was curtailed over three hundred years ago! I realize that even today commas make readers pause, but so do periods and semicolons and colons. So how do you know, when your ears detect a pause, that you shouldn't be inserting one of those other marks instead of a comma? Even worse, you might pause simply because of the rhythm of the sentence, or to catch a your breath, or to emphasize a certain word; and maybe no punctuation mark at all should be placed where you paused. My advice about commas and pauses is:

> *Writers should not inject commas into sentences because they hear pauses, for the same reason that doctors should not inject antibiotics into patients just because they hear sneezes.*

Another even more unreliable method for placing commas is the "salt-and-pepper" method. That's the one where your pen turns into a salt shaker; then you use it to sprinkle your papers with commas during your final revision. Some students sprinkle commas generously and others sprinkle more sparingly—all according to individual taste. But regardless of the amount of comma seasoning applied, the salt-and-pepper approach to punctuation usually produces writing with too few commas in some sentences and too many commas in others.

OOD INFORMATION ABOUT COMMAS

If neither the pause nor the salt-and-pepper approach works, then what does? There are three considerations you need to weigh as you decide where to insert commas and other punctuation marks in your sentences:

1. First is the **kinds** of structures in your sentence. For example, sentences containing two independent clauses are punctuated differently from sentences containing one independent clause and one dependent clause:
   Two independent clauses: *I use commas in my writing,* but I don't know any comma rules. (insert a comma after the first clause and before the conjunction)

One independent clause followed by one dependent clause: *I use commas in my writing although I don't know any comma rules.* (no comma needed here)

2. Second is the *placement* of structures. A sentence containing one independent clause and one dependent clause is punctuated one way if the dependent clause is placed at the beginning of the sentence and another way if the dependent clause is placed at the end. Different placement requires different punctuation even though both versions contain the same kinds of structures:

   Dependent clause at the beginning: *Although I don't know any comma rules,* I often use commas in my writing. (insert a comma when the dependent clause is written **first**)

   Dependent clause at the end: *I often use commas in my writing although I don't know any comma rules.* (no comma when the dependent clause is written **last**)

3. Third is *meaning.* Meaning also helps writers decide where to place commas. When information in a relative clause is *essential* to the meaning of the main sentence, that clause <u>*is not*</u> enclosed in commas. Yet the same kind of clause containing information that is *not essential* to the meaning of the main sentence <u>*is*</u> enclosed in commas.

   Essential relative clause: *The guidelines that relate to comma use* could help me in my writing. (The information in the clause beginning with "that" is necessary if the reader is to understand which "guidelines" the writer is talking about; therefore, the clause is <u>not</u> enclosed in commas.)

   Non-essential relative clause: *Comma guidelines,* which I have never before understood could help me in my writing. (The information in the clause beginning with "which" is not necessary in order for the reader to understand which "guidelines" the writer is talking about; therefore, the clause is enclosed in commas.)

As you make your final decisions about where to place commas in your writing, think about the kinds of the sentence elements you are using, their placement, and their intended meanings.

C AN WE TALK?

Frankly, I have a confession. Commas are tough to teach. They are tough to teach because there are so many different comma rules. Depending on which English handbook you pick up, you may find anywhere from ten to fifteen different rules for just the comma. Then check out the semicolon: you'll find maybe three or four semicolon rules. That's a big difference.

There are commas for almost everything: commas for introductory parts of sentences, commas for lists, commas for parenthetical expressions (whatever they are), commas for dates and addresses—and that's not the half of it.

I can figure out how to *explain* all these different rules. That's not the hard part. I just can't figure out how to tell if my students have learned them or not. Simple, you say, just write some sentences in a paragraph and have the students insert the commas.

But all commas *look alike.* A comma after introductory information in a sentence looks no different than does a comma setting off a parenthetical expression. How do

I know what a student is thinking when he or she places a comma in a spot early in a sentence? I don't. Or at least I didn't—until now. For you see, I have just devised the world's first foolproof comma system, a system that will truly tell me what students have learned about commas. It works like this: Every comma rule, or guideline, is indicated by *a different-looking comma.*

Comma Guideline #1: A comma follows the first of two independent clauses joined by a coordinating conjunction (BOYFANS words: *But, Or, Yet, For, And, Nor, So*). Using my new, foolproof system, you will write this comma like this: ⏐ /,

The slash mark in front of the comma is a reminder that this comma is reinforced by the conjunction that follows it. That kind of reinforcement can make the comma as strong as a period.

DO IT YOURSELF! *Insert the* /, *After the First Independent Clause*

Directions

A. *Combine the following sets of sentences joining them with the conjunction provided in parentheses. Rewrite the resulting sentence inserting a* /, *after the first independent clause. The first one is done for you as an example. CIRCLE the punctuation you insert.*

1. I watch the news on television. I listen to radio talk shows. (and)

    I watch the news on television (/,) *and I listen to radio talk shows.*

2. The television news is informative. The talk shows are more entertaining. (but)

    _____

    _____

3. Most talk show hosts talk about politics. Dr. Joy Brown talks about personal problems.(but)

    _____

    _____

4. I think she gives excellent advice. I listen to her frequently. (so)

    _____

    _____

5. Dr. Brown gives good advice. She has an excellent sense of humor. (and)

    _____

    _____

    _____

B. *The following sentences all contain coordinating conjunctions (BOYFANS words), yet NOT all of them contain more than one independent clause. If a sentence contains at least two independent clauses joined by a coordinating conjunction, insert the comma* /, *where needed. Otherwise, make no mark. CIRCLE any punctuation you insert.*

1. I have never called in to a radio talk show but I have thought about it.

2. I would probably become nervous and sound embarrassed.

3. But someday I may call Dr. Joy Brown.

4. Once someone called and had a problem similar to mine.

5. I listened very carefully and I followed the doctor's advice.

C. *Insert commas into the following paragraph if they are needed to separate two independent clauses joined by a coordinating conjunction. Use the mark* /, *and circle the punctuation you insert.*

Sometimes radio talk show hosts make me angry. They are extremely opinionated and their listeners often seem misinformed and gullible. Many of the hosts treat the callers rudely and hang up on them. They cut off people who don't share their views. The callers must be insulted by this treatment but they still keep calling. My friend and I decided to call the Bill Gallagher show one day. We called and called but we never got through to Bill Gallagher. Maybe we were calling at the wrong time or maybe we were calling the wrong number.

How many commas did you insert in the above paragraph? If you inserted more than four commas, you need to rethink your decisions.

JOURNAL PROMPT

Do you listen to the radio regularly? Do you ever listen to talk radio? How do you think talk radio is different from other kinds of radio offerings? Who is your favorite talk radio show host? Why? Whom do you like the least? Why? Have you ever been a caller on a radio or TV show? Describe your experience. Is there a show you would like to call? If you could be on the radio for a few minutes, what would you say?

INDEPENDENT CLAUSES AND RUN-ON SENTENCES

The comma that separates independent clauses joined by a coordinating conjunction is particularly important for you to understand if you have ever been corrected for writing run-on sentences. When you write run-ons, you are simply running sentences together without adequate punctuation:

I have not learned much about punctuation I frequently write run-on sentences.

This kind of run-on sentence could easily be repaired with a single period:

I have not learned much about punctuation. I frequently write run-on sentences.

Another way to repair this run-on would be to add a coordinating conjunction and then separate the two complete ideas with a comma.

I have not learned much about punctuation, <u>and</u> I frequently write run-on sentences.

HE COMMA SPLICE RUN-ON

Another kind of run-on is called a **comma-splice**. Do you understand the meaning of "splice"? In the electrical trade a splice is used to connect two bare wires; you simply make sure they are touching and then wrap the point where they connect with electrical tape to keep the wires together. In the same way, to splice two sentences, you simply make sure they are touching and then wrap the point where they connect with a comma, like this:

I have not learned much about punctuation, I frequently write run-on sentences.

Even though a comma was sufficient to connect two independent clauses when it was backed up by a conjunction, the comma *alone* is not strong enough to separate one complete idea from another. Therefore, a comma splice is simply another way of running one sentence into another without adequate punctuation—a comma splice is a type of run-on.

COLLABORATE! *Repairing Run-On Sentences*

Directions

Work together with a group or on your own.

A. The following sentences include run-ons, including comma splice run-ons. Repair each sentence by using a comma plus a suitable coordinating conjunction (but, or, yet, for, and, nor, so). Write the comma you insert as /, to remind you that this comma is reinforced by a conjunction when separating two complete ideas. CIRCLE the punctuation you add.

1. My husband is allergic to grasses and house dust, I am allergic to the cold.

_____

_____

2. Mike's allergies make him sneeze my allergy makes me itch.

_____

_____

3. I never take medicine for my allergy Mike is constantly taking pills.

_____

_____

4. We always keep our house warm, that prevents me from having an allergic reaction.

_____

_____

5. I try to vacuum and dust frequently, Michael still sneezes and takes his medicine.

_____

_____

B. *Read the following student paragraph. This paragraph is punctuated as if it contains only one sentence, yet it actually contains many sentences. Insert periods to mark where one sentence ends and the next one begins. Insert commas where complete ideas are separated by a coordinating conjunction. CIRCLE any punctuation you insert.*

Mohammed is allergic to everything he can't come to visit me for he is allergic to my cat he is also allergic to flowers so he doesn't enjoy being outside certain times of the year I feel sorry for him but I also feel frustrated there are hardly any activities the two of us can enjoy together I wish he would take pills to help his allergies or maybe shots would make him better then perhaps he could enjoy life more and he could "smell the roses" like everyone else.

JOURNAL PROMPT

Do you have any allergies? What are they? What kinds of reactions do your allergies cause? Do you have friends who are allergic to things you enjoy? Have allergies ever affected your relationship with someone? How? What would be the worst thing you could possibly imagine being allergic to? Why?

Comma Guideline #2: **A comma is used to separate introductory elements from the main sentence.**
Using my system, you will write this comma like this: $\boxed{<,}$

This sign (called a "less than" sign) located in front of the comma is a reminder that the less significant information in front of the comma is leading up to the more significant information in the main clause of the sentence.

Commas setting off introductory elements are the commas most frequently omitted by student writers. Introductory elements vary; they range from single words, to phrases, and even to clauses. Yet they all share the same function: they *introduce* the main sentence.

 OMMAS AFTER INTRODUCTORY WORDS AND TRANSITIONS

Many different single words can introduce sentences. At one time, nearly any single introductory word was followed by a comma. For this reason, many people still write the following sentence with a comma:

Now, I understand why we use punctuation marks.

Nowadays requirements for placing commas after single introductory words have been relaxed. So writers often opt to leave this comma out.

One kind of introductory information that is still consistently followed by a comma, however, is a single *conjunctive adverb or a short transitional phrase.* Conjunctive adverbs are transitional words like *however, furthermore, consequently, nevertheless, moreover, and meanwhile.* They are followed by a comma when they introduce the main idea of a sentence. Shorter transitional words consisting of only one syllable—*then, next, thus*—do not need to be set off by commas:

Furthermore, I improved my writing. (comma after conjunctive adverb)
Then I improved my writing. (no comma after one-syllable conjunctive adverb)

Transitional phrases such as *for example, in fact, as a result, on the other hand,* and *in addition* also are followed by a comma when they introduce sentences.

In addition, I improved my writing.

Another introductory comma that *cannot* be left out is the comma that prevents misreading. If a sentence could be misread when the comma is left out, it becomes important to put a comma after an introductory word.

Carefully baked bread was removed from the hot oven.

The above sentence could be interpreted two different ways:
The bread was *baked* carefully.
OR
The bread was *removed* carefully.
With the comma in place after the introductory word, the sentence would read:

Carefully, baked bread was removed from the oven.

Now the reader can read the sentence only one way; the bread was *removed* carefully but not necessarily *baked* carefully.

When it comes to introductory words, you need to consider both *structure* and *meaning* as you decide where to place the comma.

DO IT YOURSELF!   *Insert the Introductory Comma*

Directions

The following sentences all contain introductory information. Using the guidelines explained above, decide whether a comma is necessary to set off the introductory information from the main sentence. Write the introductory comma like this ⌄, to remind you that it is setting off lesser information introducing the more important information in the main sentence. CIRCLE the punctuation you insert.

1. Finally Sean has a full-time job.

2. However he still needs to budget his money carefully.

3. Furthermore he should avoid going into debt.

4. In fact he might think about cutting up his credit cards.

5. Then he could reduce the amount of money he spends on interest.

6. After all credit cards usually require high interest payments.

7. For example some credit card companies charge 22% interest.

8. Next Sean should start a retirement account.

9. Thus he could ensure his future security.

10. Unfortunately invested money cannot always be accessed easily.

Compare your answers to those of your classmates. If you have any disagreements, discuss your reasons for deciding to place commas where you did.

 OMMAS AFTER INTRODUCTORY PHRASES

A common structure in sentences is a phrase. Sentences can contain prepositional phrases, participial phrases, infinitive phrases, and gerund phrases. Any of these phrases could occur at the beginning of a sentence. Sometimes they are introductory; sometimes they are not. Sometimes they are followed by commas; sometimes they are not. Let's look at them carefully.

Introductory Prepositional Phrases

Writers frequently introduce sentences with prepositional phrases. In fact, sentences that begin this way are often more interesting-sounding than sentences in which the subject comes first. When deciding whether to use a comma after an introductory prepositional phrase, follow these guidelines:

1. A comma should follow a *long* introductory prepositional phrase but is not needed after a short one. I usually consider four or more words to be a long phrase:
   In a modern affluent society, most people have checking accounts. (a comma after a long prepositional phrase)
   In America most people have checking accounts. (no comma necessary after a short prepositional phrase)

2. If a sentence begins with two or more prepositional phrases in a row, the series of phrases is followed by a comma:
   In this part of the world, most people have checking accounts. (a comma after two prepositional phrases in a row)

DO IT YOURSELF!   *Punctuate Introductory Prepositional Phrases*

Directions

In the following paragraph, the sentences all begin with introductory prepositional phrases. Insert commas where needed. Write the commas like this **◁,** *to remind you that the material you are setting off is introductory to the main sentence. CIRCLE the punctuation you insert.*

In June I opened my first checking account. Into it I deposited my first paycheck from my part-time job as a receptionist. For a very long time I had wanted my own checkbook. To me it was a symbol of being an adult. On the last day of my first month of work I finally realized my dream—my own checking account. At the bank the teller let me look at all the different checks I could order. On some were pictures of flowers or wildlife or even scenery. After considerable serious thought I decided on the checks with the flowers even though they cost more than the plain checks. On that day in June I took an important step toward managing my finances.

JOURNAL PROMPT

Write about some of your budget concerns. Do you use credit cards? Why or why not? Do you have a checking account? Do you prefer to pay with cash or by check? Why? Have you ever taken a class on money management? Do you think such a class would be valuable for you? Why or why not?

*I*NTRODUCTORY VERBAL PHRASES

A common way to introduce an idea is with a participial phrase. Usually such a phrase describes the subject of the main sentence. Participial phrases begin with participles: words that end in -ING, -ED, or look like irregular verbs:

> <u>Wearing heavy garden gloves</u>**,** *Mrs. Myers dug holes for next year's daffodils.*
> <u>Covered with loose soil</u>**,** *the bulbs are protected from harsh winter weather.*
> **<u>Known</u>** <u>for their brilliant color</u>**,** *the tulips create a showy display each spring.*

Some participial phrases look very much like gerund phrases which also begin with words ending in ING. When gerund phrases begin sentences, however, they are not introductory. They are instead acting as a part of the main sentence, usually the subject. Therefore they should not be set off with commas. Compare these two sentences:

> *Working in the yard*, *Mrs. Myers felt energized.* (The introductory participial phrase is followed by a comma.)

> *Working in the yard energized Mrs. Myers.* (The gerund phrase is a part of the main sentence and, therefore, should not be followed by a comma.)

How can you tell when a phrase beginning with an ING word needs a comma and when it does not? If you can remove the phrase and still have a complete sentence, then you should set it off with a comma. But if you remove the phrase and no longer have a complete idea, then you should *not* set the phrase off with a comma.

COLLABORATE! *Pick the Participial Phrases and Punctuate Them*

Directions

Work together with a group or on your own. The following sentences begin with either a participial phrase or a gerund phrase. Using the guidelines explained above, decide which is which. Place commas <, *only as needed after introductory <u>participial phrases</u> NOT after <u>gerund phrases</u>. CIRCLE the punctuation you insert.*

1. Watering flowers too often can kill them.
2. Planning my garden I ordered seeds from the seed catalogue.
3. Using the clippers I trimmed the hedge.
4. Using the clippers is difficult when I'm wearing garden gloves.
5. Pruning the bushes is an annual chore.
6. Carrying the young plants in a tray I walked to the far end of the garden.
7. Pushing her wheelbarrow Mrs. Myers moved dirt from one spot to another.
8. Pushing the wheelbarrow was not easy for her.
9. Watching flowers grow makes me happy.
10. Watching her flowers grow Mrs. Myers enjoys her summers.

INFINITIVE POSSIBILITIES

Another type of verbal phrase that can be introductory to a sentence is an infinitive phrase. An infinitive phrase begins with the word "to" plus a verb stem:

> *To plant daffodils, Mrs. Myers often uses a special tool called a "bulb planter."*

Infinitive phrases, too, can cause confusion for writers because they are not always introductory. Like gerund phrases, they can actually be acting as the subject of the main sentence. The way you can tell whether or not to place a comma after an infinitive phrase coming at the beginning of a sentence is to decide whether the phrase is necessary for the sentence to be complete. If it is necessary, you place no comma. If the phrase is not necessary to make the sentence complete, you set the phrase off with a comma:

> *To grow a beautiful garden is not easy. (Insert NO comma because the infinitive phrase is necessary for the sentence to be complete; it is a part of the main clause of the sentence rather than introductory to it.)*
> *To grow a beautiful garden, a gardener must invest time and energy. (Insert a comma because the infinitive phrase is NOT necessary for the sentence to be complete; it is introductory material that needs to be set off.)*

COLLABORATE!   *To Comma or Not to Comma—You Decide!!*

Directions

A. *Working together with a classmate or on your own, read the following sentences and insert commas when needed after* <u>introductory</u> *infinitive phrases. Write the commas like this* <, *to remind you that the purpose of the comma is to set off material that introduces the main sentence. CIRCLE the punctuation you insert.*

1.   To build a deck requires some carpentry skills.
2.   To start the process you must first draw a plan for the deck.
3.   To ensure that the deck is level you must have the right tools.
4.   To create a perfectly level deck is not easy.
5.   To do the job right you must be willing to invest time as well as money.

B. *In the following paragraph, all the sentences begin with verbal phrases (participial, gerund, or infinitive). Decide which ones are introductory and set them off with commas that look like* <, *and CIRCLE any punctuation you insert.*

Working in the yard seems to be my neighbors' favorite pastime. To create glorious rows of color next to her house Mrs. Greenthumb plants many different kinds of perennials each summer. Working by her side Mr. Greenthumb also takes pride in the landscape. To build things is his contribution. Watching him build fences and trellises I always marvel at how easy he makes it look. Working with wood has always been difficult for me. Using a power saw I once managed to build a bird house. Making it took three days. To attract some birds I planted a garden with berries. Being too eager for the berries to grow I overwatered them and killed them. Comparing me to my neighbors is depressing since I live next door to Mr. and Mrs. Greenthumb.

JOURNAL PROMPT

Do you ever work around the house either planting or building things? Do you enjoy this kind of work? Why? Do you have neighbors who work in their yards? Describe what they do. Have you ever built something yourself, like a shed or a deck or something else useful? Are you clever with power tools and building things? Describe an experience you have had building something.

*I*NTRODUCTORY SUBORDINATE CLAUSES

Another type of introductory information is *introductory subordinate clauses*. Subordinate clauses are word groupings that contain subjects and verbs and begin with one of the following **subordinating conjunctions**:

after	before	unless
although	if	until
as	since	when
as if	so that	whenever
as long as	than	whenever
because	though	while

The following is an example of a sentence introduced by a subordinate clause:

After he ate, *the dog slept.*

If the writer had forgotten to insert the comma in this sentence, the reader would read "After he ate the dog . . ." before figuring out that no one was really eating a dog. Without a comma, a reader might have to read the above sentence several times before figuring out which word groups belong together. To prevent this kind of confusion, subordinate clauses are always set off by commas when they are introductory to the sentence.

However, sentences with subordinate clauses can usually be reversed. When the subordinate clause comes at the end of the sentence, the possibility of misreading is eliminated because the subordinating conjunction then separates one clause from the other:

The dog slept after he ate. (With this word order, no comma is needed because the word "after" separates the two clauses.)

DO IT YOURSELF!   *Punctuate Introductory Subordinate Clauses*

Directions

Apply what you have just learned about punctuating introductory subordinate clauses.

A. In the following sentences, decide whether or not a comma is needed to set off the subordinate clause. Insert a **<,** *to remind yourself that the subordinate clause is a lesser element that is* <u>introductory</u> *to the main sentence. CIRCLE any punctuation you insert.*

1. Jennifer began smoking when she was in the sixth grade.

2. Because she was a rebel she did not quit smoking even though her parents asked her to stop.

3. When she first started smoking only a few of her friends smoked.

4. After they began high school many more of Jennifer's friends became addicted to cigarettes.

5. They skipped classes whenever they needed a nicotine "fix."

6. Although children under eighteen cannot legally buy tobacco products Jennifer and her friends had no trouble obtaining cigarettes.

7. Since Jennifer has become an addicted smoker she can hardly run a block without becoming winded.

8. Jennifer has not quit smoking although her mother now has lung cancer and her father has emphysema.

9. Because she is really "hooked" Jennifer has not been able to give up smoking.

10. Whenever she has an opportunity she warns other young people of the danger of beginning smoking.

B. *In the following paragraph, insert any commas* **<,** *needed because of introductory subordinate clauses. CIRCLE any punctuation you insert.*

Today smokers are made to feel like criminals although smoking is not against the law. Whenever students in my classes want to light up they have to go outside to smoke. Unless they are in specially designated areas they will be asked to extinguish their cigarettes. Before researchers published information about the dangers of second-hand smoke people were allowed to smoke nearly everywhere. Although I have never been a smoker I remember being in college classes where students smoked during class. If my professor was a smoker he or she would usually smoke while teaching! Such scenes will probably never be repeated in college classrooms because society has changed its views about smoking. While I do not think smokers are criminals I am glad that I do not have to teach in a smoke-filled room.

JOURNAL PROMPT

Are you a smoker? Have you ever been a smoker? Have you ever tried to quit smoking? Explain. If you are not a smoker, what are some of your opinions on smoking? Do you think today's rules about smoking are unfair? Why or why not?

Comma Guideline #3:   Commas are used to separate items in a list or a series. Using my system, you will write this comma like this: $\boxed{+,}$

The plus sign in front of the comma is a reminder that commas in lists act like plus signs adding one item on a list to another.

Using commas to separate items in a list is a common comma guideline that most students know and follow. Lists can consist of a series of single words:

I try to eat well balanced meals that include fruits, vegetables, meats, and grains.

Lists can consist of a series of phrases:

I brush my teeth in the morning, after meals, and before bedtime.

Lists can consist of a series of clauses:

I enjoy reading for pleasure after I finish my work, before I fall asleep at night, and when I have days off.

If you look carefully at the above examples, you may disagree with some of the commas I have inserted. Some writers do not insert the last comma before the "and" in a list. The logic is that the conjunction *takes the place* of the comma.

Actually most punctuation references consider the comma before the conjunction in a list as "optional." In other words, you would be correct if you inserted it; and you would be correct if you didn't insert it.

Personally, I *always* insert this final comma in the lists I write. I believe doing so reduces my chances of writing a sentence that can be misunderstood. Look at this example:

I am having a party. You are invited. Please bring <u>celery, carrots, pork and beans</u>.

If you receive this note, what will you bring? Will it be celery, carrots, and a can of pork and beans? Or will it be four items: celery and carrots and pork and beans? Do you see the problem? If I were planning to make Chinese food and wanted pork and green beans for a stir-fry dish, I would be very disappointed if you showed up with a can of pork and beans. (You'd probably be disappointed, too, since you wouldn't get any stir fry.)

Here is another example of the potential hazards of leaving out the comma before the conjunction in a list:

The estate will be divided equally among Jim, Fred, Dale, Sam and Della.

Who gets what? Do all the people on the list receive one fifth of the estate? Or do Jim and Fred and Dale all receive one fourth of the estate while Sam and Della have to share the last fourth? Actual court cases have hinged on the omission of commas in lists, and people like Sam and Della have come out as losers.

That is my case for inserting the final comma before the conjunction in a list: it eliminates confusion!

DO IT YOURSELF!   *Punctuate the Lists*

Directions

The following paragraph contains some sentences with lists. Punctuate these correctly with commas that look like **+,** *to remind you that each comma is helping you add an item to your list. CIRCLE any punctuation you insert.*

Carbon monoxide is difficult to detect because it is odorless colorless and tasteless. For that very reason, carbon monoxide may present a health hazard in your home. Carbon monoxide may be produced by the incomplete combustion of fuels like coal oil kerosene natural gas propane or wood. This dangerous gas is found in cars wood stoves gas stoves kerosene heaters open fires and even cigarettes. Whenever you use any of these, you should make sure you are in a well-ventilated area.

Exposure to low levels of carbon monoxide can cause headaches dizziness nausea and other flu-like symptoms. Exposure to high levels of the gas can cause death. For this reason you should have your house checked often for carbon monoxide leaks. Each year you should hire a professional to check any furnaces gas dryers space heaters water heaters wood stoves fireplaces and chimneys. This is especially important if you plan to caulk around your windows seal your doorways or insulate your walls. Call your gas company immediately if you notice that your houseplants are dying soot is building up around your furnace vents your hot water supply fluctuates from hot to cold or your furnace is making strange noises.

JOURNAL PROMPT

Are you aware of the dangers and symptoms of carbon monoxide poisoning? Do you know of anyone who has ever been injured by this dangerous gas? Have you thought about installing a carbon monoxide detector in your home? Why or why not? What kinds of precautions do you take regularly to make sure your home is a safe place?

Comma Guideline #4:   Commas are used to enclose non-essential and parenthetical information.
Using my system, you will write this comma like this: $\left(,\right)$
The parentheses around the comma are reminders that the information enclosed by commas is non-essential and could easily be left out of the sentence.

ESSENTIAL INFORMATION RESTRICTS

Non-essential information is also called **non-restrictive** information. So another way of stating this comma rule is *commas are used to set off non-restrictive elements in sentences.*

If there are non-restrictive elements, that must mean there are also *restrictive* elements in sentences. Restrictive elements restrict or limit a statement. Non-restrictive elements don't. Look at these examples:

Non-restrictive: *Police officers,* <u>*who are civil servants*</u>*, are public employees.*
Restrictive: *Police officers* <u>*who drink on duty*</u> *are a menace to the city.*

In the first sentence, the clause "who are civil servants" is interesting additional information in the sentence, but it does not change what the main sentence intends to say—it does not restrict the meaning of the sentence. Police officers are, in fact, public employees whether the reader thinks of them as "civil servants" or not. Since the additional information contained in this relative clause is *not necessary* to the reader's understanding of the main sentence, I *enclose* the clause in commas.

But in the second sentence, the clause "who drink on duty" is necessary because it restricts what I want to communicate. If I were to remove this relative clause, my sentence would read, "Police officers are a menace to the city." I did not intend to say that police officers in general are a menace to the city. But I did intend to say that a restricted group of police officers—those "who drink on duty"—are a menace to the city. The clause "who drink on duty" is a very important *restrictive* element that changes the meaning of the main clause. Since it is *necessary* information, I do **not** enclose it in commas.

COLLABORATE!   *Restrictive or Not Restrictive*

Directions

Working with a group or on your own, decide when and where to insert commas. Write the commas as ⟨,⟩ *to remind you that the information you are enclosing is not necessary information. CIRCLE any punctuation you insert.*

1. Lancaster Avenue which happens to be the street where I live is being resurfaced.

2. The street that leads to my house is being resurfaced.

3. Mary Perkins who works in the personnel office won the award.

4. A woman who works in the personnel office won the award.

5. Room 350 with a western exposure is the best room for watching the sunset.

6. The room with a western exposure is the best room for watching the sunset.

7. My only brother John is a teacher. (Should there be commas around "John"?)

8. Of my three brothers, my brother John is a teacher. (Should there be commas around "John"?)

9. President Clinton wearing a jogging suit hurried across the White House lawn.

10. The man wearing a jogging suit hurried across the White House lawn.

- Here's a trick for deciding when to use commas around clauses beginning with the word "who": A restrictive (necessary) clause will "sound right" if you substitute the word "that" for "who," but a non-restrictive (not necessary) clause will not. Double check your answers for numbers 3 and 4 above.

- When deciding whether you should use "which" instead of "that," the preferred form is "which" for non-restrictive (not necessary) information and "that" for restrictive (necessary) information. However, in practice, these are often confused even by experienced writers, or forgetful writers—like me.

PARENTHETICAL EXPRESSIONS

Parenthetical information consists of expressions that interrupt the main flow of the thought in a sentence *and* are not essential to the meaning of the sentence. All the following commas are enclosing parenthetical information:

She was, <u>in my opinion</u>, an outstanding candidate.
He, <u>on the other hand</u>, has not earned my vote.
The election results, <u>however</u>, may surprise us.

Other common parenthetical expressions include the following: *as a matter of fact, incidentally, namely, in the first place, of course, thus, consequently, therefore, moreover, furthermore, nevertheless, too, likewise.* At times you may feel some of these words are not interrupting the flow of your thoughts. In such cases, you may decide not to enclose them in commas. Remember, your intended meaning is a valid consideration when making punctuation decisions.

COLLABORATE!   *Enclosing the Parenthetical Expressions*

Directions

Work together with a group or on your own. In the following paragraph, locate parenthetical expressions and non-restrictive information. Enclose these sentence elements in commas that look like this (,) CIRCLE any punctuation you insert.

Justice Oliver Wendell Holmes who was a famous Supreme Court justice led a remarkable life. He was tall and handsome even more so as he aged with piercing eyes and a prominent moustache. He was a veteran of the Civil War in fact a veteran who had been wounded three times. Holmes was educated at Harvard and not surprisingly had many scholarly friends. Longfellow, Lowell, Emerson, and William James who were all well-known American authors were his acquaintances. Holmes gained recognition for writing *The Common Law* one of the classic works of American legal scholarship and served with distinction on the Supreme Court of the United States for thirty years. Holmes a great proponent of free speech was actively involved in the Supreme Court's work into his nineties.

Which sentences were most difficult for you? About which items, if any, did you and your classmates disagree? Explain.

JOURNAL PROMPT

Are there any famous people in history you particularly admire? Who are they? Why do you admire them? Have you ever read a biography of a person you admire? How did the biography affect your opinion of that person? If you could have lived your life as a certain person in history, who would that be? Why?

Putting It All Together

Let's review the four most important comma guidelines for writers and the special marks that help us keep them straight.

The Comma	The Guideline
/,	A comma follows the first of two independent clauses joined by a coordinating conjunction (BOYFANS words: *But, Or, Yet, For, And, Nor, So*)
<,	A comma is used to separate introductory elements from the main sentence.
+,	Commas are used to separate items in a list or a series.
(,)	Commas are used to enclose non-essential and parenthetical information.

Of course I don't expect you to use these strange-looking marks together with your commas for the rest of your life. But I do expect you to use them while you are studying commas in this chapter. Think of them as "training wheels." When you are learning to apply a new guideline, the extra little mark will be the training wheels that remind you of how you support your decision to place a comma where you place it. Once you master all the comma guidelines and leave this chapter behind, you can cast off the training wheels; but maybe you will still visualize those supports every time you use a comma in your writing.

COLLABORATE! *Using All the Training Wheels at Once*

Directions

Together with a group or on your own, insert all the commas that should be contained in the following paragraph. Be certain to use the appropriate "training wheels" for each comma you insert. If necessary, refer to the above chart of commas and guidelines. CIRCLE all your punctuation marks.

From a report in the Daily Planet newspaper a major research study has begun in three counties in Nevada. When it is finished it will be the first comprehensive study of the effects jet airplane testing has on the sense of humor of people who work near test sites. This study which is funded by a grant from a private corporation is headed by Dr. Lois Lane. Dr. Lane an expert on kryptonite and flying newspapermen is a clinical professor at the Metropolis School of Medicine. Her primary goal is to learn the adverse effects of airplane testing on area workers and a secondary goal is to analyze the effects of sonic booms on the local cactus crop. All the workers who take part in the study will receive an autographed picture of Superman Dr. Lane's one-time boyfriend. In order to gather as many participants as possible Dr. Lane had to fly some workers in from nearby Orem a town in Utah that makes computer software. There are no testing sites in Utah but the workers were more than willing to participate in the study. The symptoms Dr. Lane will be looking for in all the workers is lack of response to joke punch lines presence of facial wrinkles caused by scowling and absence of smile response. In the cactus crop she will be analyzing prickliness plumpness and color. Since Dr. Lane spent the first ten years of her career as a newspaper reporter she is certain to arrive at some interesting if not entirely accurate conclusions.

WRITE RIGHT FOR THE JOB: Punctuation Matters

On the job, punctuation can become a volatile issue. The most common questions I'm asked by employees who attend my training workshops are questions about punctuation. And comma use is usually number one on the list of concerns. I have actually heard reports of major office battles about whether or not to place a comma before the "AND" in a list and about how many commas to use when writing a date in a document. Such questions seem trivial in the more casual setting of academia, but in the professional world they become hotbeds of debate. Therefore, I feel responsible to mention some of the minor "rules" that pertain to the use of commas.

The following rules, or guidelines, address more specialized comma uses. You will not find occasion to apply them as often as the first four guidelines discussed in this chapter. You should read them, however, and familiarize yourself with the examples:

Comma Guideline #5:   Enclose appositive in commas. (Appositives or nouns in apposition, are simply nouns positioned right next to other nouns that they rename.) This rule is a variation of *non-restrictive* **comma use.**
Examples: *America's first president,* <u>*George Washington*</u>*, married Martha Custis.*
("George Washington" is the appositive)
My dog, <u>*Fido*</u>*, has black and white spots.*
("Fido" is the appositive)

Comma Guideline #6:   Enclose nouns of direct address in commas. (These are people to whom you are talking.)
Examples: <u>*Henry*</u>*, have you voted yet?*
("Henry" is the noun of direct address.)
After the performance, <u>*ladies and gentlemen*</u>*, you may attend a reception for the performers.*
("Ladies and gentlemen" are nouns of direct address.)

Comma Guideline #7:   Use commas to separate direct quotations from explanatory words such as *she said.*
Examples: *"I love you," she whispered.*
"And I," he replied, "have a severe case of indigestion."
(Notice that quotations always come **after** the comma.)

Comma Guideline #8:   Use commas with dates in the following ways:
Place commas before and after the year in a three-part date:
Example: *My son was born on August 15, 1969, at the city hospital.*
Use no commas when writing dates in a military or international style:
Example: *The captain ordered the men into action on 17 September 1992.*
Also, use no commas when the date includes a month and year only:
Example: *We moved into our new house in October 1995.*

Practice writing your own dates using commas correctly when needed:

1. I was born on _____ (write month, date, and year).

2. I started school this year on _____ (write the date military style).

3. I moved here in _____ (provide month and year only).

WRITE RIGHT FOR THE JOB: Other Commas that Matter

One of the main reasons commas are so important on the job is the impact they have on meaning. The misplacement of a comma can cause a sentence to mean something entirely different from what the writer intended. That could make a company liable, or responsible, for something that was written by accident thanks to a carelessly placed comma. Look at this example from *The Boston Herald*, February 23, 1983:

> *A misplaced comma cost nurse Angela Penfold her job in a health center in England. Penfold wrote to health authority officials to complain about her supervisor: "I have come to the opinion Mrs. Pepperell is out to make my life hell, so I will give in my notice." In fact, Penfold did not intend to resign.*

What did nurse Penfold intend? She just meant to say that her supervisor was making life miserable; she felt the supervisor was intentionally doing this to make her quit her job. Instead, thanks to the comma, Penfold gave notice without meaning to and did lose her job—with the stroke of a powerful comma.

COLLABORATE!   *Letting Commas Decide What You Mean*

Directions

Working with a group or on your own, carefully read the following sentences. Consider where commas could be inserted. Write at least two versions of each sentence. (One version may use no commas.) Explain the meaning of each version.

1. William James and Fred will play cards.

   Punctuation option 1:_____

   Explain meaning: _____

   Punctuation option 2:_____

   Explain meaning: _____

2. Mrs. Carnegie is a pretty generous lady.

   Punctuation option 1:_____

   Explain meaning: _____

   Punctuation option 2:_____

   Explain meaning: _____

3. Mr. Franklin the secretary called in sick.

   Punctuation option 1:_____

   Explain meaning: _____

   Punctuation option 2:_____

   Explain meaning: _____

4. The body the police discovered was gone.

   Punctuation option 1:_____

   Explain meaning: _____

   Punctuation option 2:_____

   Explain meaning: _____

5. We are going to eat Fred before we leave camp.

   Punctuation option 1:_____

   Explain meaning: _____

   Punctuation option 2:_____

   Explain meaning: _____

6. The prime minister who was recently ousted by the Greek citizens and his wife

   flew to Spain.

   Punctuation option 1:_____

   Explain meaning: _____

   Punctuation option 2:_____

   Explain meaning: _____

THE READING CONNECTION

1. Look through books, magazines, and newspapers. Find examples of all four of the main comma guidelines you studied in this chapter. Bring back your findings to class.

2. Go to your school library or bookstore and find resources such as English handbooks, style guides, or usage guides that contain explanations of punctuation. Compare the rules of two different sources to each other. Also compare what the sources say about comma use to what this chapter says about comma use (specifically the use of commas with lists, with prepositional phrases, with introductory words, and with dates). What, if any, areas of disagreement did you find? What thoughts do you have about "rules" for punctuation after reading and comparing different sources? Share your findings with your classmates.

3. Go back through previous entries in your own journal. Read your entries and insert any commas that you may not have inserted before. Which comma guidelines were you employing in your writing before reading this chapter? Which comma guidelines were you not employing? Does the insertion of commas make your journal more readable? Explain.

THE WRITING CONNECTION

While punctuation is important to mark the way for your reader, not all writers are particular about punctuation marks. Many fiction writers, in particular, have developed their own style of punctuating. One of those writers was Mark Twain, the author of *Tom Sawyer* and *Huckleberry Finn* and other notable masterpieces of American literature. Twain didn't always see the need for punctuation marks in his writing. This frustrated his editor, who then complained. In response Mark Twain sent in an entire page full of punctuation marks in random order. With the list he attached a note that said, "Put them wherever they seem to fit." His editor never complained about punctuation again.

Unfortunately for you, turning in a page full of random punctuation marks with your writing assignments is not an option. Maybe after you have established yourself as an eccentric author, you will be able to get away with it—but as a student and a worker, you're stuck with acknowledging certain prescribed conventions of punctuation in your writing. Select one or several topics to write about. In the revision step, pay careful attention to your use of commas.

1. The unexpected creates humor. Write a piece that includes some humor. Catch your reader off guard. Just when you set the reader up to expect one thing, write something surprising and unpredictable in the next sentence. Share your writing with one or several classmates and note their response to your attempt at humorous writing.

2. Read one or more chapters from a novel. It may be a novel you have read before. Try to write a short sequel to one of the chapters. Try to imitate the writer's style including his or her use of punctuation.

3. Develop one or several of your journal prompts into a finished piece of writing. Pay careful attention to your use of commas. Ask a classmate to read what you have written and look for possible errors in comma use. If you are not sure of some of your punctuation decisions, go back over the comma guidelines in this chapter and in outside punctuation resources. Strive for a perfectly punctuated paper!

SELF TEST FOR CHAPTER 13

1. The word "punctuation" comes from the Latin word "punctus" meaning _____.

2. The purpose for using punctuation in your writing is to help _____ (who?) get through your writing smoothly without having to backtrack or becoming confused.

3. The three considerations you should weigh when making punctuation decisions are _____, _____, and _____.

4. Commas should be placed after the first of two independent clauses joined by _____.

5. The subject of the sentence is not considered _____ information and is therefore not set off by a comma at the beginning of a sentence.

6. Information that *limits* a statement the writer makes in a sentence is called _____ or necessary information.

7. Non-restrictive information is ALWAYS/NEVER (circle one) set off by commas.

8. Whether or not to insert a _____ before the "and" in a list is optional, but many writers think its presence can avoid costly misreading.

9. The noun of _____ is the person the writer is talking to.

10. An _____ renames the noun it appears next to in a sentence.

FINAL JOURNAL WRITING

Write in your journal about any lights that were turned on for you in this chapter about punctuation. After reading about commas, how will you make punctuation decisions differently? If you won't punctuate differently, explain why? What unanswered questions do you still have about commas? Where could you find answers to those questions? Were the punctuation guidelines difficult to read and understand? Why or why not? After reading this chapter do you feel less frustrated or more frustrated about commas—or were you never frustrated to begin with? Explain your response.

*S*EMICOLONS AND *C*OLONS: *V*ALUABLE *W*ORKERS THAT *N*EED *M*ORE *E*MPLOYMENT

*I*t is almost always a greater pleasure to come across a semicolon than a period. . . . You get a pleasant little feeling of expectancy; there is more to come; read on; it will get clearer.

—*GEORGE F. WILL*

QUESTIONS TO THINK ABOUT WHILE READING CHAPTER 14:

1. What is a semicolon, and where should I use it?
2. What are some options for using semicolons, colons, or commas?
3. In which situations should I NOT use semicolons and colons?
4. How can semicolons and colons help me write clearer lists?
5. Which punctuation "rules" will be useful for me as I write and revise?

The semicolon and colon are two useful marks for writers. But how often do you use them? Occasionally? Rarely? Never??!! Do you avoid using semicolons and colons because you aren't sure you will use them "correctly"? If your answer is "yes," you're not alone. Even though semicolons and colons qualify for several important jobs in sentences, they aren't always employed by writers—especially student writers.

SEMICOLON IS BORN

When the Greeks first introduced the semicolon into writing, its original meaning was that of a question mark. As the mark moved into Latin, it changed: the period and the comma traded places and the comma part became larger and more curved, giving us our present day question mark. Yet the semicolon reappeared in its original shape in later Latin manuscripts. This time it was used to create a long pause. An Italian scholar and printer named Aldus Manutius (1450–1515) is credited with standardizing semicolon use and giving the mark its name.

In importance, the semicolon, ranks just behind the period and the comma. By looking at it, you can see it is closely related to those two punctuation marks. Think of it this way: The semicolon is a hybrid mark. Its mother is a period. Its father is a comma. It inherits all its strength from the mother **.....** and all its gentleness from the father **,,,,,** Put these two marks together and they produce a semicolon **;;;;;** This mark is a gentle period or a strong comma depending on how you choose to view it.

The semicolon's use to signal a pause stronger than a comma but less final than a period was firmly established by Justus George Schottelius in 1663 in his *Detailed Treatise on the German Language* in which he described the *Strichpunktlein* (stroke with a little point.)

MODERN SEMICOLONS

Today, when we use semicolons in our writing, we follow several guidelines:

Semicolon Guideline #1:   **Use a semicolon between two sentences or independent clauses that are closely related in subject matter.**
Semicolons, like periods, are used between complete ideas, or independent clauses. The only special requirement for using semicolons in place of a period is that the independent clauses must express *closely related ideas*.
—Two independent clauses punctuated with **periods**:

Jerry just bought himself a motorcycle. *He loves it*.

—The same two independent clauses punctuated with a **semicolon**:

Jerry just bought himself a motorcycle; he loves it.

When we studied commas, we also learned that a **comma** can connect two independent clauses IF a **conjunction** is present:

Jerry just bought himself a motorcycle, and he loves it.

Each of the above examples contains two complete ideas or independent clauses. As you can see, as long as the ideas are closely related, you have at least **three options** for punctuating them.

WHEN SHOULD YOU EMPLOY WHICH MARK?

So how do you decide which way to punctuate two closely related sentences?

- Sometimes the decision is just personal preference. You may simply like periods better than semicolons. Or you may prefer semicolons because you think they make your writing look more sophisticated.

- Sometimes you may decide on a semicolon to connect two closely related sentences because the sentences are short and you think your writing would sound less choppy if you joined them with a semicolon instead of using a period after each one. But sentences don't necessarily have to be short to be joined by semicolons; they only have to be *related in subject matter*.

- You might argue that all sentences in the same paragraph are closely related, yet you don't connect them all with semicolons. True, but if you look carefully, you will find that some sentences *belong* together more than others. This is especially true if you are comparing ideas, contrasting ideas, or discussing two events that occur simultaneously. For example, the following paragraph contains six related sentences. However, the writer chooses to use a semicolon only twice:

David used to complain that he didn't have time to read; his job kept him on the road many hours of the day. I decided to order him a different kind of book. The subject matter was something I knew he would enjoy, a fast-paced adventure. On Monday morning the book arrived in the mail. David was pleasantly surprised. The book was not on paper; it was on audio tape. That week during his long daily commute, he "read" all four tapes and enjoyed his drive like never before.

Compare the sentences with semicolons to the other sentences in the paragraph. What is special about their relationship? _____

_____

_____

COLLABORATE!   *Use Semicolons in Paragraphs*

Directions

Work together with a group or on your own. In the following paragraphs, the independent clauses are divided by slash marks (/). Replace each slash mark with some kind of punctuation: either a period, a comma, or a semicolon. Be able to give reasons for the mark you choose. Add capitalization, when necessary, after all periods. CIRCLE the marks you insert.

A. My mother loves tiny things/ in the spring she constructs a miniature garden on her balcony/ a sea shell becomes a pond/ a golf tee transforms into a bird bath/ I delight in her inventions/ and she delights in my praises.

B. I look at my fellow fire fighters/ and I start to grin/ I love my work/ the helicopter is approaching/ it will take us to the fire/ we pick up our tools and prepare for another hot day.

DO IT YOURSELF!   *Try the Semicolon as an Option*

Directions

Combine each of the following sets of sentences using three different punctuation options:
a. *A period after each sentence.*

b. *A semicolon after the first sentence and a period after the second.*
c. *A comma and a coordinating conjunction (but, or, yet, for, and, nor, so)*
CIRCLE all the marks you insert.

1. I need absolute quiet when studying

    I can't concentrate when the television is on

a. _____

_____

b. _____

_____

c. _____

_____

2. the new company policy was discussed

    all the departments were represented

a. _____

_____

b. _____

_____

c. _____

_____

3. I prefer seafood restaurants

    my husband likes steak houses

a. _____

_____

b. _____

_____

c. _____

_____

4. my father told me to get an education

    I'm glad I listened to him

a. _____

_____

b. _____

_____

c. _____

_____

5. the veterinarian's office is full of hissing cats

the pediatrician's office is full of crying babies

a. _____

_____

b. _____

_____

c. _____

_____

In the space provided, copy guideline #1 for using the semicolon: _____

_____

_____

_____

_____

Semicolon Guideline #2:   **Use a semicolon instead of a comma between two independent clauses that are joined by a coordinating conjunction when there is a comma or commas within at least one of the clauses. Instead of placing a comma before the conjunction (BOYFANS word) joining two independent clauses, you place a semicolon in that position *on one condition*—if one or more commas appear elsewhere in either independent clauses:**

> *My mother, who is Norwegian, speaks with an accent; and most people enjoy listening to her.*

In the above sentence, a SEMICOLON appears before the conjunction because of the commas around "who is Norwegian."

The logic of this semicolon guideline has to do with which mark is doing the toughest job. Imagine punctuation marks as workers with a hierarchy:

- The period is the strongest worker.
- The semicolon is not as strong as a period, but it is stronger than a comma.
- The comma is weaker than the period and the semicolon.

Typically a compound sentence with two independent clauses and a conjunction presents two job openings for punctuation marks:

1.   a period at the end of the sentence;
2.   a comma before the conjunction that connects the second independent clause.

But if the compound sentence presents three **different** job openings for punctuation marks, we need hire three different workers. But who does which job. That depends . . .

- Job #1 is to mark a full stop at the end of the entire compound sentence. This is the toughest job. So we hire a period.

- Job #2 is to mark the end of the first independent clause. That is still a tough job because this worker, too, must separate two complete ideas. Because it receives some help from the conjunction, the mark after the first idea doesn't have to be quite as strong as the period. For this job, the second toughest job, we hire the semicolon.

- Job #3 is simply to separate out a few unnecessary words from one of the independent clauses. This is the easiest job. After all, the mark is not separating one complete idea from another. So we employ the weakest mark, the comma, for this position.

Study the following examples of compound sentences that use semicolons after the first independent clause, because there are already interior commas elsewhere:

The Hollywood Cinema, a new theater on State Street, features horror movies; and everyone flocks to see them.

    Since Richard is a professional musician, he often attends concerts; and I usually accompany him.

    I like peanuts, apples, and grapes in my salad; but I do not like bananas.

COLLABORATE!   *Add Commas and Semicolons to Compound Sentences*

Directions

Working in a group or on your own, fill in commas and semicolons as needed in the following compound sentences. Some sentences will require commas only; others will require both semicolons and commas. If you need to review comma uses, refer to the guidelines in Chapter 13. CIRCLE any mark you insert.

1. If you finish the job you may go home early but if you do not finish you will need to stay late.

2. Rob Bibler my art professor is very talented and his wife is also an artist.

3. The cafeteria offered garlic bread spaghetti and salad for lunch but dinner included dessert as well.

4. Mrs. Baker manages the bookstore and I enjoy working for her.

5. Sue collects stamps and I collect records coins and baseball cards.

6. Jerry ate the raw fish but Lucy refused to taste it.

7. While watching the movie I felt a chill rush down my back and I had to remind myself that it was only fiction.

8. Who for example will paint the house and who will do the yard work?

9. Thursday July 27 is my birthday and Friday July 28 is my wedding anniversary.

10. Your dinner Mr. Smith will be served in the dining room but dessert will be outside by the pool.

In the space provided copy guideline #2 for using the semicolon:

_____

_____

Semicolon Guideline #3: **Use a semicolon between independent clauses joined by a conjunctive adverb (therefore, however, nevertheless, thus, moreover, also, besides, consequently, meanwhile, otherwise, then, furthermore, likewise, still)**

    This third semicolon application is probably the one writers use most frequently. Conjunctive adverbs are a special group of adverbs that can be used like conjunctions between sentences to connect complete ideas. As you can see, these adverbs signal transitions from one idea to another:

We reached the bus stop late; therefore, we missed the bus.

Notice that the semicolon is used to separate the two independent clauses and a comma is used to off set the conjunctive adverb from the clause in which it appears. In other words, conjunctive adverbs need punctuation on both sides.

DO IT YOURSELF! *Surround the Conjunctive Adverb*

Directions

In the following paragraph, many compound sentences contain conjunctive adverbs. Add semicolons and commas to these sentences as needed. CIRCLE any punctuation marks you insert.

    I usually enjoy going to the movies however I often end up sitting by inconsiderate people. Last week I sat behind a man who refused to remove his hat consequently I had to move my head from side to side to see the entire screen. His girlfriend was wearing strong smelling perfume furthermore she sprayed herself with a fresh dose while I was eating my popcorn. The man sitting next to me bought his little girl a large soda therefore she had to leave to go to the rest room during the middle of the film. The people behind me were having an argument likewise the woman next to me couldn't stop talking to her husband. Next weekend I am not going to the movies however I might rent a movie to watch at home all by myself.

JOURNAL PROMPT

Have you ever sat near annoying people in a movie theater, at a concert, or at a sports event? What particular actions annoyed you? Did you say anything to anyone to stop the annoying behavior? Explain what happened. When you are in an audience, do you act with consideration to others around you? For example, how do you act in a full theater that may be different from the way you act when a theater is almost empty?

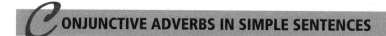

CONJUNCTIVE ADVERBS IN SIMPLE SENTENCES

You may remember seeing some of the adverbs on the conjunctive adverb list used as parenthetical expressions in the previous chapter on commas. If a conjunctive adverb occurs *within* a simple sentence, it is considered to be parenthetical and, therefore, is set off by commas:

> *We, nevertheless, missed the bus.*

DO IT YOURSELF!   *Enclose in Commas or Use Semicolons*

Directions

Insert semicolons and commas into the following sentences as needed. CIRCLE any punctuation marks you insert.

1. Mark is tall therefore he usually sits in the back row.
2. Maria is short however sitting in an aisle seat enables her to see the movie screen.
3. Maria therefore always tries to find an aisle seat.
4. The only place Bernie buys popcorn is at the movies likewise that is the only place I buy candy bars.
5. Consequently I do not eat many candy bars.
6. Fred can be annoying because he has a loud laugh furthermore he laughs at some things that aren't funny.
7. I go to movies with him nevertheless because he is good company.
8. I like to go to movies with friends otherwise I feel out of place at the movie theater.
9. I enjoy watching television alone however.
10. I can watch anything I like moreover I can change the channel anytime I like.

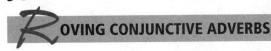

ROVING CONJUNCTIVE ADVERBS

Since conjunctive adverbs are adverbs, they possess that quality we have seen in adverbs before: they can move around in sentences. Most adverbs move easily from the beginning of the sentence to the end of the sentence or the middle of the sentence. The same is true even of conjunctive adverbs:

> *We arrived at the bus stop late; <u>therefore</u>, we missed the bus.*
> *We arrived at the bus stop late; we, <u>therefore</u>, missed the bus.*
> *We arrived at the bus stop late; we missed the bus, <u>therefore</u>.*

Notice how the above sentences are punctuated. The semicolon *always* separates the two independent clauses regardless of where the conjunctive adverb is placed. Commas are inserted, when needed, to set off the conjunctive adverb.

DO IT YOURSELF!   *Punctuate the Roving Conjunctive Adverb*

Directions
Insert semicolons and commas correctly into the following sentences. CIRCLE any marks you insert.

1. We enjoyed the picnic however a cold wind started up after we had eaten.
2. We enjoyed the picnic a cold wind started up after we had eaten however.
3. Skiing is my favorite sport consequently I look forward to winter.
4. Skiing is my favorite sport I consequently look forward to winter.
5. Rod likes to travel to exotic places therefore he visited Borneo last year.
6. Rod likes to travel to exotic places he therefore visited Borneo last year.
7. We thought the heavy traffic would make us late nevertheless we managed to cross town in fifteen minutes and arrive on time.
8. George scheduled the staff meeting for Thursday afternoon everyone will not be able to attend however.
9. George scheduled the staff meeting for Thursday afternoon however everyone will not be able to attend.
10. George scheduled the staff meeting for Thursday afternoon everyone however will not be able to attend.

WHEN NOT TO USE SEMICOLONS

Like periods, semicolons separate one complete idea from another; that is, they separate one independent clause from another independent clause. Semicolons, however, **do not separate** *subordinate* clauses from independent clauses.

Subordinate clauses are word groups that contain subjects and verbs but don't express complete ideas. They begin with words such as *after, although, because, if, since, unless, when,* and *while.* Subordinate clauses are punctuated like this:

When the subordinate clause comes first, use a comma:

Since I am going to church, I cannot meet you for breakfast.

When the subordinate clause comes last, comma use no punctuation:

I cannot meet you for breakfast since I am going to church.

However, if these same ideas are expressed in independent clauses instead, the semicolon would be appropriate:

Two independent clauses:

I am going to church; I cannot meet you for breakfast.

OR

I am going to church; therefore, I cannot meet you for breakfast.

This is an example in which structure decides the punctuation more so than meaning.

COLLABORATE!   *Deciding between Semicolons and Commas*

Directions

Working with a group or on your own, decide where to place commas and semicolons. Remember you need a complete idea on each side of a semicolon. Some of the sentences will need no punctuation. Insert marks where needed and CIRCLE them.

1. After the ball game was over we went out for pie and coffee.
2. The student received an "A" on his test therefore he was very happy.
3. Because the student received an "A" on his test he was very happy.
4. The door opened the woman entered the room.
5. She did not seem to be upset when I saw her.
6. When I saw her she did not seem to be upset.
7. I saw her however she did not seem to be upset.
8. I saw her she did not seem to be upset however.
9. Mike bought a computer because it would save him time and money therefore it would make his office more efficient.
10. Mike bought a computer consequently he can save time and money and operate his office more efficiently.

DO IT YOURSELF!   *Write Sentences and Punctuate Them*

Directions
Change the structure of the following sentences in a variety of ways with the help of the words in parentheses. Insert semicolons and commas as needed. CIRCLE all punctuation marks.

1. Brooke is a vegetarian

   her husband eats meat

(nevertheless) _____

_____

2. some vegetarians eat fish

   some do not

(however) _____

_____

3. Brooke became a vegetarian

   she wanted to lose weight

(because) _____

_____

4. she became a vegetarian

   she did lose weight

(after) _____

_____

5. she became a vegetarian

   she did lose weight

(therefore) _____

_____

6. Matt is careful about what he eats

   Matt is not a vegetarian

(however) _____

_____

7. I enjoy many ethnic foods

   I will probably never become a vegetarian

(since) _____

_____

8. eating healthful foods is important

    exercise plays a significant role in staying fit

(likewise) _____

_____

9. eating healthful foods is important

    exercise plays a significant role in staying fit

(although) _____

_____

10. eating healthful foods is important

    exercise plays a significant role in staying fit

(while) _____

_____

    In the space provided, copy guideline #3 for using the semicolon: _____

_____

_____

_____

_____

_____

THREE SEMICOLON GUIDELINES UP FOR REVIEW

Semicolon Guideline #1:   Use a semicolon between two sentences or independent clauses that are closely related in subject matter.

   My mother is a teacher; my father is a truck driver.

Semicolon Guideline #2:   Use a semicolon instead of a comma between two independent clauses that are joined by a coordinating conjunction when there is a comma or commas within at least one of the clauses.

   Tom's boss, Harriet Brown, called the meeting; and everyone arrived late.

Semicolon Guideline #3:   Use a semicolon between independent clauses joined by a conjunctive adverb (therefore, however, nevertheless, thus, moreover, also, besides, consequently, meanwhile, otherwise, then, furthermore, likewise, still).

   The tailor shortened my pants; however, they are still an inch too long.

COLLABORATE!   *Applying All Three Semicolon Guidelines*

Directions

Working with a group or on your own, fill in semicolons where needed in the following paragraphs. CIRCLE any marks you insert.

In today's society most people can eat as much as they want whenever they want. This kind of affluence means many people are overweight. Being overweight is dangerous it can shorten life expectancy. Although most people understand the health risks posed by being overweight, the majority of people eat whatever they like and they become fat and unhealthy as a result. I do not recommend that everyone should go on a diet however, I do believe that people should eat only when they are hungry. Many of us eat even when we are not hungry therefore, we gain weight. We are lucky to live in society where food is not scarce but, too often, having so much means eating too much.

JOURNAL PROMPT

What are your views of the eating habits of Americans? Do you think people eat when they are not hungry? If so, why do you think they eat? Have you ever been in a situation where food has been scarce? How do you think that has affected the way you feel about food? Do you ever use food for purposes other than satisfying hunger? For example, do you use food for comfort, or to ease loneliness, or to help you deal with anxiety? Discuss these uses of food.

THE COLON, A SIGN OF WHAT IS TO COME

The colon, another mark used for interior punctuation, looks like two periods stacked one on top of the other : : : : : Colons are used in business letters (*To whom it may concern:*), in time schedules (*1:30 pm*), in play scripts (*Act I: scene iii*), in church programs (*Psalms 23:3*), and in bibliography entries (*Upper Saddle River, New Jersey: Prentice Hall*). A complete style guide will explain these uses in detail.

For writers, colons are also useful for clarifying relationships of elements in sentences. In the world of punctuation traffic signs, the colon is a flashing yellow light that alerts a reader that something is coming up ahead—specifically, an explanation is coming up.

WHEN A LIST IS COMING UP

The most common use of the colon within a sentence is to introduce a list, or a series. The colon tells the reader "a list is coming up ahead." Frequently the words "the following" or "as follows" precede the colon when lists are introduced. Look at these examples:

> *The winner may select one of the following:* a gold watch, a diamond ring, or a fur coat.
> *He gave instructions as follows:* lift the lid, insert the key, and turn it clockwise.

Sometimes, however, the expressions "the following" or "as follows" are left out. In such cases a colon may still be used **if** the statement introducing the list is a complete sentence:

> *Thomas Peel Wasson owned three cars:* a Honda, a pick-up, and a jeep.
> *Maggie brought everything:* the hot dogs, the potato chips, and the lemonade.

The introductory statements preceding the above lists end with a summarizing or a collective noun. And the list simply breaks down that collective noun in detail.

A situation in which a list requires **no colon** to precede it is the situation where the list follows the verb and serves as a direct object or subject complement of a sentence. The following are examples:

Direct objects after action verb:

> *George collects stamps, coins, and baseball cards.* (No colon)

Subject complements after being verb:

> *Hannah was a student, a mother, and a wife.* (No colon)

> *The same hold true if the items on the list are all objects of the same preposition:*

Objects of a preposition:

> *Young Eric Eide opened his knapsack filled with candy, cookies, and soda pop.* (No colon)

The guideline for using the colon with lists then reads as follows:

Colon Guideline: Use a colon to introduce a list that is preceded by the expression "as follows" or "the following" or a list that is preceded by a complete sentence, usually containing a collective noun or a summary statement.
Do not use a colon before a list that does not meet these requirements.

DO IT YOURSELF!   *Decide Where to Use the Colon*

Directions

A. *Insert a colon to precede a list, if needed, in each of the following sentences.*

1. My daily exercises include the following twenty sit-ups, ten curl-ups, and fifteen leg lifts.

2. My next car must have certain extras air conditioning, power door locks, power windows, and a stereo CD player.

3. Last Saturday we watched three old movies *Casablanca, Vertigo,* and *Ben-Hur.*

4. Last Saturday we watched *Casablanca, Vertigo,* and *Ben-Hur.*

5. Kristie enjoys walking her dog, working in the yard, and running along the beach.

6. Kristie enjoys outdoor activities walking her dog, working in the yard, and running on the beach.

7. The treasures in my daughter's toy box include the following a doll house, a pop-up book, a set of blocks, a stuffed teddy bear, and a music box.

8. The chef seasoned the stew with oregano, garlic, and basil.

9. During our vacation we drove through three western states Washington, Idaho, and Nevada.

10. During our vacation we drove through Washington, Idaho, and Nevada.

11. On your schedule your courses will be listed as follows math at 8:30, economics at 10:30, and biology at 1:30.

12. Your research paper should include the following a title page, a thesis statement, an endnote page, and a bibliography.

13. Susan was a wife, a mother, and a full-time student.

B. *In the space provided write five of your own sentences containing lists. Structure the sentences so that three of them require the use of colons and two of them do not. CIRCLE any punctuation marks you use.*

1. _____

_____

_____

2. _____

_____

_____

3. _____

_____

_____

4. _____

_____

_____

5. _____

_____

*L*OOKING INSIDE THE LISTS

Do you recall that one function of the comma was to separate the items in lists from one another? The interior punctuation of lists looked like this:

I invited Mary, Pat, Terry, and you to my party.

Sometimes, however, lists become quite complicated.

Imagine for a moment that I am going to have a party. I list my guests in the following way:

I will invite Mary, my teacher, Pat, her husband, Terry, the coach, and, of course, you.

If I then asked you to furnish a party hat for each of my guests, would you know how many hats to bring? Will there now be eight different people at the party (remember I, the host, will be there, too)? Or could there be seven, or six, or only five? Who is who on this list? Is Mary the teacher? Is Pat her husband? Or is Mary just someone without a title, and is Pat the teacher? Is Terry Pat's husband or is Terry the coach? (Maybe I should just cancel the party!) These are not the only possibilities the reader might entertain if such list were to contain only commas. Let's clarify the list by writing it in a vertical arrangement:

Person 1: Mary, my teacher

Person 2: Pat, her husband

Person 3: Terry, the coach

Person 4: you

I can achieve the same clarity in my original sentence by using a SEMICOLON each time I come to a new person.

I will invite Mary, my teacher; Pat, her husband; Terry, the coach; and, of course, you.

Now you can rush right out and buy five party hats. One for me, one for you, and three for the rest of my friends. Notice the commas that remain in the list are being used to set off information belonging to each of the items on the list; they are not being used to separate one list item from another. The *semicolons* are doing that—after all, on the punctuation hierarchy, semicolons are a step stronger than their relatives, the commas. In our exploration of how to punctuate lists, then, we have discovered a fourth semicolon guideline:

Semicolon Guideline #4:   Semicolons should be used to separate items in a series when one or several of these items themselves contain commas.
This guideline should be followed even if only one item in the list contains a comma, for example:

I invited Joe; Mary, my teacher; Janice; and Mark.
(Only the second item contains a comma, but that means semicolons must be used to separate item from item.)

DO IT YOURSELF! *Punctuate Complex Lists*

Directions

Practice incorporating lists into your sentences and punctuating them correctly using commas, semicolons, and colons.

A. *Insert the lists provided into the following sentence settings. CIRCLE all punctuation marks in the sentence you write.*

1. Items to be listed:

—Fred Hansen, owner of Fred's Market

—John Player, president of the First Bank

—and Donald Norton, manager of Fast Food Farms

Sentence:

_____

_____

_____

_____ were three members of the City Council.

2. Items to be listed:

—a hair dryer

—an electric toothbrush

—a bottle of cologne

—and some bath oil

Sentence:

In her overnight case, Barbara packed the following _____

_____

_____

_____

3. Items to be listed:

—his mother

—his father

—his twin sister

—and Sammy, the dog

Sentence:

Darren's entire family consisted of _____

_____

_____

_____

4. Items to be listed:

—writing computer programs

—entering them into her computer

—and testing them

Sentence:

Jill spends her time doing the following

_____

_____

_____

_____

5. Items to be listed:

—writing computer programs

—entering them into her computer, which is an IBM

—or testing them

Sentence:

Jill spends her time as follows _____

_____

_____

_____

6. Items to be listed:

—Friday, January 3

—Monday, January 6

—or Wednesday, January 8

Sentence:

You may schedule your check-up on _____

_____

_____

_____

7. Items to be listed:

—buying a new car

—sending my son off to college

—living in a more expensive apartment than last year

This year has required me to budget more carefully because I am _____

_____

_____

_____

8. Items to be listed:

—kiwi fruit

—honey tangerines

—and strawberries, the everbearing variety

Sentence:

At the buffet our club was served a tantalizing assortment of fresh fruit _____

_____

_____

_____

B. *Write your own complex list requiring both commas and semicolons. Incorporate it into a sentence and decide whether a colon is an appropriate mark to precede your list. CIR-CLE all your punctuation marks.*

_____

_____

_____

_____

_____

_____

WRITE RIGHT FOR THE JOB: Being Prepared to Punctuate

In addition to understanding in-depth the uses of the comma and the semicolon and the use of the colon to punctuate lists, you will find it useful to understand the uses of other punctuation marks, especially when you write on the job or for your classes. Memorizing the "rules" that apply to every punctuation mark, however, may not be a particularly rewarding effort, nor would it be an exciting way to spend your precious time. The best strategy for insuring that you are prepared to punctuate your writing correctly is to keep a set of punctuation guidelines handy at all times. On the job, most employers provide style guides or usage guides or secretarial handbooks for their employees. In college, the most universal recommendation of professors is an English handbook—nearly every textbook publisher offers one. In the past you may have found looking up rules in handbooks and guides to be less than satisfying. Many of those sources explain punctuation rules by using much grammatical terminology. By now, if you have worked through many of the chapters in *Writing with the Lights On*, grammatical terminology should not be unfamiliar to you. Yet having access to a set of "simply stated guidelines" for punctuation may benefit you in your future writing and revising. Therefore, here in the final part of this chapter, the final part of this book, I have prepared for you my own collection of simply stated punctuation guidelines.

PUNCTUATION GUIDELINES FOR WRITING WITH THE LIGHTS ON (SIMPLY STATED)

Use Commas *, , , , ,*

1. Only when you know exactly why you are using them. This is the first rule of comma use.

2. Before the words *but, or, yet, for, and, nor, so (coordinating conjunctions)* when these words connect two complete sentences *(or independent clauses)*.
    Example: *Silence is golden, but the squeaky wheel still gets the grease.*

3. After introductory words, phrases, or clauses. Introductory *words* are typically transitional; introductory *phrases* are usually prepositional (beginning with *in, on, by, for*, etc.) or verbal (beginning with *running, singing, ignored, known, to be, to sneeze*, etc.); introductory *clauses* are dependent clauses beginning with subordinating conjunctions *(although, since, because, while*, etc.).
    Examples

    Definitely, good things come in small packages.
    On a visit in Rome, you should do as the Romans do.
    Although a penny saved is a penny earned, the love of money is the root of all evil.

    NOT, however
    when the dependent clause placement is reversed.
    Example: *The love of money is the root of all evil although a penny saved is a penny earned.* (No comma)
    after *short* introductory prepositional phrases where no pause is needed for emphasis.
    Example: *On Sunday my actions spoke louder than words.* (No comma)

4. Between items listed in a series (individual words, phrases, dependent clauses.) The comma before the coordinating conjunction *(and, or, nor)* that precedes the last item on the list is an optional comma. To avoid confusion, however, you would be wise to insert such a comma.
    Example: *Tuna, pastrami, chicken salad, ham, and cheese are my favorite sandwich toppings.*

5. To enclose unnecessary or parenthetical expressions such as non-restrictive phrases and clauses; appositives; and expressions, such as transitions, that interrupt the sentence.
Example: *Paul, nevertheless, changed horses in mid-stream.*
Variety, which is the spice of life, is usually expensive.
Mrs. Snively, my English teacher, never judged a book by its cover.

NOT, however—

when the information in a phrase, clause, or appositive is necessary information.
Example: *A teacher who has green hair is difficult to ignore.*

Use Semicolons ; ; ; ; ;

1. Between two closely related sentences *(independent clauses)* that are NOT connected by the words *but, or, yet, for, and, nor, so (coordinating conjunctions)*.
Example: *Nothing was ventured; nothing was gained either.*

2. Between two complete sentences *(independent clauses)* joined by *but, or, yet, for, and, nor, so (coordinating conjunctions)* when either or both of the sentences contain one or more commas.
Example: *Actions speak louder than words; but, if you act in haste, you may repent in leisure.*

3. Between sentences *(independent clauses)* joined by *therefore, however, nevertheless, thus, moreover, also, besides, consequently, meanwhile, otherwise, then, furthermore, likewise, still (conjunctive adverbs)*.
Example: *Practice makes perfect; however, all work and no play makes Jack a dull boy.*

4. Between items in a list or series when one or more of the items contain a comma.
Example: *Never send a boy to do a man's work; to buy groceries, except snacks; or to pick up the mail.*
Grandma's hundredth birthday party was attended by her first husband, Fred; her second husband, George; her third husband, PeeWee; but not her late husband, Hermann.

Use Colons : : : : :

1. Before a list of items introduced by *the following* or *as follows* or introduced by a complete sentence that summarizes items in an upcoming list.
Example: *Absence eventually makes the heart do all of the following: grow fonder, grow older, and grow restless.*
I love all kinds of food: chocolate cake, chocolate pie, chocolate ice cream, and sandwiches with chocolate spread.

NOT, however—

after an action or being verb

Example: *The classes I am taking this semester are Cooking with Chocolate, Decorating with Chocolate, and Communicating with Chocolate.*

2. Between two sentences *(independent clauses)* when the second sentence explains the first:
    Example: *Researchers have determined why so many commuters are buying recreational vehicles: they need a place to live while waiting in traffic.*

3. Preceding a quotation.
    Example: *The sign above the robbery detective's door read: "A man's reach should not exceed his grasp."*

4. Between hours and minutes—5:15
    Between Act and scene of a play—IV:iii
    Between titles and subtitles—*Writing with the Lights On: From Sentences to Paragraphs*

Use Apostrophes ′ ′ ′ ′ ′

1. With a word or words from which one or more letters have been left out *(contractions).*
    Example: *They're (they are)*
    Can't (cannot)
    It's (it is)

2. To show ownership or possession
    A. If the owner, or possessor, does not already end in an "s" or "z" sound, add an apostrophe plus an "s."
    Example: *Edith ran into the men's room accidentally.*
    B. If the owner, or possessor, already ends in an "s" or "z" sound, add an apostrophe only.
    Example: *They were at Amos' Diner.*
    Archie went into the ladies' room looking for Edith.

3. To show joint ownership, add the apostrophe (or apostrophe plus "s") only to the last owner's name.
    Example: *I bought this white elephant at Lord and Taylor's safari sale.*
    To show separate ownership, add the apostrophe (or apostrophe plus "s") to each owner's name.
    Example: *I went to Nordstrom's and Penney's sales looking for more white elephants.*

Use a Hyphen - - - - -

1. Between two or more words that combine to express *one idea*—only when those words appear immediately before the word they are describing.
    Example: *King Kong is a well-known gorilla.*
    (but—King Kong is well known.)

2. Between compound numbers and in fractions if these are written out in words.
    Example: *That particular pair of jeans costs ninety-one dollars.*
    Two-thirds of my paycheck goes to pay my telephone bill.

Use a Dash — — —

1. To emphasize information.
   Example: *I have only one interest——chocolate!*
2. To set off a parenthetical element when commas could be confusing.
   Example: *The basic skills——reading, writing, and speaking——are important to master if you want to become a reader, writer, or speaker.*
3. To show a sudden break in thought:
   Example: *Of course, I remember what he said——now, what was it he said again?*

Use Quotation Marks " "   " "   " "

1. In pairs, to enclose direct quotations, whether from a written or spoken source.
   Example: *Will Rogers once said, "I tell you folks, all politics is applesauce."*

   "Everything is funny," said Will Rogers, "as long as it is happening to someone else."

   "Politics is has got so expensive that it takes lots of money to even get beat with," wrote Will Rogers.

   (In the above examples pay attention to how **commas** are used with quotation marks to set off quoted sentences.)

   Note: To set off a quotation inside a quotation use single quotation marks

   Example: *When asked if he would run for President, Will Rogers replied, "I will say 'won't run' no matter how bad the country will need a comedian by that time."*

2. To use words in a special sense:
   Example: *My old car was a "lemon."*

3. To set off titles of poems, songs, short stories, articles, and other parts of longer works.
   Example: *John Keats wrote a sonnet entitled "On the Grasshopper and the Cricket."*

4. Together with other marks:
   Always place an ending *comma* or *period INSIDE* the quotation marks.
   Example: *"When I'm good, I'm very good, but when I'm bad, I'm better," said Mae West with a shrug of the shoulder.*

   Mae West once said, "Between two evils, I always pick the one I never tried before."

   Always place a *colon* or *semicolon OUTSIDE* the quotation marks.

   Example: *Oscar Wilde once said, "A poet can survive everything but a misprint"; I now know what he meant by that.*

   Place a *dash, question mark,* or *exclamation point INSIDE* the *quotation marks* only if it applies to the quotation.

   Examples: *Didn't he say, "I don't have any money"?*

   (Question mark **does not** apply to quotation.)

   No, he said, "Will you lend me some money?"

   (Question mark **does** apply to quotation.)

Use <u>Underlining</u> or Italics

(Underlining is a substitute for italics in handwritten manuscripts.)

1. To create emphasis where you cannot convey it by means of word order.
   Example: *You are **so** wrong.*
2. For the titles of books; names of newspapers and magazines; titles of movies, works of art, television and radio shows, and record albums.
   Example: *At Lafayette College, the underground newspaper, edited by Ross Gay and Matt Shapiro, is called **The Toilet Paper.***
3. To indicate the names of ships and aircraft.
   Example: *Charles Lindbergh crossed the Atlantic in **The Spirit of St. Louis.***

Use Parentheses (in pairs) ( ) ( ) ( )

1. To enclose incidental or explanatory information in a sentence.
   Example: *In the photograph (see above) I am riding a camel.*
2. To enclose numbers used to enumerate ideas in a sentence.
   Example: *The research paper was divided into three parts: (1) the outline, (2) the body, (3) the bibliography.*

Use Brackets [ ] [ ] [ ]

1. Within a quotation, to enclose explanatory information that is not a part of the original text.
   Example: *The school newspaper reported, "We [the students] would prefer that all final exams be take-home tests."*
2. Instead of parentheses, to enclose parenthetical information within material already in parentheses.
   Example: *You will find the information in any book about him (see My Life [Second Edition]).*

Use Ellipses (Omission Marks) ... ...

1. When letters or words in quoted material have been omitted.
   Example: *"Why don't you come up sometime and see me? ... come on up, I'll tell your fortune."*—Mae West, from the screenplay entitled *She Done Him Wrong*
2. Indicated by three dots plus a period (four dots altogether) when the omitted portion ends with a period.
   Example: *"He explained his position...."*

Use Slashes / / / / /

1. To express alternatives.
   Example: *While using he/she to avoid sexist language is acceptable, it is awkward when used too often.*

2. To write fractions.
   Example: *Adding 1/2 and 1/8 results in 5/8.*

Use Endmarks ?!.?!.?!.

1. A *period* after a complete statement.
   Example: *It is easier for an elephant to slip through the eye of a needle when lightly greased.*
   A *period* after abbreviations and initials.
   Example: *Mr. and Mrs. W. H. Auden*

2. A *question mark* after a direct question.
   Example: *Did you hear about the teacher who crossed her eyes and couldn't control her pupils?*

3. —an *exclamation mark* after a word, phrase or complete sentence.
   Example: *Ouch!*
   What a day!
   I can't believe it!

COLLABORATE!   A Punctuation Challenge

Directions

Together with a group or on your own read the following selection. Punctuate each paragraph correctly as you go. Some marks have been left out; some marks that are included are incorrect; and some are already correct. This will present quite a challenge. Remember, you may encounter sentences in which you have options to use several different marks for the same situation. Discuss your reasons for choosing the mark you choose.

On June 15 1999 Chester and Wilbur Snortly entered the unexplored regions of the jungles of Lalaland, they had just sold all their worldly belongings a television a CD player and their tractor and invested their money in coffee. They were motivated by the following (1) the natives of Lalaland were wild about coffee, (2) the natives had diamonds (3) the natives would trade their diamonds for coffee.

Chester was an unscrupulous, scheming, deceitful scoundrel. His thoughts were vile his intentions were dishonorable and his morals were non-existent. "Anything or anyone for a dollar was his motto."

His brother Wilbur; however, was good man. He hoped to use their money to bail their elderly confused mother out of jail in Los Angeles California she was in jail, because Chester had framed her. When Chester had announced his latest money making scheme gentle Wilbur although he had reservations agreed to follow him to Lalaland. Poor Wilbur still had hopes of rehabilitating his only brother Chester.

As we join them Chester and Wilbur are on the treacherous jungle trail they are without bearers for Chester has frightened them off one-by-one. The intense heat of the Lalaland jungle is affecting Chesters already fermented mind and he is ranting and raving from morning till night.

Suddenly they enter a clearing there in the bright sunlight stands a old wrinkled Lalaland native he is practicing throwing a spear into a tree. The natives rough dry skin sounds like two sheets of sandpaper grating together each time he walks to retrieve his weapon from the tree.

Chester winks at Wilbur, and smiles a wicked smile. He says Wilbur Im going to have some fun here. Coming up behind the old native Chester sarcastically hollers Ill bet you cant hit a silver dollar at one hundred paces amazingly the native understands and speaks English. Ill give you a cup of coffee if you can he continues.

Teasingly Chester flips a silver dollar high into the air. Clank Chesters laughter comes to an abrupt halt. The spear to Chesters utter amazement has struck the coin right in the center. The old native energized by the odor of the fresh hot fragrant coffee sounds like a thousand pieces of sandpaper rubbing together as he vigorously hobbles over to the coffee pot.

Chester stomps his feet and screams uncontrollably as he sees the elated native sipping the costly hot black brew. However Chester makes another bet he bets the old man cant hit a quarter with the spear at one hundred paces. The eager man smiles at Chester and pointing to the coffee pot signals Wilbur to start pouring another cup of coffee. After doing that he marches off with spear in hand.

Without hesitating for an instant the native accomplishes the amazing feat and again he is rewarded. Chester is crazy now he throws himself on the ground and screams with anguish. The coffee is dwindling however there are no diamonds in sight.

Poor poor Mother whispers Wilbur to himself.

Ill bet you cant hit a dime at one hundred paces screams Chester hysterically.

Sir my eyes are old and weak for I am ninety nine years old. I beg you to let my brother take my place he is only ninety three answers the old man.

Wilbur asks the native to call his younger brother after all Chester is near the end.

The native turns slowly in the direction of the hut at the edge of the clearing, and calls out Hey Brother could you spear a dime for a cup of coffee.

SELECTED ANSWERS

Chapter 2   Paragraphs . . . Useful Writing Blocks

Page 28   Collaborate! Choosing Controlling Topic Sentences

ANSWERS: 1. b   4. a   7. b   10. b

Chapter 4   Verbs Bringing Sentences to Life

Page 80   Do It Yourself! Look for Action

ANSWERS: 1. played   4. read   8. wiggle

Page 81   Do It Yourself! Look for All Kinds of Action

ANSWERS: On sunny Sunday afternoons my family and I often (drive) through Central Oregon. Juniper trees (grow) in this part of the state. Defiant red rim rock (surrounds) the high plateau. . . .

Page 83   Do It Yourself! Find Verbs that Are Just Being

ANSWERS: 1. was   4. became   9. am

Page 83   Do It Yourself! Distinguish Action from Being

ANSWERS: **A.** 1. being   4. action   7. action (circle "and" after "grass")   11. action   15. being   18. action (circle comma after "feet")   **B.** 1. action (circle comma and "and" after "faces")   4. action   8. action   12. being

Page 86   Collaborate! Thinking Through the Action . . . or the Being

ANSWERS: 5. being/ circle "is"/ Humidity is a treatment for croup.   10. action/ circle "trigger"/ not reversible

Page 88   Do It Yourself! Link Sentence Parts Together

ANSWERS: 4. The English *settlement* in Newfoundland (was) (old.)   7. Most *towns* in Newfoundland (are) (seaports.)

Page 89   Do It Yourself! Decide Action or Being

ANSWERS: **A.** 1. action   4. action   7. being   **B.** 1. being   5. action   9. being

Page 90 Collaborate! Going on a Verb Hunt

Answers: **A.** The wind(was) sharp and cold. The sky (threatened) snow . . .   **B.** Some
people actually (like) housework. I (am) one of them. . . .

The wind(was) — *being*; The sky (threatened) — *action*; people actually (like) — *action*; I (am) — *being*

Page 94 Collaborate! "Re-verbing" a Document

Suggested Answers: Dear Miss Ledd: It has come to my attention that you inquired about
our company's services. As manager of this office, I would like to respond. I understand
you called our office on May 15 and spoke with Mrs. Kerring about the injuries. . . .

Page 96 Collaborate! Getting Rid of Get, Got, and Gotten

Suggested Answers: 1. The weather *became* hot on Monday.   6. I didn't *hear* your last
name.   12. He will *compile* the facts for us.   20. You *may* leave early if you have *finished* your work.   32. The purpose of this committee is to *determine* the source of the
problem.   37. Let's *focus on* the matter at hand.   47. Joe *recovered* from his illness and
is healthy again.   53. *Do you have* the tickets?

Page 98 Do It Yourself! Using Verbs for the "Good" of Your Sentences

Answers: **A.** 1. My car runs *well*.   4. no change   8. You did *well*, Honey.

Chapter 5   Verb Tenses . . . The Writer's Timekeepers

Page 106 Collaborate! Reading for Tense Times

Answers: **A.** Examples of verbs changed from present to past: Harvest mice *were*
midget acrobats. They *stretched* and *twisted* and *swung* from one blade of grass to another. . . . Examples of verbs changed from present to future: Harvest mice *will be*
midget acrobats. They *will stretch and twist and swing* from one blade of grass to another. . . .   **B.** Examples of verbs changed from past to present: Tears *roll* down our
unshaven faces, and we *sing* "Silent Night." Suddenly we *forget* our wounds and our
hunger. We *raise* prayers of thanks. . . . Examples of verbs changed from past to future: Tears *will roll* down our unshaven faces, and we *will sing* "Silent Night." Suddenly we *will forget* our wounds and our hunger. We *will raise* prayers of thanks. . . .

Page 109 Collaborate! Convert "Bad Grammar" to "Good Grammar"

Answers: Over the years, Joe and I have *became/*(become) good friends. Yesterday he
come/(came) to me with an interesting question. He asked if I'd ever *stole/*(stolen) anything
before. . . .

Page 111 Do It Yourself! Pick the Right Verbs for the Job

Answers: Dear Mr. Jenkins: I (is) applying for a job with your company. I (seen) your ad
in the paper yesterday as I (come) out of the hardware store. I had (went) to the. . . .

I (is) — *am*; I (seen) — *saw*; I (come) — *saw*; had (went) — *gone*

Page 114   Do It Yourself! Practice Using the Highly Irregular Being Verbs

ANSWERS: Today *is* the day I *am* taking my first mid-semester exam. I *am* scared about . . . Last night, she and I *were* up until three o'clock studying together. . . .

Page 117   Do It Yourself! Make It "Simple"

ANSWERS: **A.** Fred *plays* (play) with his son. Fred *wears* (wear) blue jeans. His son *is* (being verb) in rompers . . .   **B.** In the old days, baseball *was* (being verb) a family affair. The whole country *came* (come) together during the week. . . .   **C.** The Los Chiles Mexican Restaurant *will celebrate* (celebrate) Cinco de Mayo on the fifth day of May. The featured menu *will include* (include) chimichangas. . . .

Page 120   Do It Yourself! Pick the Progressives

ANSWERS: This afternoon I will be buying a new can. I will be going on a shopping
future progressive ‾‾‾‾‾‾‾‾‾‾‾‾   *future progressive* ‾‾‾‾‾‾‾‾‾‾

spree for my dream vehicle. Last night, when I was reading the paper, I noticed all
past progressive ‾‾‾‾‾‾‾‾‾

the dealers in town are having sales. . . .
present progressive ‾‾‾‾‾‾‾‾‾

Page 121   Collaborate! Doing Business without Progressive Tenses

ANSWERS: Dear Mr. Wang: As I *look* through my stack of applications, I see that you have applied for a job with our company. Your resume demonstrates you meet all the qualifications and have the experience we *desire*. Therefore, I *will recommend* that our screening committee consider your application seriously. . . .

Page 123   Do It Yourself! Ask the Emphatic Question

SUGGESTED ANSWERS: **A.** 1. Do you like milk?   5. Does Mary speak Spanish?

Page 124   Collaborate! Reviewing the Different Tenses

ANSWERS: Too much cholesterol in the bloodstream will endanger a healthy heart.

Therefore, many Americans are monitoring their cholesterol levels carefully. Conse-

quently, today thousands of Americans jog or walk daily. . . .

Page 128   Do It Yourself! Play with "Perfect"ion

ANSWERS: 1. This year *has been* an unusual weather year.   6. The weatherman predicts, by next week, so much snow *will have melted* that we may experience some flooding in the valley.

Page 129   Collaborate! Naming the Tenses

ANSWERS: 1. *simple past* I drove my daughter to Los Angeles for transfusions daily. After a few months, the ride became routine. . . .   5. *present perfect* The businesses have changed the land. They have destroyed the wilderness. . . .   9. *present emphatic* I do attend classes regularly. I do study hard. But I do not always get good grades. . . .

Page 131   Do It Yourself! Find the Time

ANSWERS: Dear Diane, This *is* [simple present] my senior year. I *am graduating* [future progressive] on June 16. I *am* [simple present] sad. I *have attended* [present perfect] the same school my entire life. . . .

Page 133   Collaborate! Shifting Tenses Smoothly

ANSWERS: **A.** I *have* [simple present] a childhood friend. Her name *was* Katie. I *meet* her in the sixth [simple past] grade. There *have been* [present perfect] thirty students in that sixth grade class. . . .   **B.** I *bought* [simple past] a camera yesterday. Now when we *take* [simple present] our vacation next summer, I *will be taking* [future progressive] pictures of everything. . . .

Chapter 6   Nouns . . . The Pattern Makers of Sentence Design

Page 138   Do It Yourself! Decide Abstract or Concrete

ANSWERS: 1. concrete   3. abstract   7. concrete   13. abstract   17. abstract

Page 140   Collaborate! Marking the Markers and the Nouns

ANSWERS: Have you decided to buy a new mattress set? You should invest in the very best. The materials, the quality. . . .

Page 141   Collaborate! Differentiating Nouns from Verbs

ANSWERS: I *dream* (verb) about having my own apartment. I know the *dream* (noun) of having my own place will come true someday. At least, I *hope* (verb) so. To me, an apartment *means* (verb) independence. I would no longer need *support* (noun). . . .

Page 143   Do It Yourself! Search for Subjects

ANSWERS: Cats are cautious creatures. Our cat certainly is. Felix always runs and hides. . . .

Page 145   Do It Yourself! Make Subjects and Verbs Agree

ANSWERS: 1. The dancers *move* across the stage.   6. The boy *has* talent.

Page 146   Do It Yourself! Put Only "Agree"able Verbs in the Paragraph

ANSWERS: 1. attend   4. runs   10. follow   15. is

Page 147   Do It Yourself! Follow the Action to the Direct Object

ANSWERS: *Computers* [S] have changed the *world* [DO]. Today *people* [S] use *computers* [DO] at school, on the job, and even at home.

Page 149   Collaborate! Writing Sentences with Subjects and Objects

ANSWERS: **B.** Do you want a *mate* [VA][DO]? *Scientists* [S] have studied human mating *behaviors* [VA]. . . . [DO] In general, *men* [S] value physical *attractiveness* [VA] and *youth* [DO]. A pretty *woman* [DO] can give a *man* [S][VA][IO] romantic *ideas* [DO]. . . .

Page 152   Collaborate! Figuring Out Four Noun Functions

Answers: 1. The *students* S will attend (action) the *program* DO.   5. *Fred* S is (being) a *senior* SC.   10. The class *treasurer* S sold (action) his *family* IO five *tickets* DO.

Page 160   Collaborate! Taking Out the Garbage (I Mean Verbiage)

Answers: **A.** Section One has *pertinence* to any law that makes *provision* for legal fees. Although we are in *agreement* with you. . . .   **B.** Section One pertains to any law that provides for legal fees. Although we agree with you. . . .

Chapter 7   Adjectives Adding Details to Description

Page 171   Collaborate! Redundant Adjectives

Answers: 1. Not redundant   7. Redundant   14. Not redundant   21. Redundant

Page 172   Collaborate! Removing Unnecessary Adjectives from Clichés

Answers: Dear Mr. Jawb Hunter, I have read your application and have given much ~~thoughtful~~ consideration to your qualifications. The ~~written~~ document you submitted. . . .

Page 173   Do It Yourself! Question the Adjective

Answers: **A.** Circle the following: 1. what kind   5. which   8. which   **B.** "This is an emergency!" In *a neat white house* (what kind) next to the lake, *elderly Vi Sayer* (what kind) was reading in *her den* (which). She remembers hearing *no sounds* (how many). . . .

Page 179   Do It Yourself! Complement Sentences with Adjectives

Answers: The strange figure entered the dark room. Its long uncombed hair was (white.)

Page 187   Collaborate! Putting the Efficiency Experts to Work

Suggested Answers: 1. The required application fee is due by January first.   4. The retired school employees serve on advisory committees.

Chapter 8   Pronouns for Every Point of View

Page 192   Do It Yourself! Write Easier-to-Read Paragraphs with Pronouns

Answers: Dr. Craig Packer from the University of Minnesota does research on lions. *He* (Dr. Craig Packer) works together with his wife, Dr. Anne Pusey. *She* (Dr. Anne Pusey) accompanies *him* (Dr. Craig Packer). . . .

Page 193   Do It Yourself! Hunt for the Antecedents

Answers: Janell was lucky. Rolland Greene liked *her* (Janell). This was one of the reasons *he* (Rolland) tried to get *her* (Janell) to replace *him* (Rolland). . . .

Page 195 Collaborate! Clearing up the Confusion

ANSWERS: Today was a hectic day at the Smith residence. First, visiting Cousin George took the sheet off the hide-a-bed and then folded *it* (the hide-a-bed?) up. Aunt Julia, who was getting her coat on, told Mom *she* (Mom?) had a hair appointment. Uncle Fred was busy reading a book about sex; *it* (sex?) really interested him. . . .

Page 198 Collaborate! Becoming an "It is" Buster

ANSWERS: 5. I understand that this agreement will apply to all future requests. 8. Implementing the proposed procedures is expected to have a minimal effect on our company's profits.

Page 203 Collaborate! Name the Case

ANSWERS: **A.** *I* will be taking a very difficult test in math tomorrow. [*subjective*] Tom, the tutor, can help *me*. [*objective*] *He* explains things so well. . . . [*subjective*] **B.** Pronoun 1: I = subject   Pronoun 6: me = indirect object   Pronoun 12: He = subject

Page 204 Collaborate! Deciding the Case

ANSWERS: *Marco the Magician* (subject/he) ran five swords through a coffin-like box. *The box* (subject/it) was not empty. The box held *a woman* (direct object/her). . . .

Page 205 Do It Yourself! Figure Out the Case in Spite of "And" and "Or"

ANSWERS: 1. The teacher gave James and (I/me) two different tests. 4. Shannon and (I/me) attend this class. 9. The audience watched Dan and (I/me).

Page 207 Collaborate! Who's a Possessive What?

ANSWERS: *My* boyfriend, Mike, and I went to the state fair. [*adjective*] *His* friend, Ray, was selling the tickets. [*adjective*] Mike paid for *his*. . . . [*pronoun*]

Page 209 Collaborate! Stopping the Sexism

SUGGESTED ANSWERS: Dear Dr. Mann: Yesterday, we received a written complaint from a Pat Frazier about deplorable treatment received in your office. Evidently Pat came to your office needing emergency care, and your receptionist was too busy with a personal phone call to notice Pat's bleeding arm. . . .

Page 212 Do It Yourself! Be a Pronoun Sleuth

ANSWERS: *This* is Reggie Jackson. [*demonstrative*] Reggie sees *himself* as a very private person. [*reflexive*] . . . He owns several homes; at least *three* are in California. [*numerical*] . . .

Page 215 Collaborate! Fixing Pointless Points of View

ANSWERS: 1. I think I could not find the perfect spouse because I would probably find something wrong with her. I mean, she, like everyone, would have defects. I might not be able to see her defects, but my companions could see them almost instantly.

This is why I think I cannot find my perfect mate. The only thing I can do is look for someone at least close to what I desire.

Chapter 9   Adverbs Helping Writers Make the Transition

Page 223   Do It Yourself! Ask the Adverb Questions

ANSWERS: *Yesterday* Jane arrived *home* from vacation and discovered something frightening. Her house had *just* been robbed! The thieves had *clearly* known about her vacation. . . .

Page 224   Collaborate! Using Adverbs to Make a Change

ANSWERS: Yesterday was Saturday, and I *was **finally** moving* into my new apartment. Unfortunately the weather *was **not** cooperating*. But that *did **not** change* my plans. . . .

Page 228   Collaborate! Who is the Adverb Telling about Now?

ANSWERS: *Recently* I broke my tooth. It happened *here* when I was eating my lunch on campus. *Quite unluckily*, I had ordered a hamburger. . . .

Page 230   Collaborate! Reveal the Source of the Adverb with the "LY"

ANSWERS: My husband *constantly* watches talk shows. To him, they are *extremely* interesting. My feelings are *completely* opposite. I find them *incredibly* dull. . . .

Page 234   Collaborate! Inspect the Bridges

ANSWERS: Narratives may be written (primarily) to recount events. (Nevertheless) narration can (also) present a sequence of events to prove a point. (Specifically) if you write about the first time you registered. . . .

Page 236   Do It Yourself! . . . Very Carefully

ANSWERS: 1. Your comments are true.   4. The blood curdling scream was the first sound I heard.

Page 240   Collaborate! Do the Job on Adverbs

ANSWERS: **A.** <u>There are</u> many candidates running close races in the upcoming election. To be <u>very honest</u>, I am having a difficult time deciding whom to vote for. . . .

B. Many candidates are running close races in the upcoming election. To be honest, I am having a difficult time deciding whom to vote for. . . .

Chapter 10   Prepositions Creating Phrases that Position

Page 248   Do It Yourself! Find the "Positioners"

ANSWERS: As I walked (into) the room, I immediately noticed the open closet door (on) the wall (to) my left. (Inside) the closet hung a bright blue baseball cap. . . .

Page 248   Do It Yourself! Become Better Acquainted with the Not-So-Lonely Prepositions

ANSWERS: **B** As I walked <u>into the room</u>, I immediately noticed the open closet door <u>on the wall</u> <u>to my left</u>. <u>Inside the closet</u> hung a bright blue baseball cap. . . .

Page 251   Collaborate! Tell Time with Prepositions

ANSWERS: Jorge and I became engaged (at) the end (of) August just (before) my twenty-third birthday. Two weeks later he went away to college. His classes began (on) the day. . . .

Page 254   Fill in the Puzzling Prepositions

ANSWERS: ACROSS 1. toward   5. by   18. for   27. across   DOWN 2. after   8. down   15. inside   26. before

Page 263   Collaborate! Making Phrases Say What You Want Them to Say

ANSWERS: 1. Mr. Smith, together with his wife Dorothy, paid for the house.   4. In response to your questionnaire in the enclosed envelope, yes, I have given birth to a male child.

Page 264   Do It Yourself! Spot the Interference

ANSWERS: 1. Each have finished yesterday's assignment. *Each of the students* **has** *finished yesterday's assignment.*   8. All are here for my birthday. **No change.**

Page 266   Do It Yourself! Shift your "I's"

ANSWERS: *In 1964* I graduated from high school. *After high school* I attended Portland State College. . . .

Page 274   Saying It in a Word, Not a Phrase

ANSWERS: Dear Ms. Dee Lynn Quint, In February, our company sent you a letter because your payment was overdue. On January 1, 1995, you purchased a computer program and promised . . .

Chapter 11   Verbals Bringing More Life to Sentences

Page 280   Do It Yourself! Revisit Shakespeare

ANSWERS: 1. to be   2. to suffer   3. to take . . .

Page 284   Do It Yourself! Put Picturesque Participles into the Paragraph

ANSWERS: **A.** My favorite uncle is named Denis with one "N." He's a *dancing* fanatic.

Every year this *aging* man travels to Oregon from Norway just to go to *overflowing* dance halls. . . .

Page 286   Do It Yourself! Conduct the Gerund/Participle Test

ANSWERS: *Jogging* [gerund] is my addiction. For me, it is a *fulfilling* [participle] activity. My neighbor does not enjoy *jogging* [gerund]. . . .

Page 287   Collaborate! Keep All Three Verbals in the Air at One Time

ANSWERS: (Studying) [gerund] is not always fun. Sometimes it is a (dreaded) [participle] chore. (Thinking) [gerund] is hard work. I like (to read) [infinitive]. . . .

Page 287   Do It Yourself! Discover the Bigger Verbal World

ANSWERS: **B.** 1. a win: winning the big game   4. this practice: passing the ball and running with it   8. dedication: Giving your all

Page 292   Do It Yourself! Get the Picture with Participial Phrases

ANSWERS: **B.** 1. happy: Wearing a smile on her face   4. perfect: made just for canoeing

Page 295   Collaborate! Distinguishing Gerund Phrases from Participial Phrases

ANSWERS: By *digging through garbage* [gerund], researchers have discovered that we Americans throw away about 15 percent of the food we buy. *Wasting food* [gerund] is common. Cheese *covered with mold* [participle]. . . .

Page 297   Do It Yourself! Watch your P's and I's (Prepositions and Infinitives)

ANSWERS: *To fear something unnaturally* [INF] is a phobia. . . . Every time I go *to the airport* [PREP]. . . . I once loved *to fly* [INF]. . . . Once there, I boarded a carrier *to Holland* [PREP]. . . .

Page 300   Do It Yourself! Phix the Phragments (Just Testing My Spell-Checker)

SUGGESTED ANSWERS: 1. The road was paved by the county.   4. Getting high grades in all my classes was my goal.   8. I paid for the hot water heater replaced by the plumber.   12. I want to join the army during a time of national emergency.

Page 302   Do It Yourself! Help Misplaced Participles Find Their Nouns

ANSWERS: 1. *Piled high with papers*; describes "office"; revised: The professor avoided his office piled high with papers.   4. *Covered with greasy gravy*; describes "steak"; revised: I thought the steak covered with greasy gravy would be very fattening.   8. *Flying to California*; describes "passengers"; revised: The Grand Canyon was seen by the passengers flying to California.

Page 305   Collaborate! Attaching Detached Participles

SUGGESTED ANSWERS: 1. Looking down from the forty-fifth floor, Fred thought the cars looked like toys.   4. A herd of elk could be seen by the pilot flying low.   8. Speaking as an old friend, Mary said, "This purchase should not be considered."

Page 306   Collaborate! Participle Pandemonium

SUGGESTED ANSWERS: Ringing loudly, my alarm woke me. I turned it off and got out of bed. Being late for school, I decided that skipping my morning shower was my only choice. But tempted by the thought of raisin bread, I thought a quick breakfast sounded like a good idea. . . .

Page 308   Do It Yourself! Consider Calling on a Comma

ANSWERS: 1. Wearing a flowing gown, the woman entered the room gracefully. 4. To help his charity was his goal.   9. To finish her work early, Anita had to give up her lunch hour.

Page 311   Finding the Common Denominators

SUGGESTED ANSWERS: **A.** 1. >Time of injury >Date of injury >Location where injury occurred   4. >Communicating well in writing >Dealing positively with stressful situations >Working as a team member   **B.** 1. I would like a girl to be capable of supporting herself, to have her own job, to have her own apartment, and to make her own decisions without needing the opinions of others.

Chapter 12   Clauses—Sentences Inside Sentences with Complex Ideas

Page 322   Do It Yourself! Distinguish Simple from Compound

ANSWERS: 1. Simple   4. compound I enjoy reading my classmates' papers/ ,for they give me ideas to use in my own writing.   8. compound We all write rough drafts/ , and then we revise them.

Page 323   Collaborate! Simple and Compound Sentences Working Together in Paragraphs

ANSWERS: Anita's family went to the Humane Society to find a cat/ or a dog. simple The boys in the family wanted a cat/ ,but the girls wanted a dog. compound Mom/ and Dad decided the children could look at both kinds of animals. simple . . .

Page 324   Do It Yourself! Repair the Run-ons

ANSWERS: 1. Option #1: Damon doesn't like to gamble. He likes to go to shows. Option #2: Damon doesn't like to gamble, but he likes to go to shows. Option #3: Damon doesn't like to gamble; he likes to go to shows.   4. Option #1: Many attractions in Las Vegas are expensive. I cannot afford to take them all in. Option #2: Many attractions in Las Vegas are expensive, so I cannot afford to take them all in. Option #3: Many attractions in Las Vegas are expensive; I cannot afford to take them all in.   8. Option #1: Many of the restaurants offer elegant buffets. The prices are usually reasonable. Option #2: Many of the restaurants offer elegant buffets, yet the prices are usually reasonable. Option #3: Many of the restaurants offer elegant buffets; the prices are usually reasonable.

Page 334   Do It Yourself! Reverse the Clauses

ANSWERS: 4. I will ask Karen to take me to the airport since John is always late.   10. If I win the lottery$_\emptyset$ I will buy a house at the beach.

Page 336   Collaborate! Decide the Adverb Question

ANSWERS: *So* <u>that I can help prevent pollution</u>, I use the city bus system. The bus is easy to take <u>since there are bus stops every few blocks throughout the city.</u> <u>Because the public transportation system is very popular</u>, busses go everywhere in town. . . . (These first three subordinate clauses answer the question "under what condition.")

Page 337   Find the Relative Clauses

ANSWERS: **A.** Carol, who is my daughter-in-law, flew to Mississippi for Christmas. She traveled with her son, who is only two years old. . . .   **B.** Carol flew to Mississippi for Christmas. She traveled with her son.

Page 339   Collaborate! Find the Fragments

ANSWERS: 1. fragment   4. complete sentence   8. complete sentence

Page 340   Taking the First Step to Wiping out "That"

ANSWERS: From the information provided and the analytical results of the samples obtained, it appears the source of the bacteria detected. . . .

$\mathcal{I}$NDEX